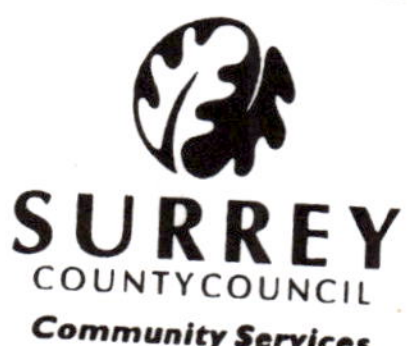

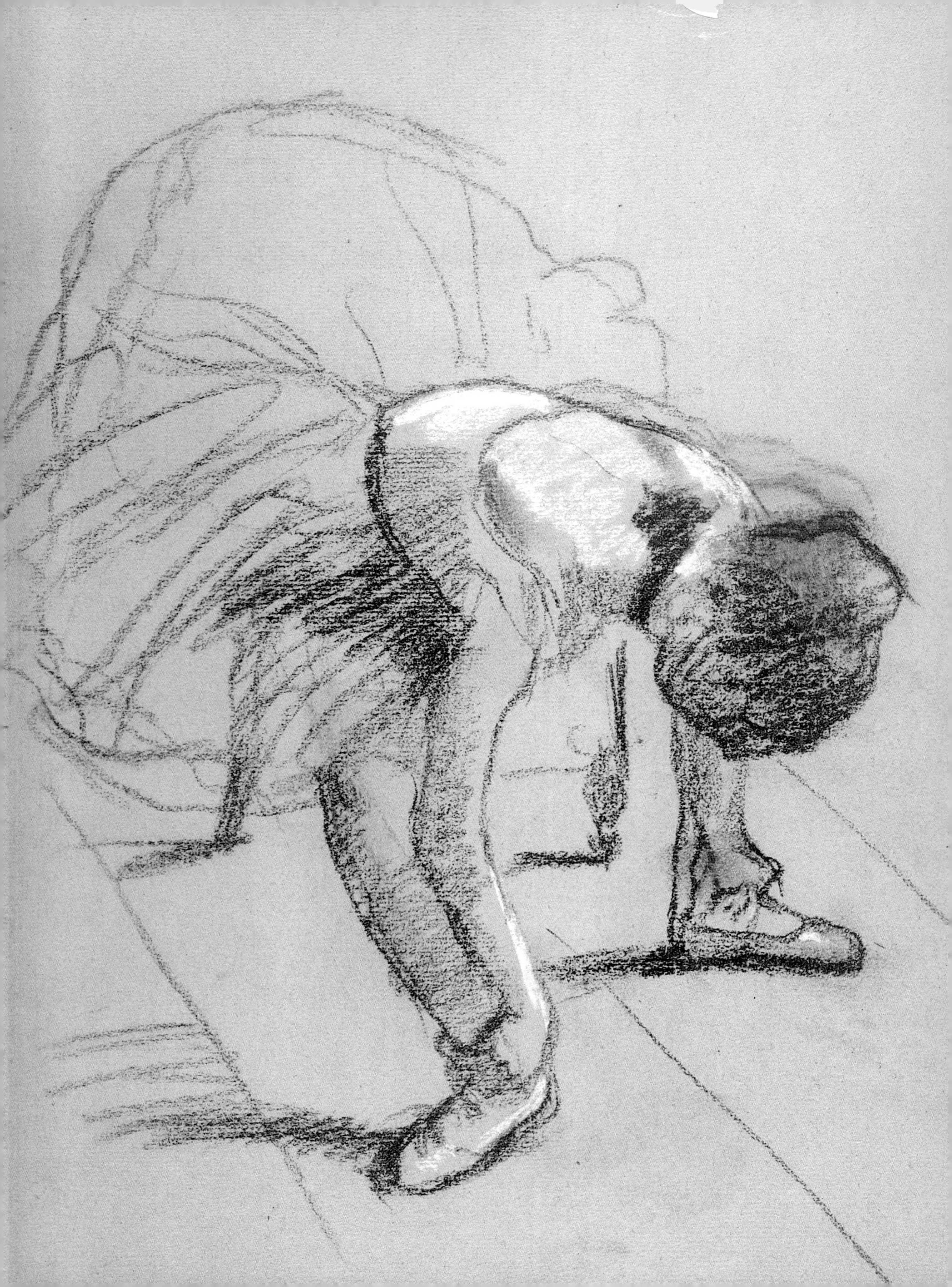

French Drawings and Paintings from the Hermitage

Poussin to Picasso

State Hermitage Museum
Hermitage Development Trust

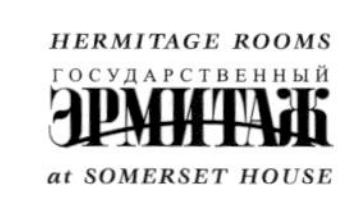

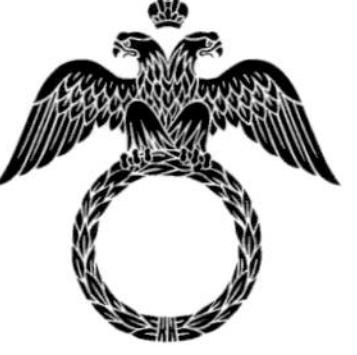

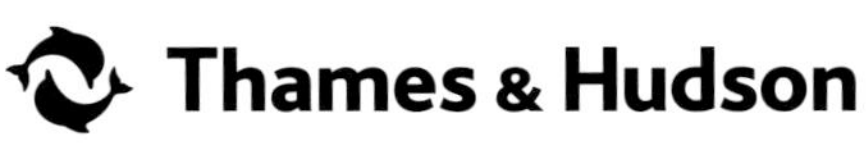

This catalogue has been produced on the occasion of the exhibition **French Drawings and Paintings from the Hermitage: Poussin to Picasso** held in the Hermitage Rooms at Somerset House, London, 3 November 2001 – 3 March 2002

Objects have been restored specially for this exhibition in the paper restoration workshops of the State Hermitage Museum, under the guidance of Valentina Kozyreva

Photography by Leonard Heifetz, Yury Molodkovets, Svetlana Suyetova and Vladimir Terebenin, and Sergey Pokrovsky

With special thanks to Mikhail Balan, Elizaveta Abramova and Alexey Mitin

Exhibition design by Jasper Jacob of JJA

Contributors to the Catalogue Entries

DRAWINGS

A.K.-G. – Asya Kantor-Gukovskaya, M.Phil
I.N. – Dr Irina Novoselskaya
V.S. – Valery Shevchenko, M.Phil

PAINTINGS

A.K. – Dr Albert Kostenevich
Y.K. – Ekaterina Deriabina
N.S. – Natalia Serebriannaia

First published in the United Kingdom in 2001 by
Thames & Hudson Ltd
181A High Holborn
London WC1V 7QX

British Library Cataloguing-in-Publication Data
A catalogue record for this book is available from the British Library

ISBN 0-500-97613-9

Translated by Catherine Phillips
Edited by Robert Williams
Designed by Isambard Thomas
Printed in Italy by EBS, Verona

All works are on paper unless otherwise stated. Measurements (height before width) are given in millimetres for drawings, in centimetres for paintings. Collectors' marks: references are to F. Lugt, *Les Marques de collections de dessins et d'estampes*, Amsterdam, 1921, supplement The Hague, 1956

Preface

Lord Rothschild

The ongoing transformation of Somerset House, one of London's architectural masterpieces, into a new cultural centre is one of the most exciting and challenging ventures with which I have had the good fortune to be involved. From time to time we have had to take our courage in both hands and back new schemes with no proven record of success. The idea of opening a 'baby' Hermitage by the Thames to show selected pieces from the vast treasure-house on the Neva was immediately appealing, but would it catch the imagination of a London that is already extraordinarily well endowed with museums and art galleries? I am delighted to say that our first exhibition, 'The Treasures of Catherine the Great', has been a resounding success, attracting over 180,000 visitors - an astonishing number given the modest size of our exhibition rooms. These visitor numbers are a huge compliment to both the charismatic personality of Catherine the Great over 200 years after her death and the quality of the exhibits that the Hermitage sent to London.

This new exhibition, 'French Drawings and Paintings from the Hermitage: Poussin to Picasso', also depends on Catherine's genius as a collector and her brilliant forays into the capitals of Europe to secure the finest art for Russia. The rich collection of French drawings and paintings that she assembled inspired her successors to add further material, so that today the Hermitage has perhaps the finest collection of French art outside France. We have therefore been able to borrow both paintings and drawings, so our visitors will be able to see the interplay between drawings by Claude and Poussin and their paintings, and to compare vigorous chalk figure studies by Greuze with the final work, *Filial Piety*.

Our Russian colleagues have also found for us two fascinating drawings with direct links with Britain. The earlier, by the once much admired French artist Gustave Doré, gives a vivid record of the now vanished rough world of Whitechapel. Picasso's exuberant drawing of Lydia Lopukhova, later the wife of the great economist John Maynard Keynes, takes us to the world of the Ballets Russes and their electrifying impact on audiences in London.

With their characteristic generosity and enthusiasm, Prof. Mikhail Piotrovski and his colleagues have guided us through their vast holdings and advised us on the selection for this exhibition. I would like to thank them for their help. Without their commitment this show could not have taken place. My fellow trustee Dr Timothy Clifford has, as always, made his expertise freely available, assisted with the selection and made a significant contribution to the catalogue with his introductory essay.

The setting up of the Hermitage Rooms in London and the mounting of this and the previous exhibition have only been possible because a group of private individuals and organizations have backed our endeavour with most generous financial support. My fellow trustees and I would like to thank them most warmly and pass on to them the thanks of the many who came to Somerset House to visit our first exhibition. I am sure they are as pleased as I am by our success so far, and that they share my optimism about the future of our partnership with the Hermitage in St Petersburg.

Foreword

Professor Mikhail Piotrovski

This elegant exhibition offers a London audience select masterpieces of French drawing and painting from the extensive Hermitage collection.

Drawing is a very specific form of art. It most visibly and vividly reveals the author's personality, the presence of which is felt almost directly. Many viewers feel they can communicate with drawings more intimately than is possible with paintings. They find themselves face to face with the artist. Drawings stimulate dialogue. Such dialogues presuppose knowledge and taste. Thus a love of drawings has always been a sign of a refined aesthetic sense, a true appreciation of artistic language.

Placing together paintings and drawings, as we have done for this exhibition, is a device that allows us better to understand the merits of each. Together they create an elegant combination that comes close to competition. French art is particularly suitable for this. Elegance and grace are its dominant features, a fact admirers and collectors throughout the world have always maintained. This exhibition informs us about the passion for French art and French style that was characteristic of both Western Europe and Russia in the 18th, 19th and 20th centuries. French works dominate the extremely rich collection of drawings that belong to the Hermitage, which tells us as much about Russian culture as it does the history of French art.

Russia's rulers and wealthy grandees collected drawings with a will. As usual it was Catherine the Great who set the highest standard. An indication of her taste for contemporary art is Greuze's superb *Filial Piety*, exhibited here alongside a whole series of the artist's preparatory drawings for this painting. Poussin's and Boucher's refined drawings fit neatly both with their own painted landscapes and with the later artistic wonders of Degas, Matisse and Picasso. Together they make up a marvellous exhibition, which we hope is characteristic of the spirit of the Hermitage and its exhibitions, both at home and abroad.

Drawing dominates this exhibition, unlike many other mixed-media presentations, where graphic works and paintings often appear together in equal numbers. Such an approach as ours allows the viewer to see something new in long-familiar works, giving them unexpected pleasure. Such has been the aim of the organizers of the exhibition. Once again, this is the fruit of a successful collaboration between the two 'Hermitages', the one on the Neva, the other by the Thames. We are pleased that our collaboration, begun so recently, is continuing with such success.

Five Centuries of French Drawings from the Hermitage

TIMOTHY CLIFFORD

The History of the Hermitage Collection of French Drawings

IRINA NOVOSELSKAYA

Style and Technique in French Drawings

VALERY SHEVCHENKO

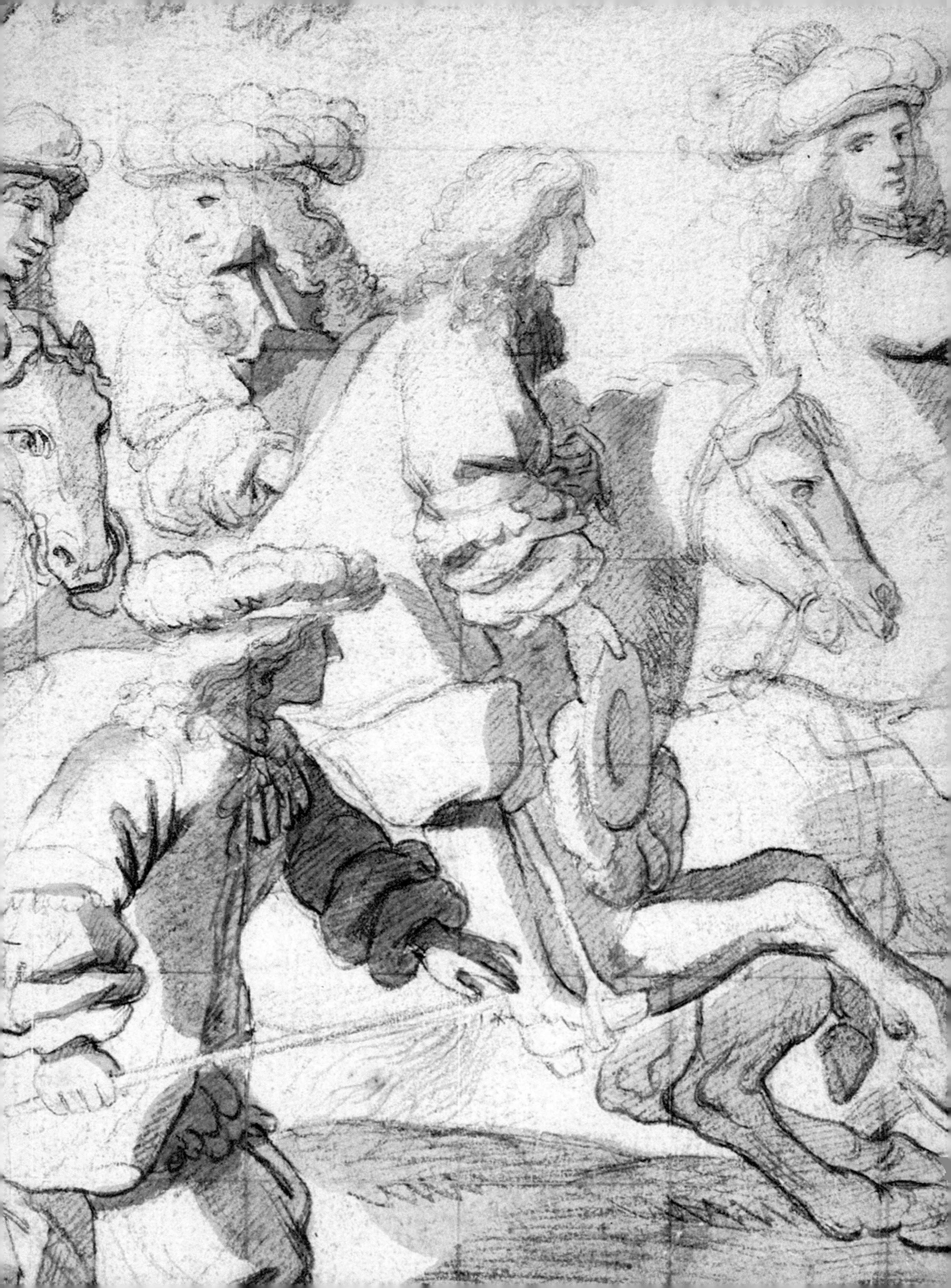

Five Centuries of French Drawings from the Hermitage

TIMOTHY CLIFFORD

The principal characteristics and distinctive stylistic developments of French art from the 1560s to the 1940s are represented in this exhibition catalogue. During that period, artists came to create their own style, one that is recognizably French. In part it grew out of an indigenous medieval Court school, but depended on infusions of artistic talent initially directly from Italy and later by way of French artists travelling there in order to study at first hand classical architecture, sculpture and advanced workshop traditions. This was the High Art tradition nurtured by the Accademia del Disegno in Florence and by both the Zuccaro and the Carracci academies in Rome. There was also the Northern realist tradition of the Netherlands, which, combined with the bravura and graphic fluency of Flanders, consistently percolated through eastern France and was accelerated by Louis XIV's wars and territorial annexations. French art, as it developed, like French bureaucracy, was centralist, and came to be based at two major institutions, one the Académie Royale de la Peinture et de Sculpture in Paris (founded 1648), the other the Académie de France in Rome (1666), which since 1804 has been based at the Villa Medici near S. Trinità dei Monti.

French art was nurtured to serve the French state, providing a propaganda machine to glorify the monarchy and later the Empire. The French Court needed to be provided not just with portraits of the monarch and his retinue, but also with palaces ornamented with sumptuous gardens, salons with grandly painted ceilings, the finest furniture, the finest ceramics, rich tapestries and silks, and above all pictures showing allegories and histories that bolstered the political system. In 1663 Louis XIV instructed his minister Jean-Baptiste Colbert to set up the Gobelins manufactory (for tapestries, furnishings and other decorative arts) under the direct supervision of a painter, Charles Lebrun, in order to disseminate French academic standards and rules among the

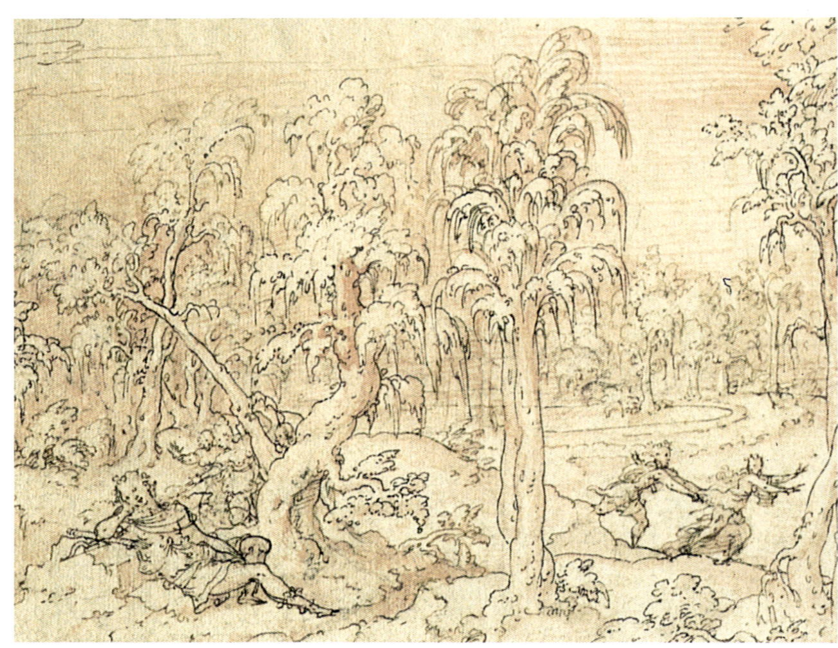

artisans. The same was to apply to other centralized state ventures, such as the Savonnerie (for the manufacture of carpets), established in 1627 by Louis XIII and granted a new contract in 1664, and the (Royal) Vincennes–Sèvres factory (for porcelain), set up in 1738 under the direct patronage of Louis XV and his mistress Mme de Pompadour. The best works by students of the Académie were exhibited each year, providing a public opportunity to judge and monitor the results of their training, a system initiated by Colbert and Lebrun that in time developed into the Salon, a prominent cultural fixture in Parisian life. The result was an immensely competent conforming art, and the most sophisticated and perfectly produced decorative arts in Europe. Nowhere else, save perhaps Papal Rome in the 17th century, was art so subservient to a system, in France's case, Absolutism.

French art had its rebels, its releases from such constraints, and this was manifested, for example, in Watteau and the birth of the Rococo in the early

fig. 1
Detail from
Jean Cousin II
Landscape with Mythological Figures (Apollo's Affairs of Love?) (cat. 5)

18th century, the development of unconventional geniuses such as Chardin and Géricault, and the opening of the Salon des Refusés in 1863, which publicly exposed the gulf between academic and 'contemporary' art and witnessed the explosive birth of Impressionism. Thus the France of the Académie, the Beaux-Arts tradition, was to spawn the reactive *vie bohème* of Paris – of absinthe, the garret, Montmartre, and an artistic milieu in which artists like Picasso could flourish. Common to all these elements were drawing and design, for without design there could never have been Court art or, for that matter, bourgeois art for private delectation. Drawings were more often than not made as a means to an end, but some were intended as an end in themselves. The dealer and patron Edme-François Gersaint, for example, explained in his 'Brief Life of Antoine Watteau' (1744) that it was not only he who 'definitely prefer[red] Watteau's drawings to his paintings', this was 'an opinion which Watteau shared. He was more pleased with his drawings than his paintings.... He derived greater satisfaction from drawing ... I often saw him mortified because his painting lacked the spirituality and truth of which he was capable with the crayons.'

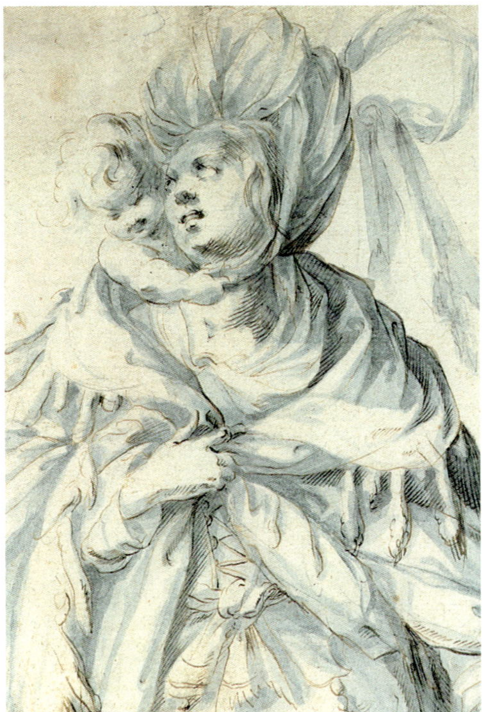

fig. 2
Detail from
Jacques de Bellange
Gypsy Woman with Two Children (cat. 8)

Back in the 16th century, French art had been hugely influenced by two Italians, Rosso Fiorentino and Francesco Primaticcio, who arrived in France in 1530 and 1532 respectively, expressly to work for François I at Fontainebleau. Their Mannerist painted and stucco'd décor for this spectacular new château in the Ile de France led to an eponymous Court style managed by French artists that pervaded and then lingered on in France for another half-century. The curious Mannerist style introduced by the Italians – broad-shouldered youths, hair tightly curled, with muscular chests, narrow hips and long legs, and mannequin-like women with elaborately coiffed hair, bare breasts and transparent draperies – was imitated by Jean Cousin II, while his landscape settings, with spiky trees formed like petrifications (fig. 1), although common to contemporaries such as Etienne Délaune and Antoine Caron, developed from Antwerp Mannerist precedents.

The final flowering of Mannerism in Europe was at Nancy in the independent Duchy of Lorraine, where both Jacques de Bellange and Jacques Callot were employed at the ducal Court. Bellange was principally a draughtsman and etcher of quite extraordinary imagination and fancy, who forged from a variety of Italian sources a wild and ethereal world of his own, with tousle-haired, wild-eyed girls wrapping themselves with attenuated fingers into tattered and elaborately fringed draperies, a private world of flame-like figures always teetering on the edge of ecstatic climax. Bellange's drawings in pen and ink, invariably with explosive surges of cross-hatching describing naked forms lightly draped, remind one of earlier, and indeed tamer, 16th-century drawings by followers of Michelangelo. His drawings in pen with brush and wash, sometimes with colour added, with their soft tonal range describing mass and the fall of light on billowing forms, recall paintings by early Florentine Mannerists like Pontormo.

Like Bellange, Callot was born in Lorraine, and may have studied under Bellange in his youth. He travelled to Rome, then in 1611 moved to Florence. There he amused himself drawing hunchbacks, beggars and gypsies, which he subsequently etched. His drawings are full of insect-like figures performing the rituals of etiquette, strutting in a balletic manner with self-conscious refinement. In 1621, after the death of his patron, Cosimo de' Medici, Duke of Tuscany, Callot returned to Nancy, where he shrugged off Florentine elegance. Twelve years later Louis III invaded Lorraine. This, with its attendant horrors, clearly shocked Callot, and it triggered off a series of drawings of grim intensity, with rich *chiaroscuro* that prefigure Goya's *Disasters of War*.

France, like Lorraine, continued with a type of late Mannerism into the first quarter of the 17th century, a style dispelled with the return from Rome in 1627 of Simon Vouet, whose Baroque altarpieces and interior decorative schemes were soon in great demand in Paris. His drawings, harking back to the Carracci tradition, are mostly in black chalk and are highly resolved, confident studies of figures and drapery, as can be seen in a late sheet of studies (cat. 15). The artists of the next generation who trained in his studio included Charles Lebrun and Eustache Le Sueur, but the two most notable and celebrated painters of 17th-century France – Claude and Poussin – reacted against the centralized constraints of France and

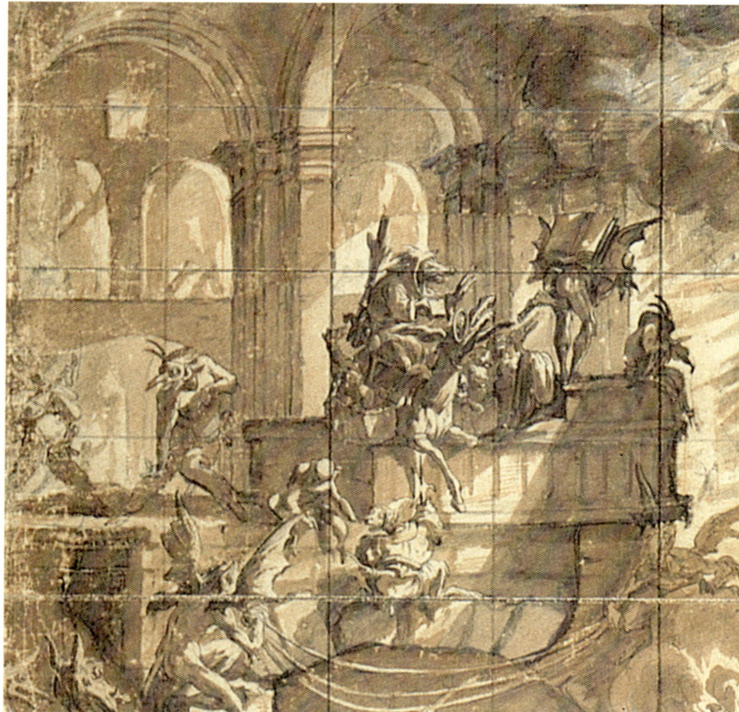

fig. 3
Detail from
Jacques Callot
The Temptation of St Anthony (cat. 14)

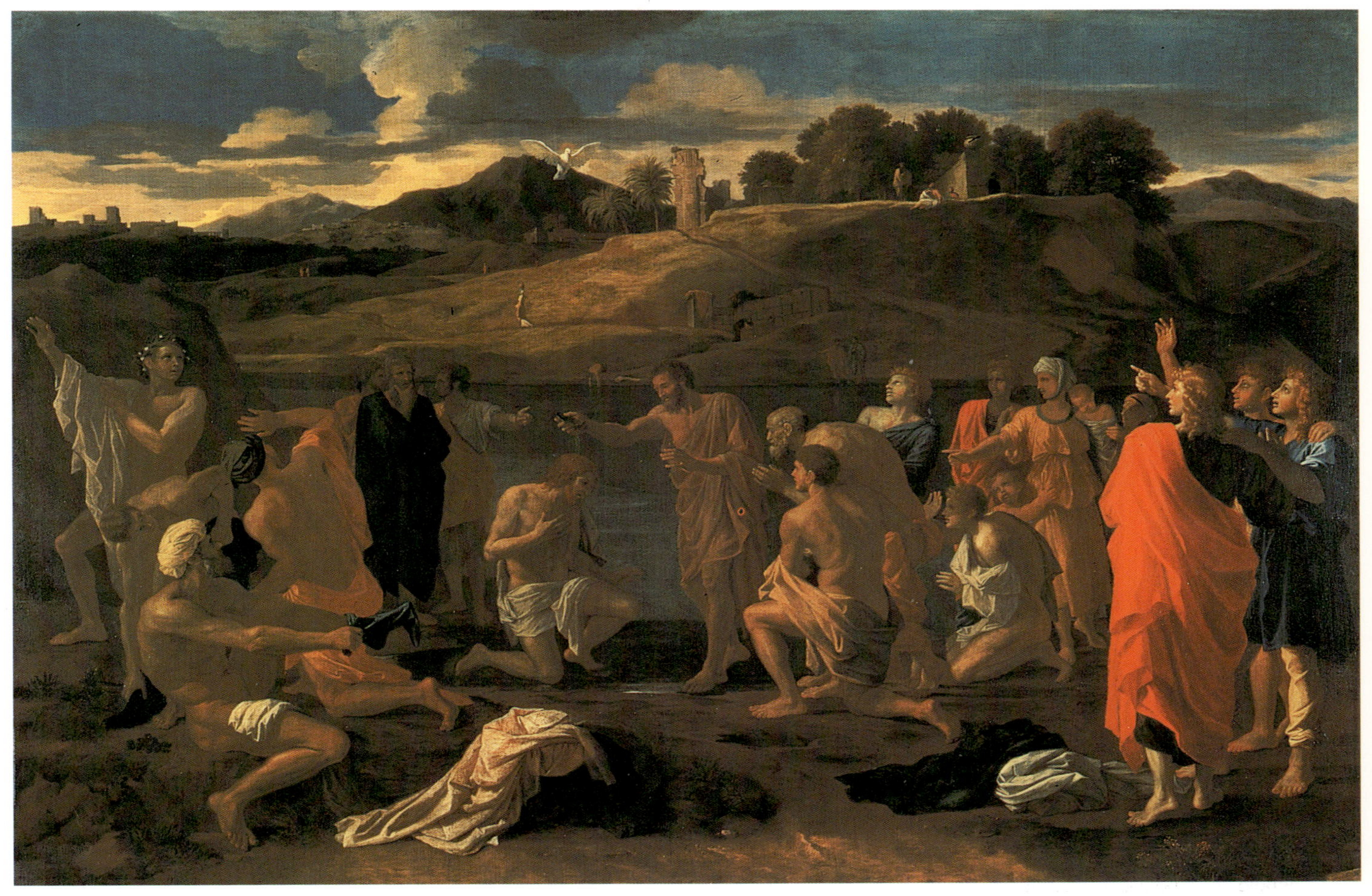

fig. 4
Nicolas Poussin,
The Sacrament of Baptism,
1646

oil on canvas, 117.5 × 177 cm.
The Duke of Sutherland Collection, National Gallery of Scotland, Edinburgh / Bridgeman Art Library

its Court and spent most of their working lives in Rome.

Claude's ideal landscapes in oils (see cat. 21), painted in a contrived, disciplined manner learned from Agostino Tassi in Rome, have gradations of colour that develop from dark greenish-brown foregrounds to lighter greens in the middle distance and finally to distant ethereal blues, all framed with *coulisses* (like theatre wings) that give a sense of almost infinite recession. His working drawings, free and loose, with a liberal use of wash, were often made *en plein air*, and contrast with his carefully crafted oils painted in the studio. He remained a poor figure draughtsman and in his early years often relied on others for the *staffage* in his landscapes. Almost his entire *œuvre* was painted in and around Rome, and his influence had more effect on British art than on French.

Nicolas Poussin, originally from Normandy, studied in Paris before settling in Rome. Among the drawings included here is one (cat. 19) of four compositional studies for *The Sacrament of Baptism* (fig. 4), a painting in Poussin's second series of 'The Seven Sacraments' in the collection of the Duke of Sutherland and today on loan to the National Gallery of Scotland. The study seems to be an example of Poussin drawing from wax models placed in one of his contrived little puppet theatres, using a system to establish composition and *chiaroscuro* similar to that which Gainsborough employed a century later, where rocks, moss and plaster models were arranged as aids in landscape composition. Poussin excelled as a figure draughtsman, although he eschewed virtuosity for its own sake, using broken lines and mottled washes to explore and represent form. It was the influence of the Classical Poussin, through the studios of artists such as Lebrun and the later Neoclassicist Jacques-Louis David, that demarcated the two great rival academic traditions of French art for more than two centuries. The *Poussiniste* tradition was to develop as one of austerity, harmony and stoicism, whereas the *Rubénistes* sought exuberance, rich Venetian colour and Baroque flutter.

Charles Lebrun, by the 1660s the dominant figure in the Paris art world as director of both the Gobelins and the Académie Royale, had become a follower of Poussin's theories of art while working in Poussin's studio in Rome in the early 1640s. The prodigiously energetic and well-organized Lebrun provided the Court with all that was required for the royal palaces and aristocratic châteaux – paintings, decorative schemes, sculptures and furnishings. As his designs and sketches demonstrate (see cats. 26–8), he was a fine draughtsman in the academic tradition. His solid, assured and sculptured drawing manner, combined with his doctrinaire taste for flattering allegory and sumptuous splendour, appealed to the obsessive Absolutism of Louis XIV. Drawings for architecture, sculpture and the applied arts in France were never considered as anything separate from 'art' in general, for the art of the royal palaces was all-pervasive and all-embracing, with major artists designing not only buildings, gardens and fountains but textiles, furniture, clocks and other furnishings too.

The measured classicism noticeable in many designs of the later 17th century and early 18th is apparent in a large highly wrought drawing by Gilles-Marie Oppenord comprising alternative ideas for an elaborated clock-case on a tall pedestal (fig. 5). Oppenord was a designer, etcher and architect who had trained at the Académie de France in Rome for eight years before returning to Paris to design, among many other tasks, the high altars of St Germain-des-Prés and St Sulpice. Indeed, there was not then much difference between designing an altar or an elaborate and costly clock-case, for both required the collaboration of a variety of skilled executants. The clock's case could have been supplied by the cabinetmaker André Charles Boulle (1642–1732),

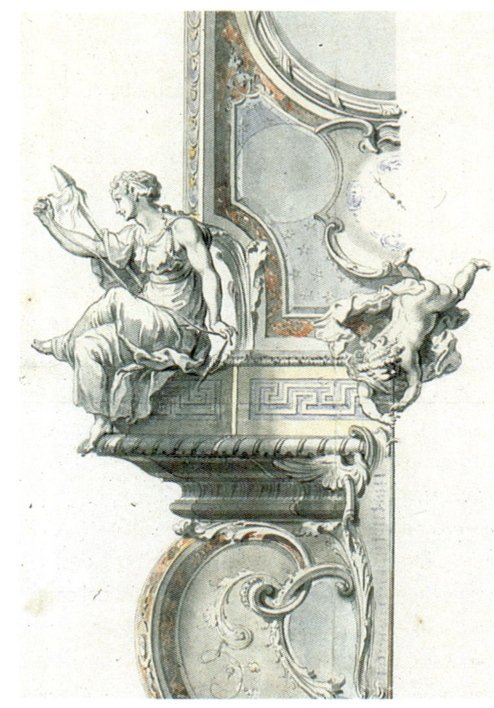

fig.5
Detail from
Gilles-Marie Oppenord
Design for a Clock-case and a Barometer (cat. 30)

while the gilt-bronze sculptured figures were probably modelled by someone such as François Girardon (1625–1715) or the Slodtz brothers, sculptors otherwise engaged in carving figures for the royal palaces and gardens. Such a highly finished drawing (cat. 30) would have given the patron a clear understanding of the completed work's appearance, and would have served as vital guidance to the team of sculptor, *ébéniste* and clockmaker. Other examples of designs requiring a team of skilled artists and craftsmen for their realization include a drawing by Claude Gillot for decorating a harpsichord (cat. 32), which shows the instrument in a painted case supported on a carved and gilded trestle with cabriole legs. The drawing, probably intended for the client, gives an indication of the kind of work the painter Antoine Watteau undertook in Gillot's workshop. Major artists were frequently involved in creating what we now choose to identify somewhat dismissively as 'minor arts'. Watteau also worked for a while under Claude Audran III, to whom a worked up, coloured design for the back of a tapestry covered sofa (cat. 31) is attributed. This sheet has a label hinged at the centre providing, in another hand (probably that of the painter Jean-Baptiste Oudry), an alternative central reserve or compartment.

Watteau, Oudry, other painters and numerous craftsmen were all to be infected by the Rococo, the new style popularized in the reign (from 1715) of Louis XV, which developed out of the ornamental vocabulary of Jean Bérain (1640–1711), son of a Lorraine gunsmith. Watteau, who arrived in Paris from Valenciennes in 1702, made drawings using butterfly-like caresses of red chalk (and often of red, black and white chalks together, the so-called *aux trois crayons*) that conjured up landscapes, figures and delicate Singeries – ornament that included trellises, canopies, festoons and, above all, monkeys. His contemporary, Oudry, was a successful painter of hunting scenes and still-lifes in particular, and a major designer for the tapestry manufactory at Beauvais.

The Hermitage collection provides us with the unique opportunity to follow the development of one of Jean-Baptiste Greuze's painted compositions, *Filial Piety* (cat. 50), by means of eight studies in chalk for individual figures and the dog (cats. 51–8). Greuze admired women, yet he drew them not as objects of desire but in all their variety as newly-weds, disconsolate widows and aged crones. Like Lebrun he became obsessed with the passions, and in expressing physiognomy shared an interest with both William Hogarth and the Swiss philosopher Johann-Kaspar Lavater. Drawings from the Napoleonic era by Pierre Prud'hon and Ingres reveal how differently these two artists drew – Prud'hon almost painting with his soft crayons, producing moody tonal images (cat. 67), while Ingres, using a very hard pencil, sharply delineated his portraits, allowing only the faintest bruise of a shadow (cats. 68, 69).

The Hermitage's collection of 19th-century drawings is far less comprehensive. An elegant little chalk drawing by Edouard Manet shows a pretty girl out on a promenade in her smart new hat and cloak (cat. 72). Its confident slashing diagonal shading betrays a respect for Fragonard and the 18th-century world so much beloved by the Goncourt brothers. Edgar Degas provides a delightful study of a ballet dancer, a rapid annotation but acutely observed, with her wired tutu riding up as she reaches down (cat. 73). The Hermitage is celebrated for its matchless series of paintings by Henri Matisse, that bard of colour, but it is less well known that the collection also has a number of his fine drawings (cats. 75–79). In these characteristic works – spare, bold and fluent – we experience a world reaching back to the engraved backs of Etruscan mirrors, contemporary admiration for Japanese prints and a shared infatuation for line that we also see in Picasso and in Ingres' portrait drawings. Early Picasso is a world away from the French tradition. In two great gouaches (cats. 81, 82) Picasso looked back to the mannered melancholy of El Greco, for here Spain rather than France exerted a powerful influence on this great painter of the 20th century, domiciled in France, whose presence continues to be felt by French draughtsmen today.

The History of the Hermitage Collection of French Drawings

IRINA NOVOSELSKAYA

The Hermitage has one of the world's largest collections of drawings, renowned for both its high quality and incredible variety, which covers the French, Italian, Flemish, Dutch, German and other national schools from the 15th century to the early 20th. Despite its name, the Department of Drawings is not limited to drawings alone: incorporating something in the region of 40,000 items, it includes illuminated manuscripts, a collection of portrait and landscape miniatures and works in pastel.

The Hermitage's collection of works on paper was put together more or less in parallel with that of paintings. Catherine II acquired her first significant group of paintings in 1764 from the German merchant Johann Ernst Gotzkowsky (the year that has since come to be seen as marking the foundation of the Hermitage), and just four years later she purchased her first cache of drawings from the connoisseur Carl Cobenzl. She thus laid the foundation of the Hermitage art collections – which were to reach great heights over the next decade – during the first five years of her reign. Royal collections had come to include works on paper – drawings and prints – as early as the 17th century. Louis XIV of France, for instance, made a number of important purchases and acquired drawings produced in the studios of leading Court artists.

Count Carl Cobenzl (1712–70), Plenipotentiary Minister to the Austrian Empress, Marie-Thérèse, in the Southern (Austrian) Netherlands, was a renowned patron, founder of the Academy of Arts in Brussels and of a free school of drawing there. It was probably after his appointment to Brussels in 1753 that he embarked on his collecting activities. In the early 1760s Cobenzl entrusted his nephew Philipp Cobenzl with the task of putting his collection in order and creating a cataloguing system. All the drawings were glued onto violet mounts (five sizes of mount were used, depending on the dimensions of the drawing); the greater

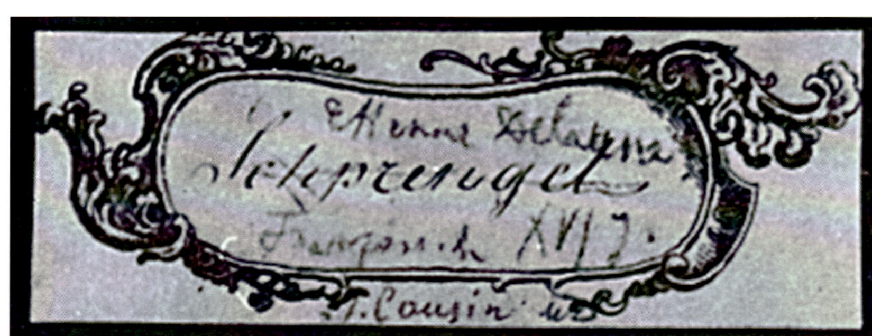

8

Catalogue de Desseins.

N.° I. Un Livre relié en Maroquin rouge contenant 930. Desseins de l'Histoire Sainte par Van Orley.

Première Grandeur
Dans le Premier Carton N.° II.

Numeros.		Noms des Auteurs.
1.	Les Egiptiens	Monixo.
2.	Loth et ses filles	Leli.
3.	une tête d'Enfant	Mignard.
4.	une autre	
5.	une autre	
6.	une autre	Polidore.
7.	une autre	
8.	Deux Enfans	Mazzuolo.
9.	Deux autres	
10.	une tête de Vierge en Couleurs	Correge.
11.	La Coupe trouvée dans le Sac de Benjamin	
12.	La Purification	Corneille
13.	Mercure et un Berger	
14.	une tête	J. Sarti.
15.	S.te Marguerite	
16.	N. S. guérissant le Paralitique	Raphaël.
17.	un Genie avec la forge de Vulcain	
18.	L'Adoration des Bergers	Cavedone.
19.	un Croquis	
20.	une S.te Vierge	Van Deyck.
21.	Portrait de Van Deyck et du fils de Rubens	
22	un homme appuié sur une table	
23.	une S.te Vierge	Tintoreto.
24.	une Histoire	
25.	une S.te Vierge	Farinati.
26.	un Buste d'Eveque	

fig. 6
Cartouche from a Carl Cobenzl mount

fig. 7
A page from the Cobenzl 'Catalogue de desseins' in the Hermitage's Department of Drawings

part are still attached to these mounts, as can be seen with some of the works shown here. Philipp then glued onto each mount a piece of paper ornamented with a cartouche in which he wrote the artist's name. These cartouches today serve as the easily recognizable collector's mark of Carl Cobenzl (fig. 6).

Catherine purchased the Cobenzl collection in 1768 through the mediation of Prince Dmitry Golitsyn, Russian envoy in Paris. It consisted of a small number of paintings and prints and around 4,000 drawings of various European schools. Alongside Italian and Flemish works was a large body of French drawings. Philipp Cobenzl had also compiled a brief manuscript catalogue of the works in his uncle's collection according to size: he gave each one a chronological number, and provided a brief description of the image and the likely identity of the artist. Some of the attributions are still accepted today; others – like the subject-matter of a number of works – have been dropped. The Cobenzl catalogue is kept, along with the drawings themselves, in the Hermitage's Department of Drawings (fig. 7).

Cobenzl's selection of French 16th-century crayon portraits is of particular interest. Thanks to this acquisition the Hermitage has the largest collection of such portraits outside France itself, some 120 in all. Along with old copies, often produced from lost originals (of great iconographical, cultural and historical significance), there are masterpieces by the most important portraitists of the age: François Clouet, 'L'Anonyme Lécurieux', Pierre Dumoustier the Elder and others. The Cobenzl collection is particularly rich, both in quantity and variety, in 17th-century works. It includes all the leading names – Daniel Dumoustier and Lagneau, Jacques Callot and Simon Vouet, Poussin and Claude, the epitome of Academicism, Charles Lebrun – and all the genres. A notable group of 40 portraits by Claude Mellan – a rare visual record of the times in which he lived – depicts members of the royal family, courtiers, military leaders, clergymen, writers and scholars. Only the group of works by Mellan in the Nationalmuseum, Stockholm, can compare with the Hermitage's holdings. Although 18th-century works are less numerous (for obvious reasons, bearing in mind the years in which Cobenzl was collecting), some of the most outstanding artists of the first half of the century are represented, among them Watteau, Nicolas Lancret, François Boucher and Jean-Baptiste Oudry.

In 1769, only a year after acquiring Cobenzl's collection, Catherine bought a large number of drawings from Count Heinrich Brühl's heirs, firm evidence of her serious intentions as a collector. Brühl had been all-powerful Minister of the Saxon Court, and with the aid of his secretary and adviser in artistic matters, Carl-Heinrich Henneken, had played a major role in the formation of the Dresden Picture Gallery and Cabinet of Prints and Drawings. With Henneken's assistance Brühl also put together his own, by no means insignificant, collection. In addition to a good number of paintings and prints, Catherine received from Bruhl's heirs 14 *in-folio* albums in leather bindings (figs. 8, 9), stuck into which were something in the region of 1,000 drawings, mainly of the French, Italian and Dutch schools. Although Brühl's collection of drawings was inferior to that of Cobenzl both in quantity and quality, it was none the less an extremely valuable acquisition. Drawings by Simon Vouet and Eustache Le Sueur enriched the French collections, along with several works by Poussin, including *The Dromedary* (cat. 17) and *The Conversion of Saul* (cat. 20).

Firm cultural ties between Russia and France were largely responsible for further additions to the collection of Western European – above all French – drawings. The enthusiasm in Russia for French art and literature began during Catherine's reign, and at the very height of her collecting

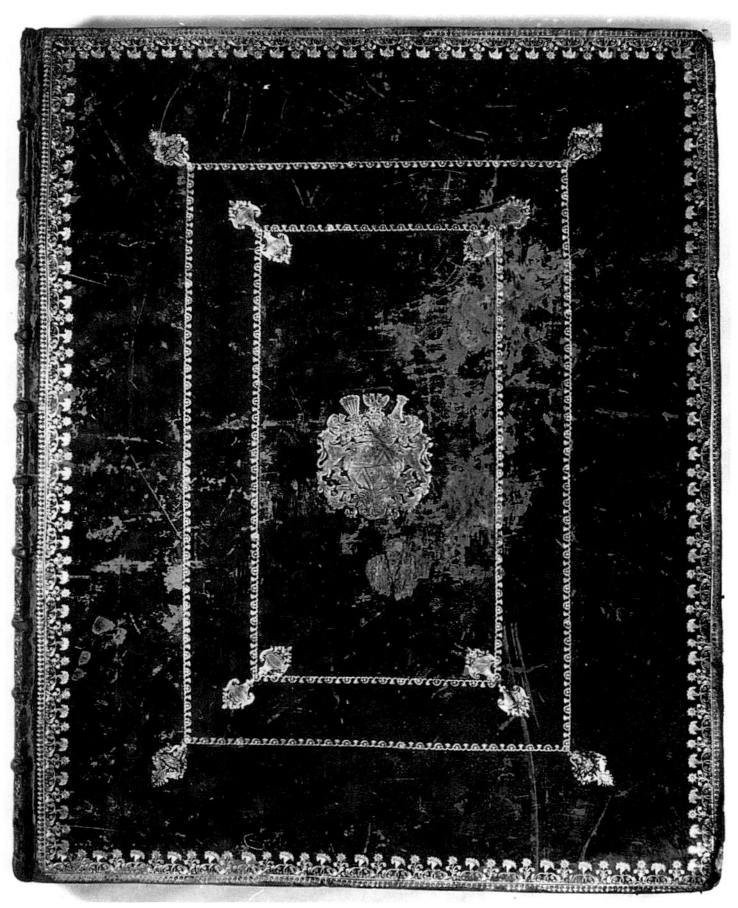

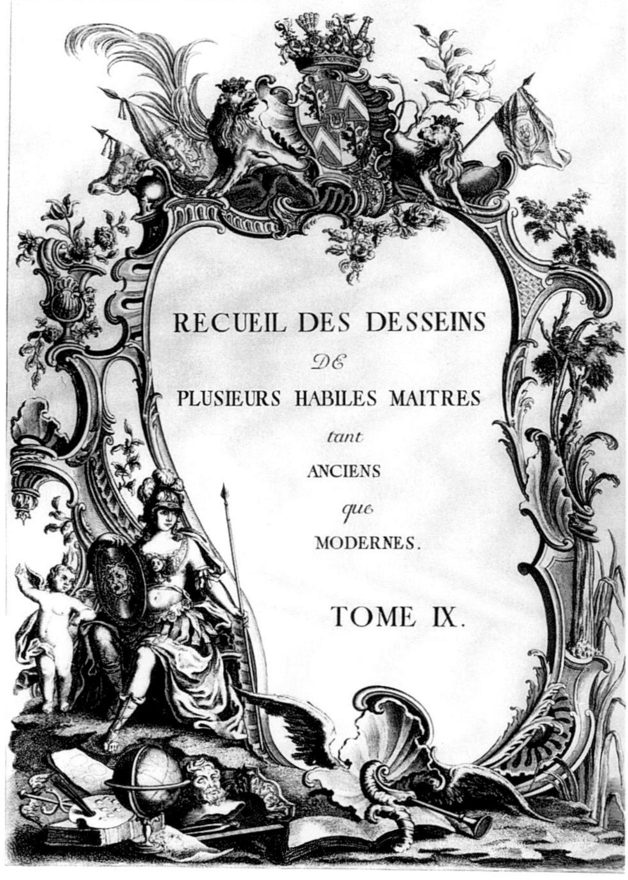
RECUEIL DES DESSEINS
DE
PLUSIEURS HABILES MAITRES
tant
ANCIENS
que
MODERNES.
TOME IX.

fig. 8
Leather binding from one of Count Heinrich Brühl's *in-folio* albums

fig. 9
A page from Brühl's album, 'Recueil des desseins de plusiers habiles maitres tant anciens que modernes'

fig. 10
The collector's mark of Paul I: the *P* beneath the crown

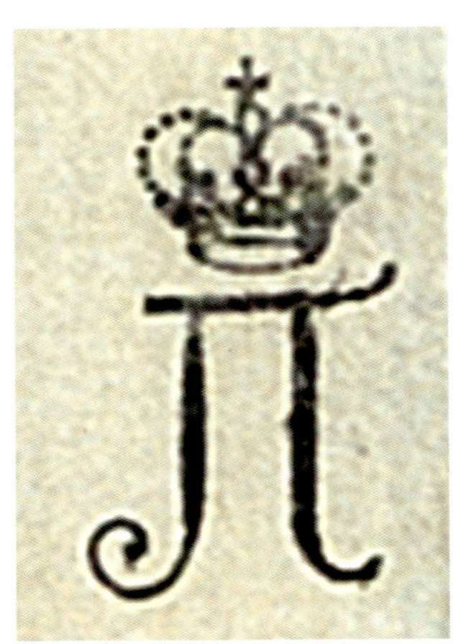

activities, from the 1760s to the 1780s, she was in close contact with a number of leading Enlightenment figures. She corresponded regularly with both Voltaire and Diderot, and she took advice from the French sculptor Maurice-Etienne Falconet (who was in St Petersburg working on a vast equestrian statue of Peter the Great, known today as *The Bronze Horseman*), from the draughtsman and engraver Charles-Nicolas Cochin, Secretary to France's Académie Royale, and from Baron Melchior Grimm (1723–1809), a German diplomat, connoisseur and journalist based in Paris. The result was a pronounced 'French' orientation in her collecting activities.

Catherine began assembling a collection of architectural drawings, one dominated by French masters, in the 1770s. The scale of her building activities in St Petersburg and its environs, and the extensive redecoration of her country palaces, was well known elsewhere in Europe and excited the interest of various foreign architects. In 1773, for instance, she received a gift in the form of an album of designs for a Pavilion of the Sciences and Arts (see cat. 64), which the architect Charles de Wailly dreamed of building at Tsarskoye Selo, her summer residence south-east of St Petersburg. In 1780, through Grimm, Catherine purchased a large collection of designs and drawings by the French architect Charles-Louis Clérisseau, something in the region of 1,120 sheets. She was keenly interested in architects like Clérisseau, whose neo-Antique and Greek Revival designs reflected the fashionable passion for Antiquity, and acquired yet more designs and drawings by de Wailly, 'ruins' paintings by Hubert Robert, and in 1782–3, on Grimm's recommendation, a large selection of views by Jean Houel, a friend of Jean-Jacques Rousseau and a regular visitor to Mme Geoffrin's well-known literary salons. These mainly showed various ancient sites in Sicily, and many had been published in the artist's *Voyage pittoresque des îles de Sicile, de Malte*… (4 vols, Paris, 1782–7). At 264 sheets, the Hermitage's collection of drawings by Houel – like the Clérisseau group – is the most numerous of any in the world.

At some date before 1797 the Hermitage acquired an album of drawings by Jacques Callot, formerly part of the celebrated Paris collection of Jean de Jullienne. The album consists of around 800 drawings by this outstanding draughtsman, mainly small format figure sketches, a considerable number of which were the basis for Callot's prints. If one adds to these sketches individual sheets by Callot – *Soldier with a Sword and Shield* (cat. 12) from the Cobenzl collection, *Parterre at Nancy* (cat. 13) and *The Temptation of St Anthony* (cat. 14), both from Jean de Jullienne – it becomes clear that Callot occupies a significant position in the French collection.

Initially the drawings, like some other works of art, formed part of Catherine's private collections and were kept with her library. She called for individual sheets to be brought to her from time to time, while those works Clérisseau had sent framed were hung in her boudoir and the various private rooms known as her 'attics' (a practice continued by Catherine's heirs). Only specialists were allowed to examine the drawings, in connection, for instance, with commissions for building works; later, the director of the porcelain factory was given access, as were members of the administration of the Imperial theatres. The architects Charles Cameron and Giacomo Quarenghi, both great admirers of Clérisseau, were given access to his drawings when working on projects at Tsarskoye Selo.

After Catherine's death the rate of the collection's growth slowed considerably. In 1804 Dmitry Buturlin, head of the museum, addressed a report to Emperor Alexander I (Catherine's grandson) in which he argued that the drawings collection had reached a sufficiently high level to require no further expansion, nor any further expenditure. Although some additions continued to be made, the heyday of the formation of this collection, in terms of both quantity and quality, had ended.

During the first decades of the 19th century the most notable acquisitions came in the form of architectural drawings and views, and among the works of the French school were albums with views and plans of buildings in Paris (1809–15), a gift to Alexander I from the celebrated architects Charles Percier (1764–1838) and Pierre Fontaine (1762–1853), as well as numerous designs and drawings by Auguste Montferrand (1786–1858) and Thomas de Thomon (1760–1813), who contributed so much to St Petersburg's architectural scene. Other significant collections of drawings acquired in the 19th century include those of V. P. Divov (1833) and Luigi Grassi (1862). The latter collection included Watteau's *Avenue in a Park* (cat. 35).

Even during Catherine's reign, specialists (members of the Academy of Arts, leading painters and printmakers) were invited to help select drawings, and in 1796 Paul I, Catherine's son, who had just succeeded to the throne, had brought in the architect Vincenzo Brenna to take charge of the Imperial collection of prints and drawings. In 1797 members of the Academy compiled the first inventory of drawings: although it covered just 6,798 items, all of these were stamped with an initial *P* (for Paul I) beneath a crown (fig. 10). In 1805, when the museum was reorganized under Alexander I, the Department of Drawings became an independent unit and a storage system was established, dividing works into five standard formats and within them according to author and school. Based on the principles of storage employed by Cobenzl, this system, in its main features, is still in use today.

In the wake of the Revolution in October 1917 a considerable amount of new acquisitions arrived. The number of drawings almost doubled, due both to the nationalization of private collections and the redistribution of collections within existing museums. In 1924, for example, some 2,000 of the most valuable Western European drawings were transferred from the museum and library of the St Petersburg Academy of Arts. The Academy's collection dated back to the time of Catherine's first acquisitions. In 1767 Lt.-Gen. Ivan Ivanovich Betskoy, the Academy's President, had given 7,000 drawings to the Academy, donating over 363 more in 1769. The first donation's contents were extremely uneven in quality. Alongside superb sheets (such as drawings by Jacques de Bellange) were many indifferent works, often supplementary or study sheets by little-known, and even unknown, artists. A considerable number of them are life studies, which were used by students for copying: many sheets today bear the traces of oils and paints. All the drawings donated in 1767 have a small stamped asterisk, the collector's mark Betskoy adopted (fig. 11).

Outstanding amongst the Betskoy drawings, however, is a collection of studies by Jean-Baptiste Greuze 'sent from the Most Honourable Mr Betskoy' in 1769. Of this, 240 sheets were by Greuze. None bears Betskoy's asterisk, and the Academy gave these drawings a mark in the form of a two-headed eagle (fig. 12). It is not clear why so successful an artist as Greuze parted with such a large body of working material, but Betskoy, who lived abroad between 1756 and 1762, was close to literary and artistic circles in Paris, where he attended Mme Geoffrin's salon and was acquainted with Baron Grimm and Diderot. It was, perhaps, on Diderot's recommendation and with his help that Betskoy was able to purchase Greuze's drawings.

For many years the Betskoy collection was shuttled to and fro between the Academy's museum and library, stored in closed boxes. It was only in 1863 that the first album with ten

opposite, top to bttom

fig. 11
A stamped asterisk, the collector's mark of Ivan Ivanovich Betskoy

fig. 12
The collector's mark of the St Petersburg Academy of Arts

fig. 13
The collector's mark of Alfred Beurdeley

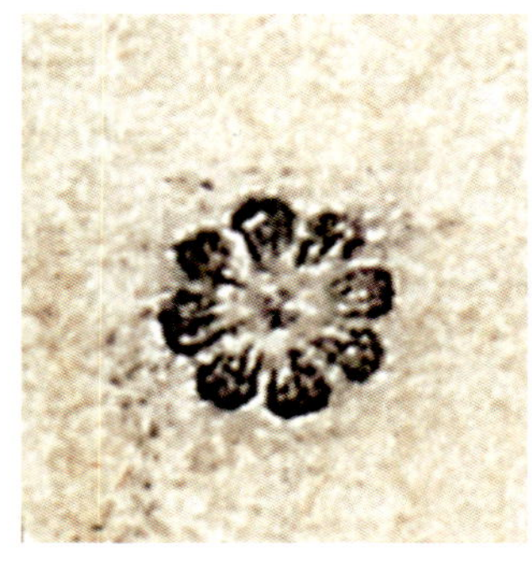

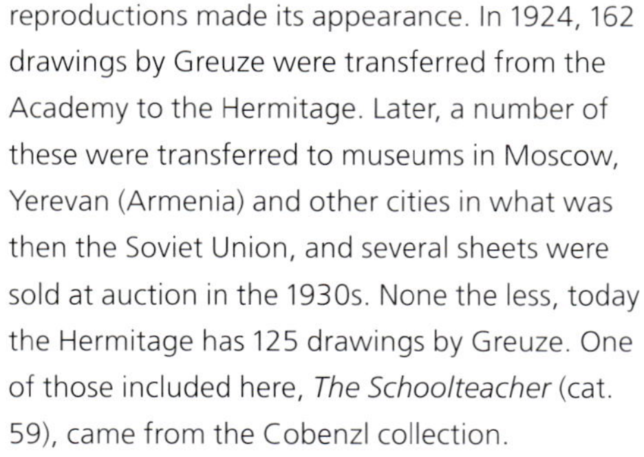

reproductions made its appearance. In 1924, 162 drawings by Greuze were transferred from the Academy to the Hermitage. Later, a number of these were transferred to museums in Moscow, Yerevan (Armenia) and other cities in what was then the Soviet Union, and several sheets were sold at auction in the 1930s. None the less, today the Hermitage has 125 drawings by Greuze. One of those included here, *The Schoolteacher* (cat. 59), came from the Cobenzl collection.

In quantity and composition the Hermitage's collection of drawings by Greuze is unique. It is far superior to the collection in either the Louvre or the Musée Tournus in the artist's home town. There are 30 studies of nude models made during Greuze's time at the Académie in Paris and 16 of female heads and several compositional sheets, but most numerous and precious are the preparatory studies of figures, heads and hands used for his paintings in oils. Thanks to Catherine's felicitous purchase of *Filial Piety (The Paralytic)* (cat. 50), which arrived at the Hermitage in 1766, both the painted canvas and eight preparatory drawings can be displayed together, revealing much of interest in the artist's method of work.

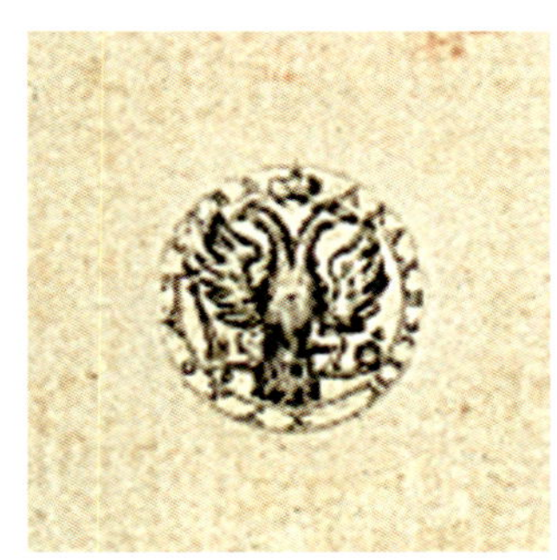

Between 1924 and 1928 a collection of works on paper was transferred to the Hermitage from another educational establishment, the library and museum of the former Baron Stieglitz Central School of Technical Drawing. This brought the Hermitage more than 5,000 drawings by architects, decorative artists and masters of ornamental and applied graphics, above all of the French school. Collections of such ornamental works first appeared in the 18th century, although that of the Stieglitz School had been acquired from the Paris antiquary Alfred Beurdeley in 1888, and included the former collection of Jules Carré. The Hermitage also has the manuscript catalogue of the Beurdeley collection, compiled by the owner himself. All the drawings from his collection bear a mark consisting of the first and last letters of his surname (fig. 13).

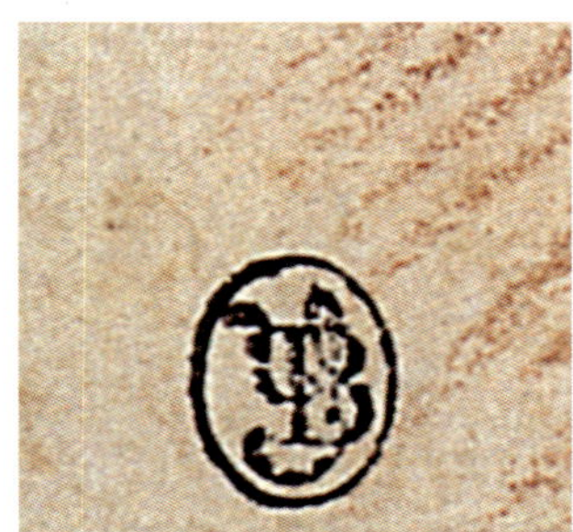

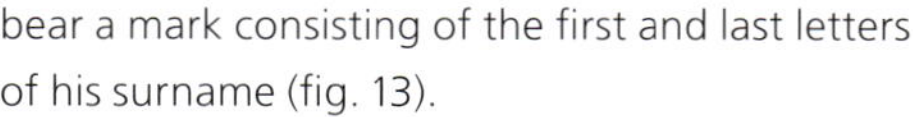

Paris was also the source of acquisition, in 1891, of ornamental drawings from the collection of Charles-Etienne Bérard, a considerable part of which was bought for the Stieglitz School by its honorary patron and Chairman of the Council, the renowned Russian statesman Alexander Polovstov. Next to the School building was a Museum, specially built by the architect Maximilian Messmacher, where students were able to improve their skills through the study of ornamental works of all kinds. Although part of Bérard's collection was afterwards transferred to other museums, the remaining body is still extremely valuable, with the most outstanding French ornamental artists of the 17th and 18th centuries – including Daniel Marot the Elder, Giles-Marie Oppenord and Jean-Guillaume Moitte – well represented.

Numerous other additions were made in the 1920s and 1930s. The basis of the 19th- and 20th-century collection, for instance, was laid by more than 30 sheets transferred from the State Museum of New Western Art in Moscow (in two lots, in 1934–5 and 1948–9), bringing works by Georges Rouault, Degas, Odilon Redon and Picasso. A large collection of drawings by Matisse (26 sheets) came in the form of a gift from one of the Museum's great friends and donors, Matisse's secretary and assistant, Lydia Delectorskaya, of which five are included here.

From the mid-1930s to the present day, additions have been made largely via the Hermitage Expert Purchasing Commission. This has brought the Museum an important work by Manet, *Mme Guillemet* (cat. 72), as well as drawings by Hubert Robert, Edmé Bouchardon and François Boucher. Today, the collection continues to expand, thanks to gifts made by Russian and foreign artists and collectors.

Style and Technique in French Drawings

VALERY SHEVCHENKO

By the end of Catherine the Great's reign, French works dominated the Hermitage's collection of drawings. Their number was doubled in the 1920s through the acquisition of the vast collection belonging to the Stieglitz School, which means that today we can trace all the main developments in French drawing from the 16th century onwards. Only a limited number of sheets survives from the 16th century, the most admired of which are crayon portraits. Initially intended as preparatory drawings for paintings, they were executed in black chalk but could easily be tinted with red chalk, known as *sanguine*. Sitters were usually shown in a three-quarters view, with costume details marked with just a few sparing touches of crayon. The most striking drawings are those that appear least finished, although they actually contain everything from volume to individual characterization. Thanks to interest among the aristocracy the genre developed rapidly in the 16th century, and collecting crayon drawings became popular. One gruesome legend, however, records that such portraits played a terrible role in 1572 in the St Bartholomew's Eve Massacre, by making it possible to identify the Huguenot victims.

Portrait drawings were valued even more highly than histories or mythological works, and as a result have survived in greater numbers. Leading portraitists – François Clouet, the unidentified artist known as 'L'Anonyme Lécurieux' and Pierre Dumonstier the Elder – are represented in the Hermitage by outstanding examples of their work. Clouet, superbly talented, succeeded his father, Jean, as Court artist under François I. His crayon portraits (fig. 14) are not sketches, they are highly finished and keenly perceptive in their analysis of personality. Drawn in black chalk with faces modelled in red chalk, black and red are combined for the eyes and hair, sometimes with additions of coloured pencil. Such portraits, which record real-life individuals in careful detail, existed alongside

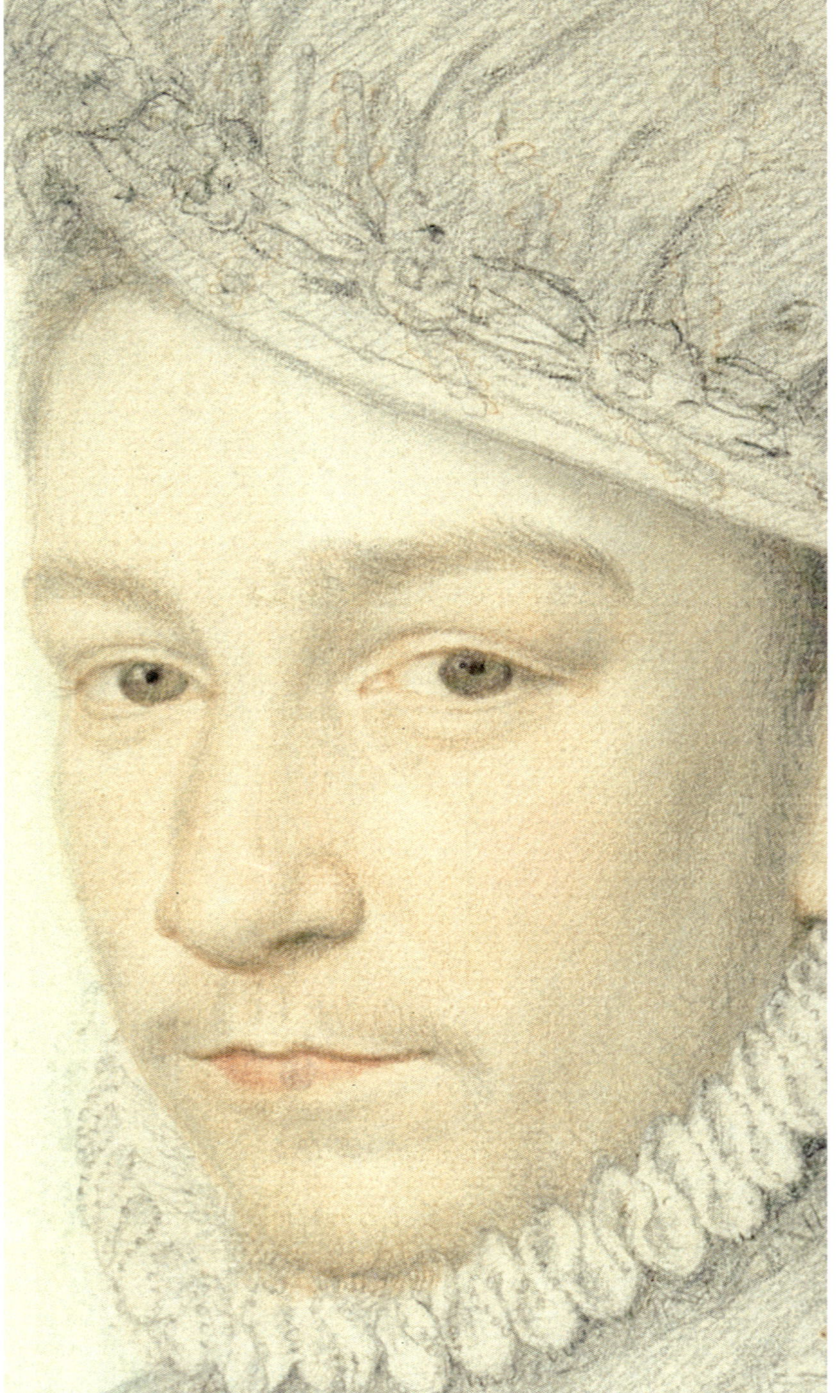

fig. 14
Detail from
François Clouet
Charles IX
(cat. 1)

more generalized compositional portrait studies. An extremely rare example of that kind of 16th-century drawing is the double portrait *Etienne and Pierre Dumonstier* (cat. 3) by Dumonstier the Elder, probably a preparatory work for a lost painted portrait. Almost as rare is the portrait of a boy by the artist known by the name of the collector who possessed many of his works, Lécurieux (cat. 2). But despite the popularity of portraits, the two Mannerist drawings by Jean Cousin the Younger included here (cats. 5, 6) show how the first School of Fontainebleau established by Rosso and Primaticcio in the 1530s radically influenced French drawing in the later 16th century, a trend that continued into the first quarter of the 17th century.

The lingering effects of Mannerist art and design explain why scholars of 17th-century French art prefer to begin with 1627, the year Simon Vouet returned to Paris from Italy, when Paris once again became an artistic centre. Vouet introduced a new style of Italian painting, a tempered Baroque classicism that determined the early phase of the French academic tradition, later developed by his numerous pupils. His own studies in black chalk are remarkable for their clarity of construction and for the elegant gestures and poses of his figures, as well as for their technical skill.

While in Italy drawing was becoming an increasingly independent genre, in France it was just as closely tied to paintings and prints in the 17th century as it had been in the 16th. Drawing continued to play a practical preparatory role, only very rarely taking on independent significance. Of the great abundance of excellent 17th-century artists, some would seem to have felt no need to precede their paintings with studies – or their drawings have simply not survived – while other artists celebrated as painters in their day are currently known largely through their drawings. One such is an outstanding representative of Late Mannerism in the early 17th century, Jacques de Bellange, painter to the Court of Lorraine. Attributions of paintings to him are subject to much heated discussion, and agreement among scholars is largely limited to his drawings. These reveal a brilliant and quirky personality. Another Lorraine artist, Jacques Callot, is also known only for his prints and drawings, which present a startling combination of unbounded fantasy and cruel realism, based on a profound knowledge of contemporary life and events. His metaphorical language and grotesquely fantastical images are revealed in a compositional sketch for *The Temptation of St Anthony* (cat. 14), for which he used a variety of materials, combining sweeping brushwork with fine pen lines to achieve striking and effective contrasts of light and shade. His more restrained manner when delineating townscapes and gardens is exemplified in his preparatory drawing for an etching, the *Parterre at Nancy* (cat. 13).

By the 17th century, draughtsmen had a varied repertory of drawing techniques to choose from. Black chalk with accents in white chalk was the most common method, adopted by Vouet, Eustache Le Sueur and Charles Lebrun under the influence of the Venetians and Annibale Carracci. It allowed for both broad, sweeping works, like those of Vouet, and for the fine restraint of Claude Mellan in his portraits and engravings. Red chalk could be combined with black, and artists began to develop the technique known as *trois crayons*, so highly valued by Rubens. A few might produce fine pen drawings, but mixed techniques were in general the fashion. Both Poussin and Claude combined pen drawing with brown wash, frequently adding gouache or white highlights. Colour could be introduced by means of watercolour or gouache, or even pastel (known since the 16th century), and artists made use of tinted paper that offered a variety of colours and textures.

fig. 15
Detail from
Claude Lorrain
Landscape with Figures
(cat. 23)

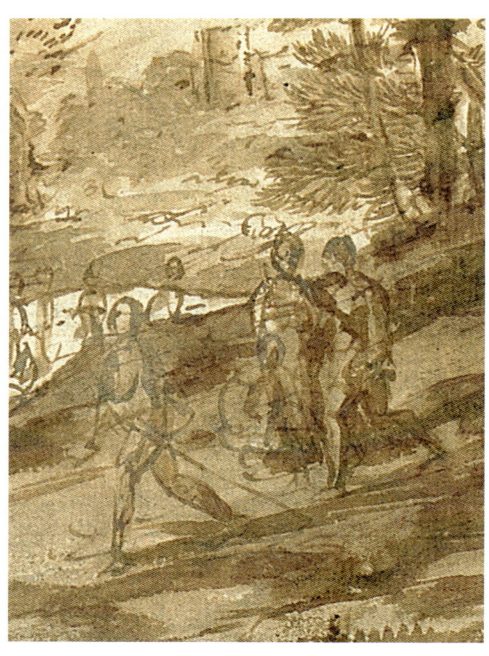

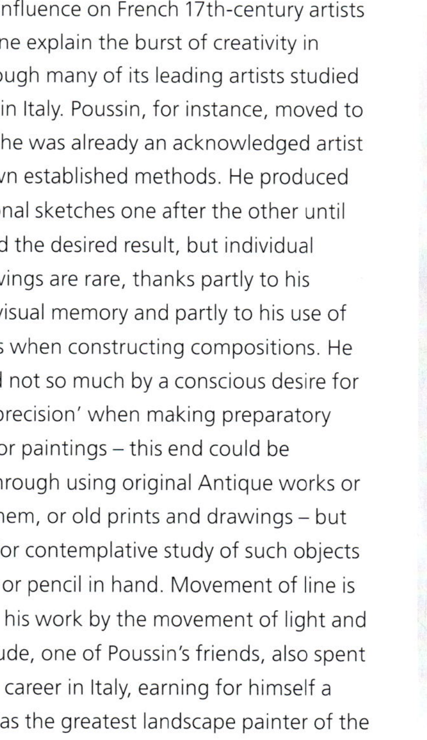

Italian influence on French 17th-century artists cannot alone explain the burst of creativity in France, though many of its leading artists studied or worked in Italy. Poussin, for instance, moved to Italy when he was already an acknowledged artist with his own established methods. He produced compositional sketches one after the other until he achieved the desired result, but individual figure drawings are rare, thanks partly to his incredible visual memory and partly to his use of wax figures when constructing compositions. He was moved not so much by a conscious desire for 'historical precision' when making preparatory drawings for paintings – this end could be achieved through using original Antique works or copies of them, or old prints and drawings – but by a need for contemplative study of such objects with brush or pencil in hand. Movement of line is replaced in his work by the movement of light and shade. Claude, one of Poussin's friends, also spent most of his career in Italy, earning for himself a reputation as the greatest landscape painter of the age. His drawings are more expressive and painterly, more virtuoso, than his works in oils (fig. 15). There is a freshness in his perception of nature in the drawings, which are well composed and reveal a mastery of technique. Both Turner and the Impressionists claimed him as their teacher.

Drawings were particular vital as preparatory material for professional engravers too. Claude Mellan, faultless draughtsman that he was, usually engraved portraits after his own sketches. Rejecting luxurious frames, he concentrated the viewer's attention on the sitter, although his original impression, expressed in the drawing, often underwent transformation in the course of transferring it to the print. His *Cardinal Mazarin* (cat. 25) is a plain and straightforward work, yet penetrating and strikingly effective. Mellan's near contemporary, Charles Lebrun, one of the

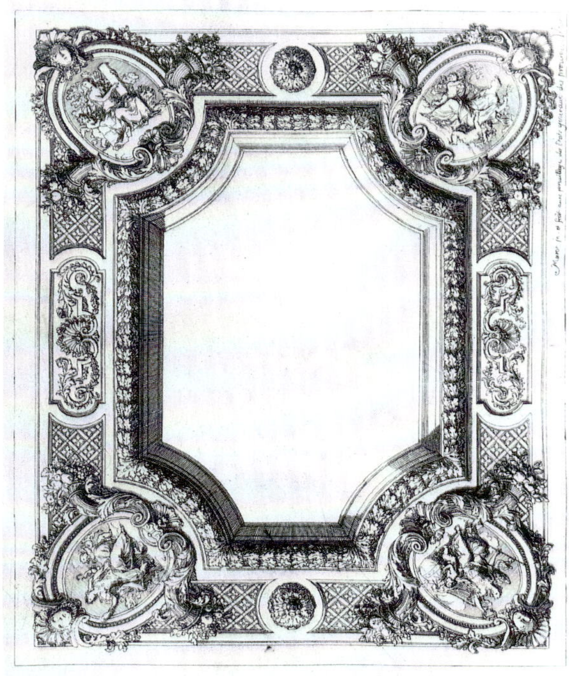

fig. 16
Daniel Marot the Elder
Design for a Ceiling

fig. 17
Detail from
Claude Audran III
Canape: Design for Upholstery
(cat. 31)

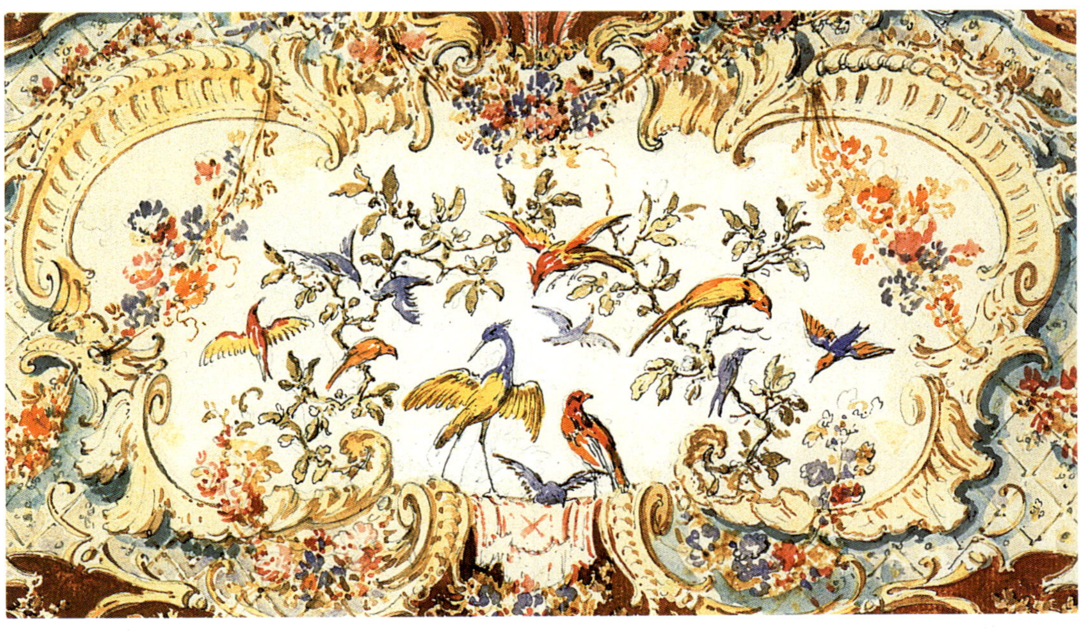

promoters of the academic Grand Style that dominated the second half of the 17th century, also appreciated the importance of making drawings during preliminary stages of work, and his own include examples of dashing bravura, simplicity and creative expression.

Ornamental drawings best express the essence of the changes that occurred in the late 17th and early 18th centuries. As the Grand Siècle came to an end, so the apparently unassailable position of the Grand Style weakened: contemporaries now saw it as pompous and heavy. The transition from bombastic luxuriance to whimsical lightness and flutter, formulated by Louis XIV's leading decorator and designer, Jean Bérain the Elder (1640–1711), led to the evolution of the Rococo style. Bérain's influence reached beyond France: for example, Daniel Marot facilitated the spread of 'French taste' to England and Holland when he quit France in the mid-1680s due to the renewed persecution there of Protestants (fig. 16). Other decorative artists, among them Claude Audran III and Claude Gillot, not to mention their brilliant pupil Antoine Watteau (whose career began with work on Arabesque panels), were also affected by the insuperable charm of Bérain's style. Audran none the less created his own style, the elegant refinement of his ornamental designs heralding many of what were to become staple Rococo motifs (fig. 17). Gilles-Marie Oppenord, a pioneer of 'picturesque taste', revealed his own rich fantasy and graphic skills in numerous variations on fountains and grottoes, vases, clocks, illustrated letters for books and more. Fountain motifs attracted many artists, although they treated them very differently, as we see if we compare examples by the decorator and sculptor Edmé Bouchardon (cat. 40) and a master of still-life, landscape and animals such as Jean-Baptiste Oudry. While Bouchardon sought to immortalize his name in monumental form, Oudry's fountain (fig. 18) in his *Hunting Trophies by a Fountain* is but a sketch for a Salon painting. Even so, he could draw daring and expressive hunting scenes

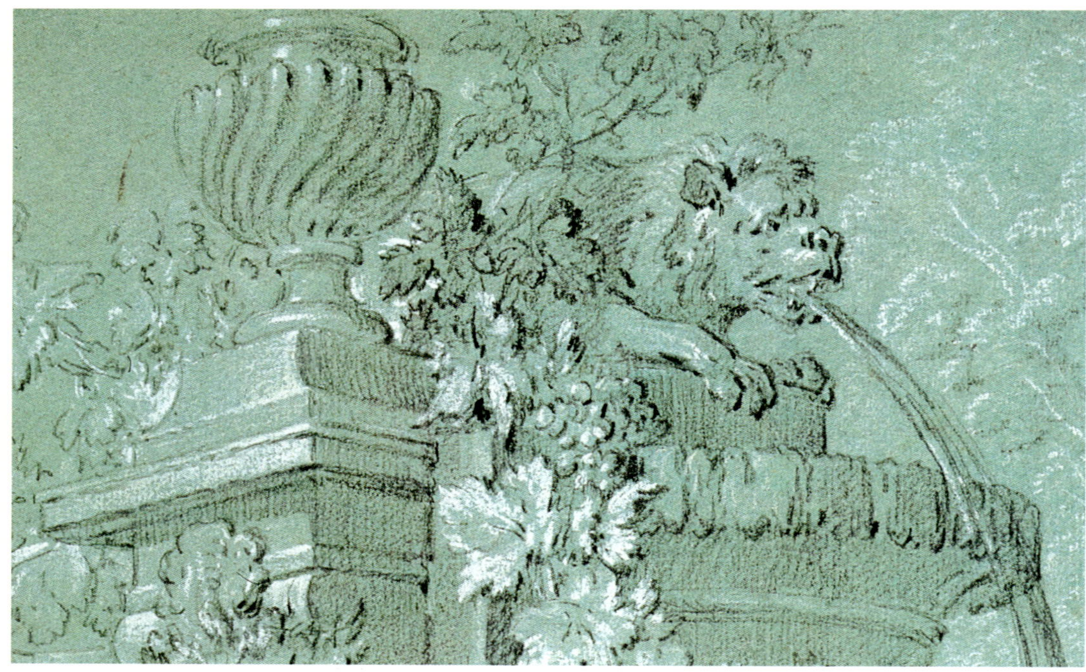

fig. 18
Detail from
Jean-Baptiste Oudry
Hunting Trophies by a Fountain
(cat. 38)

and observant records of the garden of the Arcueil estate (cat. 39).

Alterations in artistic perceptions during the first decades of the 18th century owed much to Watteau. Somehow his magical world of *fêtes-galantes* captured elusive moods, asserting the poetic value of fine nuances of feeling. His lyricism greatly influenced the further development of both French drawing and painting. In his best works using red chalk Watteau achieved a rich tonal vibrancy, not least in his exceedingly rare landscapes. Red chalk, combined with black and white chalk or white heightening, was also one of François Boucher's favourite materials. His *trois crayons* technique, combined with pastel, proved ideal for depicting the naked female body, yet inherent within it was a danger of breaking down the borders of graphic art, marking the first step towards purely painterly problems and effects. He exacerbated the dilemma through his use of tinted papers, from yellow and pale brown to a pale bluish-grey.

Fanciful motifs, dominated by curving and spiralling lines, invented by various artists were widely disseminated in prints by Jacques Gabriel Huquier (1695–1772), which spread a new decorative language that gave free rein to the unbridled imagination. Jacques Lajoue captured the essence of Rococo style not only through drawn and painted fantasies but through designs for applied art too. His *Autumn* and *Winter* (cats. 41, 42) are related in purpose to Watteau's frames for his *Autumn* and *The Birth of Venus* (cats. 33, 34), but unlike Watteau's graceful painted ornament, Lajoue's incredible *rocailles* are illusory in their sense of volume, materiality and weight. Lajoue set out his concepts as clearly as he could, whether for client or craftsman.

French drawing reached its highest point in the later 18th century. With but a few exceptions,

Europe's leading draughtsmen of the age were French, and it was they who discovered endless variety and revealed new potential in works on paper. Still a method for studying nature, drawings also served as a means of individual artistic expression. Artists often preferred materials and techniques that allowed them to work easily and quickly, preserving all the spontaneity of the hand's swift reactions to thoughts, feelings and sensations. This is manifested in some cases in drawings that are far more vivid and dynamic than the same artist's paintings, as with works by Boucher, Hubert Robert and Greuze. During this period, beauty came to be seen for the first time as a drawing's primary purpose. Previously unheard of refinements in technique and elegant decorative effects achieved through combinations of red, black and white chalks and pastel on tinted papers contributed to the increasing popularity for drawing. A variety of shades of red chalk, from warm, almost orange, to cold red and even lilac were employed. In keeping with the tendency towards increasing use of colour, artists enriched brown wash or black ink with watercolour, gouache and pastel. Paper might be yellow, brown, grey, pale blue, even pink.

Drawings were now acquired not only by specialists but by ordinary followers of fashion, who often used them to decorate their walls. Drawing had at last been raised from subordinate status to that of an independent art form. Artists with particular skills or interests might now devote themselves to it almost entirely, and the results were for the first time exhibited at the annual Paris Salons. Drawings were collected avidly and discussed by critics, and the century's most famous auctions were of drawings. Perfection of technique combined with natural artistry of execution represented the ideal, but while connoisseurs tended to prefer elegantly careless,

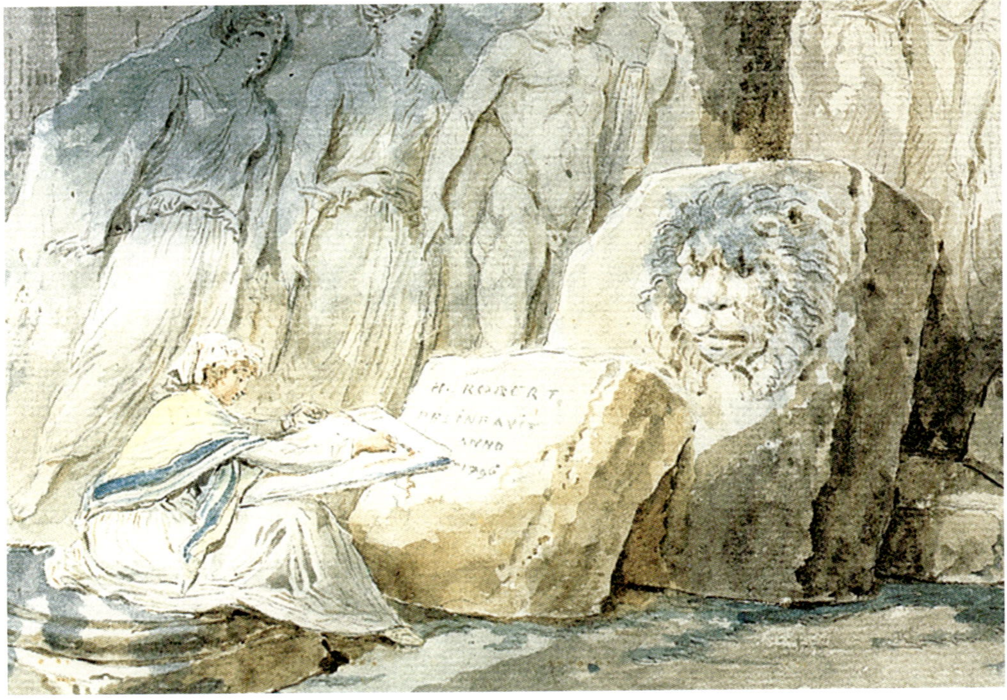

fig. 19
Detail from **Hubert Robert**
A Young Lady Drawing Amid Antique Ruins
(cat. 63)

hasty sketches, the broader public most appreciated highly finished compositions.

Rococo art may have been admired in some circles, but it also aroused keen dislike in others, who saw in it the expansion of 'bad taste'. Behind such criticism lay loyalty to classical norms, to balance and clarity, which made a return to them inevitable. Neoclassicism was a reaction to Rococo eccentricity, but despite its self-imposed task of reforming, purifying and 'antiquating' art, in many cases it simply gave a slightly new appearance to the dominant fashion. The wild fantasy of Rococo was merely contrasted with a different form of 'non-realism', a kind of classical eccentricity. While drawings by Rococo masters are wonderfully light and airy, impermanent and changing, those by Neoclassicists strive consciously for sculptural precision, their models often being three-dimensional reliefs. This last is ideally illustrated in the work of Jean-Guillaume Moitte, epitomizing decorative French Neoclassicism (cat. 66).

One of Jean-Baptiste Greuze's most important moralizing works, *Filial Piety* (cat. 50), together with eight of the Hermitage's nine studies for the painting, enable us to take a closer look at the working method of one 18th-century artist. Diderot wrote an impassioned eulogy of Greuze's obsession as he prepared each new composition, rethinking the subject and seeking exactly the right models. No other French 18th-century painter was so consistent and committed a draughtsman. Greuze saw nothing wrong in spending several years on a painting. Studies were produced for both main and secondary figures, their dimensions in the studies frequently in accordance with those in the resulting canvas. There are at times small changes in the poses, but usually each study was 'mounted' in its place. Vivid, expressive, brilliantly executed, the Hermitage studies (late 1750s–1760s) are almost totally free of the sentimental didacticism so insistently registered in the paintings.

Among the great variety of genres characteristic of French art of the second half of the 18th century are the landscapes with Roman monuments and ruins, a feature of the fascination for Antiquity that gripped the age. Architectural fantasies by such consistent *ruinistes* as Charles-Louis Clérisseau and Hubert Robert (fig. 19) were in great demand on the art market. Such works were represented each year at the Salon and were highly valued by collectors. Architects and others refused to limit themselves to designing plans, elevations and cross-sections, and set their projected buildings in superbly drawn landscapes enlivened with little genre scenes (Charles de Wailly) or presented them as part of colourful theatrical festivities (Louis-Jean Desprez). Both De Wailly, a prizewinning Parisian architect, and Desprez, architect to the Swedish Court, sent designs to Catherine II in the vain hope of winning the approval and patronage of the fabulously rich Russian Empress.

The trend in French drawing throughout the 16th to 18th centuries reveals a gradual movement away from contour and line towards areas of colour and tone, a qualitative transition from a purely supplementary role to an independent form of creativity. For the 19th century, however, it is impossible to continue tracing this development through a schematically organized sequence of Neoclassicism, Romanticism, Impressionism and Post-Impressionism. Drawing loses its unity in the 19th century, not just because of the appearance of various new national schools, endless innovative trends and tendencies, but also because of its division into numerous genres. In addition to accepted kinds of drawing, there were illustrations for books, periodicals and newspapers, industrial graphics, posters, caricatures and yet more. During the Napoleonic period, Pierre-Paul Prud'hon, with his unmistakable elegant rhythmic lines enveloped in soft mists of black chalk modelling, from which he produced incredibly fine poetic effects, had preserved the traditional concept of drawing, as did Ingres, an admirer of Raphael and the most talented pupil of the great Neoclassicist Jacques-Louis David (1748–1825). Ingres understood himself to be a painter first and foremost, seeing his considerable skill as a draughtsman merely as a necessary part of his craft. Hugely irritated when his drawings were praised above his paintings, he none the less set a standard of draughtsmanship still respected today. His combination of precise lines with softness and light allowed him to play not with contours so much as with light. Right into old age he composed each drawing with confident lines of his Conté pencil, unalterably consistent, careful and committed.

Drawing continued to serve different functions for different artists. While a series of dynamic, emotional sketches (see cat. 70) for the painting *Death and the Woodcutter* was for Jean-François Millet merely a means of establishing the composition for a single canvas, for Gustave Doré, who achieved unheard-of recognition as an illustrator and inventive caricaturist, each drawing might in itself become a finished work ready to be reproduced in books and periodicals (cat. 71). Edouard Manet's bewitching summary sketch of a young Parisian woman who seems to have appeared briefly in front of the artist's eyes before disappearing once more into the urban throng is a superb example of his 'impressions' of life (cat. 72). As for Edgar Degas, never had any artist used pastel so daringly and with so much energy. His drawings brought out new potential in the technique. Degas' main aim was unity of composition and drawing: by studying repeatedly and untiringly the same poses and gestures, he became caught up by a desire to encapsulate them in the dynamics of soft, colourful line.

In the late 19th century and early 20th, the dividing line between finished composition and hasty sketch disappeared almost completely. Henri Matisse's pencil drawings do not describe specific reality, rather they capture reality's movement, its tempo, its expressive foundation, omitting everything superfluous, sacrificing visual or anatomical precision for the sake of force of expression. Unity of artistic vision and temperamental execution animate the previously unthinkable use of lines of identical pressure and quality set off by the whiteness of the paper. A defining feature of 20th-century drawing was to be its intellectual nature, in which the artist was less concerned with depicting visible reality, rather creating a graphic analogy for it, purified of empirical, chance qualities. Picasso sought that same integrity and unity of the paper's space. An artist of true genius, a joker, an overturner of accepted ideas, a persistently curious student and experimenter, he turned to a stupefying kaleidoscope of changing styles and art forms, now working with unbroken lines like calligraphic symbols, now producing various combinations of abstract line with areas of colour, now approaching closer to painting in his technique and use of materials.

So small a selection as this one from the Hermitage's wealth of French drawings cannot trace all the stages, styles and techniques in so long a period of evolution, but the inspired works presented here allow us a glimpse of the main features in the history of almost five centuries of drawing.

CATALOGUE

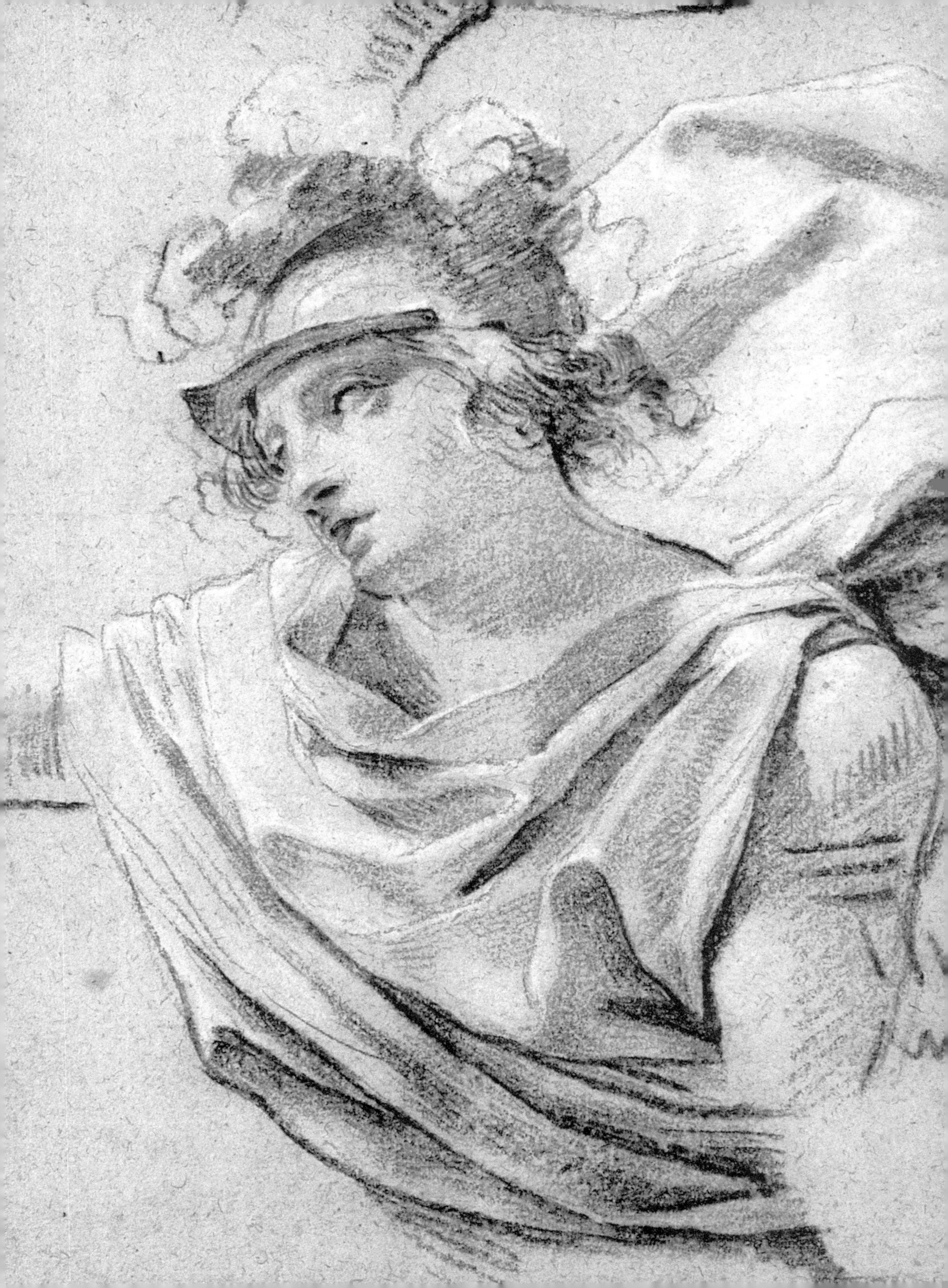

1

François Clouet

c. 1522 – 1572

Charles IX

Black and red chalk.
335 × 225 mm

Old inscription in pen and brown ink top right: *le roi Charles IXe*; above in black chalk: *1566* and *1569* (in which the *9* covers a second *6*)

PROVENANCE: collection of Count Carl Cobenzl, Brussels (collector's mark L. 2858b); 1768 acquired for the Hermitage: collector's mark L. 2061

Inv. no. OR 2893

EXHIBITIONS: 1867 St Petersburg, no. 404 (as Dumonstier); 1926 Leningrad, no. 193; 1955 Moscow, p. 77; 1956 Leningrad, pp. 89, 90; 1969 Leningrad, no. 19, ill.; 1969 Leningrad–Moscow, no. 34, ill.; 1972 Vienna–Graz, no. 13, ill.; 1982 Florence, no. 86, ill.; 1987 Delhi, no. 75, ill.

LITERATURE: Moreau-Nélaton [1908], vol. I, pp. 24, 38; vol. II, p. 84; vol. III, p. 137, no. 17; Moreau-Nélaton 1908b, p. 57, fig. VII; Marcel 1911, p. 12, ill.; Moreau-Nélaton 1924, vol. I, pp. 75, 76, fig. 23; Dimier 1924–6, vol. II, p.120, no. 471; Kamenskaya 1949, p. 25, ill.; Maltseva 1958, p. 65, ill.; Kamenskaya 1962, p. 41, ill.; Maltseva 1963, p. 35, no. 15, ill.; Kamenskaya, Novoselskaya 1969, no. 30, ill.; Maltseva 1978, pp. 126, 127, ill.; Hermitage 1994, no. 345, ill.; Jollet 1997, pp. 241–5, fig.

Crayon portraits first appeared as preparatory studies for painted portraits, but their popularity grew rapidly in 16th-century France and they soon became widespread. Readily portable and inexpensive, crayon portraits could be presented to friends, taken on one's travels, used to compose portrait galleries and be glued into albums. Numerous copies could be produced of such portraits, either by the original artists or, more usually, by pupils.

François Clouet, who studied under his father, the portraitist Jean Clouet, was the leading master in the genre in the mid-16th century. He worked at the French Court producing designs for royal processions and ceremonies, but enjoyed particular fame for his portraits.

The once extensive body of works attributed to Clouet is gradually being reduced in number, as scholars identify works in a similar manner that are, in fact, by artists of his school – including some high-quality drawings that are none the less copies. This portrait of Charles IX, King of France (reigned 1560–74), is, however, one of Clouet's recognized masterpieces. It was the basis for a full-length portrait in oils of the King (fig. 20), which is also dated to 1566 on the basis of the date on the drawing. **I.N.**

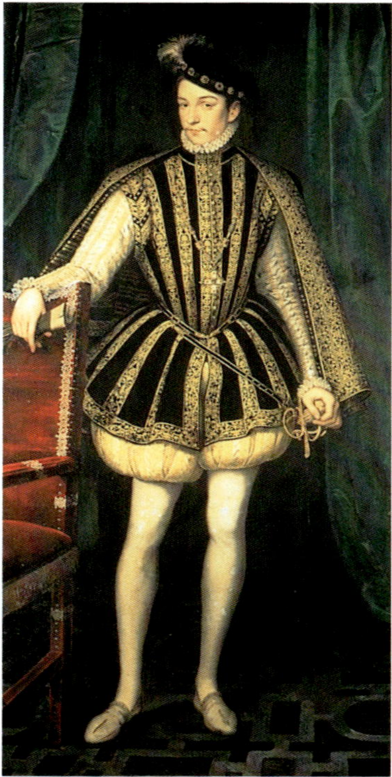

fig. 20
François Clouet
Charles IX, 1566

oil on canvas, 222 × 115 cm.
Kunsthistorisches Museum, Vienna / Bridgeman Art Library

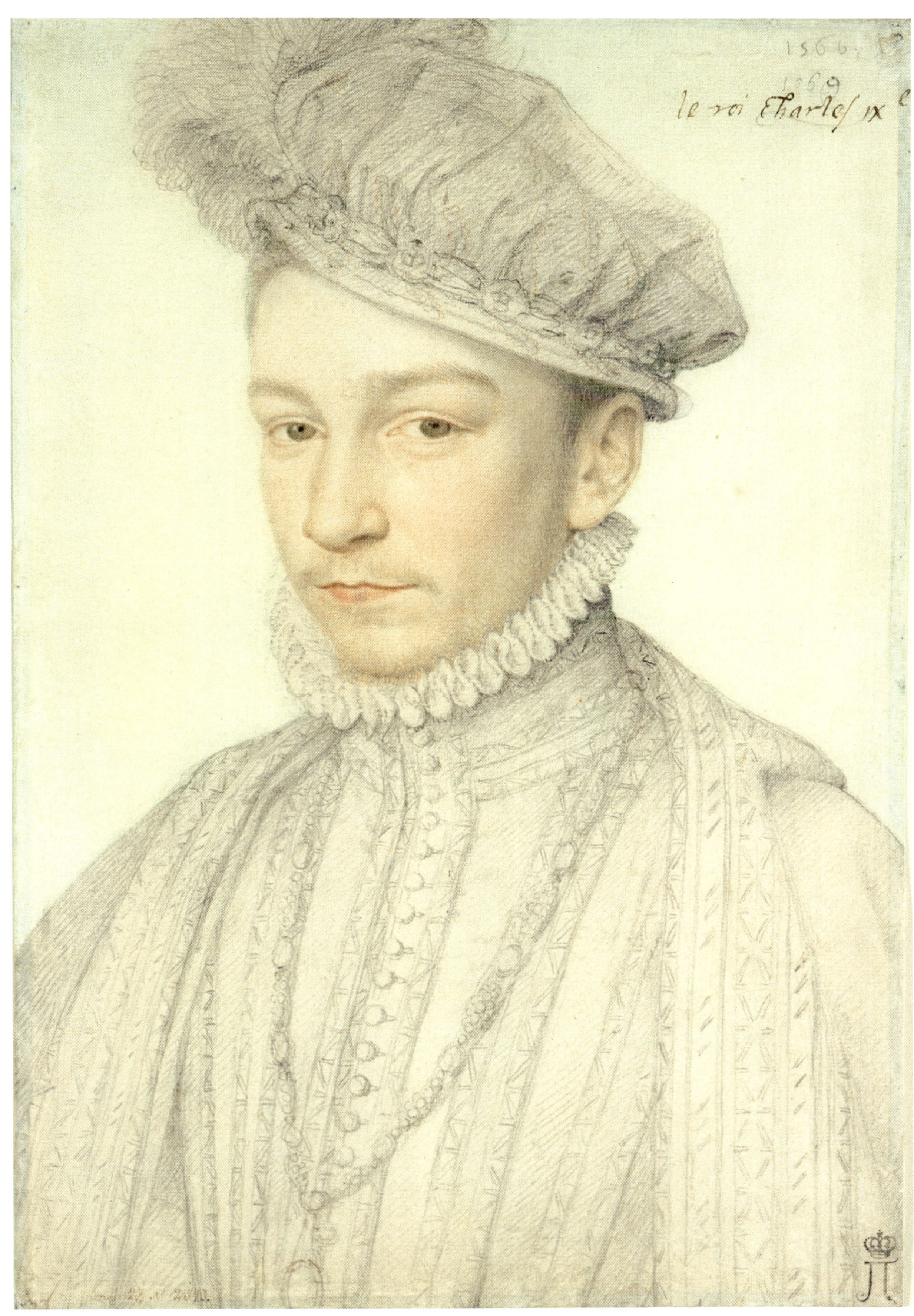
1566
1569
le roi Charles IX

2

'L'Anonyme Lécurieux'

Second half of the 16th century

Boy with Brown Eyes

Black and red chalk, pastel.
315 × 220 mm. Lined

Old inscription in pen and brown ink beneath the drawing in a cartouche: *Du Monstier*

PROVENANCE: collection of Count Carl Cobenzl, Brussels (collector's mark L. 2858b); 1768 acquired for the Hermitage: collector's mark L. 2061

Inv. no. OR 2916

EXHIBITIONS: 1955 Moscow, p. 85; 1956 Leningrad, p. 93; 1963 Stockholm, no. 24; 1969 Leningrad, no. 1; 1970 Budapest, no. 2, ill.; 1972b Leningrad, no. 434; 1975 Berlin, no. 19, ill.

LITERATURE: Dimier 1924–6, vol. II, p. 155, no. 4; Kamenskaya 1960b, no. 64, ill.; Kamenskaya 1962, p. 44, ill.; Kamenskaya, Novoselskaya 1969, no. 1, ill.

Among the artists who followed François Clouet in the genre of crayon portraits was 'L'Anonyme Lécurieux', named after the owner of a collection that included a group of his drawings. Several of his works are now in the Hermitage. Like those by Clouet, they are remarkable for their delicate modelling in light and shade, combined with a more graphic approach to contours. One feature of this drawing is the relatively strong intensity of the colour.

Portraits of children were not common in the 16th century, and this particular example stands apart even among the excellent works by contemporaries for its vivid directness. **I.N.**

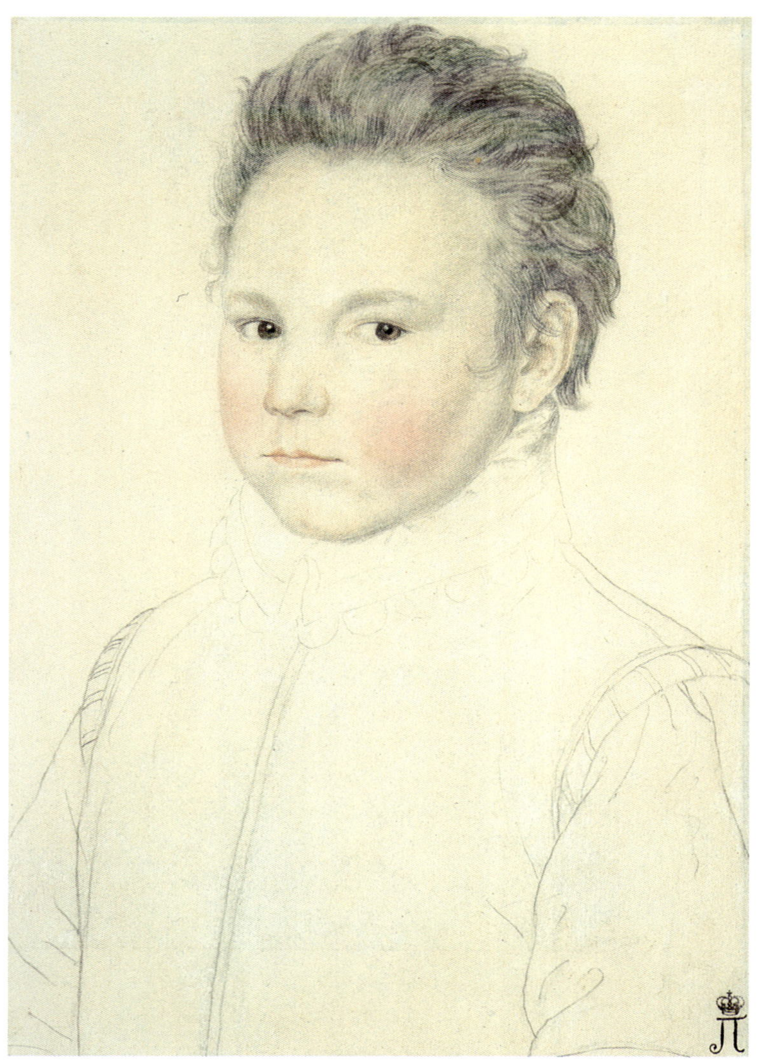

3

Pierre Dumonstier I
[the Elder]

c. 1545 – 1625 Paris

Etienne and Pierre Dumonstier

Black chalk; squared in black chalk. 225 × 310 mm. Lined

Inscription in pen and brown ink in the hand of Pierre Dumonstier the Younger above the heads: Estienne du Monstier l'aisné and Pierre du Monstier son frère; beneath, an old inscription in pen and brown ink in a cartouche: Du Monstier

PROVENANCE: collection of Count Carl Cobenzl, Brussels (collector's mark L. 2858b); 1768 acquired for the Hermitage: collector's mark L. 2061

Inv. no. OR 2866

OLD MANUSCRIPT CATALOGUES: Cobenzl – 'Catal[ogue] de Cabin[et], Catalogue de Desseins, Seconde Grandeur', p. 39v., Carton no. 33, no. 1, 'Monstier, du Monstier Père et fils'

EXHIBITIONS: 1926 Leningrad, no. 197; 1938 Leningrad, issue III, no. 50; 1956 Leningrad, p. 88; 1968 Leningrad no. 10; 1969 Leningrad–Moscow, no. 24; 1970 Budapest, no. 34, ill.; 1972, Vienna–Graz, no. 19, ill.; 1975 Berlin, no. 25, ill.; 1982 Florence, no. 89, ill.; 1998–9 New York, no. 85, ill.

LITERATURE: Moreau–Nélaton 1908a, p. 5, ill.; Moreau–Nélaton 1924, vol. I, pp. 182, 213; vol. III, p. 137, fig.; Dimier 1924–6, vol. II, p. 204, no. 804; Nothaft 1936, pp. 11, 12, 20, no. XII, ill.; Kamenskaya, Novoselskaya 1969, no. 21, ill.; Maltseva 1978, p. 176, ill.

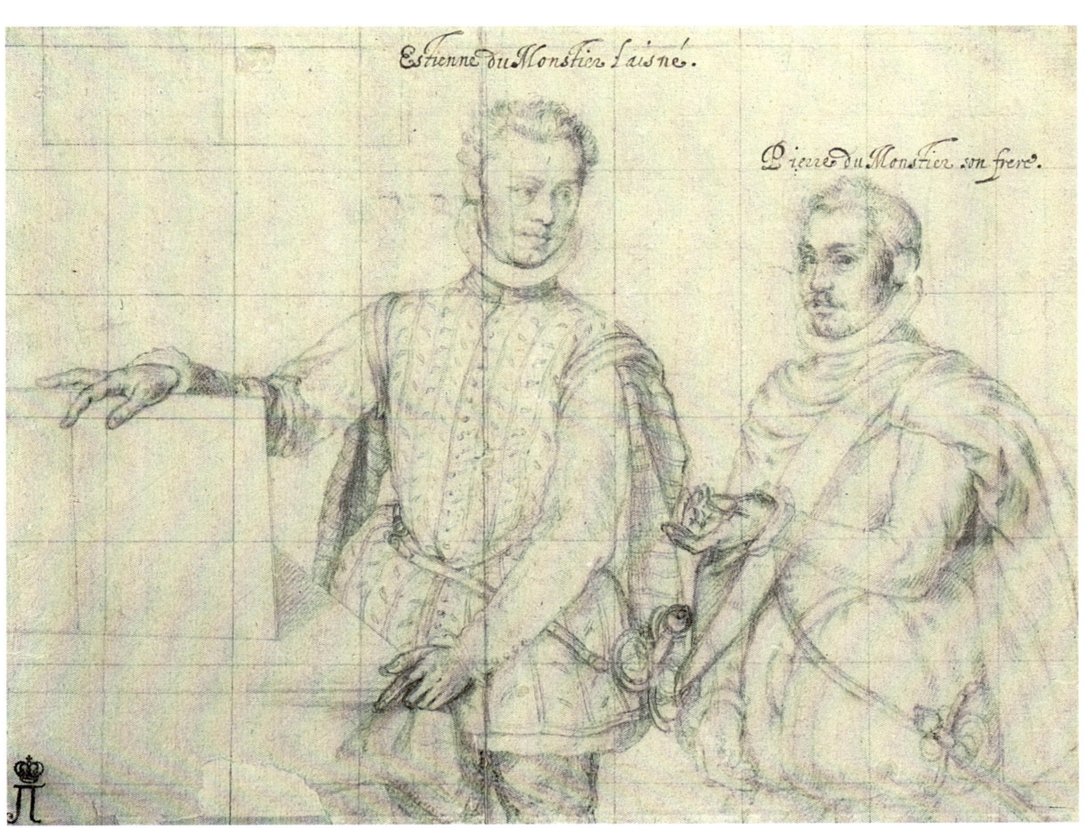

Pierre Dumonstier the Elder was the most talented member of the extensive Dumonstier (Dumoustier) family of artists, which included his father Geoffroy (c. 1510–1573), his brother Etienne (1540–1603), shown in this portrait, and his two nephews, Pierre the Younger (c. 1585–1656) and Daniel (1574–1646), the latter a famous portraitist. Pierre the Younger and Etienne, who was for a time a diplomat at the Court of Catherine de' Medici, specialized in portraits too.

The Hermitage has several works by Pierre the Elder, including this extremely rare work, a double-portrait of the two artist brothers. Its rarity lies not only in the paired portrait type but in that it depicts artists, people of relatively lowly status, rather than members of the royal family or courtiers.

The brothers are shown in relaxed poses, apparently in conversation. Etienne, with one hand resting on the edge of a table, with the other holds a book (or folder?) while turning towards his brother. This sharp turn of the head, Etienne's glancing eyes and Pierre's gesturing hand together indicate that the artist sought to avoid the static poses common in contemporary portraiture. Since the sheet is squared for transfer, it is clearly a preliminary study for a larger portrait in oils, though no such work is known. I.N.

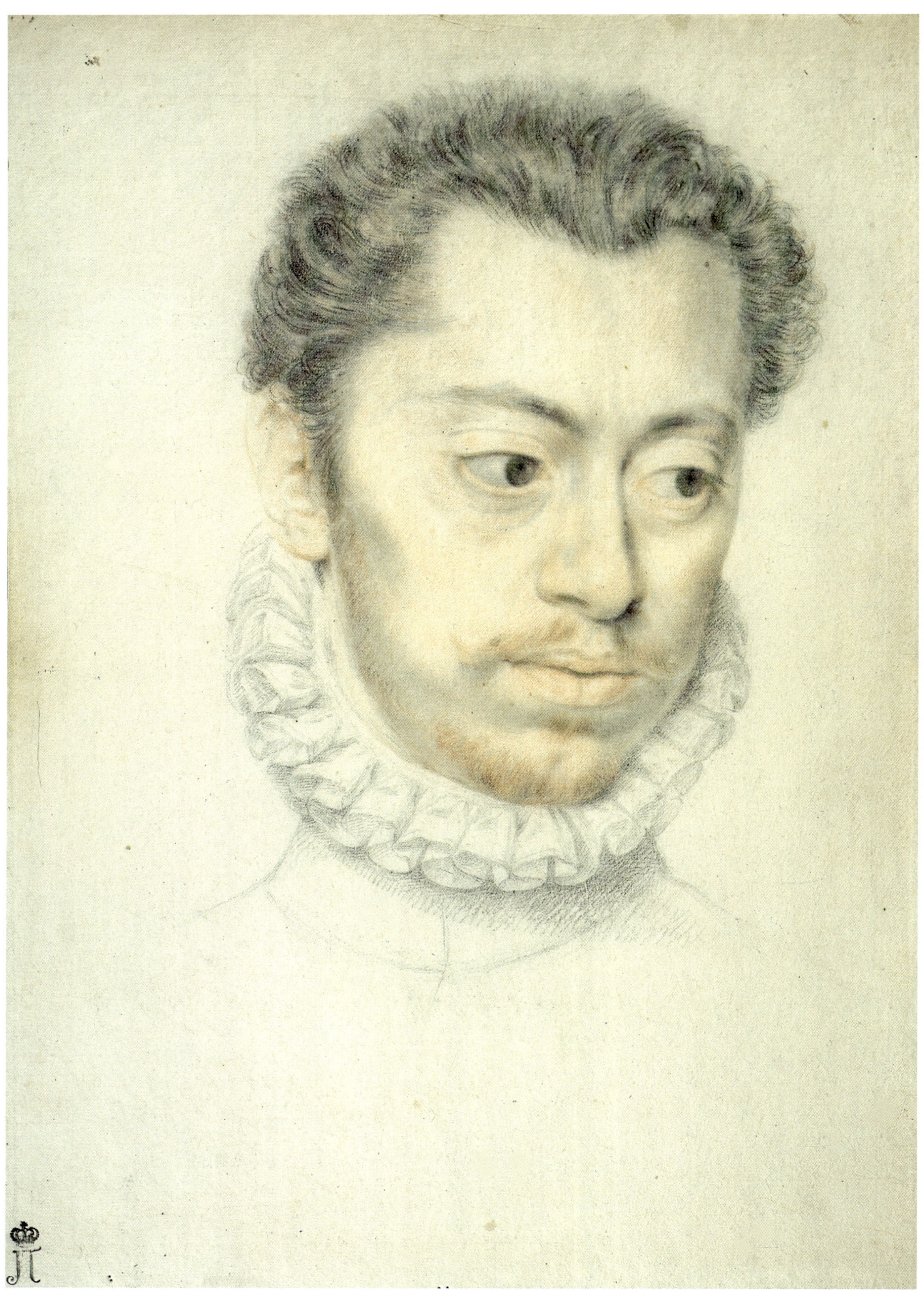

4
Pierre Dumonstier I [the Elder]

Etienne Dumonstier

Black and red chalk, pastel.
400 × 270 mm. Lined

PROVENANCE: collection of Count Carl Cobenzl, Brussels (collector's mark L. 2858b); 1768 acquired for the Hermitage: collector's mark L. 2061

Inv. no. 7400.

EXHIBITIONS: 1926 Leningrad, no. 198; 1938 Leningrad, issue III, no. 48; 1963 Stockholm, no. 26; 1969 Leningrad–Moscow, no. 25; 1972 Vienna–Graz, no. 20, ill.; 1988–9 New York, no. 84, ill.

LITERATURE: Moreau-Nélaton [1908], III, p. 137, no. 20; Moreau-Nélaton 1908a, p. 5, fig. 5; Moreau-Nélaton 1908b, p. 182, fig. 104; Dimier 1924–6, vol. II, p. 104, no. 803; Nothaft 1936, pp. 11, 20, ill. XIII; Krol 1938, p. 156, ill.; Kamenskaya 1960b, no. 35, ill.; Kamenskaya, Novoselskaya 1969, no. 20, ill.; Maltseva 1978, p. 173, ill.

In addition to the double-portrait of Pierre and Etienne Dumonstier (cat. 3), the Hermitage has another two drawings of Etienne's head, also by Pierre. One of these is dated 1569 (fig. 21), and since all three images are similar in terms of the clothing and the sitter's age, they must all have been executed in the same period.

This portrait study of Etienne clearly represents a further stage of work after the sketch in the double-portrait, and was surely used in finishing Etienne's head in the unknown painting.

The beautiful head, with its curling hair and large protuberant eyes, has a commanding presence, which is reinforced by the large size of the image and the broad texture of the drawing. The light touches of fine pastels to the face add to the highly attractive nature of this work. I.N.

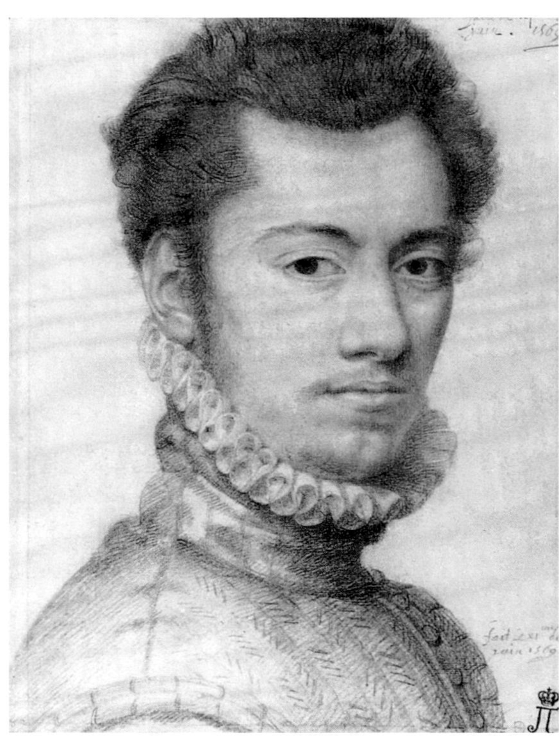

fig. 21
Pierre Dumonstier I
Etienne Dumonstier, 1569
(inv. no. OR 2868)

Jean Cousin II [the Younger]

Sens c. 1522 – c. 1594 Paris

Drawings by the Mannerist artists Jean Cousin the Elder (1490–c. 1560) and his son could not for many years be differentiated, largely because there were so few works in existence on which to base an analysis. Through his study of the manuscript 'Le Livre de fortune' (1568; Institute Français, Paris), illustrated with emblem drawings by Cousin the Younger (published as *Le Livre de fortune, recueil de deux cents dessins inédits de Jean Cousin* in 1883), Otto Benesch was at last able to establish a small *œuvre* for the younger Cousin (Benesch 1939–40, pp. 271–80).

There are four drawings in the Hermitage by Cousin, all showing mythological figures in a landscape, all of which arrived in 1768 with the collection of Carl Cobenzl. In the manuscript catalogue of the collection the drawings were given to an unidentified master. Later they were attributed to Bartholomeus Spranger (1546–1611), according to the old inscription in a cartouche beneath the drawing, to Etienne Delon, and finally to Cousin (Dobroklonsky 1932, pp. 44–7).

The attribution to Cousin was made by T. Kamenskaya: the dimensions of the sheets, the nature of the compositions, the treatment of figures and landscape and the technique are so close to accepted works – *Diana and Endymion* (Albertina, Vienna, inv. no. 24.468) and *Mercury Stealing the Cattle of Admetus* (Bibliothèque Nationale, Paris, inv. no. 2259) – that his authorship can be considered to have been firmly established (Kamenskaya, Novoselskaya 1969, nos. 33–6).

Cousin's compositions usually consist of several planes, with scenes in the foreground, middle and background linked by a single subject, and individual motifs – Eros with his bow and arrows, river gods and nymphs, baskets with flowers and fruits – frequently repeated. None the less, there are complications in identifying his subjects: Veronika Birke (1986, no. 14) notes that Cousin generally depicted non-specific scenes from classical mythology, full of puzzling features that today elude identification.

Two of the four Hermitage sheets bear traditional titles: *Landscape with Apollo* (fig. 23) and *Jupiter and Semele* (fig. 22), but only a hypothetical identification of the two landscapes with mythological figures shown here (cats. 5, 6) can be made. All four sheets are listed in the manuscript catalogue of the Cobenzl collection merely as 'Landscapes'. The similarities between them and the illustrations to 'Le Livre de fortune' suggests that they date from Cousin's mature period.

In composition, subject and style, the drawings in the Hermitage, Albertina and Bibliothèque Nationale are sufficiently similar to indicate that they form a series, or part of a series. Clearly, there is good justification for Kamenskaya's suggestion (Kamenskaya, Novoselskaya 1969, 'Foreword'), supported by Béguin (1972 Paris, no. 68), Knab and Widauer (1993, no. F–64), that they may have been intended as designs for tapestries. Their decorative nature and the pinkish-violet colouring supports this interpretation, although no specific tapestries have been identified.

fig. 22
Jean Cousin II
Jupiter and Semele

pen and brown ink and violet wash over black chalk, 285 × 415 mm (inv. no. OR 5603)

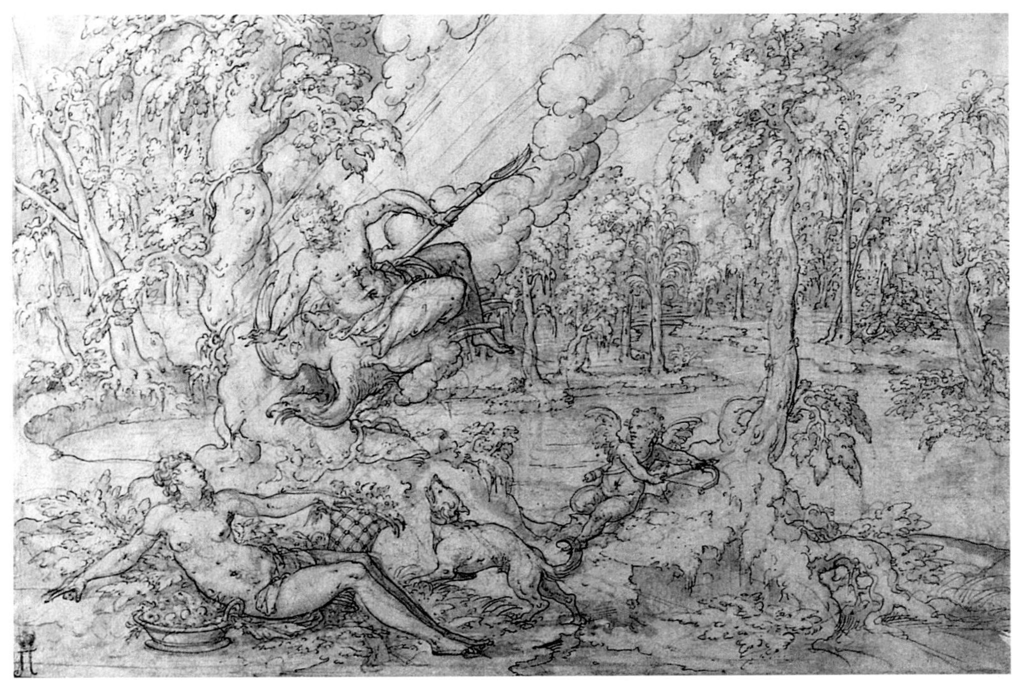

fig. 23
Jean Cousin II
Landscape with Apollo

pen and brown ink and violet wash over black chalk, 285 × 415 mm (inv. no. OR 5604)

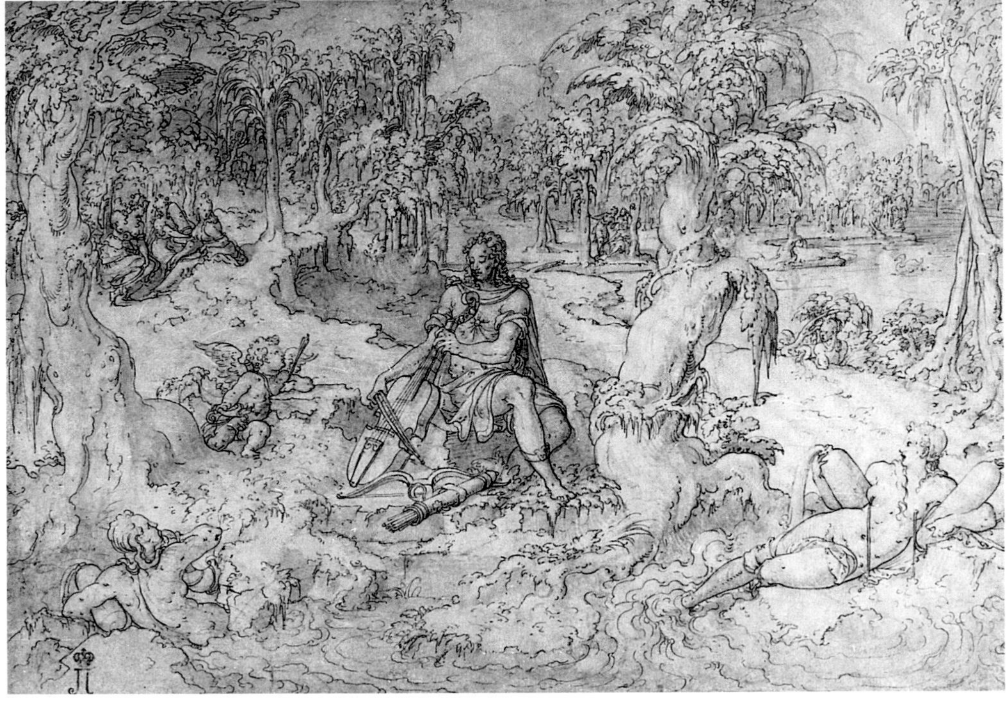

5

Jean Cousin II [the Younger]

Landscape with Mythological Figures (Apollo's Affairs of Love?)

Pen and brown ink, violet wash, over a black chalk sketch. 272 × 429 mm. Lined

Old inscription in pen and brown ink beneath the drawing in a cartouche: *Schprengel*

PROVENANCE: collection of Count Carl Cobenzl, Brussels (collector's mark L. 2858b); 1768 acquired for the Hermitage: collector's mark L. 2061

Inv. no. OR 5601

OLD MANUSCRIPT CATALOGUES: Cobenzl – 'Catal[ogue] de Cabin[et], Catalogue de Desseins, Troisième Grandeur', p. 45v., Carton no. 7: no. 28 'Inconnus, un Paysage'

EXHIBITIONS: 1959 Leningrad, p. 27; 1969 Leningrad–Moscow, no. 37; 1972 Vienna–Graz, no. 15, ill.; 1972 Paris, no. 68

LITERATURE: Dobroklonsky 1932, pp. 46–7; Kamenskaya, Novoselskaya 1969, no. 33

This drawing, close in compositional terms to the Albertina's *Diana and Endymion*, although in reverse, shows a number of scenes from the life of Apollo. In the middle ground we see him resting. The god pursuing a nymph in the background, as was suggested by Sylvie Béguin (1972 Paris, no. 68), may represent Apollo and Daphne; the spring to the right would thus represent Daphne's father, the River Peneus, and the putto to the right would be Eros,responsible for making Apollo fall in love with Daphne as revenge for the god's mocking comments regarding his archery.

The loving couple in the foreground can hardly be Apollo and Daphne, but Mannerist artists were not renowned for precision in their iconography. Apollo's love affairs were numerous, and the woman might be the Thessalian nymph Cyrene, or the Cumæan Sibyl, or the shepherdess Issa, a heroine in Ovid's *Metamorphoses*.

Individual details have analogies in other drawings: the group with Apollo chasing Daphne – as Béguin noted – is close to Pan and Syrinx in a sheet of that name in the Louvre (Département des Arts Graphiques, inv. no. 20.901), while the basket with its fruits or flowers reappears in *Jupiter and Semele* (fig. 22) and in *Landscape with Mythological Figures (Allegory of Spring?)* (cat. 6). I.N.

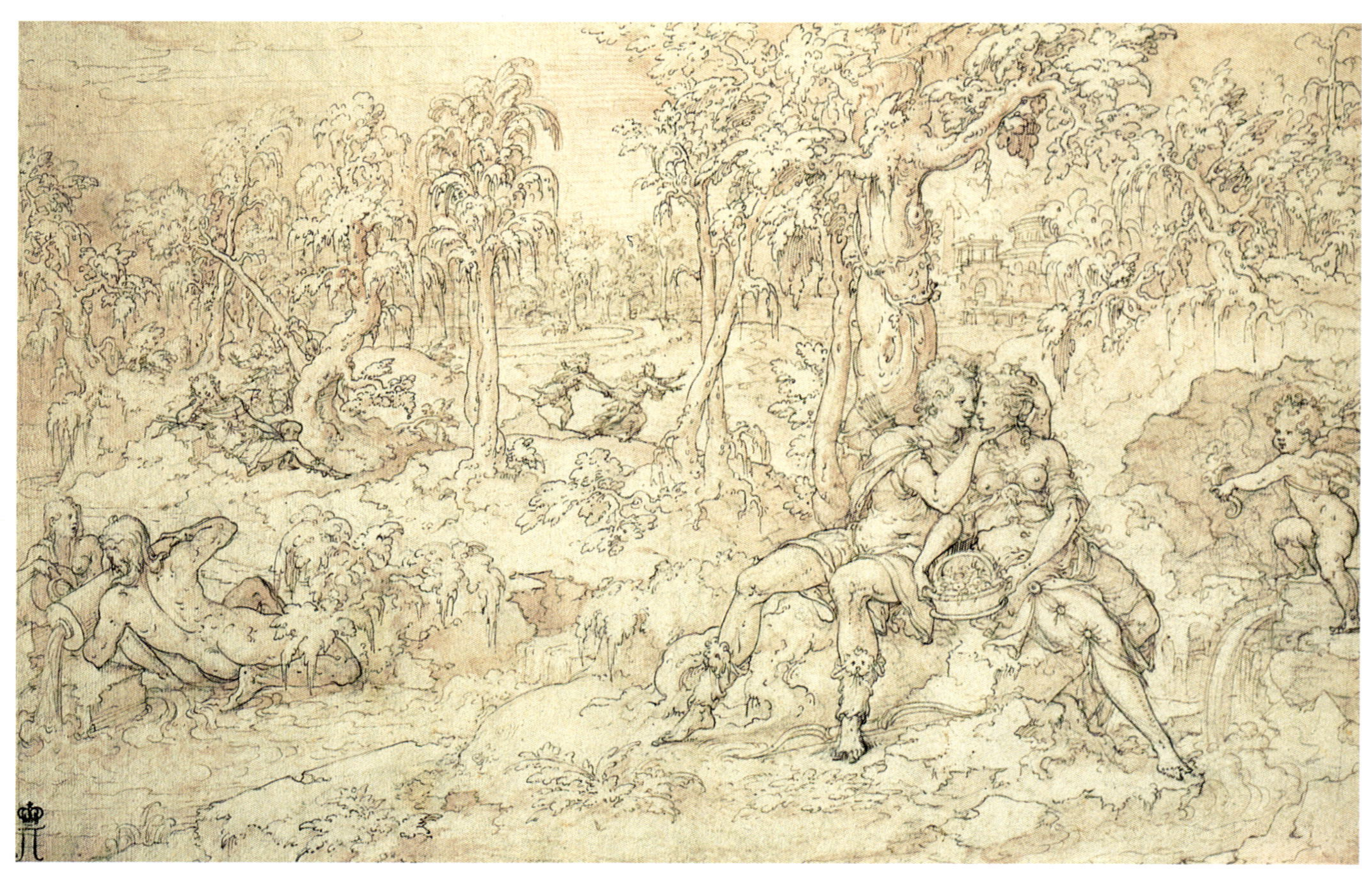

6

Jean Cousin II [the Younger]

Landscape with Mythological Figures (Allegory of Spring)

Pen and brown ink, violet wash, over a black chalk sketch. 277 × 408 mm. Lined

Old inscription in pen and brown ink beneath the drawing in a cartouche: *Schprengel*

PROVENANCE: collection of Count Carl Cobenzl, Brussels (collector's mark L. 2858b); 1768 acquired for the Hermitage: collector's mark L. 2061

Inv. no. OR 5602

OLD MANUSCRIPT CATALOGUES: Cobenzl – 'Catal[ogue] de Cabin[et], Catalogue de Desseins, Troisième Grandeur', p. 45v., Carton no. 7: no. 29 'Inconnus, un Autre' [i.e., landscape/paysage]

LITERATURE: Dobroklonsky 1932, p. 45; Kamenskaya, Novoselskaya 1969, no. 36

In this allegory Venus is surrounded by young maidens crowning her with a garland of flowers; nor is Eros forgotten, aiming an arrow from his bow. Charmian Mezentseva (personal communication) links the group of musicians on the right side of the sheet, like the merrymakers in the distance, with the Spring bacchanalia, as manifested in celebrations honouring Dionysus, Bacchic processions, turning cattle out to pasture, and other activities.

This *Allegory of Spring* differs from the other Hermitage compositions by Cousin in the large number of figures present in the main scene. The poses and attire of the group of male musicians recall those of a group of shepherds in *Mercury Stealing the Cattle of Admetus*; an identical dog also lies at their feet. I.N.

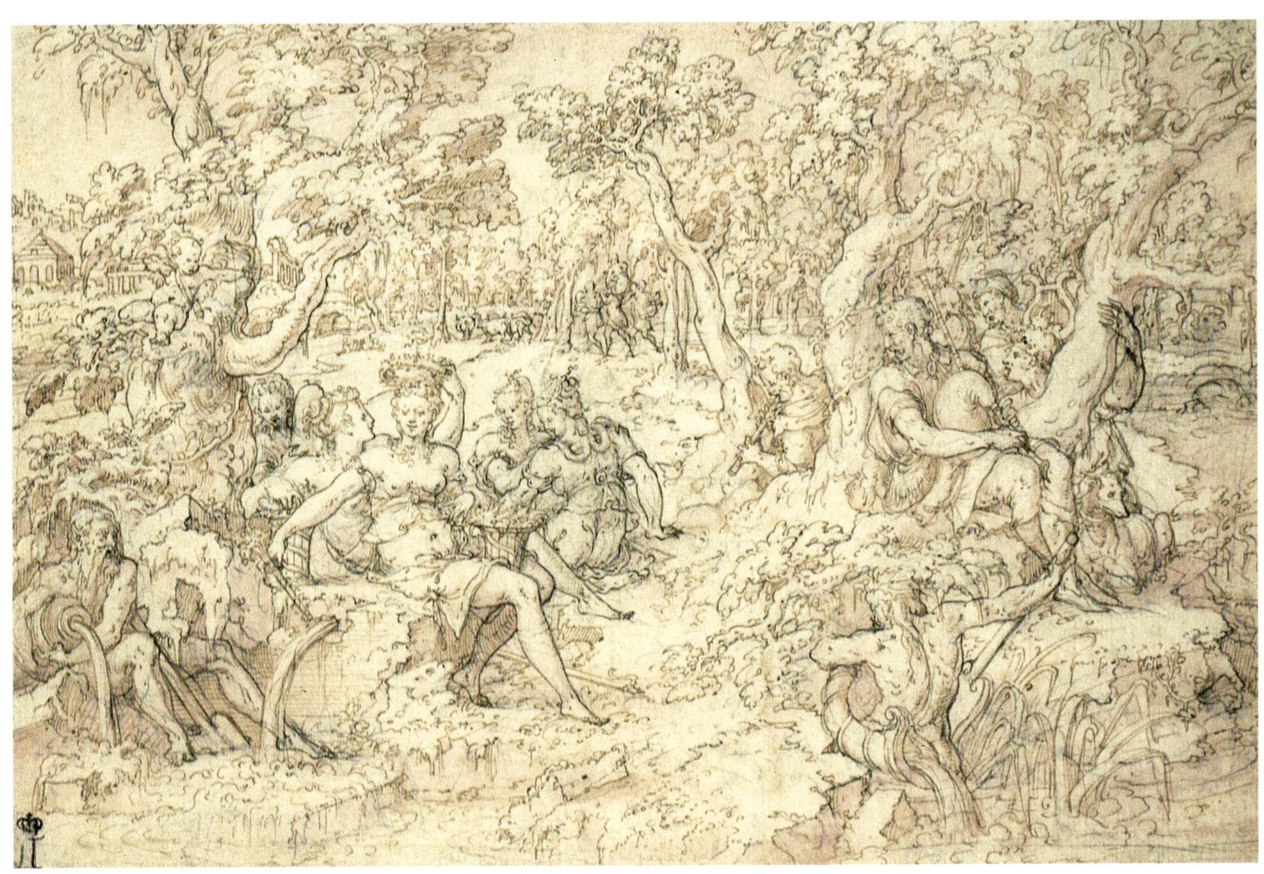

7

Jacques de Bellange

c. 1575 – 1616 Nancy

The Lamentation

Oil on canvas. 116.3 × 173 cm

PROVENANCE: to 1925, collection Khanukian, Moscow; 1967 acquired for the Hermitage through the Purchasing Commission, from a private collection in Tallinn

Inv. no. GE 10032

EXHIBITIONS: 1973a Leningrad, p. 9, no. 4; 1973b Leningrad, p. 14, no. 1; 1977b Leningrad, p. 11, no. 3; 1988 Meaux, no. 24; 1992b Nancy, no. 4; 1996–7 Washington–Fort Worth, no. 37

LITERATURE: Linnik 1973a, pp. 8–12; Linnik 1973b, pp. 65–70; Chouix 1973–4, pp. 235–6; Cat. 1976, p. 183; Worthen 1976, p. 124; Comer 1980, pp. 240–1, no. 61, fig. 115; Rosenberg 1988, p. 110; Serre, Leegenhoek 1988, pp. 7–8; Thuillier 1990–91, pp. 16–18; Thuillier 2001, pp. 128, 131–2

When this painting was in the Khanukian collection in Moscow, it was thought to be by the Spanish artist Francisco Ribalta (1565–1628). Linnik (1973a) identified it as the work of Jacques de Bellange on the basis of a drawing, *Pietà with Donors* (Musée des Beaux-Arts, Dijon), already attributed to this artist by Pariset (1948, p. 101).

Linnik supposed that Bellange's paintings would have passed through the same evolution as his prints and drawings, which moved from elegance and refinement in his early period to tragedy in his later years. It was on this basis that she dated *The Lamentation* to the last year of Bellange's life, the date also given to a preparatory drawing for the painting (see Georgel 1985, p. 168). Doubts have been expressed regarding the attribution (Thuillier 2001), but the objections are not convincing.

Bellange, whose paintings are today extremely rare, was among those Northern painters influenced by Caravaggio, notably *chiaroscuro*, sharply contrasting areas of light and dark introduced for greater dramatic effect. In *The Lamentation* the brightly lit white drapery over Christ's body stands out from the gloom of the dark background. A flickering candle is the sole source of illumination, and the figures in the middle ground, only lightly picked out, seem almost unreal. One face to the right, however, is clearly visible: that of the man who must have commissioned the painting. Although Bellange was known to contemporaries as a marvellous portraitist, this painting contains the sole surviving example of his work in this genre.

Rosenberg (1988) has argued that the figure behind the donor is Antoine de Lenincourt, while alongside the donor – whom Pariset (1962, pp. 42–9) identified as Cardinal Alphonse de Rambervillers and Comer (1980) as Charles of Lorraine (1567–1607) – is a man who might perhaps be his patron saint, for in Linnik's opinion the face recalls that of St Charles Borromeo (1538–84), the Archbishop of Milan who was canonized in 1610. Linnik has also suggested that an engraving by Francesco Parmigianino, *The Lamentation*, was Bellange's source for the central part of the composition. Rosenberg (1988) notes in addition works by Bartolomeo Passarotti (1529–92), which he felt provided the sources for the faces in the middle ground.

Numerous analogies are to be found among Bellange's drawings and etchings for elements in the painting: the image of the Virgin is reflected in an etching of the same subject, *The Lamentation* (Walch 1971, no. 17), while the face of Simon the Cyrenian (Matthew xxvii, 32: 'And as they came out, they found a man of Cyrene, Simon by name: him they compelled to bear his cross') appears also in the etching *The Carrying of the Cross* (Walch 1971, no. 23).

A variant of the composition was exhibited in Paris in 1988 (Serre, Leegenhoek, no. 1), and is now in the Musée Historique Lorrain, Nancy. N.S.

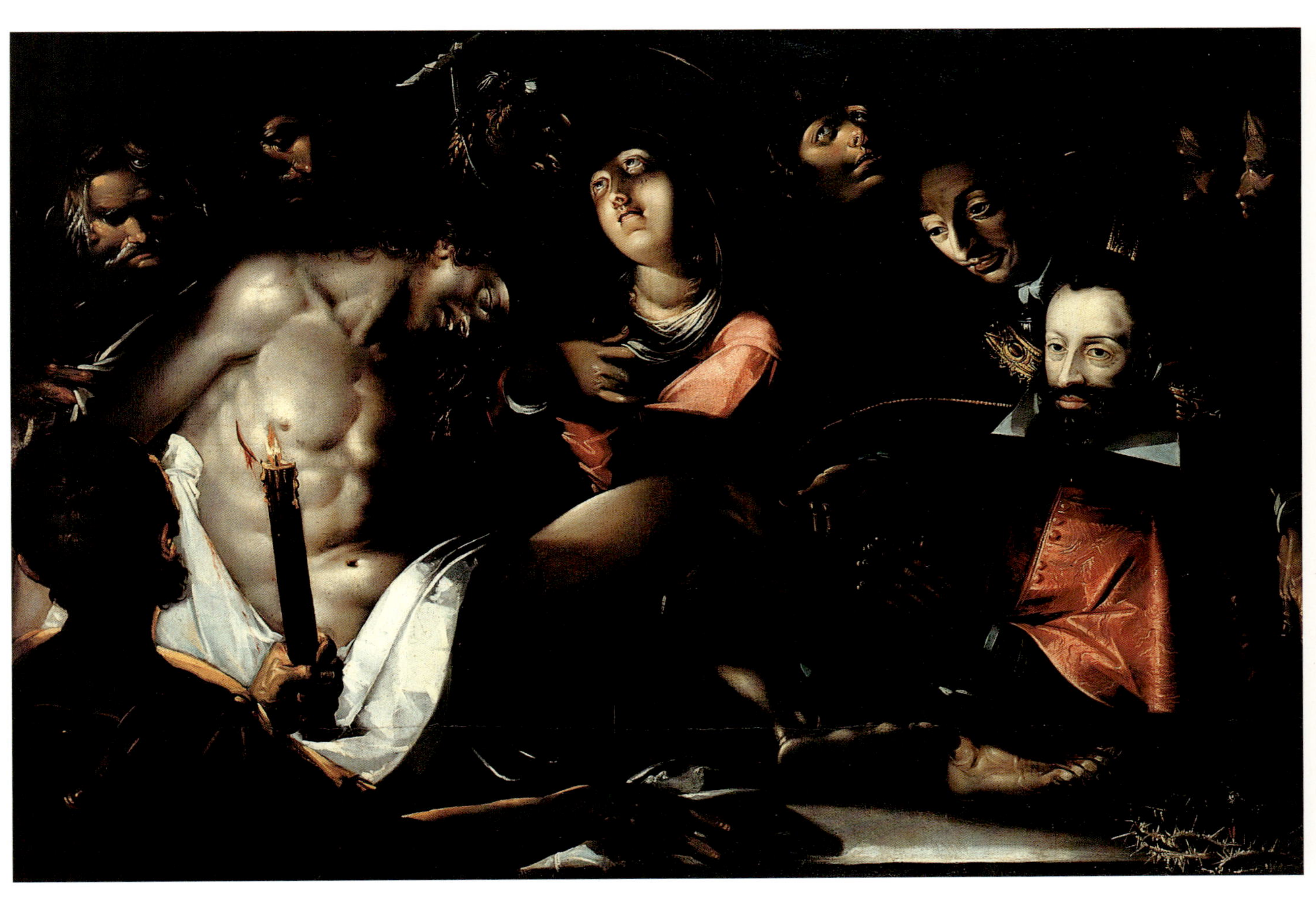

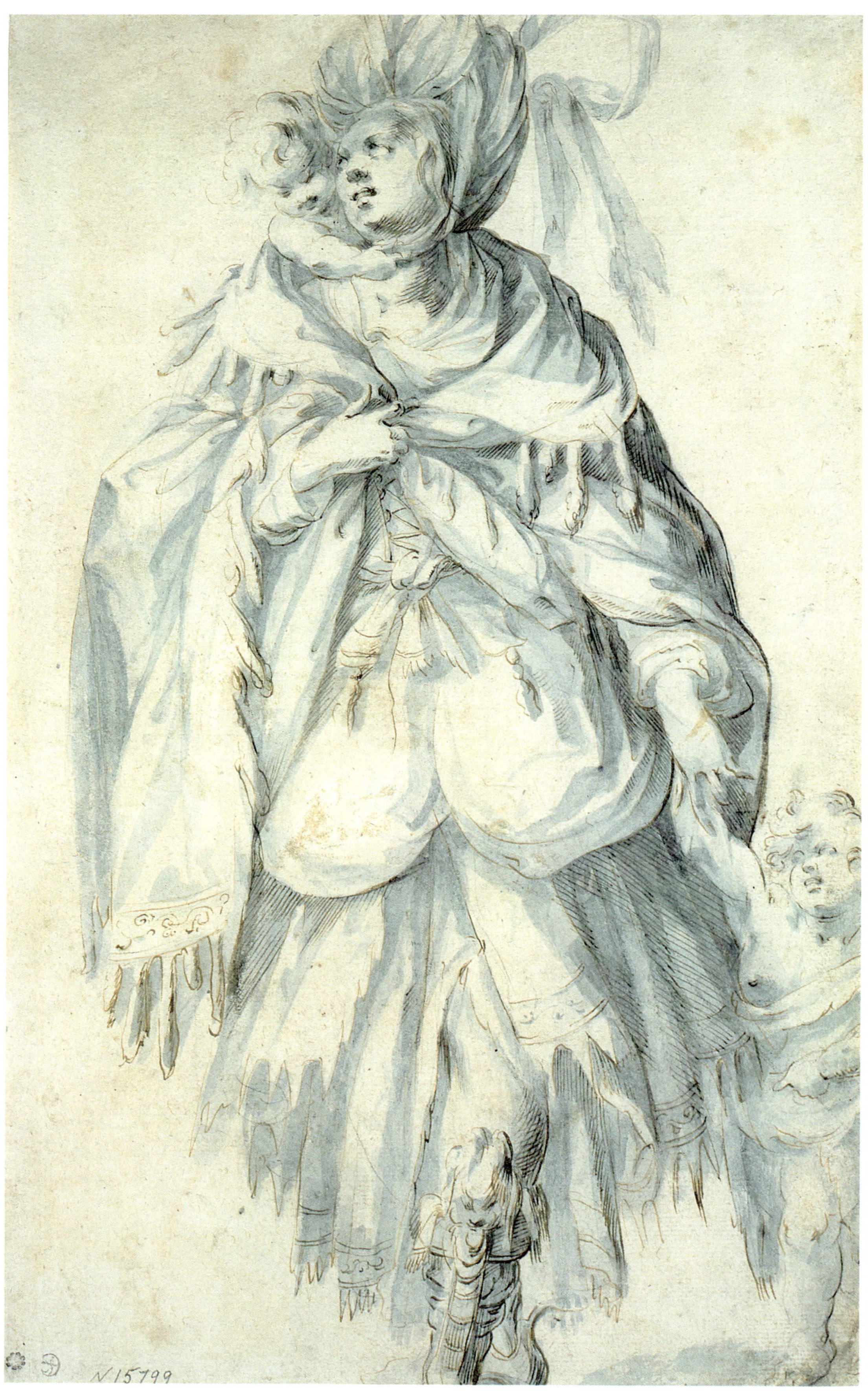
N 15799

8

Jacques de Bellange

Gypsy Woman with Two Children

Pen and brown ink, blue wash.
323 × 193 mm
On the reverse: *Gypsy with a Child on her Back*, black and red chalk

PROVENANCE: collection of Ivan Betskoy, St Petersburg (collector's mark L. 2878a); 1767 given by Betskoy to the Academy of Arts, St Petersburg; 1924 transferred to the Hermitage

Inv. no. OR 15799

EXHIBITIONS: 1955 Moscow, p. 71; 1956 Leningrad, p. 83; 1963 Stockholm, no. 29; 1986 Bogota, ill.; 1986 Buenos Aires, no. 39, ill.; 1986 Montevideo, no. 39, ill.; 1987–8 Belgrade–Ljubliana–Zagreb, no. 61; 1992b Nancy, no. 81, fig.; 1997 Bonn, no. 90, ill.; 1998–9 New York, no. 85, ill.; 1999 St Petersburg, no. 1, ill.; 2001 Rennes, no. 34, fig.

LITERATURE: Kamenskaya 1929, p. 75; Dahlbäck, Pariset 1954, p. 76; Kamenskaya 1960, pp. 96-7, no. 5?, fig.; Pariset 1962, pp. 34, 45, fig.; Linnik 1973a, p. 9; Western European Drawing 1981, no. 65, ill.; Thuillier 1992, p. 264, fig.; Novoselskaya 1999, pp. 4, 5, 12, ill.; Thuillier 2001, pp. 187, 188, 190, fig.

The Court at Nancy, where Bellange worked for over fourteen years as 'artist to Madame' (i.e., the Queen), was celebrated for its ballets and masquerades. Jacques Thuillier, the leading scholar of Bellange's work, has suggested that a number of Bellange's drawings relate directly to the ballet (Thuillier 2001, pp. 187, 188), for instance a number of images of female dancers and musicians (*Gypsy Girl with a Tambourine*, NGA, Washington, DC, inv. no. 181.43.1; *Woman Making a Curtsy*, British Museum, London, inv. no. 1870.5.14.1207).

Four drawings by Bellange or his pupils depicting gypsy women with children are now in the Hermitage: this sheet (both recto and verso) and two more (inv. nos. OR 15793, OR 15795). This drawing is the most finished of the four, and whereas the others are of poorly dressed beggars, this gypsy woman is shown in a romantic light: head erect, she wears a rich fringed shawl, a turban with streaming ribbons and buskins (the thick-soled boots worn by players performing tragedy). Thuillier (2001) suggests that this drawing should also be understood as depicting a character from a ballet. Although the heavy layers of clothing and the half-naked children – the younger one borne on the mother's back – evoke the realities of gypsy life, the suggestion of a connection with the world of ballet is a convincing one.

The drawing on the reverse of this sheet is more in the nature of a sketch (fig. 24). The heavy folds of the shawl covering mother and child are only roughly indicated, its braiding picked out in places, but by contrast with the grey mass of the clothing, the gypsy woman's face, turned towards the child, is skilfully modelled in black and red chalks. She has expressive bulging eyes, framed by locks of hair peeking out from beneath her shawl.

As regards dating, much remains unclear with regard to Bellange's graphic work, but Thuillier (2001, p. 188) reckons that Bellange's 'costume' drawings should be dated to the period 1603–16, i.e., the years spent at the Court of Lorraine. None the less, there are several features worthy of note that can help us to date this particular drawing: it has no trace of the uncertainty or the static qualities of the earliest ones; it is skilfully executed and beautiful in its painterly resolution, combining pale blue wash and daring brown lines; the Mannerist features that are so characteristic of the artist's mature period are very restrained; the grotesque features (also typical of the artist's late sheets) are relatively weak. These features support a relatively early dating of before 1610. I.N.

fig. 24
Gypsy with a Child on her Back
(reverse of cat. 8)

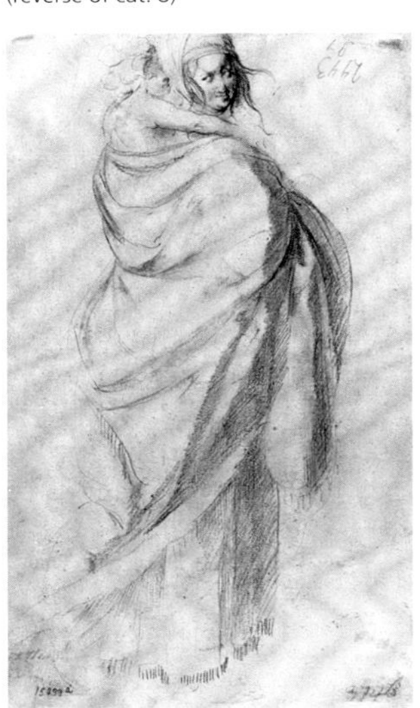

9

Jacques de Bellange

Study for the Figure of an Apostle (?)

Pen and brown ink, brown wash. The border outlined in red chalk. 283 × 143 mm

PROVENANCE: collection of Ivan Betskoy, St Petersburg (collector's mark L. 2878a); 1767 given by Betskoy to the Academy of Arts, St Petersburg; 1924 transferred to the Hermitage

Inv. no. OR 15791

EXHIBITIONS: 1955 Moscow, p. 71; 1956 Leningrad, p. 83; 1992b Nancy, p. 156, no. 13, fig.; 1997 Bonn, no. 91, ill.; 1999 St Petersburg, no. 4, ill.; 2001 Rennes, no. 29, fig.

LITERATURE: Kamenskaya 1929, p. 76; Pariset 1950, p. 342; Kamenskaya 1960a, pp. 97, 101, no. 9, fig.; Thuillier 1992, p. 156, fig.; Novoselskaya 1999, pp. 4, 5, 18, ill.; Thuillier 2001, p. 178, ill.

Formerly considered to show 'an invented figure', this image should possibly be linked – as was rightly suggested by Thuillier (1992) – with Bellange's series of prints of *Christ and the Apostles* (Thuillier 1992, nos. 14–25), which comprises 17 sheets (several of the figures are shown in two versions). Certainly the drawing is related in the placing of the figure, its relationship to the sheet, and the manner of hatching with the pen as if in imitation of an print. Similarities are also to be found in the contrast of light and shade and the sharply defined contours. The apostle's raised head with its curly locks almost repeats the head of St Philip (Thuillier 1992, no. 20à); in pose and modelling the figure recalls those of Christ, St Paul, St John and others (nos. 14, 16, 19a, b): there is the same hollow chest and rounded stomach, the foot projects forward from the long robes, and the hands have the same attenuated, curving fingers. The pronounced Mannerist features in this drawing – the foreshortening of the uplifted head on its elongated neck, the distorted facial features and fluttering curls, the nervous movement of the hands with their long slender fingers – all support a relatively late dating.

No true preparatory drawings for the various apostles have survived, which makes the Hermitage drawing of particular value, for although no such figure appears in the series of prints, it is likely that this drawing represents an unrealized version of one of the apostles. I.N.

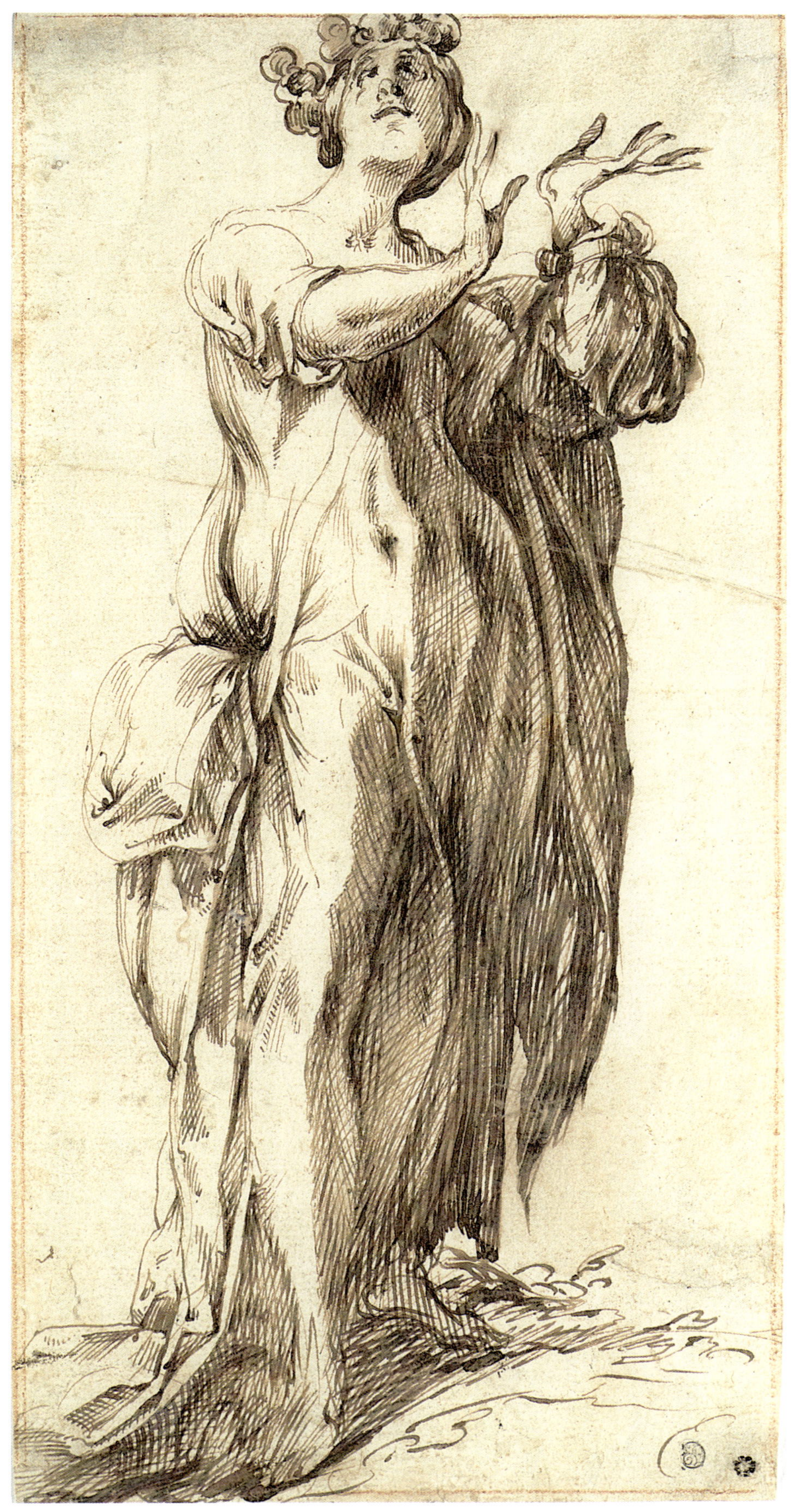

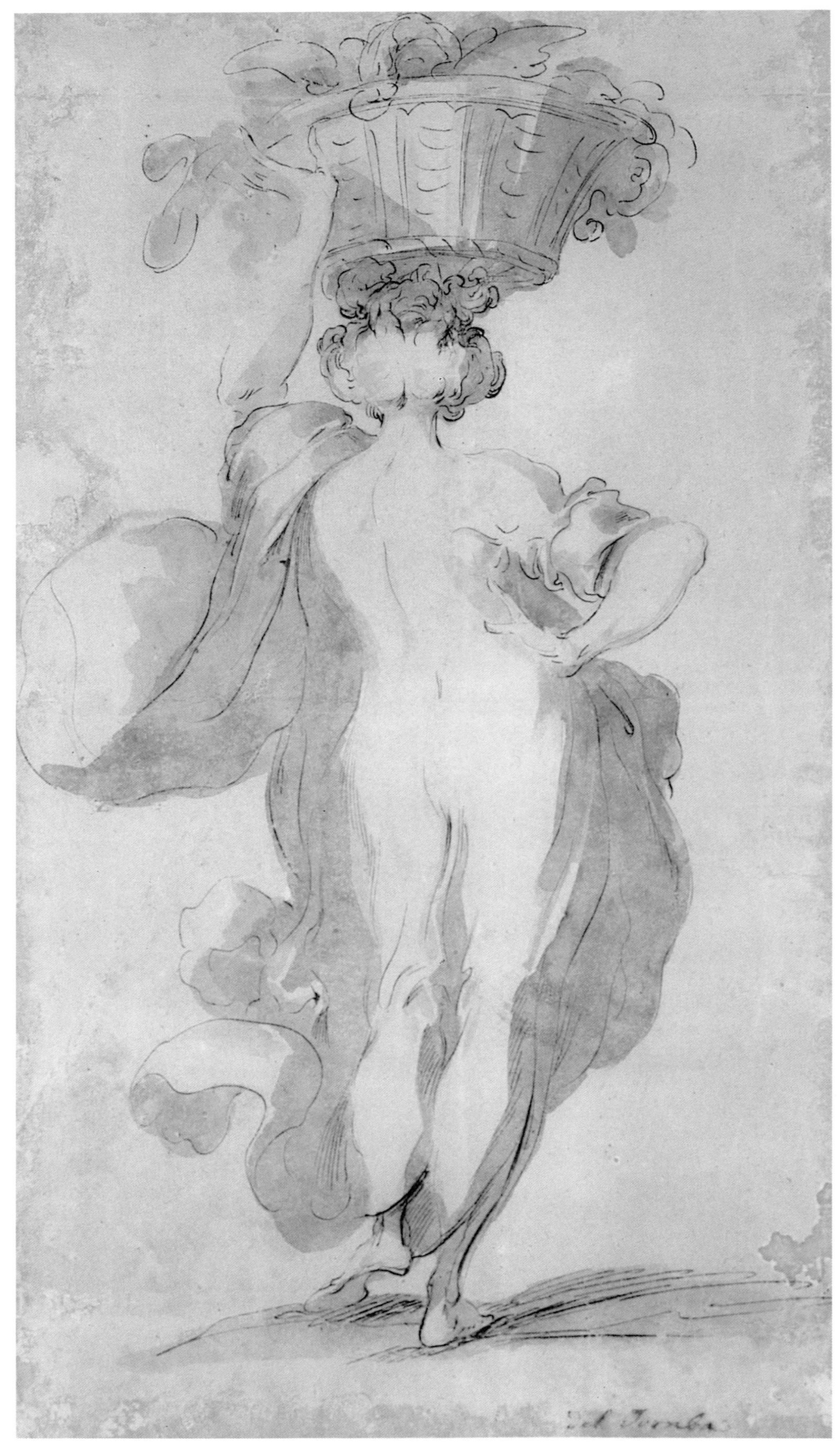

10

Jacques de Bellange

Woman with a Basket of Flowers on her Head

Pen and black ink, greyish-blue wash on pale brown paper. 387 × 215 mm Lined

Illegible inscription in pen and brown ink at the bottom edge to right: *del Imola*(?)

PROVENANCE: State Russian Museum, St Petersburg; 1935 transferred to the Hermitage

Inv. no. OR 42233

EXHIBITIONS: 1963 Stockholm, no. 28, ill.; 1968 Leningrad–Moscow, no. 5; 1970 Budapest, no. 8; 1972 Prague, no. 7; 1982 Florence, no. 79; 1992b Nancy, no. 111, fig.; 1999 St Petersburg, no. 6, ill.; 2001 Rennes, no. 48, fig.

LITERATURE: Kamenskaya 1957, pp. 36–7, ill.; Kamenskaya 1960a, pp. 97, 101, fig.; Pariset 1962, pp. 44–5, fig.; Walch 1971, pp. 104, 143; Thuillier 1992, p. 318, fig.; Novoselskaya 1999, pp. 4, 5, 22, ill.; Thuillier 2001, p. 218, fig.

This image should be linked with a series of gardening figures that is closely connected with Bellange's interest in ballet motifs. Three prints (Thuillier 2001, nos. 38–40) and three drawings (Thuillier 2001, nos. 41–3) depict female 'gardeners' (the figures are elegant and noticeably removed from reality) wearing costumes typical of the time in Lorraine (fig. 25).

Thuillier (2001, no. 48) does not include the Hermitage drawing in the *Gardeners* series, linking the woman's dress not with the theatre but with the traditions of the *Canephorus* – the figure of a woman carrying a basket upon her head that was widely used in the decorative arts and architectural decoration – and suggests that it recalls Italian images, both sculptural and painted, and the paintings of the school of Fontainebleau. The posture and the long fluttering robes shown in this drawing do indeed contrast with the less animated *Gardeners*, with the exception of one drawing in the Louvre, the *Walking Gardener with a Large Vase* (Thuillier 2001, no. 42).

In technique this drawing is close both to *Gypsy Woman with Two Children* (cat. 8) and the *Gardeners* series, yet it has its own particular tonal unity. Overall, the dynamism, elegance and sensuality of the figure (seen from behind in the favourite Mannerist pose), the way that the figure is picked out through transparent cloth and the tonal resolution are all in accord with a new, higher level in Bellange's work. I.N.

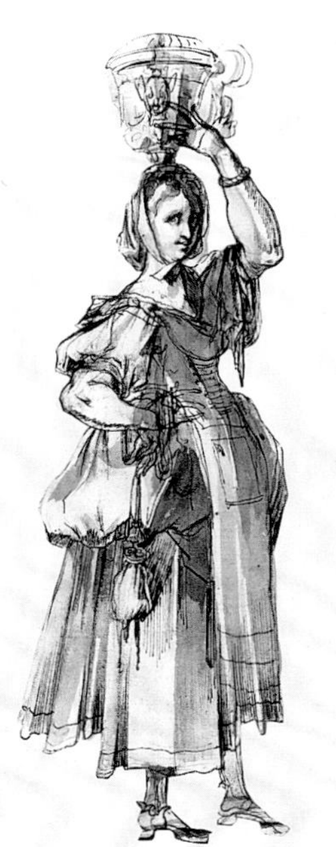

fig. 25
Jacques de Bellange,
Gardener with a Vase (Hortulana)

pen and brown ink, blue wash,
327 × 104 mm.
Nationalmuseum, Stockholm

11

Jacques de Bellange

Seated Woman in Profile

Pen and brown ink, brown wash; the border outlined in red chalk. 202 × 156 mm

PROVENANCE: collection of Ivan Betskoy, St Petersburg (collector's mark L. 2878a); 1767 given by Betskoy to the Academy of Arts, St Petersburg; 1924 transferred to the Hermitage

Inv. no. OR 16124

EXHIBITIONS: 1963 Stockholm, no. 30; 1992b Nancy, no. 27, fig.; 1999 St Petersburg, no. 7, ill.; 2001 Rennes, no. 50, ill.

LITERATURE: Kamenskaya 1929, p. 76, ill.; Kamenskaya 1960a, p. 101, no. 8, ill.; Pariset 1963, p. 123; Walch 1971, p. 119, ill.; Clifford 1973, p. 378; Thuillier 1992, p. 164, fig.; Novoselskaya 1999, pp. 4, 5, 24, ill.; Thuillier 2001, p. 222, fig.

This is clearly the latest of Bellange's drawings in the Hermitage, a work revealing the most extreme Mannerist features – elongated proportions, angular and broken contours, keen characterization taken almost to the extent of being grotesque. In technique and style of execution, using hatching to imitate a print, this drawing is close to the prints of the *Apostles* series and to the related Hermitage drawing (cat. 9), but the hatching is lighter and more delicate, and the contours of the neck, the break of the shoulder and back and the drapery folds are carefully managed.

Thuillier (2001, nos. 50, 51) notes the similarity between this *Seated Figure* and a weeping St Veronica in the etched *Carrying of the Cross* (fig. 26), suggesting that it may have been intended for use in a religious composition. Many of the artist's drawings include a version of just such a female figure in profile, body leaning forwards, hair piled high, the broad skirt falling in heavy folds (e.g. *Woman Kneeling*, Musée Historique Lorrain, Nancy, inv. no. 49.2.3; *Study for a Half-naked Woman*, École Nationale Supérieure des Beaux-Arts, Paris, inv. no. M.790). Mannerist features gradually fall away in Bellange's last years, so this drawing should be placed some time after the *Figure of an Apostle* (cat. 9) and the *Woman with a Basket of Flowers on her Head* (cat. 10). I.N.

fig. 26
Jacques de Bellange
The Carrying of the Cross
etching

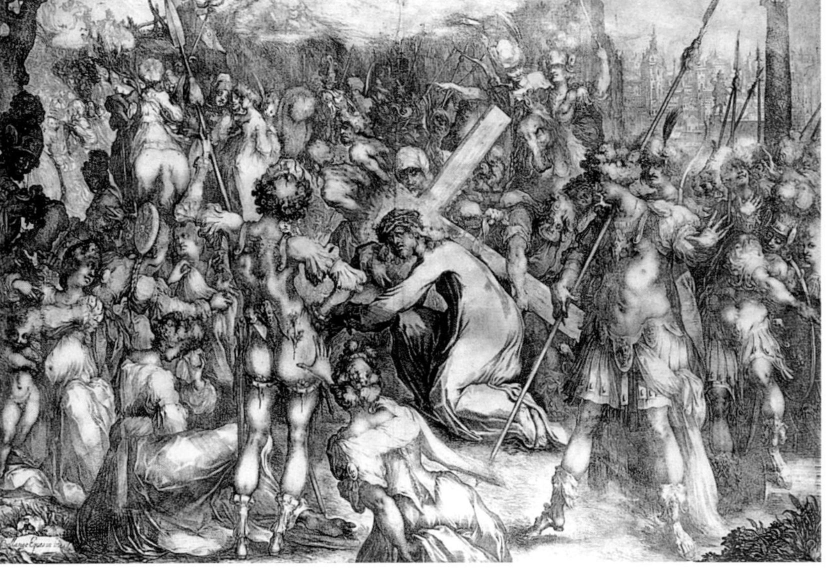

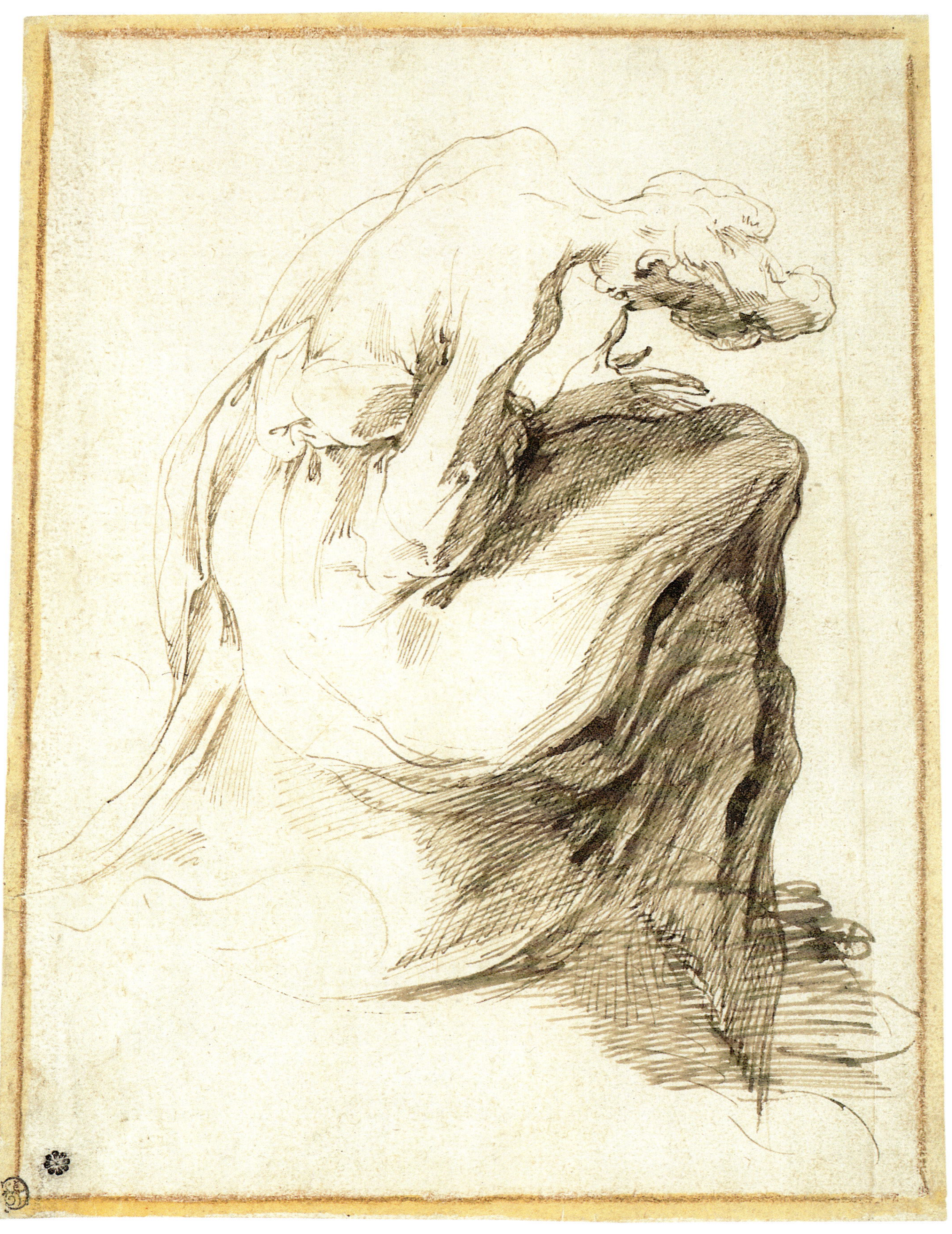

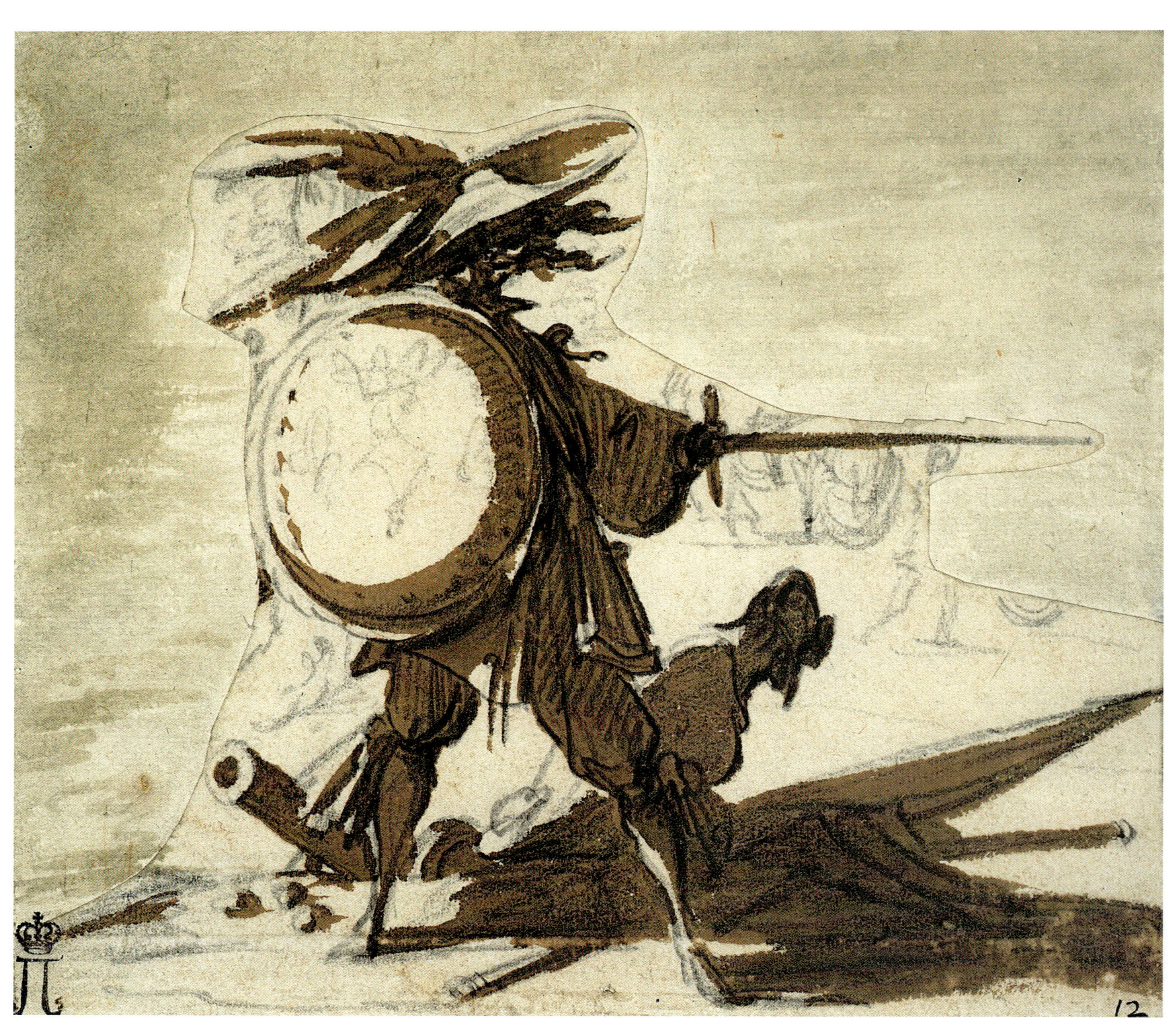

12

Jacques Callot

Nancy 1592 – 1635 Nancy

A Soldier Bearing a Sword and Shield

Black chalk and brown wash over a black chalk sketch. 180 × 210 mm

The sheet has been cut out round the contours and lined on 18th-century paper.
In the lower right corner an old number in pen and brown ink: *12*
Old inscription in pen and brown ink beneath the drawing in a cartouche: *Callot*

PROVENANCE: collection of Count Carl Cobenzl, Brussels (collector's mark L. 2858b); 1768 acquired for the Hermitage: collector's mark L. 2061

Inv. no. OR 586

EXHIBITIONS: 1926 Leningrad, no. 179; 1969 Leningrad–Moscow, no. 28; 1972 Vienna–Graz, no. 8, ill. 36; 1975 Washington, DC, no. 227a, ill.; 1986 Bogota, ill.; 1986 Buenos Aires, no. 40, ill.; 1986 Montevideo, no. 40, ill.; 1987–8 Belgrade – Ljubliana – Zagreb, no. 67, ill.; 1992a Nancy, no. 478, ill.; 1997 Bonn, no. 95, ill.; 1999 St Petersburg, no. 21, ill.

LITERATURE: Glikman 1959, no. 717, ill.; Ternois 1962a, p. 53; Ternois 1962b, no. 69, ill.; Novoselskaya 1999, pp. 5, 50, ill.

Callot, a native of Lorraine, witnessed many of the tumultuous events that took place there, and he often depicted soldiers, skirmishes, prisoners and the various sufferings caused by war. In this drawing the sihouetted young woman seated at the soldier's feet and various figures barely indicated in the distance introduce a sense of narrative to the occasion.

In an album of his drawings from the collection of Jean de Jullienne and now in the Hermitage is another version of this drawing (inv. no. OR 589). That soldier, shown in a similar pose, although without a sword, is executed in the same technique and he is also cut out around the contours. Neither sheet was etched, although in type and motif they can both be linked with several of the author's *Capricci* (a series of 50 sheets showing scenes from life in Florence during the reign of Cosimo II Medici).

Due to the keen and grotesque nature of this image – the angular figure, elongated proportions and unusual attire – specialists have been led to date the drawing *c.* 1617, although the combination of black chalk and wash might well be evidence of a slightly later date. It is possible that it is a fragment of work for a particular composition, although it may well have been an independent production. Whichever is the case, its expressive and striking qualities and the freedom of its modelling in light and shade make it one of Callot's best – albeit unfinished – works. I.N.

13

Jacques Callot

Parterre at Nancy

Black ink wash, black and red chalk.
260 × 390 mm

PROVENANCE: collection of Jean de Jullienne, Paris (included in sale of his goods 1767); before 1797 acquired for the Hermitage

Inv. no. OR 1526

EXHIBITIONS: 1926 Leningrad, no. 177; 1955 Moscow, p. 76; 1963 Stockholm, no. 31; 1972 Prague, no. 17, ill.; 1975 Washington, DC, no. 15, ill.; 1992a Nancy, no. 450, ill.; 1998–9 New York, no. 87, ill.; 1999 St Petersburg, no. 23, ill.

LITERATURE: Bruwaert 1912, pp. 107–9; Zahn 1923, pp. 56, 57, 76, 116, 117; Marot 1958, pp. 81–3; Glikman 1959, no. 380, ill., pp. 52–3; Ternois1962b, no. 839, ill; Knab, Oberhuber 1968–9, pp. 143–4; Western European Drawing 1981, no. 67, ill.; Novoselskaya 1999, pp. 5, 54, ill.

Of particular value among the Hermitage's series of drawings by Callot from Jean de Jullienne's collection are compositional sheets or preparatory sketches for etchings. This multi-figure composition, full of a lightness and a spirit of joy so atypical of this artist, unfolds against a broad architectural and gardenscape panorama. These are the parterre gardens of the palace of the Duke of Lorraine at Nancy, although it has been pointed out that while Callot remained true to reality in his depiction of the parterres, he gave his creative imagination full rein in the architecture (1992a Nancy, no. 450). The scene is enlivened by groups of figures playing games, onlookers and others who stroll around the grounds. To the left a carriage arrives, and amid the onlookers is the Duchess Nicole, to whom the artist dedicated the etched version. At the top, in the centre of the composition, is a cartouche bearing the arms of the Duke of Lorraine.

Traditionally, it has been thought that Callot produced this drawing for an etching in 1625 (fig. 27). Naturally the print reverses the drawn image, but it also includes some significant alterations: it lacks the carriage and riders, yet the number of figures has been increased by adding to the onlookers in the foreground, the strollers in the middle ground and the gardeners; the central group of seated and standing onlookers has been removed, as has the tree to the right. But the basic composition remains intact: the general structure, the architecture, the gardens and many of the figures have been transferred directly from the drawing to the print.

There is another drawing showing the parterre at Nancy, acquired in 1958 at auction at the Hôtel Drouot for the Musée Historique Lorrain (248 × 392 mm – the size corresponds to that of the etching). In poor condition, that drawing more or less repeats this one, not only in composition but also in a number of details, such as the placing of individual groups and the inclusion of the tree to the right. None the less, it lacks the carriage and riders, bringing it closer to the etching. It should be noted too that the Hermitage has a series of figure studies linked with the making of the print (Glikman 1959, nos. 381–411).

The *Parterre at Nancy* is undoubtedly one of the artist's masterpieces. Its tiny human figures are full of movement and the whimsical patterns created by the flowerbeds fit neatly into the overall pattern of order and geometry (particularly visible in the print). At the same time there is an unusual lightness of execution, a painterly effect in this almost monochrome sheet, with its gradations of greyish tones from barely noticeable pale grey to black, enlivened by touches of red chalk, which makes this unusual panorama particularly charming. I.N.

fig. 27
Jacques Callot
Parterre at Nancy
etching

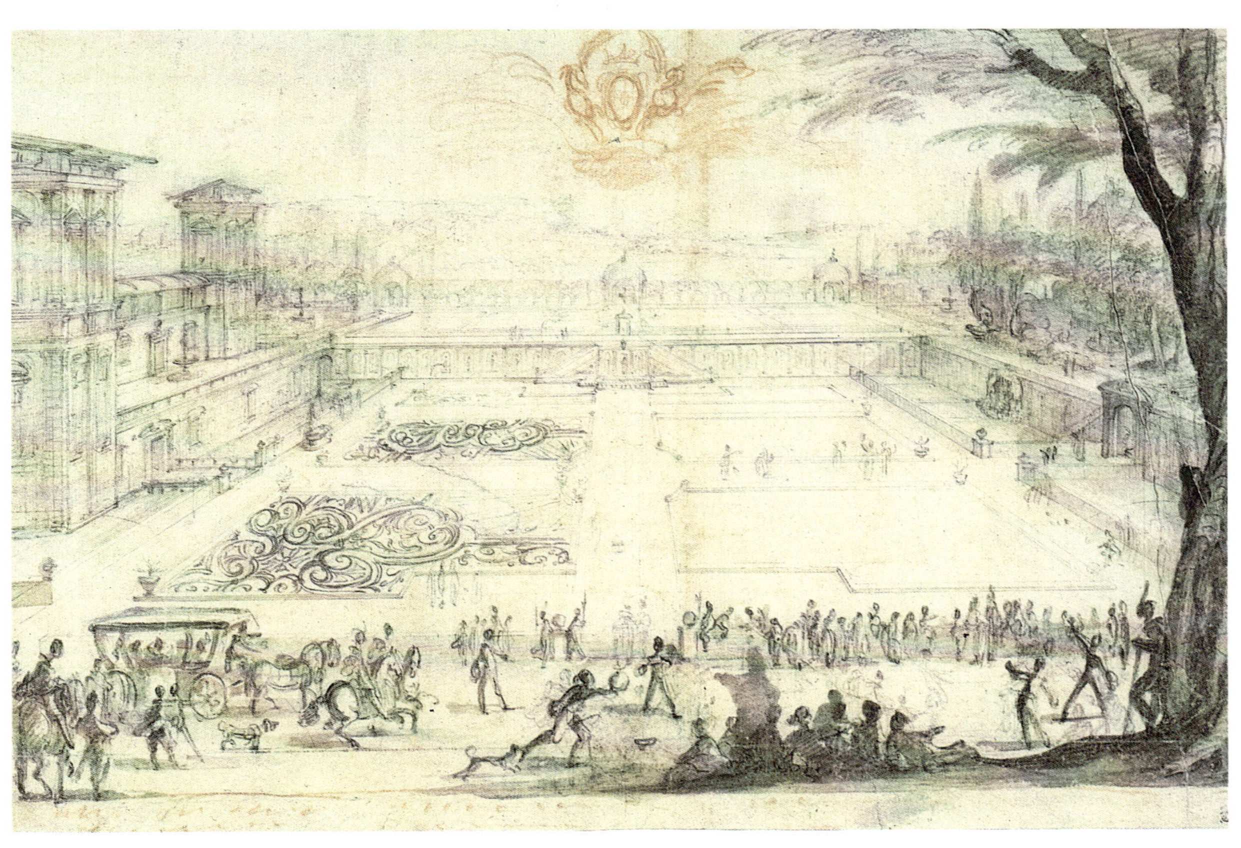

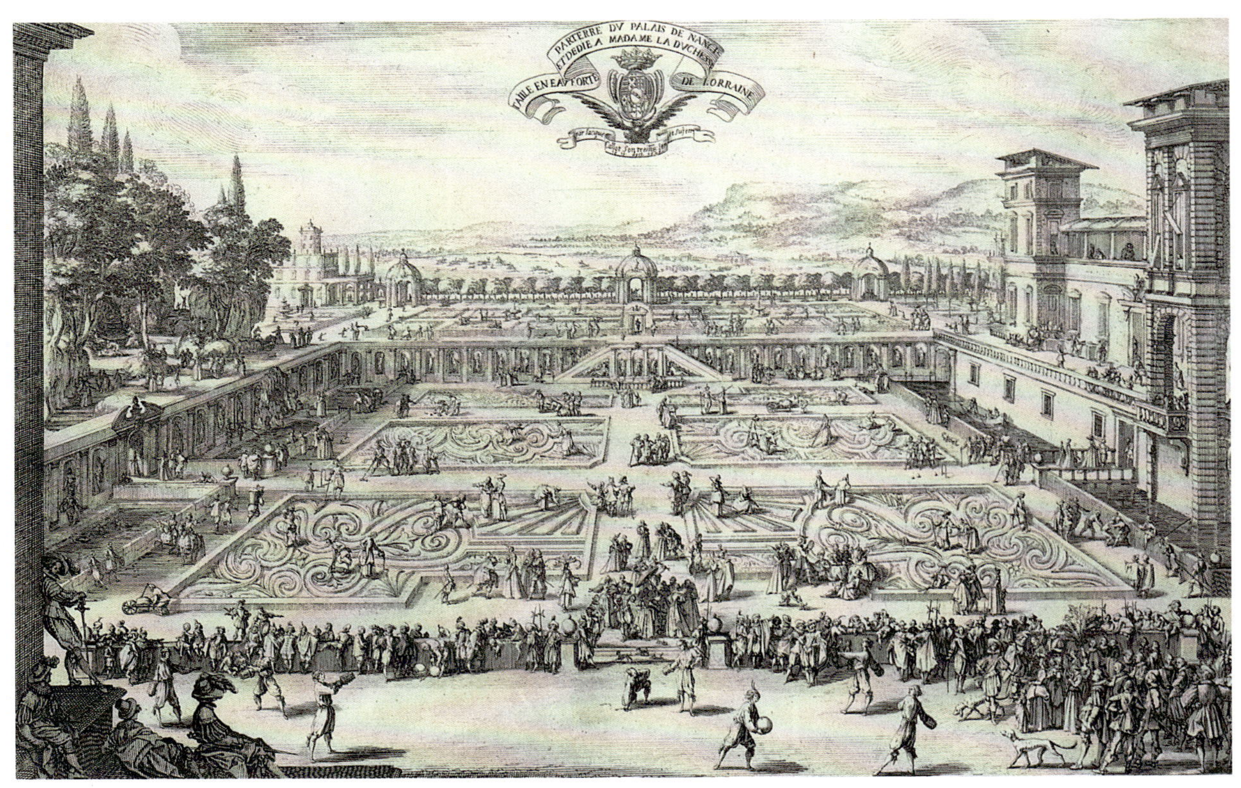
PARTERRE DV PALAIS DE NANCY
ET DEDIE A MADAME LA DVCHESSE
TAILLE EN EAV FORTE
DE LORRAINE

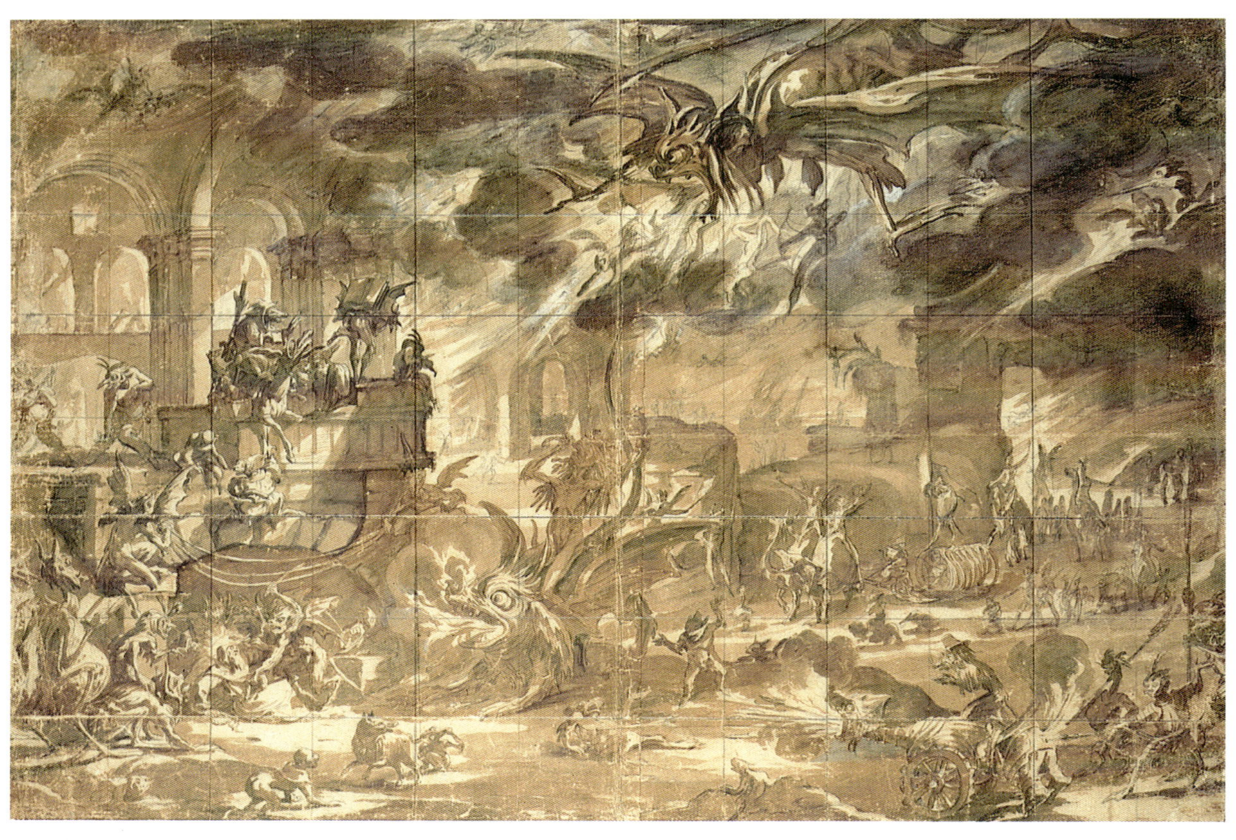

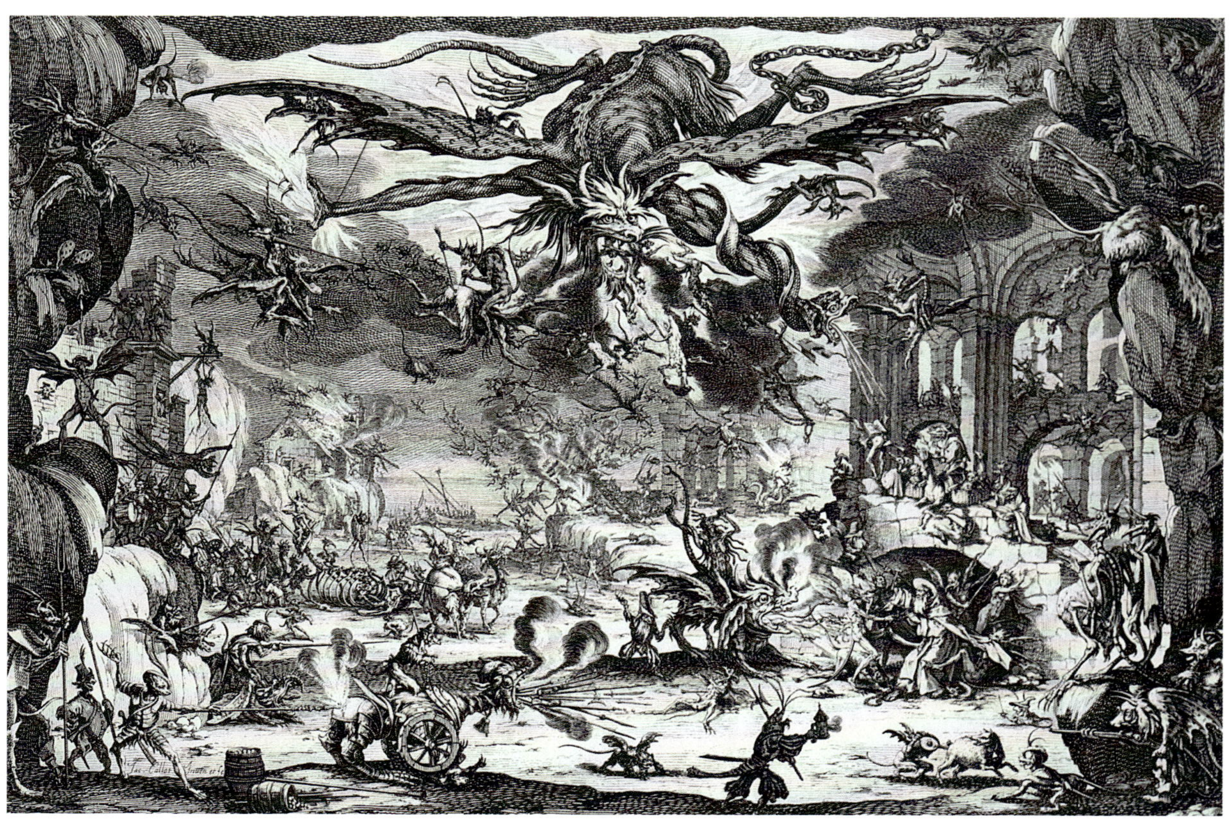

14

Jacques Callot

The Temptation of St Anthony

Black chalk, pen and brown ink, brown wash, heightened with gouache, touched with red chalk; squared in black chalk, the vertical lines pressed deep into the paper. 450 × 670 mm. Sheet glued together from two pieces arranged vertically (joined at the centre); addition glued to the middle of the left side. Lined

PROVENANCE: collection of Jean de Jullienne, Paris (included in the sale of his goods in 1767); collection of Prince Golitsyn; Academy of Arts, St Petersburg; 1924 transferred to the Hermitage

Inv. no. OR 14522

EXHIBITIONS: 1956 Leningrad, p. 89; 1963 Stockholm, no. 32; 1970 Budapest no. 14; 1972 Vienna–Graz, no. 9, ill.; 1975 Washington, DC, no. 37, ill.; 1992a Nancy, no. 532, fig.

LITERATURE: Mariette 1741, p. 117; Remy 1767, no. 693; Mariette 1851–60, vol. I, pp. 260, 285, 287; Meaume 1860, vol. I, pp. 109, 110; Bruwaert 1912, p. 70; Zahn 1923, p. 89; Ugloff 1935, pp. 220–24, ill.; Glikman 1959, pp. 102–5, no. 714, ill.; Ternois 1961, p. 21; Ternois 1962a, pp. 110, 119, 134–5, 160, 162; Posner 1977, p. 215, note 50; Hermitage 1994, no. 346, ill.

For 20 years St Anthony (AD 251–356) lived in utter solitude in an abandoned fort in the Egyptian desert. The series of spiritual temptations and visions he experienced there have been depicted by numerous Western artists, both before and since Callot. He twice took up the subject in his prints, executing the first version in Florence in 1617 and the second towards the end of his life, in 1635 in Nancy (he frequently turned to religious subjects in the 1630s).

According to Mariette (see Ternois 1961, nos. 953–6) there were four known sketches for the second *Temptation*, but certainly there are also other works relating to the subject. One is a drawing showing the landscape without the figures (Ashmolean Museum, Oxford, 373 × 652 mm). At present, three drawings are linked with Callot's second etching of the *Temptation*: the other two are in the Nationalmuseum, Stockholm (448 × 671 mm, inv. no. M 2471/1863), and the British Museum, London (310 × 347 mm, inv. no. 1861.7.13.6). The Stockholm sketch is thought to be the first of the three, after which came this one. They are identical in size and differ in only a few details – this drawing, for instance, includes a monkey in the left foreground. The last to be produced, and the closest of the three to the print (fig. 28), is the British Museum's drawing, which gave final form to the architectural motifs.

Each of these drawings is outstanding, and the merits of the Hermitage sheet are readily apparent. There is remarkable unity to this complex composition, with its multiple figures and multiple planes, while the almost monochrome sheet is extremely painterly, with an amazing wealth of nuances of brown tone. St Anthony himself occupies only a modest place in the left side of the composition, but the theme provided great scope for Callot's unbounded fantasy, filling the scene with massive buildings and fantastical monsters. Some scholars have seen in this image of Hell a grotesque spectacle or tragic carnival, while others, noting the apocalyptic meaning of the composition, read it as a satirical depiction of war. However we interpret the meaning of what is surely one of Callot's most interesting works, it unfailingly fascinates the beholder by its originality and execution. I.N.

fig. 28
Jacques Callot
The Temptation of St Anthony
etching

15

Simon Vouet

Paris 1590–1649 Paris

Sheet of Studies: Half-length Figure of a Youth in a Helmet; Part of a Draped Knee

Black chalk, touched with white chalk, on grey paper. 340 × 239 mm. Lined

Old inscription in pen and brown ink by the lower edge to right: *Vouet*

PROVENANCE: collection of Count Heinrich Brühl, Dresden; 1769 acquired for the Hermitage

Inv. no. OR 6401

EXHIBITIONS: 1999 St Petersburg, no. 29, ill.

PREVIOUSLY PUBLISHED: Marcel 1912, between pp. 20 and 21

LITERATURE: Brejon de Lavergnée 1987, p. 151, no. CXIV, fig.; Novoselskaya 1999, p. 66, ill.

Vouet habitually made use of numerous sketches, most frequently in black chalk, as preparatory studies for his large decorative compositions. Freely executed, they are marked by dynamism, daring foreshortenings and movements. It has not so far proved possible to link the study of a half-length figure on this sheet with any specific composition by the artist. Brejon de Lavergnée (1987, p. 151, no. 146) compares this drawing with a sheet of studies in the Louvre (inv. no. 33309) showing a seated draped youth. Certainly there are similarities in the facial type, with its straight nose, heavy chin, empty 'sculpted' eyes and long hair, in the line of shoulders and arms, the placing of the figure and the careful working of folds. Nor should we ignore the analogous arrangement of the sheet with a main figure and additional sketches. Lavergnée suggests that the Louvre drawing was made during the last years of the Vouet's life.

On the basis of the 'sculptural' nature of the image, the Classical facial type and the use of light and shade, as well as the care and delicacy employed in working up details, this drawing can also be placed in the final phase of Vouet's career. I.N.

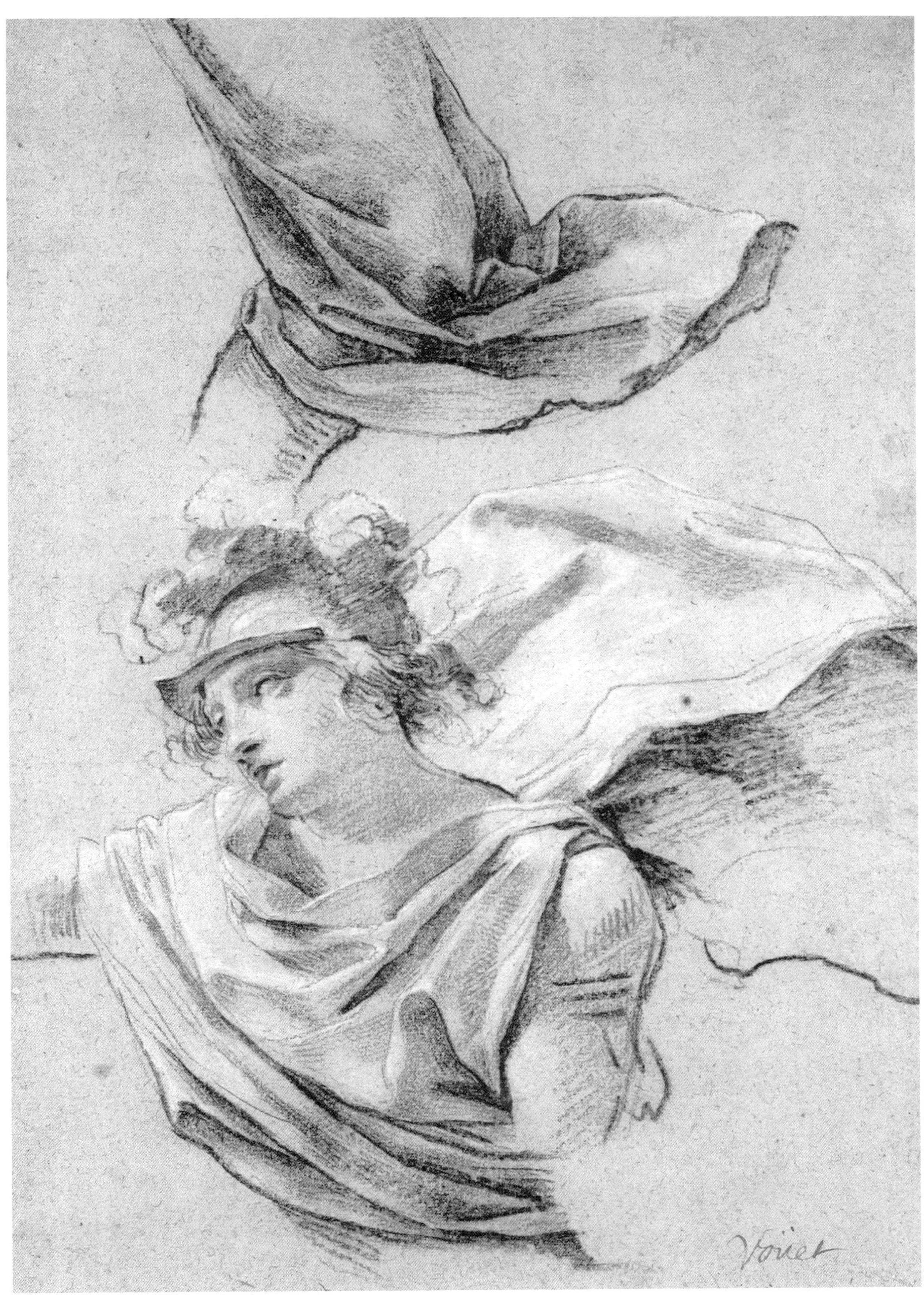
Voüet

16

Nicolas Poussin

Les Andelys 1594–1665 Paris

Tancred and Erminia

Oil on canvas (transferred from old canvas to new in 1854). 98 × 147 cm

PROVENANCE: collection of J.-A.-J. Aved, Paris; 1766 acquired by the Hermitage

Inv. no. GE 1189

OLD MANUSCRIPT CATALOGUES: Cat. 1773–85, no. 11; Cat. 1797, no. 1699; Inventory 1859, no. 3343

EXHIBITIONS: 1937 Paris, p. 59, no. 112; 1955 Moscow, p. 52; 1956 Leningrad, p. 49; 1960 Paris, p. 77, no. 42; 1965 Bordeaux, p. 12, no. 11; 1965–6 Paris, p. 31, no. 10; 1972b Dresden, no. 36; 1975–6 Washington, DC–Detroit–Los Angeles–Houston, no. 7; 1976 Mexico, no. 7; 1976 Montreal, no. 7; 1976 Winnipeg, no. 7; 1978 Düsseldorf, p. 98, no. 19A; 1981 Vienna, pp. 86–9; 1990 New York–Chicago, no. 3; 1992 Birmingham, no. 6; 1994–5 Paris, no. 35; 1995 London, no. 21

LITERATURE: Inv. Aved. 1766, no. 47, in: Wildenstein 1922, p. 209, no. 47 (106); Remy 1766, no. 106. Reimrpr.: Wildenstein 1922, p. 153, no. 106 (47); Cat. 1774, no. 11; Labensky 1805–9, vol. I, pp. 9–12; Le Breton 1809, p. 394; Landon 1814, no. 205 (CCV); Schnitzler 1828, pp. 67–8, 143 (no. 18); Smith 1829–42, part VIII, pp. 147–8, no. 290; Livret 1838, p. 171, no. 23; Dussieux 1856, p. 441; Waagen 1864, p. 284; Neustroyev 1898, p. 322; B.V. 1901, no. 5, p. 85, ill. 67 (appendix); Benois [1910], p. 156; Jouanny 1911, p. 4; Reau 1912, p. 394; Reau 1913, p. 124; Grautoff 1914, vol. I, pp. 108–9, 111, no. 39; Magne 1914, no. 339; Rouches 1921, pp. 129, 193; Reau 1929, no. 292; Hourticq 1937, pp. 84, 98; Bodkin 1939, p. 254; Vol'skaya 1946 Russian, pp. 47–9, note 36; Anikiyeva 1947, pp. 76–7; Gerts 1947; Licht 1954, p. 110; Sterling 1957, pp. 30, 23, pl. 15; Cat. 1958, p. 326; Alpatov 1960, pp. 192–3; Jullian 1960, p. 230; Blunt 1960, p. 284; Mahon 1960, p. 299; Watte 1960, p. 148; Descargues 1961, p. 160; Prokofyev 1962, no. 19; Mahon 1962, p. 28; Alpatov 1963a, p. 289; Alpatov 1963b, p. 282; Glikman 1964, pp. 42–5, 78; Friedländer 1965, p. 51; Levinson-Lessing 1965, nos. 54–5; Peyre 1965, p. 27; Grand 1965, p. 59; Blunt 1966, p. 142, no. 206; Wild 1966, p. 79, note 36; Alpatov 1967, pp. 130–35; Alpatov 1979, pp. 84–95; Lee 1967, p. 139; Blunt 1967, pp. 148, 150; Badt 1969, pp. 520–22; Novoselskaya 1972, no. 19; Thuillier 1974, no. 68; Cat. 1976, p. 222; Kojina, Herz 1977, nos. 52–3; Daniel 1979, p. 223; Zolotov 1979, pp. 49, 51, 52; Wild 1980, vol. I, pp. 57–8; vol. II, p. 55; Zolotov 1985–I, issue 5, pp. 57–8; Zolotov 1985–II, pp. 10, 12, 98; Zolotov 1988, pp. 96–8; Zolotov, Serebriannaia 1990, no. 8; Verdi 1992, pp. 10–34

Poussin created his most lyrical and poetic paintings in the late 1620s and early 1630s. Among the best of these is surely *Tancred and Erminia*, based on a subject taken from Book XIX of Torquato Tasso's epic poem *Jerusalem Delivered* (1580). Although Tasso's heroes were depicted by many 16th- and 17th-century artists, the scene of Erminia saving Tancred is unique to Poussin.

In the posthumous inventory drawn up in 1766 of the collection of J. Aved we read 'two paintings showing subjects from Tasso' – a reference to *Rinaldo and Armida* (Pushkin Museum of Fine Arts, Moscow), for many years thought to be a pair to *Tancred and Erminia*. A catalogue of the collection, however, compiled that same year, 1766, contains an incorrect identification of the subject: 'Angelica commanding the abduction of Rinaldo' and 'Angelica finding the wounded Medoro', revealing that the author had confused *Jerusalem Delivered* with Ludovico Ariosto's *Orlando Furioso* (1532). The correct identification appears in the Hermitage manuscript catalogue (Cat. 1773–85) compiled by Ernst Münich, and in Cat. 1774: 'Erminia and Tancred' and 'Armida Finding the Sleeping Rinaldo'.

The painting was not engraved in the 17th century, nor have any preparatory drawings survived, nor is it mentioned in any texts. In his study of Poussin, Wild (1980) compared the Hermitage painting with *Tancred and Erminia* of 1634 in the Barber Institute of Arts, Birmingham, which he sees as incontrovertibly by Poussin, drawing attention to the relative lack of 'tension' in the Hermitage composition, in its modelling of bodies and drapery. But a letter from Poussin to the artist Jacques Stella (Jouanny 1911) regarding *Rinaldo and Armida* throws light on this subject: here Poussin explains the different demands made by lyrical and heroic subjects, which determine whether the painting should be soft or very restrained and severe. Perpetual change in his manner of painting was one of the artist's creative principles; he felt that his individual style developed as he worked on each painting in accordance with its mood and subject.

Such an approach is perfectly illustrated by a comparison of *Tancred and Erminia* in the Barber Institute – which places the accent on Erminia's heroism – and the Hermitage painting, which concentrates on her emotions, and thus employs considerably softer and more poetic painterly language. The composition is minimal, with attention concentrated on the figure of Erminia. A somewhat melancholy mood is created by the diffused twilight, amid which Erminia is picked out by a broad stream of light, emphasizing her energy and strong will and the dynamic movement of her fragile figure, contrasting with the weakness and dependence of the fallen Tancred, outlined in soft *chiaroscuro*. The intense colouring and warm tonality of this painting shows Poussin's acquaintance with Venetian masters (the golden reflections from the armour, the soft shadows). It is undoubtedly one of Poussin's most poetic works, revealing an emotion and painterly softness characteristic of only a very short period in his career: these qualities were later overtaken by a more severe classicism.

Thuillier (1974) was surprised that a canvas of such significance and poeticism is not mentioned in primary sources, but many of Poussin's works in this 'soft' poetic manner are not mentioned in sources before the mid-18th century. These include such

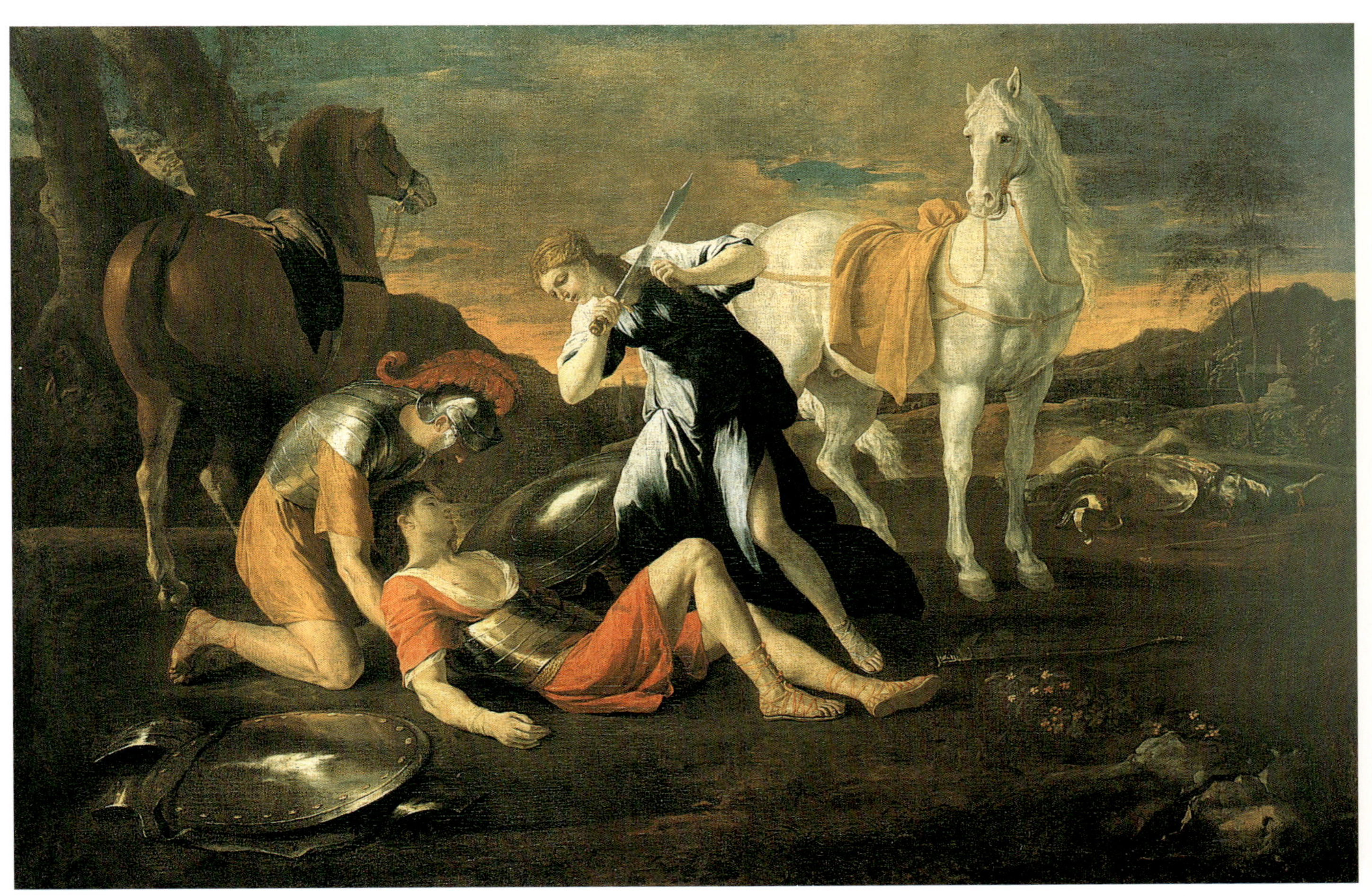

renowned works as *Cephalus and Aurora* (National Gallery, London), *Diana and Endymion* (The Detroit Institute of Arts), *Mars and Venus* (Museum of Fine Arts, Boston), and the *Inspiration of the Epic Poet* (Louvre, Paris). Perhaps the fact is that in those days heroic subjects were preferred, and discussed.

Tancred and Erminia has been dated by scholars to various years between 1625 and 1637, but the majority place it c. 1630–31. N.S.

17

Nicolas Poussin

Dromedary

Pen and brown ink, brown wash.
230 × 148 mm

PROVENANCE: collection of Count Heinrich Brühl, Dresden; 1769 acquired for the Hermitage

Inv. no. OR 8176

EXHIBITIONS: 1971a Leningrad, no. 71; 1972a Dresden, no. 76, ill.; 1987 Delhi, no. 87 ill.; 1995 St Petersburg, no. 3, ill.; 1997 Bonn, no. 111, ill.; 1999 St Petersburg, no. 31, ill.

LITERATURE: Blunt 1967, vol. I, p. 103, fig. 96; Kamenskaya 1971, p. 11, no. 3; Friedländer, Blunt 1939–74, vol. V, no. 425, p. 308, fig. 425; Zolotov, Serebriannaia et al. 1990, no. 5; Rosenberg, Prat 1994, vol. I, p. 332, no. 174, ill.; Fischer 1990, p. 7, ill.; Petrusevich 1995, p. 12, ill.; Novoselskaya 1999, pp. 5, 6, 70, ill.

The Hermitage has four rare drawings of animals by Poussin: two dromedaries, a rhinoceros and an elephant (inv. nos. OR 8174–7). While the depictions of both the elephant and rhinoceros are quite static and linear, the dromedaries are modelled in light and shade, and there is a much greater sense of movement.

We know that Poussin produced images of animals for his Roman patron Cassiano dal Pozzo, secretary to Cardinal Francesco Barberini. A surviving painting by Poussin, *Hannibal Crossing the Alps on an Elephant* (*c.* 1625–6, private collection, Paris), was also produced for dal Pozzo. In a drawing dated 1625, *The Indian Triumph of Bacchus* (The Nelson–Atkins Museum of Art, Kansas City, Missouri), the elephant is shown frontally, as in the Hermitage sheet (inv. no. OR 8174). Kamenskaya (1971, no. 1) and Petrusevich (1995, no. 1) link all the Hermitage drawings with these compositions.

Rosenberg and Prat (1994, vol. I, no. 174) were perhaps not far from the truth in suggesting that these images of animals were taken not from life but from earlier works of art: both dromedaries, it was thought, may have been taken from sculptural reliefs. A date was set on the drawings of animals of between 1632 and 1635. It was the Danish scholar Erik Fischer who indentified the works that served as the models for Poussin's dromedaries, in the catalogue of an exhibition of works by Melchior Lorich connected with Turkey. Poussin, he wrote, 'made a copy of two engravings on wood by Lorich' (Fischer 1990, p. 7). The same catalogue (p. 40) includes publication of a monogrammed woodcut by Lorich dated 1482 showing a dromedary set against a desert landscape (Melchior Lorich*: Wolgerissene und geschittene Figurren…*, Hamburg, 1626, unpag.), and the Hermitage drawing, which differs only in the lack of a landscape and the addition of a form of pedestal beneath the animal's feet. Another engraving by Lorich, monogrammed and dated 1576 (Fischer 1990), served as the model for the second image of a dromedary (fig. 29), where the animal turns his head away from the viewer. I.N.

fig. 29
Nicolas Poussin
Dromedary

ink and wash drawing
(inv. no. OR 8177)

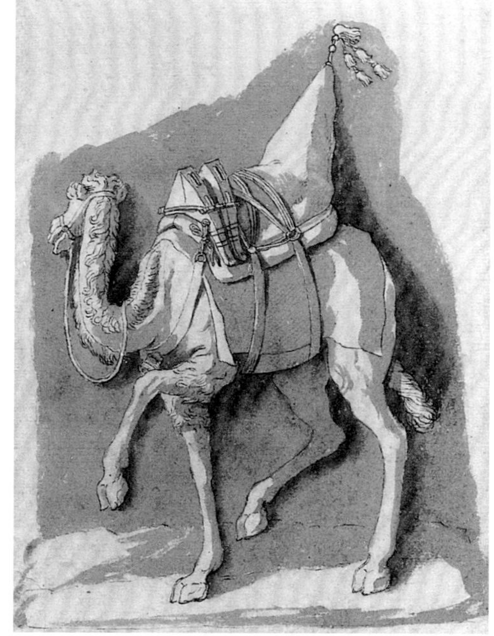

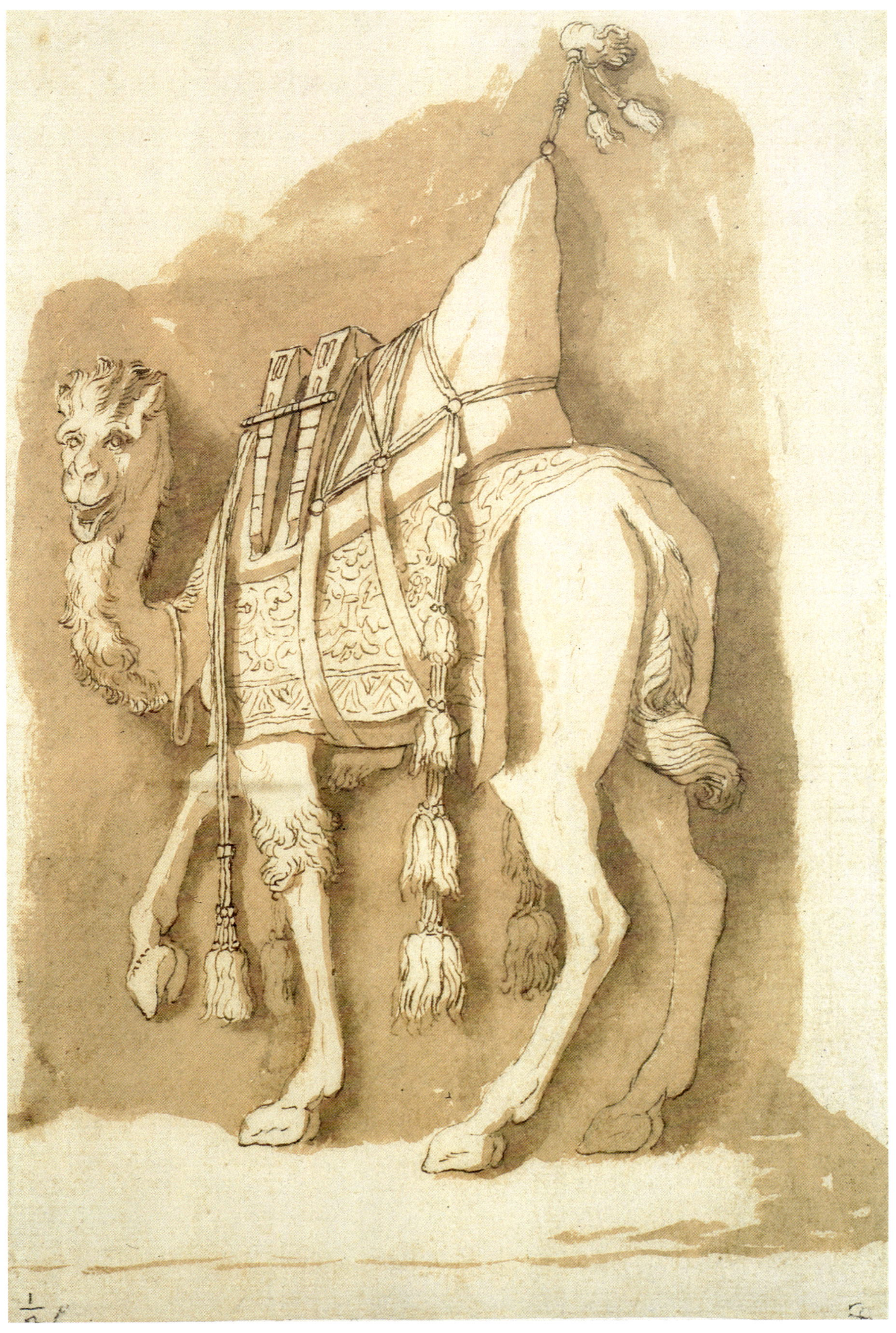

18

Nicolas Poussin

Classical Landscape with Figures

Brown wash over a black chalk sketch.
150 × 405 mm. Lined

PROVENANCE: collection of Count Carl Cobenzl, Brussels (collector's mark L. 2858b); 1768 acquired for the Hermitage: collector's mark L. 2061

Inv. no. OR 5082

OLD MANUSCRIPT CATALOGUES: Cobenzl – 'Catal[ogue] de Cabin[et], Catalogue de Desseins, Seconde Grandeur', p. 13v., Carton no. 2, no. 11, 'Poussin, un Peysage'

EXHIBITIONS: 1867 St Petersburg, no. 446; 1956 Leningrad, p. 95; 1963 Stockholm, no. 34; 1990 Edinburgh, no. 25, ill.; 1994 Paris, no. 155, fig.; 1995 St Petersburg, no. 9, ill.; 1997 Bonn, no. 113, ill.; 1999 St Petersburg, no. 33, ill.

LITERATURE: Friedländer, Blunt 1939–74, vol. IV, no. 279, pl. 216; Friedländer 1965, p. 69, fig. 238; Kamenskaya 1971, no. 9, ill.; Blunt 1979, vol. I, pp. 75, 122, 124; Wild 1980, vol. I, p. 195; Western European Drawing 1981, no. 72, Abb.; Zolotov, Serebriannaia et al 1990, no. 18, ill.; Hermitage 1994, no. 346, ill.; Rosenberg, Prat 1994, vol. I, p. 570, no. 294, fig.; Novoselskaya 1999, pp. 5, 6, 74, ill.

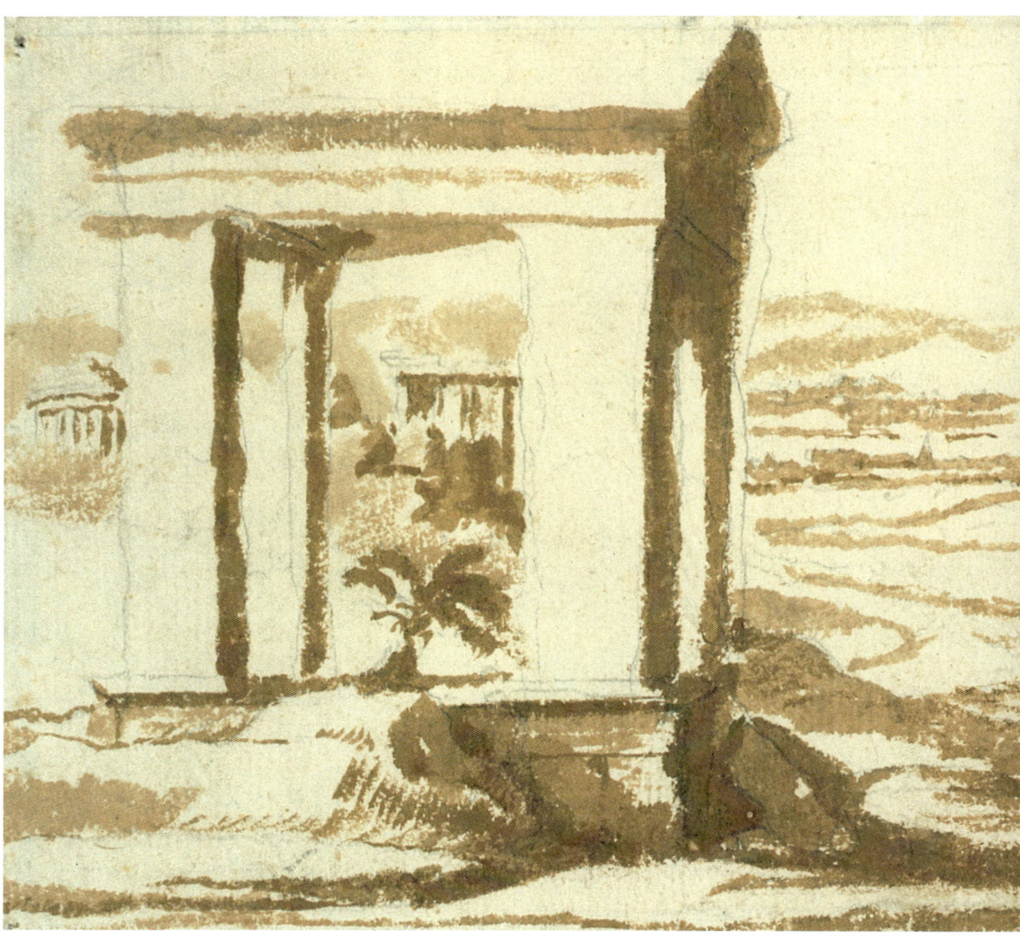

By replacing the title more commonly found in the Russian literature, *Landscape with a View of the Roman Campagna*, with one more neutral, we find ourselves moving closer to the opinion of foreign scholars, most of whom have seen in this work not the depiction of a specific locality but a composite, synthesized Italian landscape. Rosenberg and Prat gave the drawing the descriptive title *Landscape with a Small Temple to the Left and Three Seated Figures to the Right*. The same authors, noting the elongated form of the sheet and the figure types with their egg-shaped heads, dated it to 1646–7, the time when Poussin was at work on a second series of paintings of *The Seven Sacraments* (National Gallery of Scotland, Edinburgh, on loan from the Duke of Sutherland), and directly preceding his series of drawings for the *Holy Family on the*

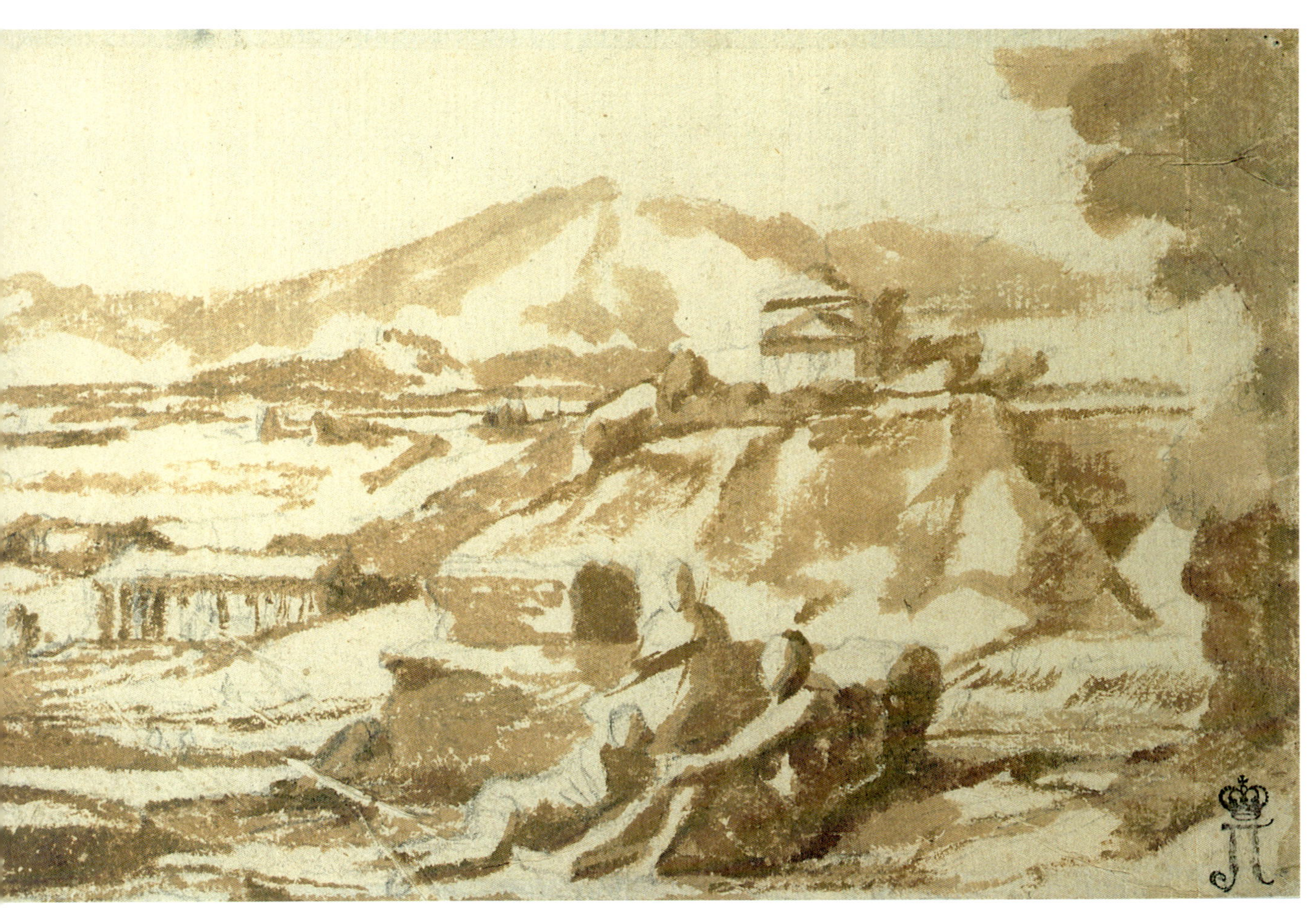

Steps (Cleveland Museum of Art, Ohio), in all of which works both figures and buildings, throwing sharp shadows, are treated in an analogous manner (Musée des Beaux-Arts, Dijon, inv. Ca 870; Pierpont Morgan Library, New York, inv. no. III.71; Département des Arts Graphiques, Louvre, Paris, inv. no. 32439; Rosenberg, Prat 1994, vol. I, nos. 313–15).

A broad, majestic panorama is spread before us in all its glory, with distant hills and a boundless valley in which stand ancient temples and ruins, the whole filled with peace and silence. Poussin has made delicate use of muted gradations of brown wash, with darker brushstrokes setting off the foreground building and resting figures, thus accentuating their importance. I.N.

19

Nicolas Poussin

The Baptism

Pen and brown ink, brown wash, over a black chalk sketch. 165 × 255 mm. Lined

PROVENANCE: collection of Count Carl Cobenzl, Brussels (collector's mark L. 2858b); 1768 acquired for the Hermitage: collector's mark L. 2061

Inv. no. OR 5081

OLD MANUSCRIPT CATALOGUES: Cobenzl – 'Catal[ogue] de Cabin[et], Catalogue de Desseins, Seconde Grandeur', p. 20v., Carton no. 2, no. 10, 'Poussin, Baptême de Jesus'

EXHIBITIONS: 1860 St Petersburg, no. 41; 1867 St Petersburg, no. 439; 1994 Paris, no. 119, fig.; 1995 St Petersburg, no. 12, ill.; 1997 Bonn, no. 112, ill.; 1999 St Petersburg, no. 34, ill.

LITERATURE: Friedländer, Blunt 1939–74, vol. I, no. 78, ill. 50; vol. V, p. 88; Blunt 1965, p. 64; Badt 1969, vol. I, pp. 225–6, 249; Kamenskaya 1971, no. 13, ill.; Blunt 1979, pp. 63, I06, ill. 122; Wild 1980, vol. II, no. 130; Zolotov 1988, p. 232, ill. 248; Zolotov, Serebriannaia et al. 1990, no. 27, ill.; Mérot 1990, pp. I90–92, ill.; Rosenberg, Prat 1994, vol. I, no. 253, ill.; 1999 Novoselskaya, pp. 5, 6, 76, ill.

This is one of four surviving sketches for a painting of the same name in the second series of *The Seven Sacraments*, commissioned by Paul Chantelou. That canvas (fig. 4) was finished at the end of 1646, to which year the drawings are also dated. As is revealed by the drawings, during the process of work the composition underwent changes both in the placing and quantity of figures and in the space set aside for those figures within the architecture.

In 1967 Blunt reconstructed the order of the artist's work on the painting, arranging the preparatory sketches in the sequence they were produced. He saw the first of these as this one and another in the Uffizi, Florence (inv. no. 903E), both of them very close in the placing of the figures and their relative setting within the composition (although there are differences, as in the background architecture and the use of light and shadow). It is possible that this drawing was the earlier of the two: it also reveals links with *The Baptism* in the National Gallery of Art, Washington, DC, from the first series of the *Sacraments* (series dated 1642), commissioned by Cassiano dal Pozzo. Both that painting and this drawing show Christ standing, while in the Uffizi sketch the figure is in a transitional state, with right leg bent: in the next two drawings in chronological terms (Département des Arts Graphiques, Louvre, Paris), Christ is kneeling.

Closest to the second painting – in the scale of the walls, the placing of groups, similarities between individual figures, and the more modest space allocated to the background, particularly in terms of the buildings – is one of the Louvre drawings (inv. no. M.I 987). Scholars have suggested, however, that there must have been at least one more drawing, which would have been closer still to the painting (Rosenberg, Prat 1994, vol. I, no. 259).

A hasty pen study for the figures of Christ and John the Baptist in this drawing is found on the back of Poussin's drawing *The Holy Family with St Elizabeth* (Musée des Beaux-Arts, Dijon, inv. no. 870). A study for a group of figures dressing is in the Pierpont Morgan Library, New York; with minimal changes this is repeated in the left side of three drawings: those in the Hermitage and Uffizi and in the first Louvre drawing (inv. no. I 990). Thus this sheet presents the original version of the composition, and yet it is striking in its unity and finished conception. The significance of the event and the atmosphere of mystery are reinforced by the generalized depiction of the figures, which are set naturally into a landscape without superfluous details, modelled simply in light and shade. All present have their attention riveted on the central figures, and the solemn nature of the scene is reinforced by the marvellously calm, hilly landscape with a river, half-destroyed temple and barely indicated tree in the distance. I.N.

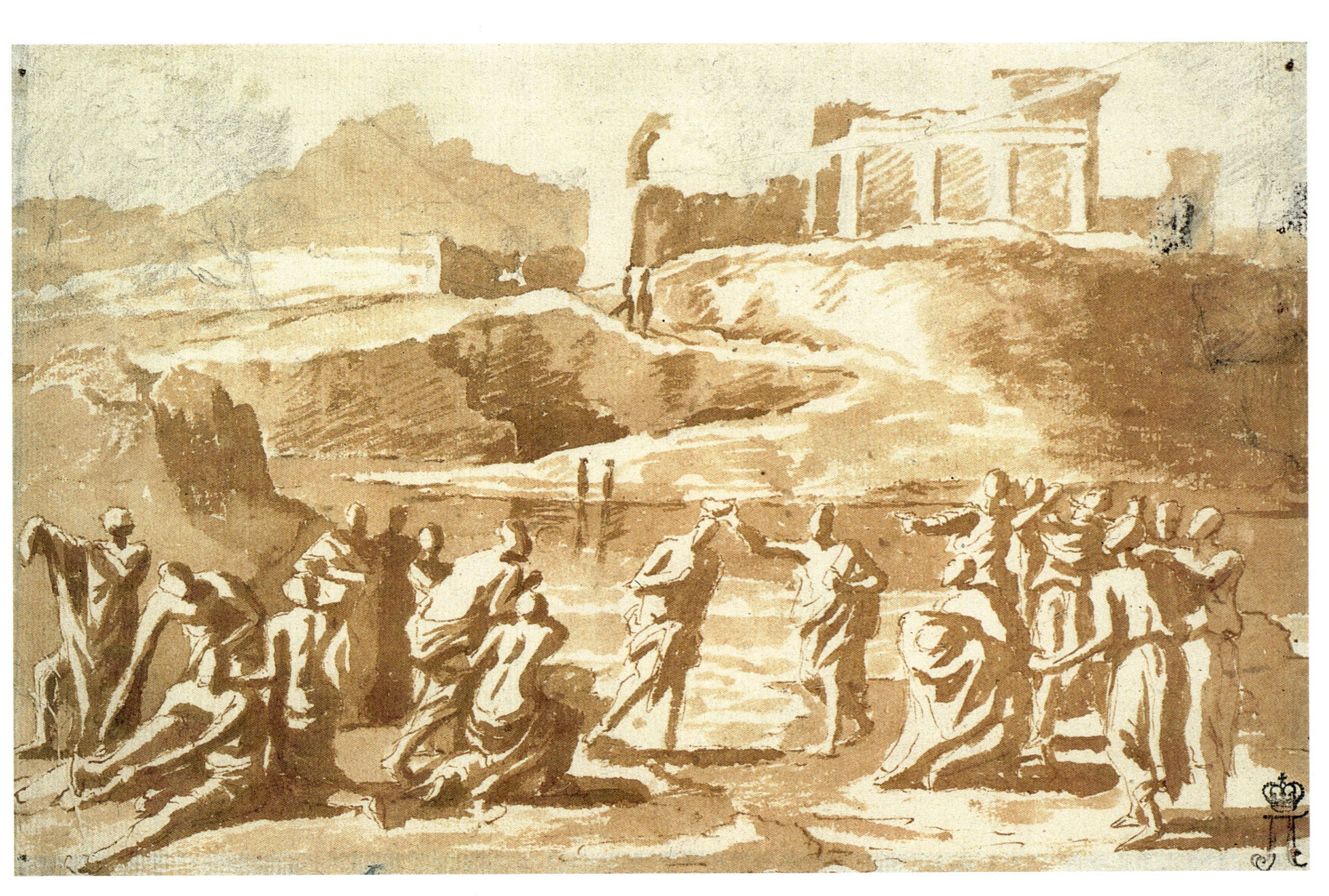

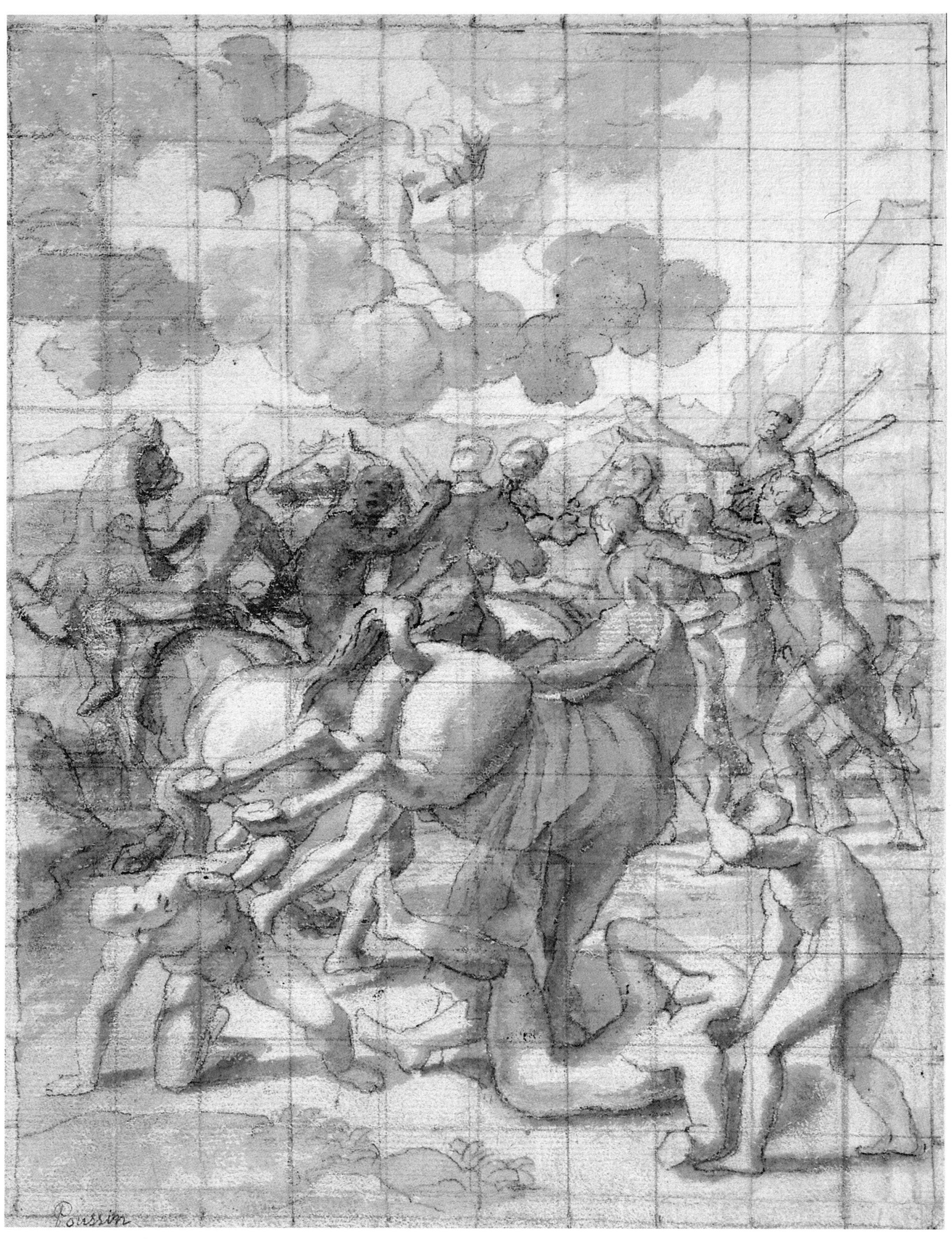
Poussin

20

Nicolas Poussin

The Conversion of Saul

Pen and brown ink, brown wash, heightened with white, red chalk; squared in red and black chalk.
310 × 227 mm. Lined

Old inscription in pen and brown ink bottom left: *Poussin*

PROVENANCE: collection of Count Heinrich Brühl, Dresden; 1769 acquired for the Hermitage

Inv. no. OR 5128

EXHIBITIONS: 1995 St Petersburg, no. 38, ill.; 1999 St Petersburg, no. 37, ill.

LITERATURE: Friedländer, Blunt 1939–74, vol. I, no. 16, pl. 71; vol. V, pp. 83, 84; Kamenskaya 1971. no. À 16, ill.; Wild 1980, vol. II, no. 197; Rosenberg, Prat 1994, vol. I, no. 369, pl.; Petrusevich 1995, p. 26, ill.; Keazor 1996, pp. 263–76, fig. 4.; Novoselskaya 1999, pp. 5, 6, 82, ill.

Poussin's authorship of this drawing was questioned for many years, a number of scholars giving it to his studio (Friedländer, Blunt 1939–74, vol. I; Kamenskaya 1971). Kamenskaya none the less qualified her assessment, noting the high quality of a work that 'was executed in the artist's workshop, possibly with his own participation'. Petrusevich (1995) placed a question-mark after the artist's name. Blunt (Friedländer, Blunt 1939–74, vol. V) and other contemporary scholars (Rosenberg, Prat 1994; Keazor 1996, pp. 268–73), however, argue that the drawing is in Poussin's own hand.

In their arguments against attributing this drawing to Poussin himself, scholars cited various features perceived as being untypical of the artist: the relatively large size of the sheet (although the squaring provides clear evidence that this is a *modello* for a painting, which would naturally be on larger paper); the combination of brown wash with intense red chalk; faults in the execution of clouds and the vegetation in the foreground. Yet none of these things weakens the impression of force and monumentality exuded by this drawing, which is surely by Poussin. Evidence of a relatively late date is to be found in the compositional skill, the unity of a group composed of a multitude of disparate moving people and horses, the contrasting use of light and shade, the particularly 'sculptural' figures in the foreground, the egg-shaped heads with barely marked facial features, the monochrome colouring that unites the scene as a whole, the vivid resonance of the red chalk, and the broken contours that indicate the artist's hand shook as he worked.

From Poussin's correspondence we know there were two stages of work on the subject of *The Conversion of Saul*, commissioned by Paul Fréart, sieur de Chantelou (Jouanny 1911, pp. 442, 458), in 1649–50 and 1657–8. The fate of any paintings that may have followed from this work is unknown. We do, however, have five drawings for them. One (Musée Condé, Chantilly, AI 171; no. I 206), a horizontal composition, is linked with the first phase (Rosenberg, Prat 1994, vol. I, no. 340); three others (one in a private collection in London, and two in the Hermitage – this drawing and fig. 30) with the second (Rosenberg, Prat 1994, vol. I, nos. 368, 369, 371). Opinions are divided with regard to the fifth (Hermitage inv. no. OR 8050).

As the largest and most finished drawing for *The Conversion of Saul*, squared for transference and executed in the artist's characteristic broken hand, this sheet is clearly the last of the sketches for the second version of the painting (1657–8), if we disregard a small hasty sketch (Hermitage inv. no. 5134) in which the movement is in the opposite direction. The latter would seem to be connected with the appearance of a fresh idea (Rosenberg, Prat 1994, vol. I, no. 371): in a letter of November 1658, Poussin wrote that he had found 'a new composition ... a thought different to my first one has come to me ' (Jouanny 1911, p. 449). I.N.

fig.30
Nicolas Poussin
Study for The Conversion of Saul
(inv. no. OR 5154)

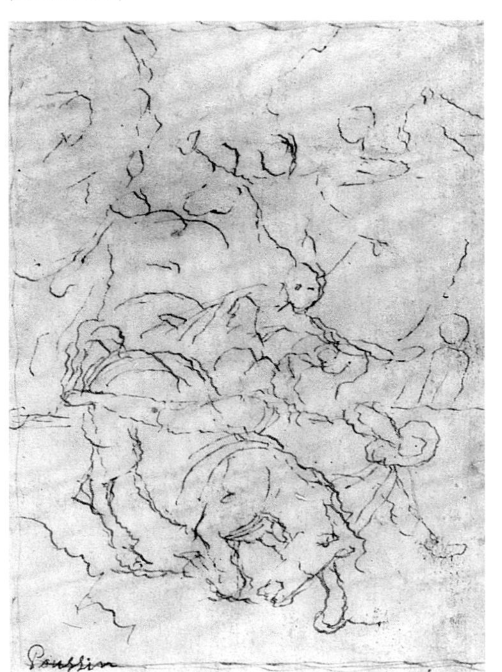

21

Claude Gellée, Le Lorrain

Chamagne (Lorraine) 1600 – 1682 Rome

Italian Landscape

Oil on canvas. 75 × 100 cm
Signed and dated bottom right on the tree: *CLAVD.. 1648 ROMAE*

PROVENANCE: collection of Louis-Antoine Crozat, baron de Thiers, Paris; 1772 acquired for the Hermitage as part of the Crozat collection

Inv. no. GE 1225

OLD MANUSCRIPT CATALOGUES AND INVENTORIES: Cat. 1773–85, no. 952; Cat. 1797, no. 1746; Inventory 1859, no. 3408

EXHIBITIONS: 1956 Leningrad, p. 35; 1968–9 Belgrade, no. 47; 1972b Dresden, no. 23; 1987–8 Belgrade–Ljubliana–Zagreb, no. 8

LITERATURE: Cat. Crozat 1755, p. 57; Cat. 1774, no. 952; Smith 1829–42, part VIII, p. 338, no. 302; Livret 1838, p. 171, no. 221; Waagen 1864, p. 291; Pattison 1884, p. 246; Cat. 1958, p. 308; Rothlisberger 1961, vol. I, p. 474; vol. 2, fig. 211; Stuffmann 1968, p. 110; Cat. 1976, p. 200; Rothlisberger 1977, p. 108, no. 172 bis

Claude's contemporaries and biographers were unanimous in underlining his great interest in the landscape of the Roman Campagna. Sandart (1675–9, p. 209) recalled that he spent many hours wandering through the groves, sketching whole views, specific motifs, trees and buildings, sometimes even working with paints outdoors, which was then almost unknown. He probably knew the Roman countryside better than any of his fellow artists in the capital.

Over time, Claude developed in his work a type of broad, flat landscape with trees dotted around to leave a clear open perspective; on distant hills he placed various structures, including ruined temples and aqueducts. Almost obligatory was a bridge in the middle distance, a river in the foreground with a herd of cattle crossing it, and on the banks, resting in the shade, shepherds or cowherds. Although they made use of one and the same set of elements, these compositions never repeated one another.

This 'ideal landscape' makes use of Claude's favourite cattle motif: they are seen returning from pasture, fording the river. The soft warm light of the setting sun envelops the figures. Everything co-exists harmoniously on this peaceful, untroubled evening.

This painting is a repetition of *Pastoral Landscape* (1647, Museum of Fine Arts, Budapest, *Liber Veritatis* 107), but differs in details. Similar figures to those in the foreground are found in the artist's *Rural Landscape* (1645, Barber Institute of Fine Arts, Birmingham) and *Landscape with Paris and Oenone* (1648, Louvre, Paris). N.S.

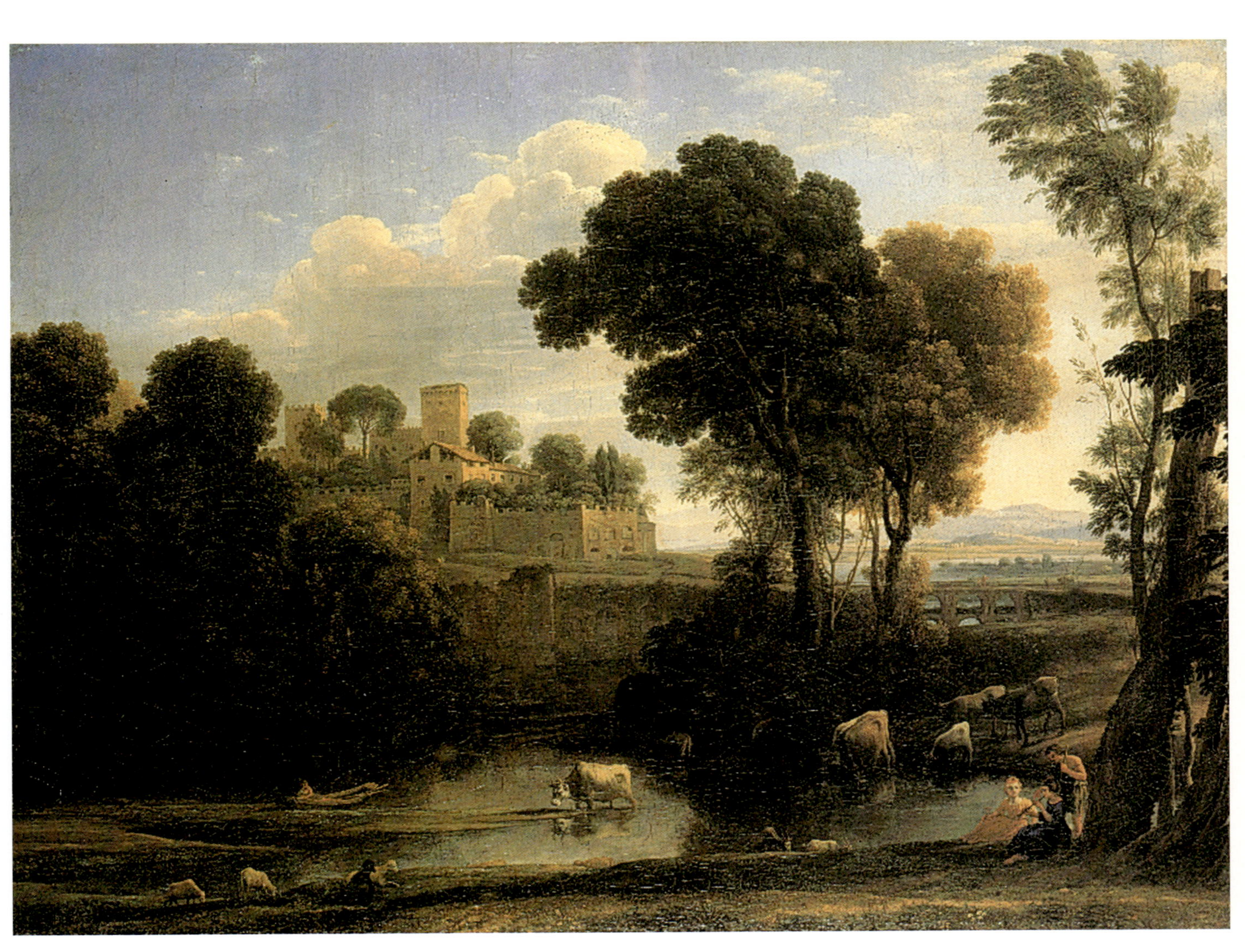

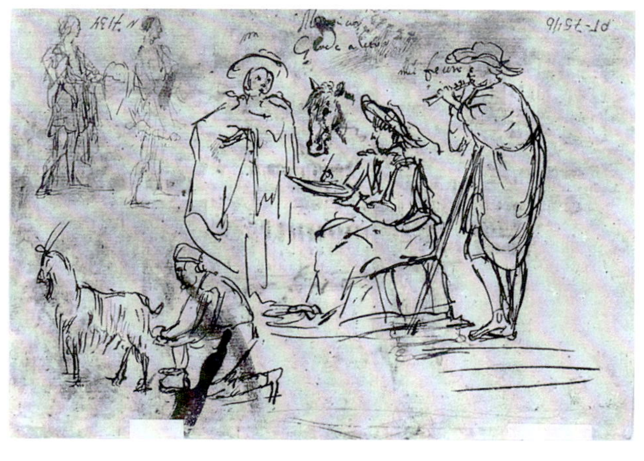

fig. 31
Claude Lorrain
Sketches of Figures and Animals
(reverse of cat. 22)

22
Claude Gellée, Le Lorrain

View of the Church of the Trinità dei Monti, Rome

Pen and brown ink, brown wash.
In places visible brown patches and lines from the drawing on the reverse.
140 × 205 mm

On the reverse: sketches of figures and animals
Inscription in pen and brown ink by the top edge in the centre: *Monsieur … Clode a …* and two illegible words above a flute in the hands of a musician
Pen and brown ink

PROVENANCE: collection of Count Carl Cobenzl, Brussels (collector's mark L. 2858b); 1768 acquired for the Hermitage: collector's mark L. 2061

Inv. no. OR 7134

EXHIBITIONS: 1959 Leningrad, p. 27; 1963 Stockholm, no. 36; 1970 Göteborg, no. 77; 1972 Prague, no. 67; 1974 Manchester, no. 29, pl. 25; 1975 Aarhus, no. 14, ill.; 1975 Copenhagen, no. 14, ill.; 1975 Berlin, no. 62, ill.; 1982 Florence, no. 85, fig. 85; 1997 Bonn, no. 108, ill.; 1999 St Petersburg, no. 40, ill.

LITERATURE: Dobroklonsky 1961, p. 395, ill.; Rothlisberger 1968, vol. I, p. 91, no. 48; vol. II, pl. 48; Western European Drawing 1981, no. 76, Ill.; Novoselskaya 1999, pp. 6, 8, ill.

Claude earned himself a reputation as 'the poet of Rome', praising the beauties of the environs of the city, where he made numerous landscape drawings, the majority of which were then used in his paintings. He drew whole compositions or parts of them, studied individual details, figures of people and animals. Sometimes he used black chalk, but most frequently he worked with pen and brown ink. This view of the Trinità dei Monti is a preparatory sketch that he used for the left side of a painting of the same name (fig. 32).

Rothlisberger (1968, vol. I, no. 48) argued that this drawing was done from the life. It certainly has a certain fragmentary nature in its composition, some motifs are incomplete, and Claude rarely allowed a building to play the main role. Thin, delicate lines and strokes have been used to convey details of the church and to pick out figures. A tree and the hill silhouetted in the background set off the architectural panorama, flooded with sunlight.

On the reverse of this sheet are figures unrelated either to the drawing or the painting, although they would seem to have been produced at the same time, and were clearly taken from life (fig. 31). There is a man milking a goat, two barely indicated figures in the upper-left corner, and a group of three men – a seated artist drawing in the middle, a musician playing a flute to the right and a man with a horse on the left. Similar motifs and figures are to be found in a number of Claude's early sketches. I.N.

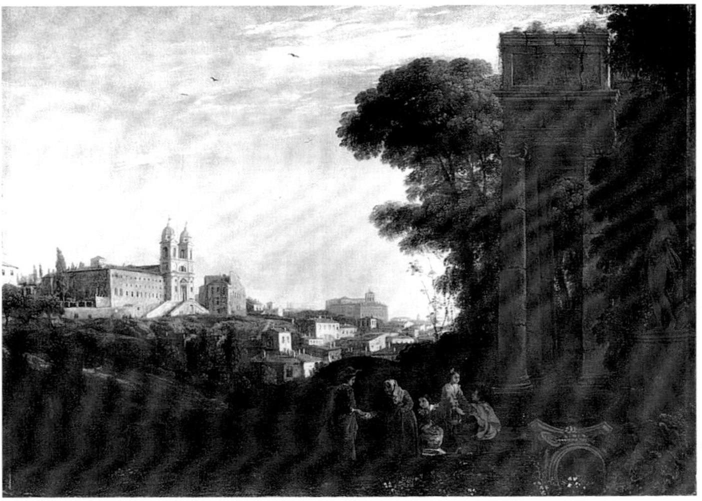

fig. 32
Claude Lorrain
A View in Rome, with the Church of the Trinità dei Monti, 1632
oil on canvas, 59.7 × 83.8 cm
The National Gallery, London

23

Claude Gellée, Le Lorrain

Landscape with Figures

Pen and brown ink, brown wash.
184 × 282 mm. Lined

PROVENANCE: collection of Count Carl Cobenzl, Brussels (collector's mark L. 2858b); 1768 acquired for the Hermitage: collector's mark L. 2061

Inv. no. OR 4368

EXHIBITIONS: 1926 Leningrad, no. 213; 1955 Moscow, p. 78; 1956 Leningrad, p. 90; 1963 Stockholm, no. 37; 1997 Bonn, no. 107, ill.; 1999 St Petersburg, no. 41, ill.

LITERATURE: Dobroklonsky 1961, p. 395, ill.; Rothlisberger 1968, vol. I, p. 133, no. 188; vol. II, pl. 188; Novoselskaya 1999, pp. 6, 90, ill.

The majority of Claude's landscape drawings are linked to his paintings. There are three sheets close in composition (Hermitage; British Museum, London, inv. no. Oo.7–214; Devonshire Collection, Chatsworth, inv. no. 873) that were created as preparatory sketches for a *Pastoral Landscape* in the collection of Lord Bute, London. By analogy with its paired and dated landscape in the same collection, that painting is dated to 1638 and the drawings are thus dated 1636–8 (Rothlisberger 1968, vol. I, p. 133, nos. 188–90). The asymmetrical construction characteristic of all three drawings supports the suggested dating.

This drawing reveals the greatest differences in comparison with the painting (the painting also includes a shepherd and shepherdess with a flock). It is executed in a hasty, sketchy manner, and clearly represents the artist's first idea. There are similarities with *The Banks of the River Tiber* (Hermitage, inv. no. OR 15928) in the manner of drawing in the left side (the foreground and hills): the same uneven quality, the same broken, hasty lines, and the same accents of small areas and dots of colour. The trees in the right-hand side of the sheet are opaque, painted with thick brown wash. I.N.

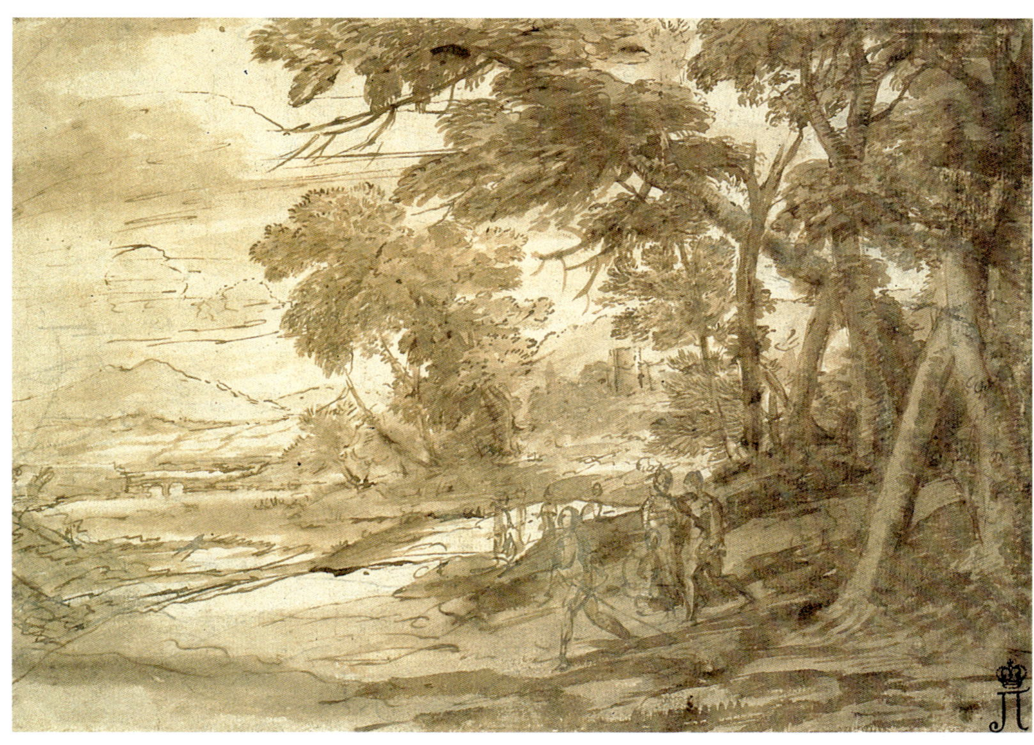

24

Claude Gellée, Le Lorrain

View of the Campagna from Tivoli

Pen and brown ink, brown wash; black chalk vertical line running through the centre; squared into rhombuses with black chalk. 209 × 309 mm. Lined

PROVENANCE: collection of Count Carl Cobenzl, Brussels (collector's mark L. 2858b); 1768 acquired for the Hermitage: collector's mark L. 2061

Inv. no. OR 4786

EXHIBITIONS: 1959 Leningrad, no. 27; 1999 St Petersburg, no. 43, ill.

LITERATURE: Dobroklonsky 1961, p. 396, ill.; Rothlisberger 1968, vol. I, p. 229, no. 572; vol. II, pl. 572; Novoselskaya 1999, pp. 6, 94, ill.

This landscape, formerly attributed to Joost de Momper, was identified as Claude's by Mikhail Dobroklonsky. In composition it is comparable with a drawing dated 1645 in the *Liber Veritatis* (an album, now in the British Museum, put together by Claude that contains sketches of all his paintings: *Liber Veritatis*, 89; Rothlisberger 1968, vol. I, no. 573; vol. II, pl. 573) and to a painting in the Royal Collection at Windsor Castle. Clearly, this drawing should also be dated to the same period.

Both the painting and the *Liber Veritatis* drawing show two apostles and a goat in the foreground that are not present in this work, and other minor differences are revealed in the proportions and in individual details. The sheets differ also in their use of colour: this sheet is monochrome, while the *Liber Veritatis* landscape is on blue paper in brown wash heightened with white, and is less delicate in its execution.

The *View of the Campagna from Tivoli* is built up of fine gradations of brown wash: the plateau and tree-trunk in the foreground are dark; as the land drops into the valley the tones become lighter and, as it rises again into the mountains, breaks up into small planes, with darker silhouettes of bushes, trees, buildings, the crevices in the hills and the paths. Gradually, as we pass from water to sky, the tones weaken and melt as if dissolving in the air. It is possible that this somewhat romanticized and quite finished drawing was produced from a detailed study taken from life. I.N.

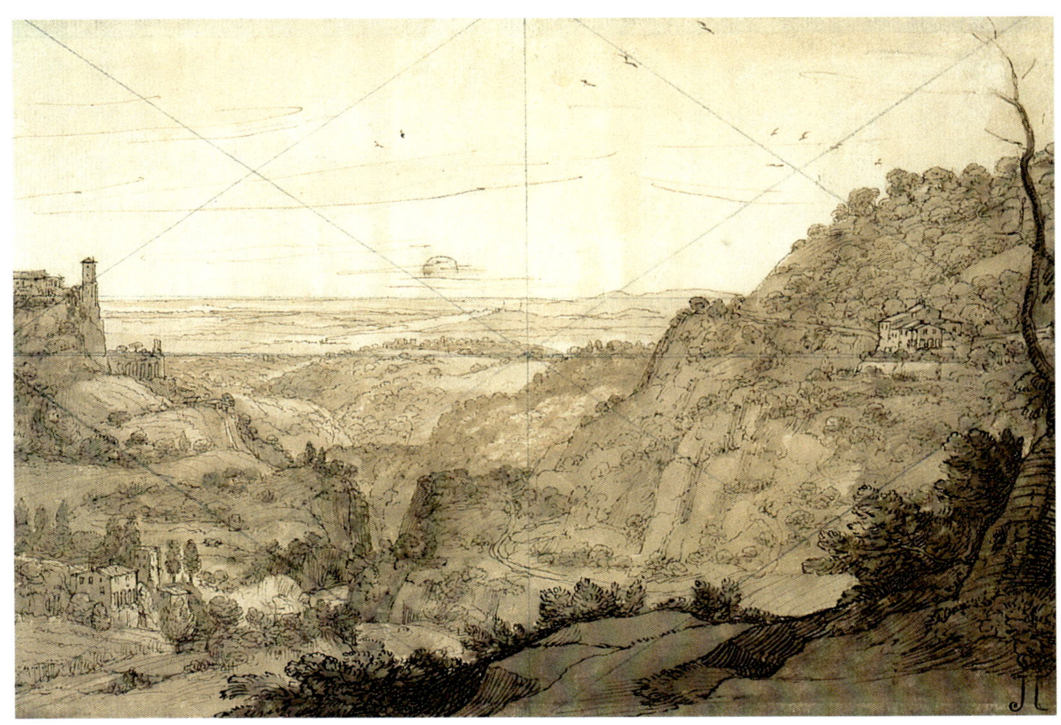

25

Claude Mellan

Abbeville 1598–1688 Paris

Cardinal Jules Mazarin

Black chalk; squared. 208 × 203 mm. Lined

Old inscription in pen and brown ink beneath the drawing in a cartouche: *Champagne*

PROVENANCE: collection of Count Carl Cobenzl, Brussels (collector's mark L. 2858b); 1768 acquired for the Hermitage: collector's mark L. 2061

Inv. no. OR 1815

OLD MANUSCRIPT CATALOGUES: Cobenzl – 'Catal[ogue] de Cabin[et], Catalogue de Desseins, Seconde Grandeur', p. 41v., Carton no. 36, no. 2, 'Champagne, un Prelat'

EXHIBITIONS: 1969 Leningrad–Moscow, no. 49; 1986 Bogota, ill.; 1986 Buenos Aires, no. 47, ill.; 1986 Montevideo, no. 47, ill.; 1988 Leningrad, no. 24, ill.; 1999 St Petersburg, no. 54, ill.

LITERATURE: Novoselskaya 1961, p. 64; Novoselskaya 1962, p. 327, no. 24, fig.; Novoselskaya 1983, p. 116, ill.; Brejon de Lavergnee 1985, p. 24, no. 24, fig.; Novoselskaya 1999, pp. 5, 16, ill.

The renowned portraitist Claude Mellan is represented in the Hermitage collection by 42 superb portrait drawings. Among the subjects are many of his leading contemporaries, including Cardinal Richelieu, Chancellor Pierre Séguier and Henri de Mesmes (President of the French Parlement).

This portrait of the Italian-born Giulio Mazarini (1602–61), the individual who established France's dominance in Europe, was used by the artist for a print (fig. 33), and the same portrait appears in one of his allegorical compositions (Inventaire 1988, no. 162). From its manner of execution and the sitter's age, the portrait can be dated to the second half of the 1640s. I.N.

fig. 33
Claude Mellan
Cardinal Jules Mazarin

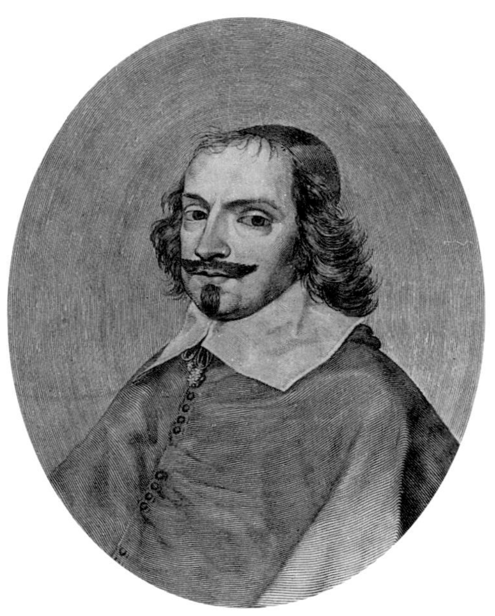

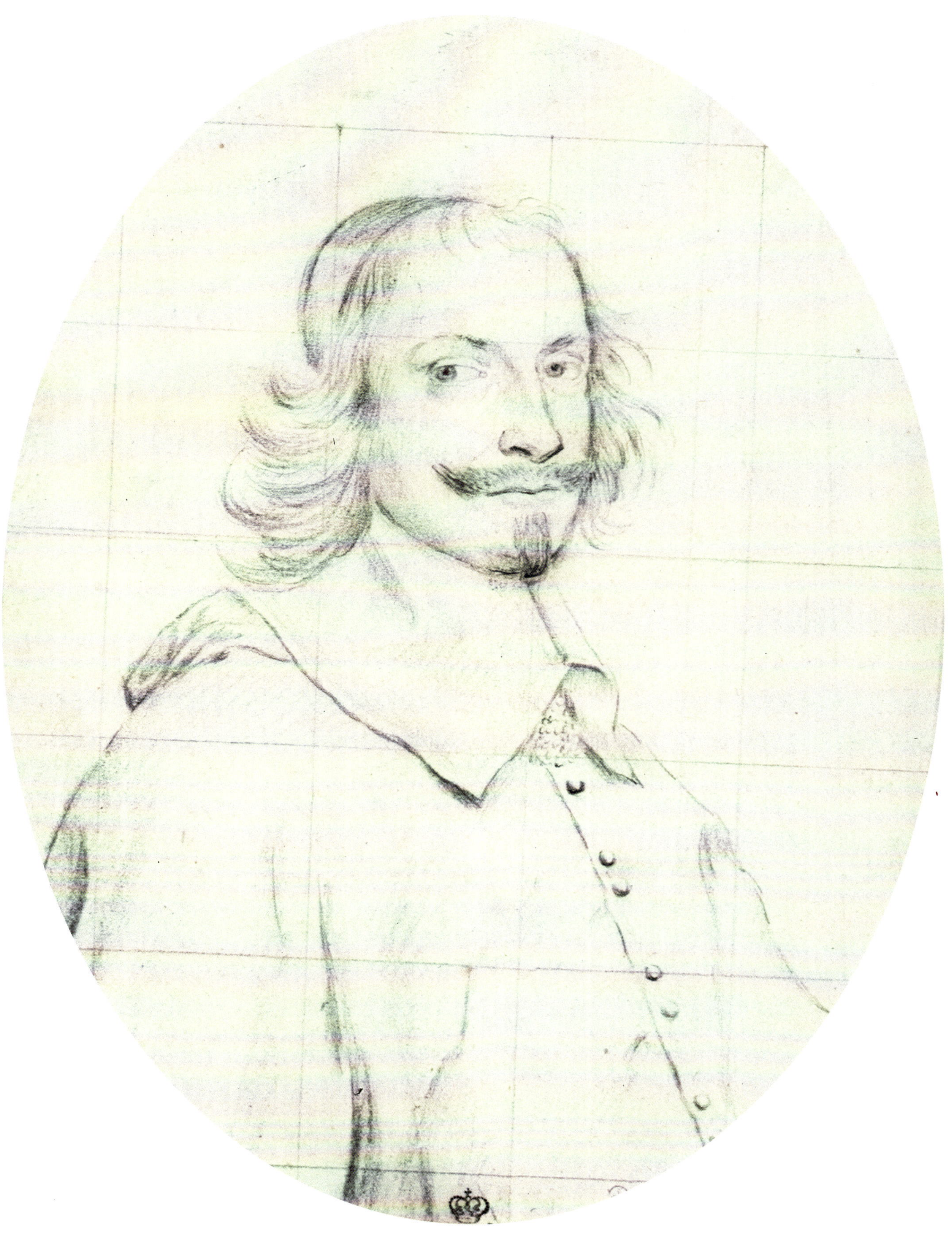

26

Charles Lebrun

Paris 1619–1690 Paris

Portière Design with the Fouquet Coat of Arms

Black and red chalk, grey-brown wash, pen and brown ink. Squared in black chalk. The border outlined in red chalk. 434 × 315 mm

Old inscription in pen and brown ink bottom left: *C Le Brun*

PROVENANCE: collection of Jean-Denis Lempereur, Paris (collector's mark L. 1740); Guichardot sale; collection of Alfred Beurdeley, Paris (collector's mark L. 421); 1889 Museum of the Baron Stieglitz School of Technical Drawing, St Petersburg; 1924 transferred to the Hermitage

Inv. no. OR 18959

EXHIBITIONS: 1912 St Petersburg, no. 209; 1970 Budapest, no. 62; 1972 Prague, no. 61; 1975 Berlin, no. 76, ill.; 1982 Florence, no. 93, ill.; 1995–6 St Petersburg, no. 37, ill.; 1999 St Petersburg, no. 62, ill.

PREVIOUSLY PUBLISHED: Guichard 1881, pl. XXI; Bonnafé 1882, p. 5; Guiffrey [1900], vol. II, pl. 196.

LITERATURE: Novoselskaya 1970, pp. 12028; Novoselskaya 1999, p. 132, ill.

In 1658 a tapestry manufactory was set up at Maincy on the initiative of Nicolas Fouquet (1615–80), Superintendent of Finances, which survived until 1661. In 1659–60 Lebrun made a number of designs for tapestries, the first being this one bearing Fouquet's coat of arms. Glorifying Fouquet's might, the tapestry *portière* that was to be woven from it was intended to be displayed at the Marquis's Vaux-le-Vicomte, the extravagant château near Melun begun in 1656.

This sketch for the *portière* is one of the artist's finished drawings, in which he carefully worked up not only the central group but the ornamental surround. The composition is symmetrical. On either side of the shield – on which we see a squirrel rampant – is a female supporter, whose lower bodies take the form of cornucopias. One (Fidelity) bears a key in her hand and has a dog in attendance, the other (Courage) wears a lion's skin and is accompanied by a lion. Above the shield are *putti* supporting the Marquis' crown, their arms entwined with a ribbon bearing Fouquet's motto: 'Quo non ascend[am]' (What shall I not achieve?). This motto also appears on the pediment at Vaux-le-Vicomte.

Another design by Lebrun for the *portière* is now in the Musée des Beaux-Arts, Besançon (Montagu 1962, p. 531, fig. 1). That drawing is more sketchy and was probably Lebrun's first attempt. After Fouquet's dramatic removal from office in 1661 (he was arrested on Louis XIV's orders and later sentenced to life imprisonment for financial corruption), the *portière* design underwent certain changes, and thus in the Besançon drawing a snake has been drawn over the top of the squirrel: the snake is the central element in the arms of Jean-Baptiste Colbert, appointed to replace Fouquet as Superintendent of Finances. Colbert commissioned several *portière* tapestries, but these do not include the cornucopias that make up the lower parts of the supporters, a cockerel has replaced the lion, and Colbert's own coat of arms that of Fouquet.

For the finished *portière* tapestries, eight sets of France and Navarre's coat of arms and eight crowns were woven to replace Fouquet's coat of arms. Later varients of the design were repeatedly produced at the Gobelins Manufactory in Paris, established in 1662 on behalf of the Crown by Colbert, who installed Lebrun there along with the Maincy team of weavers. I.N.

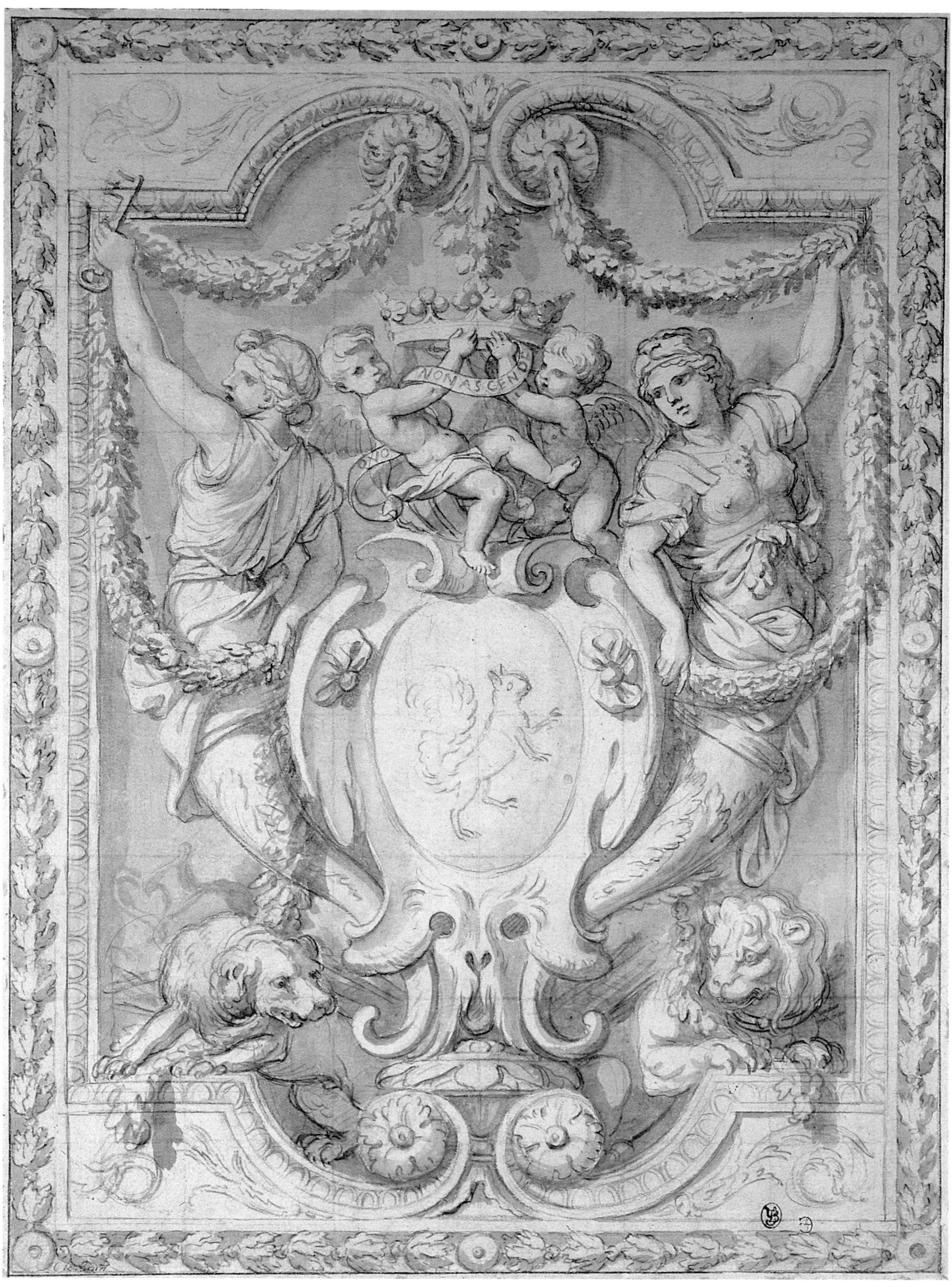

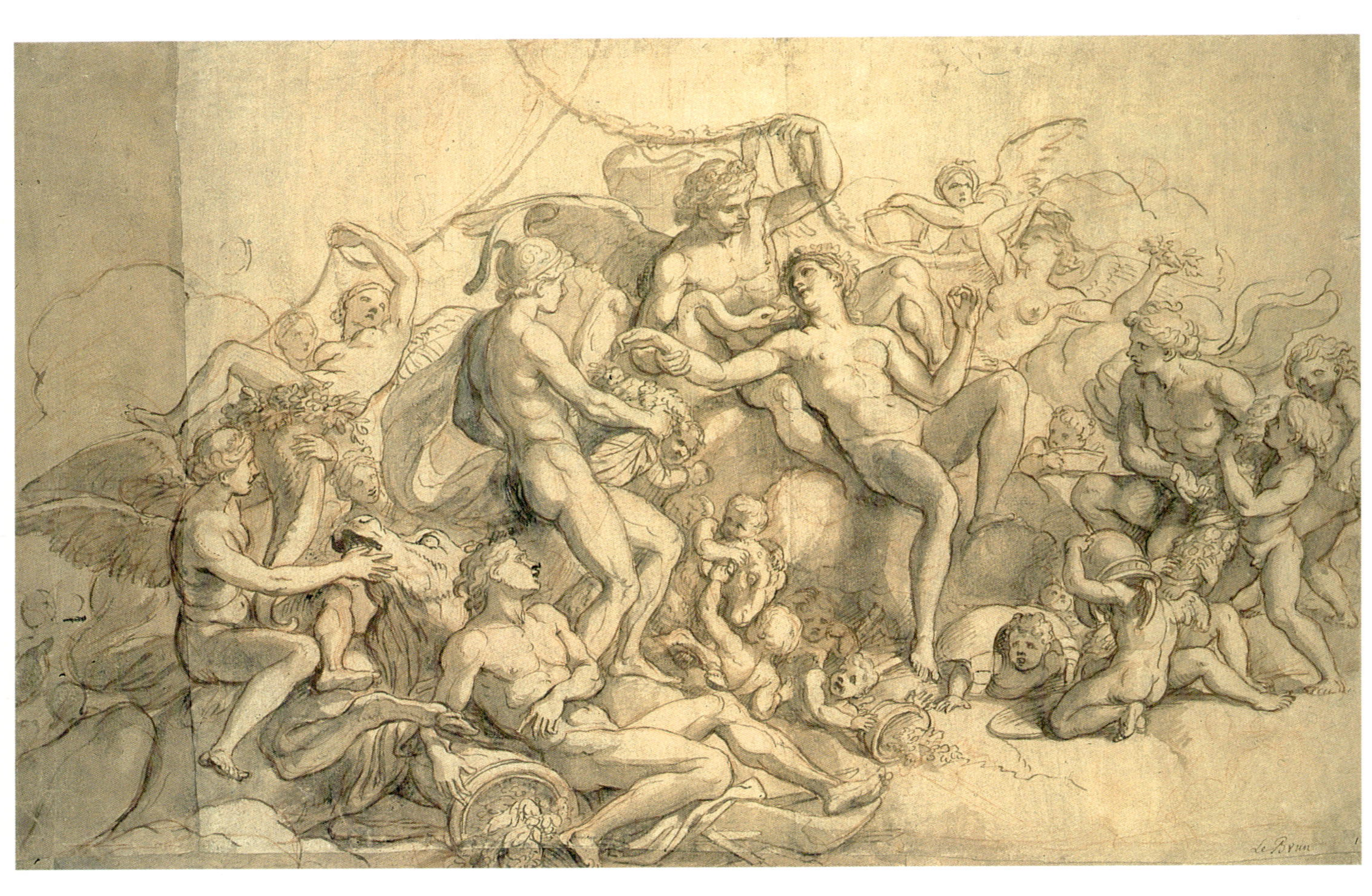
Le Brun

27

Charles Lebrun

Spring

Red chalk, pen and brown ink, black wash on pale brown paper. 385 × 615 mm. Drawing to left and bottom on attached pieces of paper. Lined

Old inscription in pen and brown ink in the bottom right corner: *Le Brun 107*

PROVENANCE: Library of the Baron Stieglitz School of Technical Drawing, St Petersburg; 1924 transferred to the Hermitage

Inv. no. OR 18960

EXHIBITIONS: 1970 Göteborg, no. 76; 1972 Prague, no. 62, ill.; 1974 Manchester, no. 42; 1975 Aarhus, no. 41; 1975 Copenhagen, no. 41; 1997 Bonn, no. 103, ill; 1998–9 New York, no. 92, ill.; 1999 St Petersburg, no. 63, ill.

LITERATURE: Novoselskaya 1970, pp. 120–2, ill.; Western European Drawing 1981, no. 79, ill.; Novoselskaya 1999, p. 134, ill.

The history and fate of works produced for the Maincy Tapestry Manufactory, such as the *Portière Design with the Fouquet Coat of Arms* (cat. 26), and for the château of Vaux-le-Vicomte – which include this drawing – are closely linked with the French Superintendent of Finances, Nicolas Fouquet.

Work at Vaux-le-Vicomte (1656–63) formed a prelude to Lebrun's large decorative works at Versailles. One of the most significant works he produced during this period was a design for ceiling paintings in the oval room at Vaux. Lebrun produced a monochrome sketch for the oval ceiling, a composition that was engraved by Gérard Audran (the engraving is known by several names: *The Palace of the Sun*, *The Four Seasons* and *Ceiling with Snakes*). At the centre of the composition is a cartouche with a coat of arms; to the sides are Jupiter and Mars, with Apollo seated beneath a portico below. Around the oval are four groups: *Summer*, *Winter*, *Autumn* and *Spring* (fig. 34), and the whole composition is encircled by a snake – symbol of wisdom – of huge dimensions.

Several drawings by Lebrun are linked to his work on the ceiling. A group showing *Autumn* is in the Louvre (inv. nos. 29.453 and I.M. 6383), as is a rough sketch for the ceiling that was clearly produced in the workshop (inv. no. I.M. 8453). This sheet in the Hermitage is a finished sketch for *Spring*. Lebrun put his great skill to good use in this large decorative composition, creating a united, harmonious whole from a multitude of figures. There is a general sense of movement towards Flora who, although she does not occupy the central position on the sheet, certainly serves as the conceptual centre. The print differs from the drawing in some poses and details of clothing, and there is a greater number of *putti*. There was also a large black chalk sketch showing the ceiling as a whole, a sketch much admired by Bernini (*Journal de voyage du Cavalier Bernin en France*, Paris, 1885, p. 224).

It seems likely that the ceiling was never executed, the consequence of Fouquet's arrest in September 1661. Jouin (1889, p. 561) tells us that after the death of Lebrun's widow in 1669, an inventory was compiled that mentions a large oval monochrome painting on canvas, *The Palace of the Sun*. This was clearly not the painting itself but a sketch, which has not survived. Bernini suggested to Colbert, Fouquet's successor, that he also make use of the composition, but the idea was not taken up. I.N.

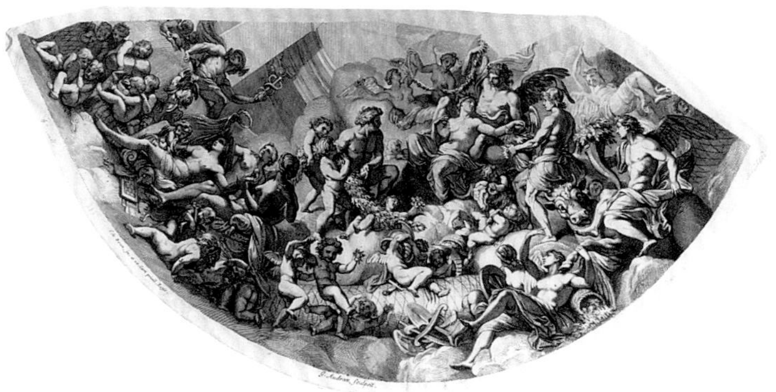

fig. 34
Gérard Audran
Spring, from the engraved *The Palace of the Sun*

28

Charles Lebrun

The Entry of Louix XIV into Dunkirk

Black and red chalk, grey wash; traces of squaring in black chalk; the border outlined in red chalk. 290 × 195 mm

PROVENANCE: collection of the Academy of Arts, St Petersburg; 1924 transferred to the Hermitage

Inv. no. OR 15820

EXHIBITIONS: 1955 Moscow, p. 78; 1972 Prague, no. 63; 1974 Manchester, no. 43, ill.; 1975 Aarhus, no. 42; 1975 Copenhagen, no. 42; 1978–9 Melbourne–Sydney–Adelaide, no. 26, ill.; 1986 Bogota, ill.; 1986 Buenos Aires, no. 48, ill.; 1986 Montevideo, no. 49, ill.; 1987–8 Belgrade–Ljubliana–Zagreb, no. 19, ill.; 1997 Bonn, no. 104, ill.; 1999 St Petersburg, no. 64, ill.

LITERATURE: Novoselskaya 1970, pp. 125, 126, ill.; Novoselskaya 1999, p. 136, ill.

Several of Lebrun's surviving sketches relate to designs for tapestries made at the Gobelins Manufactory. Notable among these is the series *The History of the King*, begun in 1662, several designs for which are now in the Louvre. Missing from these, however, is the lost sketch for *The Entry of Louis XIV into Dunkirk* (the town came under French control in 1662), of which the Hermitage drawing is a fragment showing the central scene in the left part of the composition. As the hat-doffing monarch rides forward, several riders canter behind, among them Maréchal Turenne and the Duc de Saint-Etienne; in the foreground an orderly runs alongside. Several differences, albeit insignificant, are revealed when the tapestry is compared with the sketch.

This sheet, one of Lebrun's best drawings, is typical of his work both in composition and the restrained use of light and shade, here combined with an overall sense of dynamism. I.N.

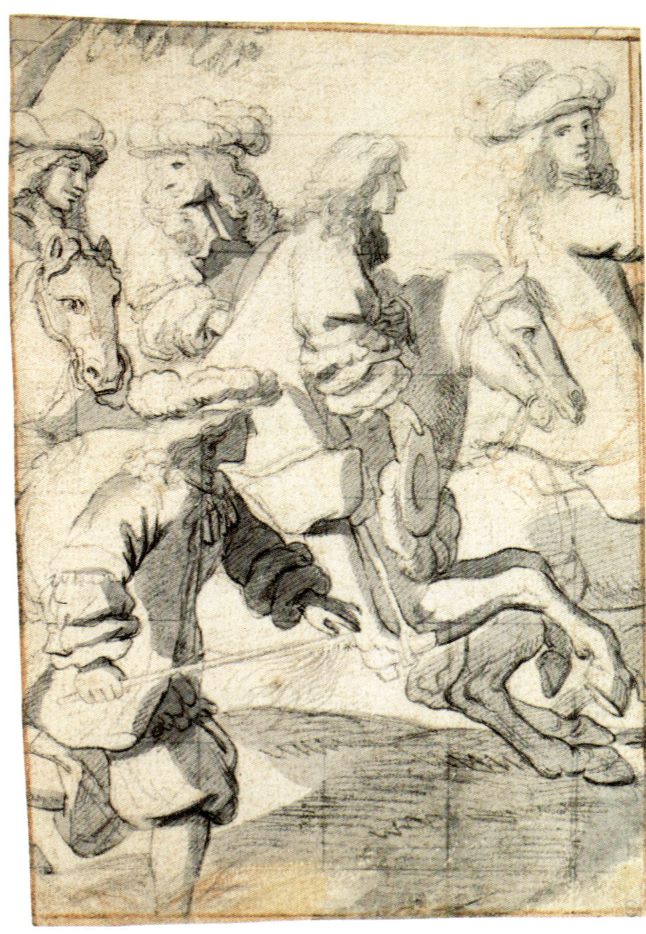

29

Daniel Marot the Elder

Paris 1663 – 1752 The Hague

Design for a Ceiling

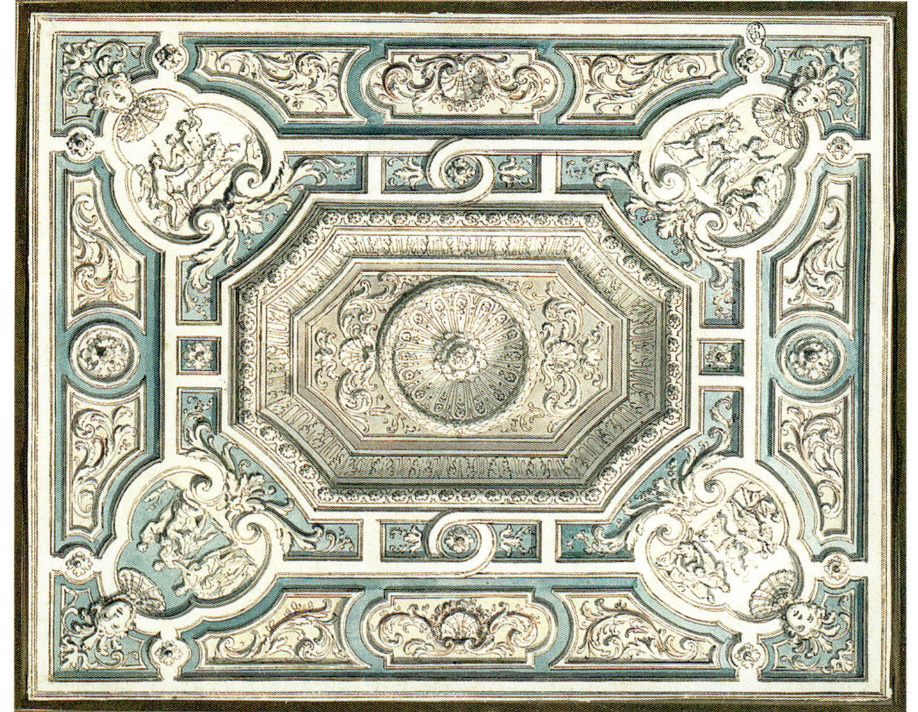

Pen and ink, wash and watercolour.
251 × 304 mm

PROVENANCE: collection of Jules Carré, Paris; collection of Alfred Beurdeley, Paris (collector's mark L. 421); 1889 Baron Stieglitz School of Technical Drawing, St Petersburg; 1923 transferred to the Hermitage

Inv. no. 28143

EXHIBITIONS: 1900 St Petersburg, no. 289; 1912 St Petersburg, no. 168; 1947 Leningrad, no. 33; 1971b Leningrad, no. 57, ill.; 1995–6 St Petersburg, no. 47, ill.

LITERATURE: Carré 1888, no. 479; Shevchenko 1995a, p. 28, ill.

Daniel Marot, son of the court architect Jean Marot, was trained in late 17th-century French Classicism, but after the revocation of the Edict of Nantes in 1685 (which had ensured Protestant freedom of worship), he, along with many other Huguenots, quitted France, a large number of them re-establishing themselves in the Dutch United Provinces, London and north German states. Marot initially chose Holland, where he worked on the interiors of the new palace of Het Loo for the Stadholder of the Netherlands, William of Orange. In 1689 William was made King of England and Scotland, and in 1694–8 Marot was in England employed at Hampton Court. He also undertook commissions both in The Hague and Amsterdam. In numerous prints, he provided his own interpretation of the most popular contemporary decorative motifs.

Marot employed an arsenal of devices, but he none the less developed a standard compositional scheme for ceilings involving combinations of a comparatively small number of elements around a central rosette. Subject medallions with mythological scenes – accompanied by obligatory female masks with characteristic feather headdresses – lost their dominant significance and were pushed into the corners. Despite a certain insistent geometry and the rather heavy articulation that was the result of training in the French 'Grand Manner', his designs were so refined as to create a minimal, easily recognizable formula. Analogous compositions and variations on decorations for ceilings are in Marot's engraved anthology, his *Oeuvres* of 1702 (fig. 16), which was reissued in an enlarged edition in 1712. V.S.

30

Gilles-Marie Oppenord

Paris 1672 – 1742 Paris

Design for a Clock-case and a Barometer with Thermometer (Two Versions)

Pen and ink, wash and watercolour.
873 × 404 mm

PROVENANCE: collection of Alfred Beurdeley, Paris (collector's mark L. 421); 1889 Baron Stieglitz School of Technical Drawing, St Petersburg; 1923 transferred to the Hermitage

Inv. no. 34673

OLD MANUSCRIPT CATALOGUES: 'Collection Beurdeley. Dessins d'architecture et d'ornements. École Française', pp. 146–7, no. 525. 'Double projet de régulateur, baromèttre et thermomèttre. Le projet de droite présente à la partie supérieure le thermomèttre figuré par la grascieuse figure de deux enfants soufflant le chaud et le froid. La figure de Diane se dresse au centre externe du projet et les attributs de la Déesse sont rappellés dans l'ornementation de la gaîne. Le projet de gauche porte à la partie supérieure et au raccordemment de la gaîne les Parques. Le thermomèttre est placé à ce raccordemment. L'artiste a repris l'idée de l'enfant qui souffle le chaud et le froid. Ce dessin est une des plus belles compositions qu'on puisse voir de ce grand Artiste. Dessin à la plume rehaussé de tons à l'aquarelle. Dessin encadré.'

EXHIBITIONS: 1900 St Petersburg, nos. 338–47; 1912 St Petersburg, no. 51; 1971b Leningrad, no. 71, ill.; 1995–6 St Petersburg, no. 68, ill.; 1998–9 New York, no. 99, ill.

LITERATURE: Shevchenko 1995a, p. 34, ill.; Shevchenko 1995b, p. 21, ill. 13.

During the first quarter of the 18th century, multi-function clock mechanisms, containing within a single case various devices and pieces of equipment, became quite common. These two versions of part of a clock-case are largely defined by their inner construction, and both continue to imitate the traditional division into clock and pedestal, albeit with a clearly visible adjustment in the relative proportions. Both versions have lost the heaviness and majesty of a piece of furniture, and the airiness resulting from the pale touches of watercolour enables us to see these designs as early examples of a tentative Rococo, although in the restrained polyphony of their materials, the variety of textures and the richness of finishes, they anticipates Rococo in its maturity.

Each version has its own theme. In the left-hand detail we can see one of the three Parcae (Roman goddesses of Destiny), a group often found decorating André-Charles Boulle's clock-cases (Samoyault 1979, p. 14, pl. 19b, 20a). Oppenord was responsible for several designs that were used in works by the renowned cabinet-maker (Shevchenko 1995a, p. 32, no. 62). In the right-hand version, which includes the figure of Diana the Huntress, Mercury's caduceus, a hunting horn, spears, nets and a boar's head are set within an elegant arabesque – hunting motifs found in another Hermitage design by Oppenord for a thermometer and barometer case (inv. 30519; see Shevchenko 1995b, p. 21, ill. 13).

In both versions the main theme is emphasized by Oppenord's characteristic floating *putti*, humorously playing around the spirit column of the thermometer: in their hands it recalls a glassblower's pipe with a burst bubble at the end, or the brass trumpet of the Goddess of Victory. In the right-hand version, the *putti* support a ducal crown, a hint that this was an official commission, which would in part explain the large format and the painstaking draughtsmanship appropriate for a presentation drawing.

This sheet was reproduced in 1881 (Guichard, pl. XL) as an anonymous design, though within a few years it was confidently described in the manuscript inventory of Alfred Beurdeley's collection as the work of Oppenord – 'one of the most beautiful compositions by this great artist which one might see'. V.S.

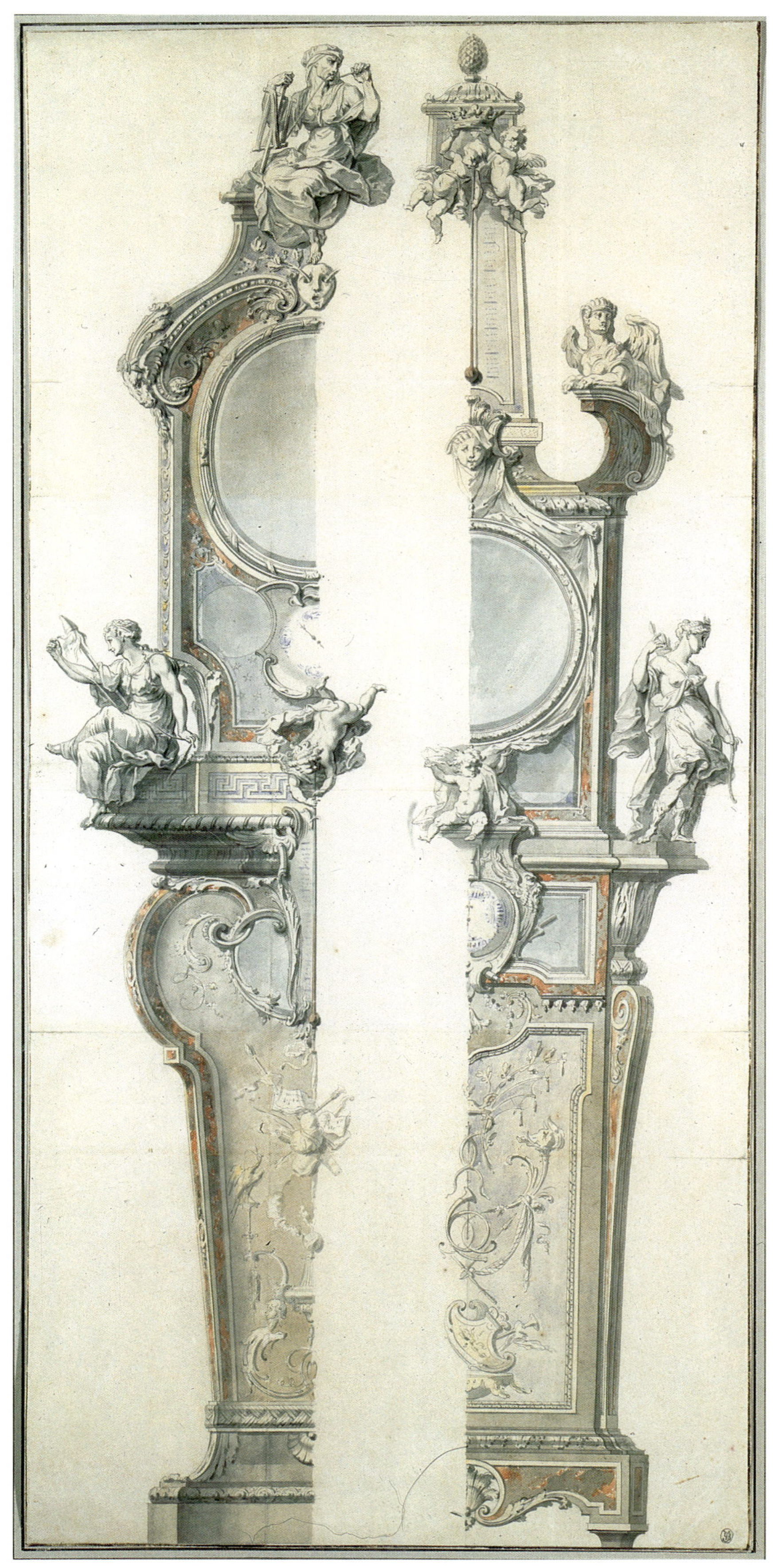

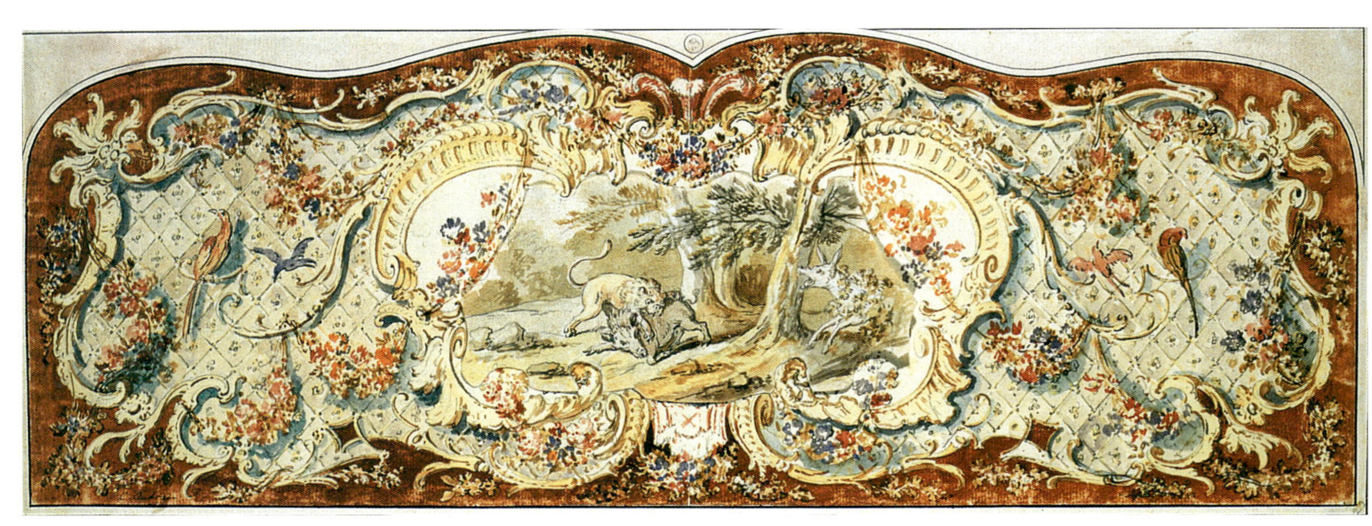

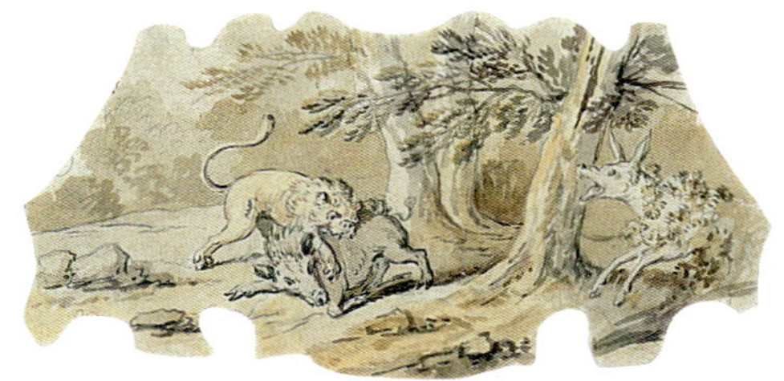

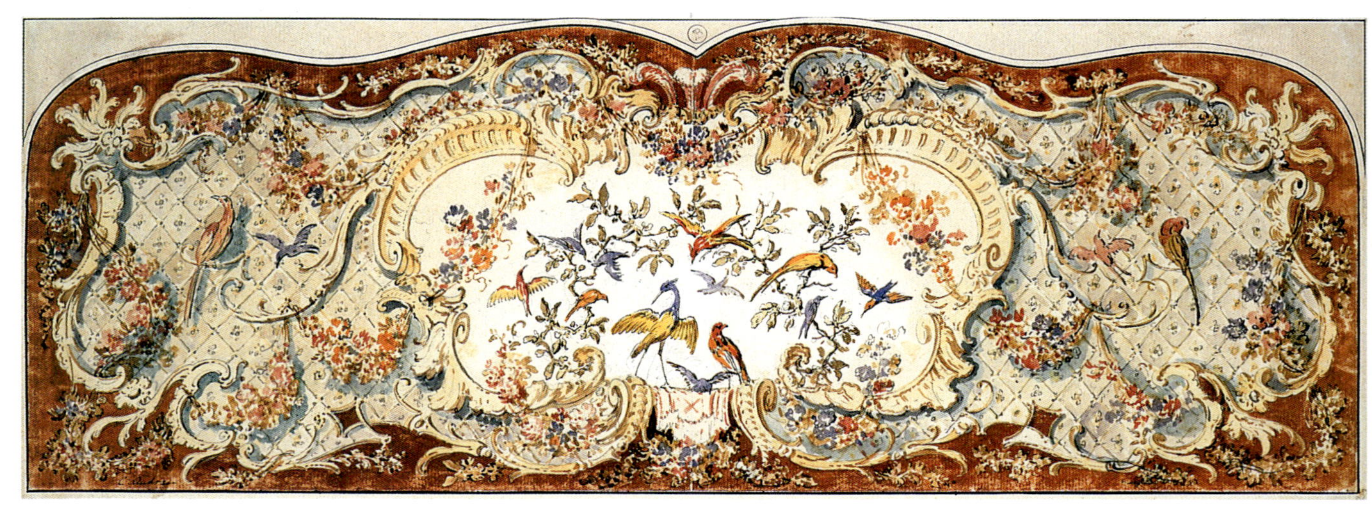

31

Claude Audran III (attributed)

Lyon 1658 – 1734 Paris

Canapé: Design for Upholstery

Signed in pen and brown ink bottom left: *C. Audran*
Watercolour over a black chalk sketch. 175 × 480 mm. Upper edge cut out around the contour

PROVENANCE: collection of Charles-Eugene Bérard, Paris (collector's mark L. 75); 1891 Baron Stieglitz School of Technical Drawing, St Petersburg; 1923 transferred to the Hermitage

Inv. no. 28010

EXHIBITIONS: 1937 Leningrad, no. 49; 1995–6 St Petersburg, no. 56, ill.

LITERATURE: Champeaux 1888/9–97/8, vol. IV, pl. 304; Bérard 1891, no. 338; Shevchenko 1995a, pp. 30–31, ill.

This upholstery design for a sofa has been attributed to various artists. It was reproduced by Champeaux, who identified it as the work of the ornamentalist François Peyrotte, who was still thought to be the author when it was acquired in 1891 for 920 francs at the sale (Hôtel Drouot, Paris) of the collection of Charles-Eugene Bérard (son of André-Denis Bérard, whose initials *AB* figure in the collector's mark). At that auction the Baron Stieglitz School of Technical Drawing was represented by the antiquary Alfred Beurdeley. He made many valuable notes (in red ink) on his copy of the auction catalogue, which he sent to St Petersburg together with the drawings he had acquired, and which today is in the Hermitage's Department of Drawings.

Peyrotte was still seen as the author when the drawing was in the Stieglitz Museum, although the sheet, in fact, bears a signature, 'C. Audran', in the same brown tone as the highlights around the garlands of flowers. This signature had either not previously been noticed or was for some reason ignored by collectors and specialists. It must have been in the Stieglitz School, however, that the inscription 'Audran Charles' was added to the mount.

Although the colour in this drawing is still intense in tone around the edge, it has gradually faded towards the centre, where the exotic birds painted with resonant bright brushstrokes were once sharply silhouetted against the white background, in a variation on the Baroque device of disrupting and breaking up space. The design and colouring were further distorted by when a watercolour insert was glued onto the central part, bearing an illustration to La Fontaine's fable of the Lion, the Boar and the Donkey. In the Bérard sale catalogue, Beurdeley added: 'Very beautiful. This is Oudry when he was director of Beauvais'. (Oudry was appointed painter at Beauvais Tapestry Manufactory in 1726; he became director in 1734, a year after Audran's death.) Beurdeley's attribution is quite convincingly confirmed by a comparison with Oudry's drawings for a series of tapestries, *The Battle of the Beasts*, particularly for a tapestry of 1745, *Battle Between Lions and Boars* (Musée Atger, Montpellier; 1982 Paris, no. 107; Roland Michel 1987, p. 171, ill. 200). In the process of work on illustrations to *The Natural History of Botanical Gardens* (Duclaux 1975, p. 140, no. 237) and La Fontaine's fables, Oudry produced many drawings of exotic beasts in the royal menagerie at Versailles. We also know that Audran and Oudry were friends, and thus collaboration between the two artists seems likely (1991 Paris, no. 8). Alterations may indeed have been introduced after Audran's death, for he left a large quantity of cartoons and designs (Mourey 1910, p. 32). (The late Bruno Pons, a leading specialist in French ornamental art, suggested to this author in 1995 in Paris that the original design may have been made and signed by a contemporary of Audran's with the same surname.) V.S.

33

Antoine Watteau

Valenciennes 1684 – 1721 Nogent-sur-Marne

Autumn (Sketch for a Decorative Panel)

Red chalk. 280 × 187 mm

PROVENANCE: collection of Alfred Beurdeley, Paris (collector's mark L. 421); 1889 Baron Stieglitz School of Technical Drawing, St Petersburg; 1923 transferred to the Hermitage

Inv. no. 40783

OLD MANUSCRIPT CATALOGUES: 'Collection Beurdeley. Dessins d'architecture et d'ornements. École Française', p. 188, no. 660. 'Deux dessins à la sanguine'

EXHIBITIONS: 1912 St Petersburg, no. 163; 1955 Moscow, pp. 72–3; 1963 Stockholm, no. 39, ill.; 1968 Leningrad–Moscow, no. 8; 1970 Budapest, N71, no. 119, ill.; 1972a Leningrad, no. 57, ill.; 1975 Berlin, no. 82, ill.; 1982 Florence, no. 100, ill.; 1983 Leningrad, no. 15, ill.; 1984 Leningrad, no. 10; 1984–5 Washington–Paris–Berlin, Drawings, no. 41, ill.; 1995–6 St Petersburg, no. 13, ill.

LITERATURE: Dacier, Vuaflart 1922, no. 141; Boerner 1931, no. 261, ill.; Parker, Mathey 1957, vol. I, p. 27, no. 197; Mathey 1959, p. 46, no. 111; Kamenskaya 1964, pp. 35–6, 37, ill. 10, p. 190, no. 1; Kamenskaya 1973, p. 149, no. 17; Zolotov 1973, p. 28; Western European Drawing 1981, no. 80; Novoselskaya 1983, Catalogue, p. 24, ill. 15; Eidelberg 1984, pp. 158, 164, note 7; Roland Michel 1984b, p. 285; Shevchenko 1995a, p. 15; Rosenberg, Prat 1996, vol. I, no. 193.

Watteau's ornamental decorative compositions are relatively few, hence the particular value of the two works presented here, *Autumn* and *The Birth of Venus* (cat. 34). Very much in keeping with the spirit of the age, the drawings none the less contain, behind their external simplicity, a mass of symbols and allegories that would have been fully comprehensible to contemporaries, but which require interpretation today.

These sheets, outstanding even in the context of the superb Hermitage collection of French drawings, were for many years dated to 1707–8 (Kamenskaya 1964, p. 190, nos. 1–2; Parker, Mathey 1957, nos. 194, 197; 1983 Leningrad, nos. 15–16; Western European Drawing 1981, no. 80), i.e., the period when Watteau was studying under Charles Audran III. But the elegant motifs and extreme freedom of execution accord with a date in the first half of the 1710s (Zolotov 1973) or *c.* 1715 (1984–5 Washington–Paris–Berlin). It is dated 1713 in the *catalogue raisonné* of Watteau's drawings (Rosenberg, Prat 1996).

Autumn is fluidly and vividly executed, and the draughting ranges from the barest skimming of the paper surface to deeply-pressed marks with red chalk. The whole nature of the drawing – its tonal variety, its exploratory and not always clear line, some discord between certain features – indicates that this is a spontaneous drawing, the work of a painter accustomed to extensive sketching from life. Even so, the influence of the school through which Watteau passed (he studied under ornamental artists that included Claude Gillot as well as Audran) is detectable in the free manipulation of varied decorative forms, in the depiction of only one half of a symmetrical composition, and in the use of devices such as the mascaron with long twisted horns – typical of Gillot's ornamental repertory (Kamenskaya 1973). This mask, in type similar to that of Momus, the personification of sarcasm, mockery and censure in Classical mythology, is found in Watteau's drawings (Zolotov 1973) and in his painting *The Commedia dell'Arte* (NGA, Washington, DC). Features associated with an 'autumnal' still-life – the wicker-bound bottle and conical glasses – also appear in his paintings *The Happy Lovers* (Mathey 1959, p. 46, no. 111) and *Occupation According to Age*, the latter known from an engraving by Charles Dupuis (Kamenskaya 1973), and in a drawing of a male figure from a private collection in Paris (1984–5 Washington–Paris–Berlin, Drawings, no. 20) and a series of prints by the engraver and publisher Gabriel Huquier the Elder after drawings by Watteau (Dacier, Vuaflart 1922: firescreen *Autumn* – no. 191, *Momus* no. 277, *The Drunkard* – no. 278).

The panel *Autumn* was published by Huquier in the series *The Four Seasons* (Dacier, Vuaflart 1922, no. 141). However, instead of reproducing Watteau's red chalk drawing, Huquier invented his own (in the Musée des Beaux-Arts, Dijon, are seven analogous preparatory drawings for prints by Huquier in pen and ink on fine paper, Dacier, Vuaflart 1922, p. 70, nos. 142–3; see also Shevchenko 1995a, p. 44). The space of the oval medallion, barely indicated in the original, was filled by the printmaker with a grape-gathering scene, while the missing left part of the frame, following usual practice, was completed by analogy with the right. The elegant virtuosity and whimsy of Watteau's drawing was turned by Huquier into pedantic dryness and precision. V.S.

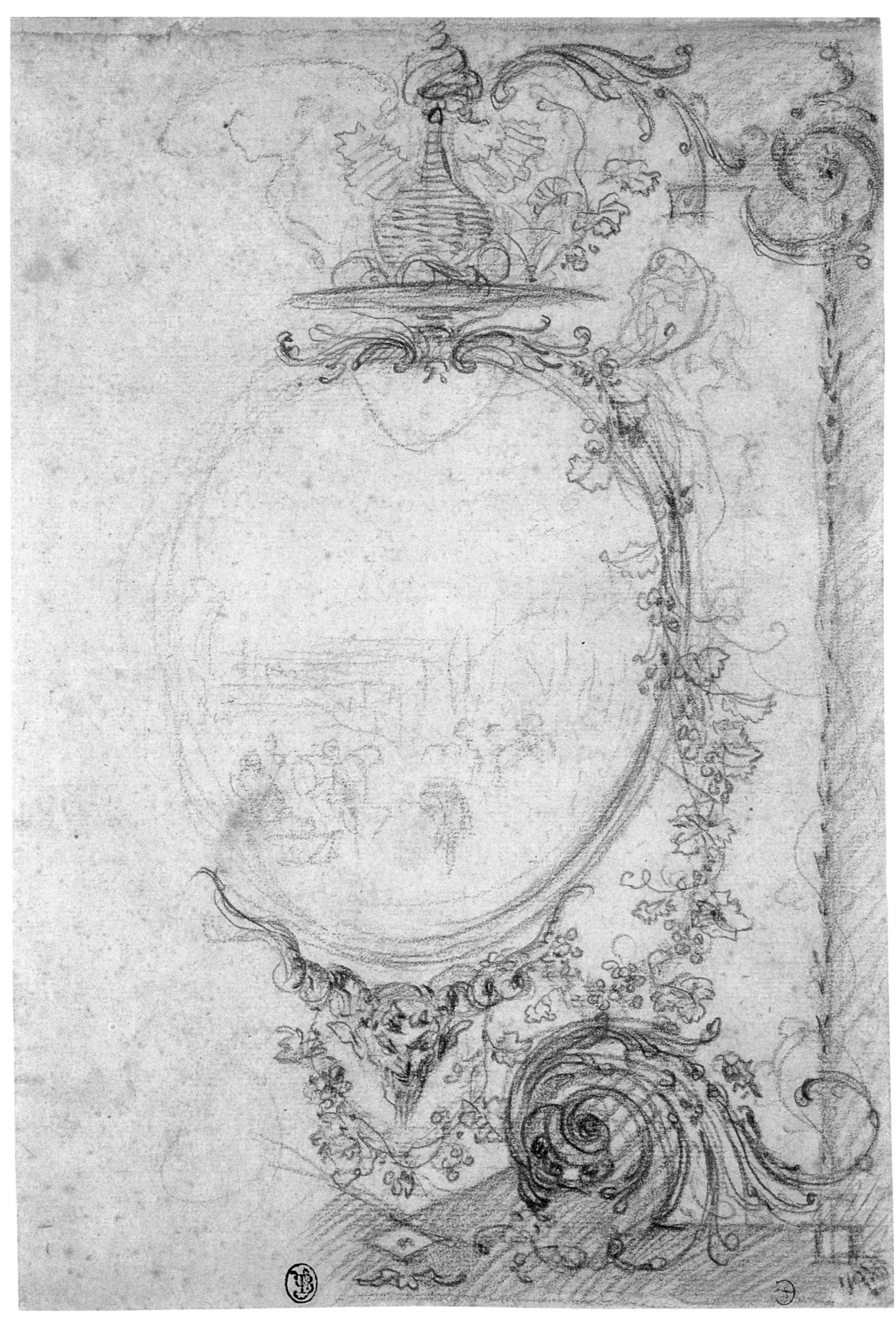

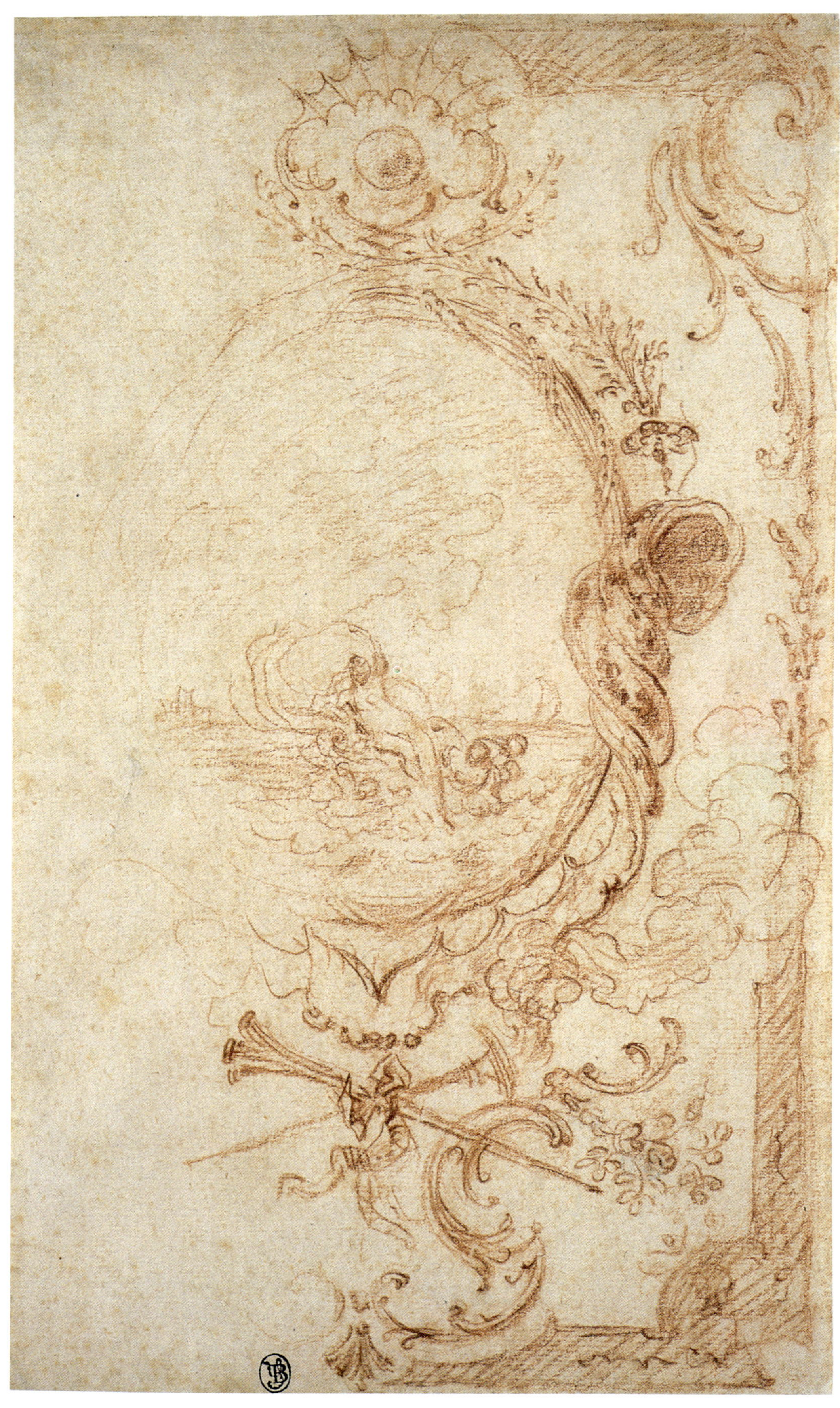

34

Antoine Watteau

The Birth of Venus
(Sketch for a Decorative Panel)

Red chalk. 297 × 176 mm

PROVENANCE: collection of Alfred Beurdeley, Paris (collector's mark L. 421); 1889 Baron Stieglitz School of Technical Drawing, St Petersburg; 1923 transferred to the Hermitage: Collector's mark L. Supplement 2681a

Inv. no. 40764

OLD MANUSCRIPT CATALOGUES: 'Collection Beurdeley. Dessins d'architecture et d'ornements. École Française', pp. 146–7, no. 525

EXHIBITIONS: 1912 St Petersburg, no. 164; 1972a Leningrad, no. 58; 1974 Manchester, no. 54; 1975 Aarhus, no. 97; 1975 Copenhagen, no. 97; 1975 Berlin, no. 83, ill.; 1978–9 Melbourne–Sydney–Adelaide, no. 32, ill.; 1983 Leningrad, no. 16, ill.; 1984a Leningrad, no. 11; 1984–5 Washington–Paris–Berlin, Drawings, no. 40, ill.; 1995–6 St Petersburg, no. 14, ill.

LITERATURE: Dacier, Vuaflart 1922, pp. 117–18, no. 283; Boerner 1931, no. 261, pl. XXI; Parker, Mathey 1957, vol. I, p. 27, no. 194; Mathey 1959, p. 46, no. 111; Kamenskaya 1964, pp. 33–5, ill. 8, p. 190, no. 2; Kamenskaya 1973, p. 149; Zolotov 1973, p. 28; Western European Drawing 1981, no. 80; Novoselskaya 1983, Catalogue, pp. 24–5, ill. 16; Shevchenko 1995a, p. 16; Rosenberg, Prat 1996, vol. I, no. 192

Despite the central place occupied by the mythological scene, the main object of Watteau's attention here was the decorative border, which seems to consist of two zones. The first is the ornamental frame itself, the second the compositional elements surrounding the oval medallion, the attributes and symbols that usually accompany the goddess of Love and Beauty: a burning torch, a rose sprig, curiously shaped seashells. The stylized shell that crowns the composition serves as a background for the precious pearl – Venus – which seems to rise from out of the foamy waves.

This panel design took shape in Watteau's mind before he embarked on the work, thus, unlike *Autumn* (cat. 33), it is unhurried, the ornamental elements are more evenly balanced and the decorative effect is more unified. Against the crests of the rushing waves, mythological figures draw the shell with the young goddess through the waters, a flimsy fabric flutters out behind her, and clouds scud across the sky. The task of capturing the animated spirit of this scene proved to be beyond the ability of Gabriel Huquier, who engraved this composition (Dacier, Vuaflart 1922). One of Huquier's seven drawings for prints in the Musée des Beaux-Arts, Dijon, was taken from this sketch (Dacier, Vuaflart 1922). V.S.

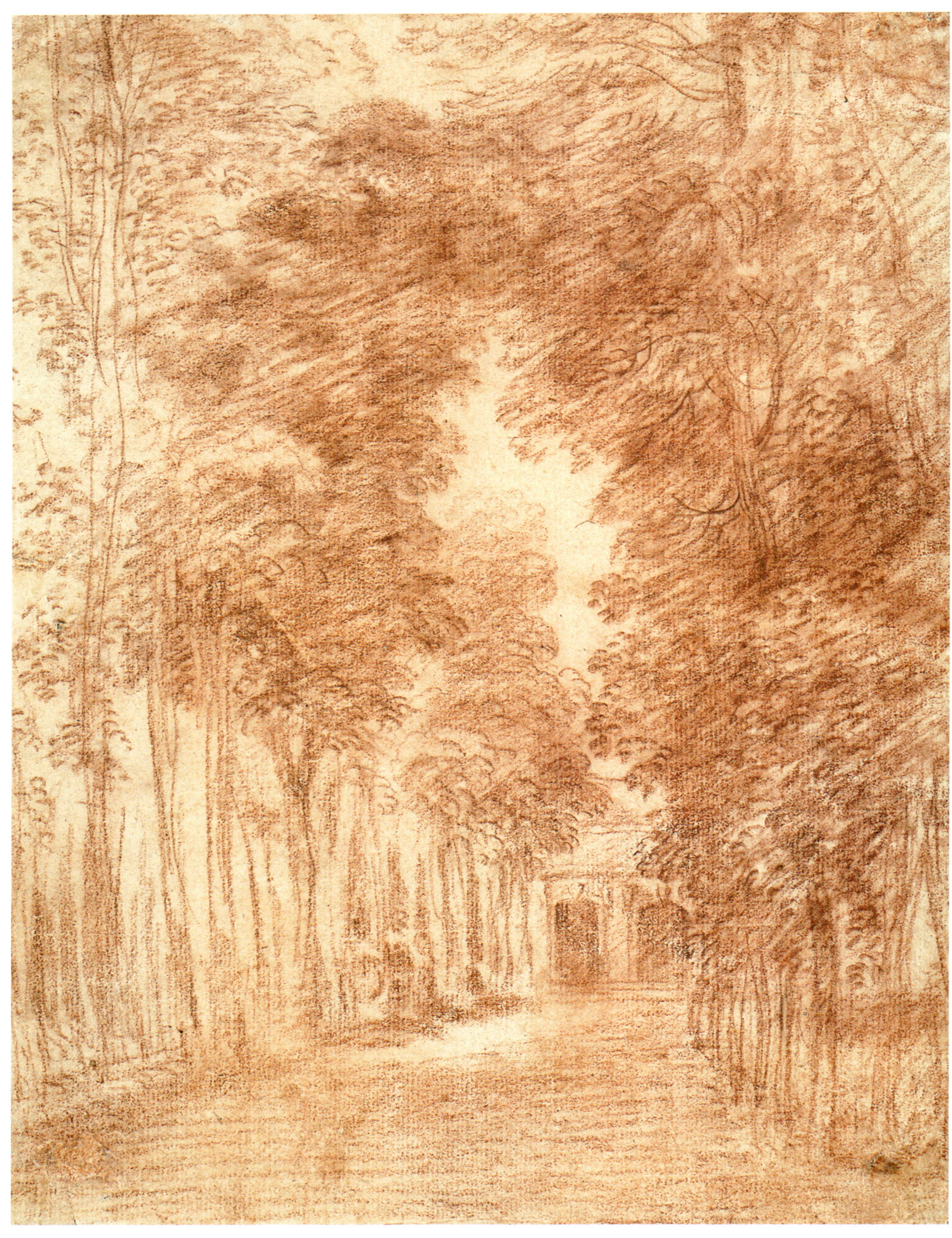

35

Antoine Watteau

Avenue in a Park

Red chalk. 210 × 170 mm

PROVENANCE: collection of Luigi Grassi, Leipzig (?); 1862 acquired by the Hermitage

Inv. no. OR 11855

EXHIBITIONS: 1867 St Petersburg, no. 482; 1926 Leningrad, no. 243; 1955 Moscow, p. 72; 1956 Leningrad, p. 84; 1959 Leningrad, p. 24; 1972a Leningrad, no. 59, ill.; 1974 Manchester, no. 55, ill.; 1983 Leningrad, no. 17, ill.; 1984 Leningrad, no. 12; 1984–5 Washington–Paris–Berlin, Drawings, no. 76, ill.

LITERATURE: Parker 1931, pp. 18, 43, no. 25, pl. 25; Parker, Mathey 1957, vol. I, no. 457, ill.; Nemilova 1964, pp. 68–9, 191, ill. 25; Kamenskaya 1973, pp. 150, 151, Drawings, no. 19, ill.; Jean-Richard 1978, no. 51; Novoselskaya 1983, p. 26, ill.; Roland Michel 1984, p. 253; Rosenberg 1984–5, p. 302, fig. 4; Kamenskaya 1985, pp. 17, 97, no. 7, pl. 7; Rosenberg, Prat 1996, vol. I, no. 238.

Along with another 13 drawings by Watteau, *Avenue in a Park* was engraved by François Boucher for the anthology *Figures de différents caractères*, a collection of etchings by various hands after Watteau's drawings published 1726–8 (fig. 35). It is the sole surviving example of those original drawings, apart from a fragmentary landscape discovered in 1980 on the verso of a drawing in Washington's National Gallery of Art.

Watteau consistently shows himself to have been a fine master of lyrical landscape in both his paintings and drawings. A similar landscape but with a three-storey house at the end of the avenue appears in his painting *The Perspective* (Museum of Fine Arts, Boston). The same building with trees to either side was engraved by Caylus with the inscription 'à Montmorency', a country house (formerly Charles Lebrun's home) belonging to Pierre Crozat, a celebrated patron and collector. Jean-Baptiste-Joseph Pater used the motif of *Avenue in a Park* in his painting *Spring* (The Cleveland Museum of Art, Ohio).

This drawing surely depicts the avenue leading up to Crozat's house, and must have been made *c.* 1714, when the artist was based at Montmorency. It is one of Watteau's most poetic creations. Half-tones are used to create gentle transitions in red chalk of different intensity, and the whole landscape seems to be wrapped in a soft haze or *sfumato*. I.N.

fig. 35
François Boucher after Watteau
Avenue in a Park

etching, from *Figures de différents caractères* (1726–8)

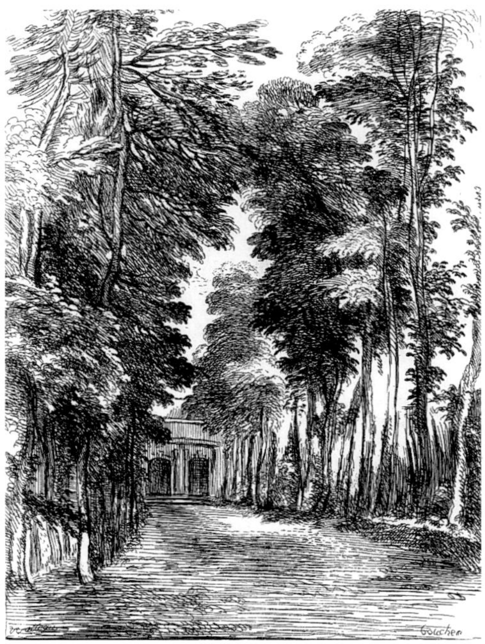

36

Jean-Baptiste Oudry

Paris 1686 – 1755 Beauvais

Dog Pointing a Partridge

Oil on canvas. 129 × 162 cm
Signed and dated lower-left corner:
J.B.Oudry 1725

PROVENANCE: 1764 acquired for the Hermitage with the collection of Johann Gotzkowski, Berlin; in the 19th century until 1925 kept at Gatchina Palace, near St Petersburg

EXHIBITIONS: 1725 Paris, Exposition de la Jeunesse (?); 1725 Paris Salon (?)

LITERATURE: Wildenstein 1924, pp. 43–4; Vergnet-Ruiz 1930, p.137; Nothaft 1941, p. 173; Cat. 1958, p. 344; Cat. 1976, p. 231; Opperman 1977, no. 245; Nemilova 1982, no. 339; Nemilova 1985, no. 167

Oudry was accepted by the Academie in 1719, and between then and 1728 he developed his own distinctive style, a transition from the purely decorative approach of the age of Louis XIV towards the *genre pittoresque* of Louis XV that was taken up in the 1720s by many leading artists: it too is decorative, the cultivation of whimsical lines, of cascades of arabesques and asymmetry. It finds expression in Oudry's work in a brilliant palette and theatrical play of light and shade. Despite his taste for the decorative, however, Oudry remained much closer to nature than other artists of his generation: 'Why not accustom youth to draw everything from nature as is done in Flanders: landscapes, animals, fruits, flowers, of which the variety is so great... This exercise would give facility in everything, since if it is true that drawing is of use in all things, I would say too that everything is of use to drawing...' (Vergnet–Ruiz 1930, p. 137).

Oudry received his first royal commission in 1724, producing in 1725 three scenes of hunting with dogs for the Salle des Gardes of the Château at Chantilly (two are still at Chantilly, one is in the Musée des Beaux-Arts, Rouen). He exhibited them together with five other works in June 1725 at the traditional Exposition de la Jeunesse (Exhibition of Youth) on the Place Dauphine in Paris. He showed another twelve paintings at the Salon later that summer. Both exhibitions included different compositions entitled 'Dog Pointing a Partridge', and the Salon also had a *Dog Pointing a Pheasant*. Both Salon paintings were of dimensions identical to the Hermitage canvas, but on the basis of their description they have been identified with a pair of hunting scenes that Oudry sold in 1740 to Sweden (Royal Palace, Stockholm: *Dog Pointing a Partridge*, dated 1724, 130 × 162 cm; *Dog Pointing a Pheasant*, dated 1725, 130 × 162 cm). Even closer to our painting is the description of a similar work shown at the Exposition de la Jeunesse. In 1732 Oudry compiled a list of his works for the Duke of Mecklenburg-Schwerin, mentioning four compositions with hunting-dogs – one with a pheasant, three with partridges – each of them priced at 400 livres. Their dimensions too accord with those of the Hermitage painting. Two of these Opperman (1977, pp. 241–4; personal communication from Pontus Grate, author of *Swedish National Art Museum, Stockholm. French Paintings*, II: *Eighteenth Century*, 1994, p. 231) identifies with the paintings in the Royal Palace, one with a work in the castle of Wilhelmshohe near Kassel (1723; 131 × 163 cm) and one sold at the Hôtel Drouot in 1950 (1725; 123 × 152 cm). It is doubtful that the Kassel painting belongs to this series, both because of the date and the fact that it does not show a partridge (as it should, if we look at Oudry's own list of 1732). More convincing is the suggestion (Nemilova 1982, 1985) that the Hermitage painting is in fact the first of the series. It displays a very similar principle of construction with the Stockholm paintings: in all three the left half is occupied by a thicket and the heavy crowns of trees, while to the right a spacious view into a valley opens up; in the foreground, on the edge of a forest, are carefully depicted flowers and grasses, or, as in our case, the edge of a wheatfield with poppies in which the pheasant or partridge hides. Near the bird's hiding-place is the stiffly pointing dog, clearly silhouetted white against the dark ground.

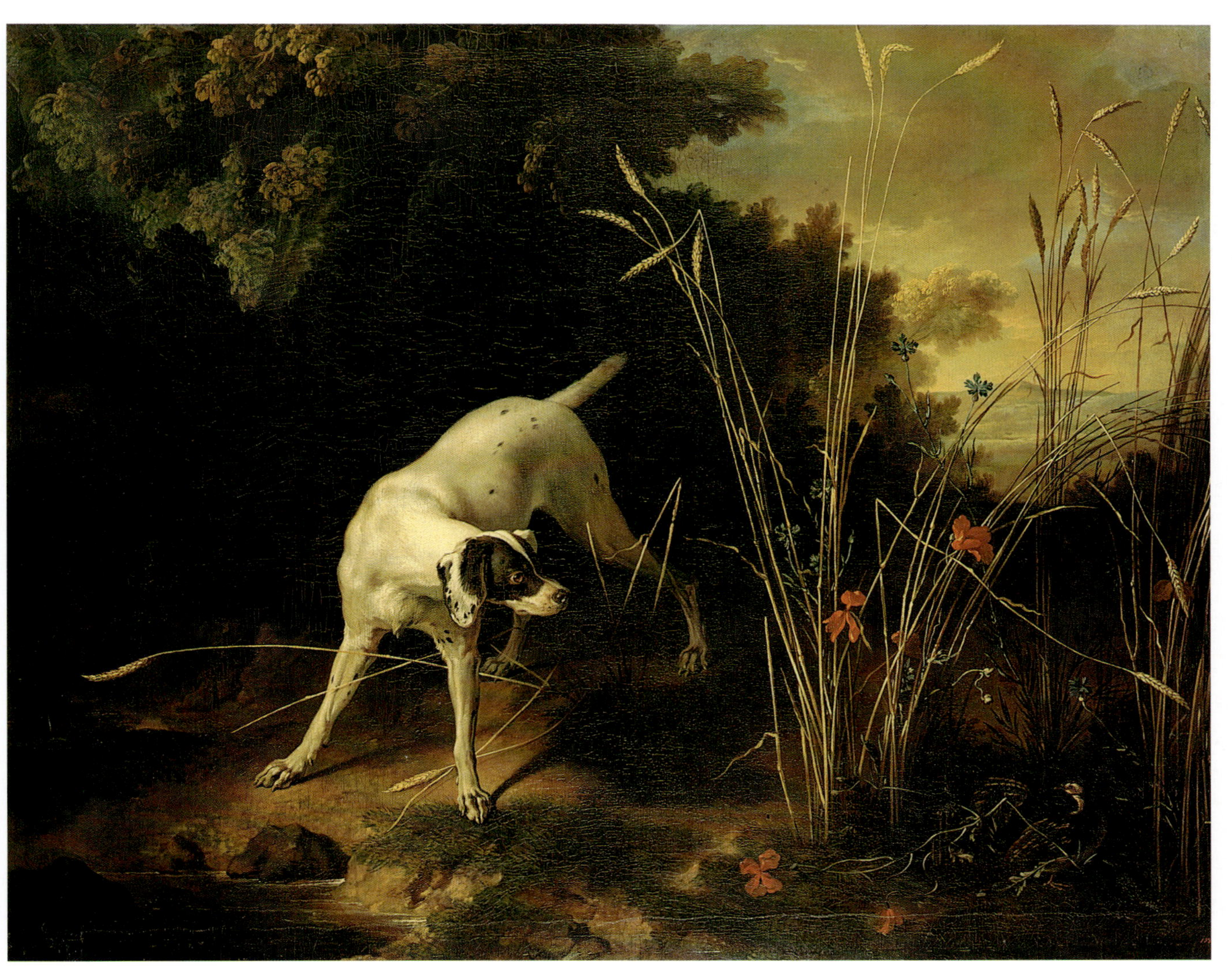

Oudry created a large number of works of similar dimensions (approximately 130 × 162 cm) on the same subject, mostly dating from the second half of the 1720s, but some from the 1730s and 1740s. Later analogies to the Hermitage canvas include a small work on copper painted for Louis XV (1747; private collection, Paris) and a version of 1748 in the Wallace Collection, London. E.D.

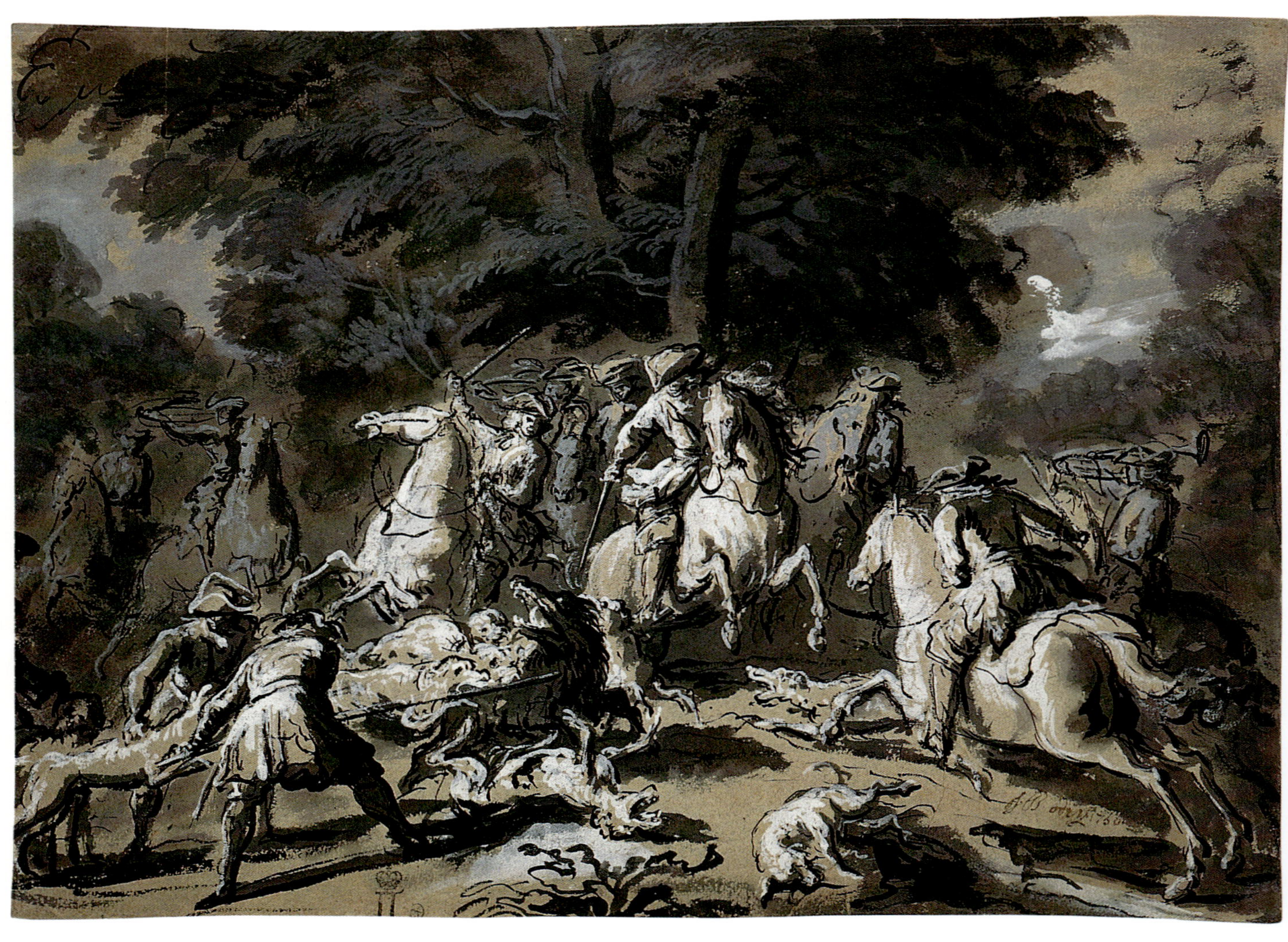

37

Jean-Baptiste Oudry

Boar Hunt

Pen and ink, black wash, highlighted with white wash on brownish-grey paper. 280 × 400 cm. Lined
Inscription in pen and brown ink to right beneath the croup of the galloping horse: *J.B.Odry 1750* [30?]

PROVENANCE: collection of Count Carl Cobenzl, Brussels (collector's mark L. 2858b); 1768 acquired for the Hermitage: Collector's mark L. 2061

Inv. no. 4872

OLD MANUSCRIPT CATALOGUES: Cobenzl – 'Catal[ogue] de Cabin[et], Catalogue de Desseins, Troisième Grandeur', p. 43v., no. 31, 'Oudry, Chasse de Sanglier'

EXHIBITIONS: 1867 St Petersburg, no. 484; 1955 Moscow, p. 85; 1956 Leningrad, p. 98; 1983 Leningrad, no. 63, ill.; 1985 Sapporo, no. 65, ill.; 1986 Bogota; 1986 Buenos Aires, no. 67, ill.; 1986 Montevideo, no. 67, ill.; 1987–8 Belgrade–Ljubliana–Zagreb, no. 84, ill.

LITERATURE: Locquin 1912, no. 672 (no mention of inscription and with incorrect dimensions of 180 × 240); Vergnet–Raiz 1930, vol. II, no. 27; Nothaft 1941, pp. 178–80, drawing 9; Opperman 1970, pp. 217–24, ill.; Novoselskaya 1983, Catalogue, pp. 4, 61–4, ill.

Seeing the signature on the drawing as Oudry's own, Nothaft read the date as 1750 and linked it with the series of *Royal Hunts* that Oudry made for the Gobelins tapestry manufactory between 1733 and 1746. We know that Oudry returned to hunting subjects after completion of this drawing, and Nothaft (1941, pp. 178, 179) places it in that period. The signature, however, is a later addition in another hand; even the artist's surname is incorrectly inscribed – 'Odry' instead of 'Oudry'.

Opperman (1970) linked this *Boar Hunt* with a group of drawings of hunts made in 1728. Analysis of the technique employed in this drawing, where highlights applied over the grey toning create a silvery effect, led to comparisons with the technique Oudry used in his illustrations of 1726 for Scarron's *Roman Comique* of 1649–57 (Duclaux 1975, no. 121). Opperman noted that such a technique is not found later than 1730 (Opperman 1970, pp. 221, 222). Yet the very natural grouping of figures and animals is a new feature that appears in Oudry's drawings no earlier than 1728. Before this, and in the majority of sheets dating from 1728, the human figures seem to be set rather clumsily between groups of dogs and wild animals. On the basis of his analysis Opperman dated the *Boar Hunt* to 1728, but a somewhat later dating cannot be excluded – which, in fact, does not contradict Opperman's own arguments. The inscribed date might better be read as *1730*, a year that suits well with the drawing's style and technique. I.N.

38

Jean-Baptiste Oudry

Hunting Trophies by a Fountain

Black and white chalk on pale bluish grey paper. 315 × 330 mm. Lined

Inscription in pen and brown ink bottom left: *Oudry fecit*

PROVENANCE: collection of Alfred Beurdeley, Paris (collector's mark L. 421); 1889 Museum of the Baron Stieglitz School of Technical Drawing, St Petersburg; 1923 transferred to the Hermitage

Inv. no. OR 28587

EXHIBITIONS: 1959 Leningrad, p. 30; 1968 Leningrad–Moscow, no. 68; 1970 Budapest, no. 82, ill; 1972 Prague, no. 82, ill.; 1975 Berlin, no. 84, ill.; 1983 Leningrad, no. 64, ill.; 1996 Karlsruhe, no. 45, ill.; 1998–9 New York, no. 94, ill.

LITERATURE: Nothaft 1941, pp. 180–81, drawing 11.; Novoselskaya 1983, p. 64, ill.

Hunting Trophies by a Fountain brings together all the elements so beloved by Oudry, a master of the genres of still-life and landscape. On the basis of a description in the Livret to the Salon of 1743, Nothaft (1941, p. 83) identified this drawing as a sketch for a large, now lost, decorative work (324 × 324 cm), which Oudry undertook for Louis XV in 1742 for the dining-room of his château at Choisy. Certainly, its description fully accords with the Hermitage drawing: 'Painting showing a fountain viewed from the corner, a vine and in the middle below a board and a wild goat; on one side a hunting dog attacking a heron in the reeds and on the other side two dogs, a pheasant and a hare tied up, and in the corner hunting baskets with various game.'

Oudry turned to such subjects on numerous occasions. In the Pushkin Museum of Fine Arts, Moscow, for example, is a drawing with a similar motif, *Hunting Trophies* (brown wash, black and white chalk; inv. no. 1006; Alexeyeva, Vodo 1977, no. 155, ill.). *Hunting Trophies by a Fountain* reveals Oudry as an outstanding colourist: the bluish-grey paper he so often used serves as a superb background for the fountain, where various gradations of black chalk are heightened and enlivened with touches of white. I.N.

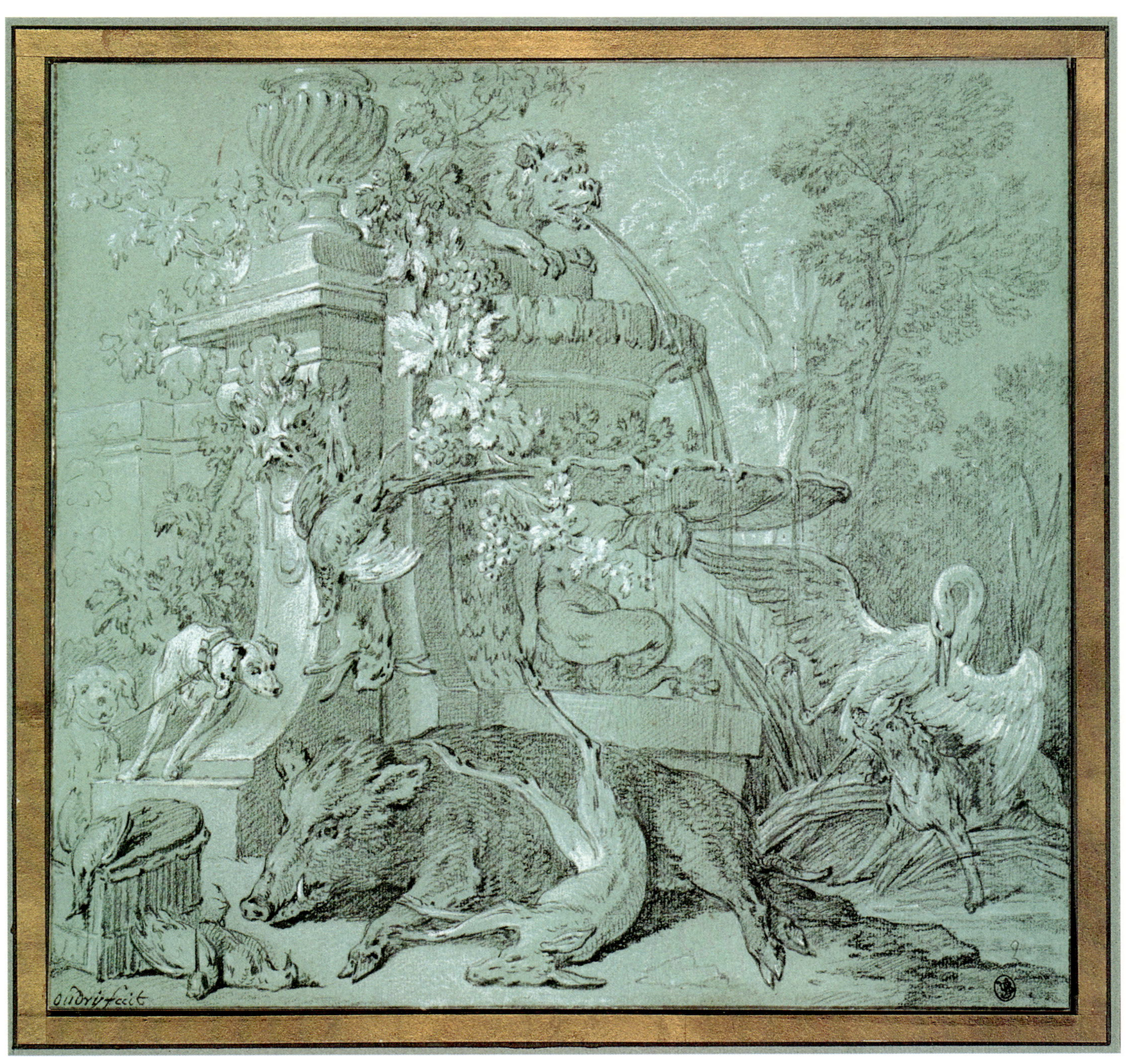

39

Jean-Baptiste Oudry

Fountain in a Park

Black and white chalk on bluish-grey paper. 325 × 520 mm

PROVENANCE: collection of Alfred Beurdeley, Paris (collector's mark L. 421); Library of the Baron Stieglitz School of Technical Drawing, St Petersburg; 1923 transferred to the Hermitage

Inv. no. 28585

EXHIBITIONS: 1955 Moscow, p. 85; 1956 Leningrad, p. 98; 1959 Leningrad, p. 30; 1983 Leningrad, no. 65, ill.; 1986 Bogota, ill.; 1986 Buenos Aires, no. 66, ill.; 1986 Montevideo, no. 66, ill.; 1987–8 Belgrade–Ljubliana–Zagreb, no. 84, ill.; 1994 Ibaraki–Mie–Tokyo, no. 60; 1996 Karlsruhe, no. 46, ill.

LITERATURE: Nothaft 1941, pp. 181, 182, drawing 12; Novoselskaya 1983, Catalogue, pp. 4, 65, ill.

This characteristic example of Oudry's parkscapes is close in motif and technique to a series of drawings made in the extensive park and gardens of the Château d'Arcueil on the River Bièvre. Between 1742 and 1747 Oudry made several paintings and numerous drawings there, which are now in various public and private collections in France and elsewhere (Duclaux 1975, pp. 150, 156). In the Louvre are four finished sheets showing Arcueil's park, like the Hermitage drawing executed in black and white chalk on pale blue paper; three of them are signed and dated 1744 or 1747 (Duclaux 1975, nos. 281–4, ills. pp. 152–5).

Not only the analogous motif and technique, but a comparison of the style provide convincing evidence of a link between the Hermitage sheet and the drawings of 1744–7: they display the same use of contrasting light and shade, of reflexes and of lines and strokes of chalk that enliven the whole. The Hermitage has another drawing of Arcueil in the same technique, *A Trellis Summerhouse in the Park at Arcueil* (inv. no. 28589), as does the Pushkin Museum of Fine Arts, Moscow, *A Corner of the Park at Arcueil* (inv. no. 7730; Alexeyeva, Vodo 1977, no. 154, ill.). Both are more sketchy than this drawing.

The series of views of the park at Arcueil are an unusual stage in Oudry's work. Their unity of colour, the combination of black, white and blue, and the architectural monuments set against marvellous landscape backgrounds give these scenes a particularly poetic feel. I.N.

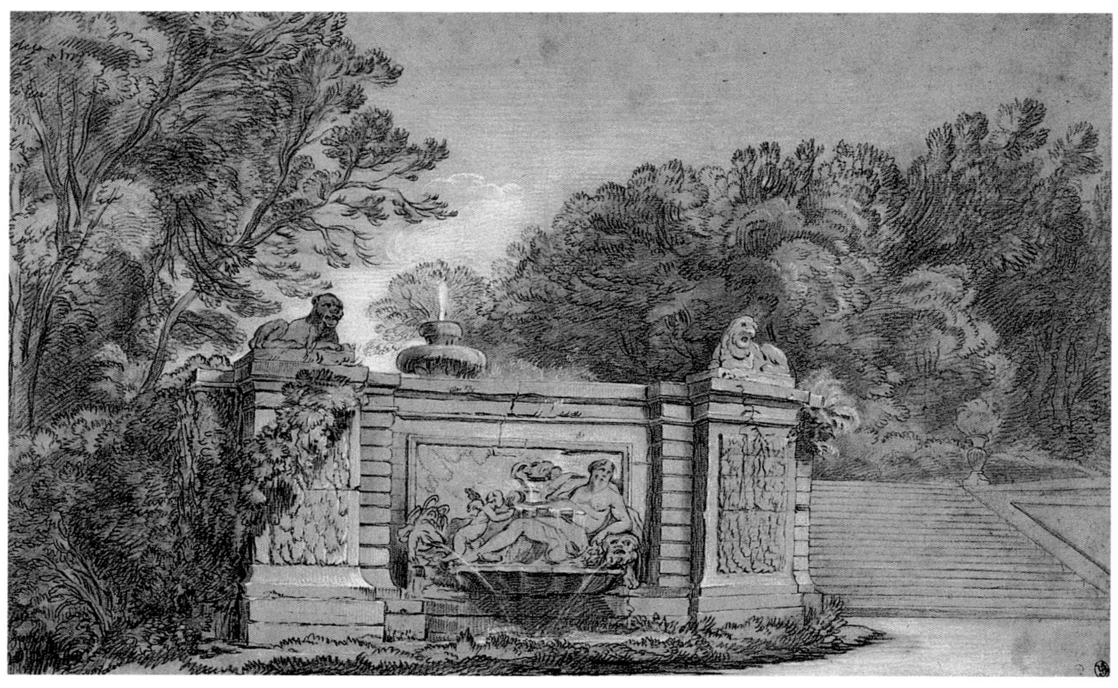

40

Edmé Bouchardon

Chaumont-en-Bassigny 1698 – 1762 Paris

Wall Fountain with a Naiad and Tritons

Red chalk. 487 × 284 mm.
Upper part of the drawing is on an attached sheet. Lined

PROVENANCE: collection of the Academy of Arts, St Petersburg; 1924 transferred to the Hermitage

Inv. no. OR 14640

EXHIBITIONS: 1983 Leningrad, no. 4, ill.

LITERATURE: Novoselskaya 1983, Catalogue, pp. 5, 14, ill.

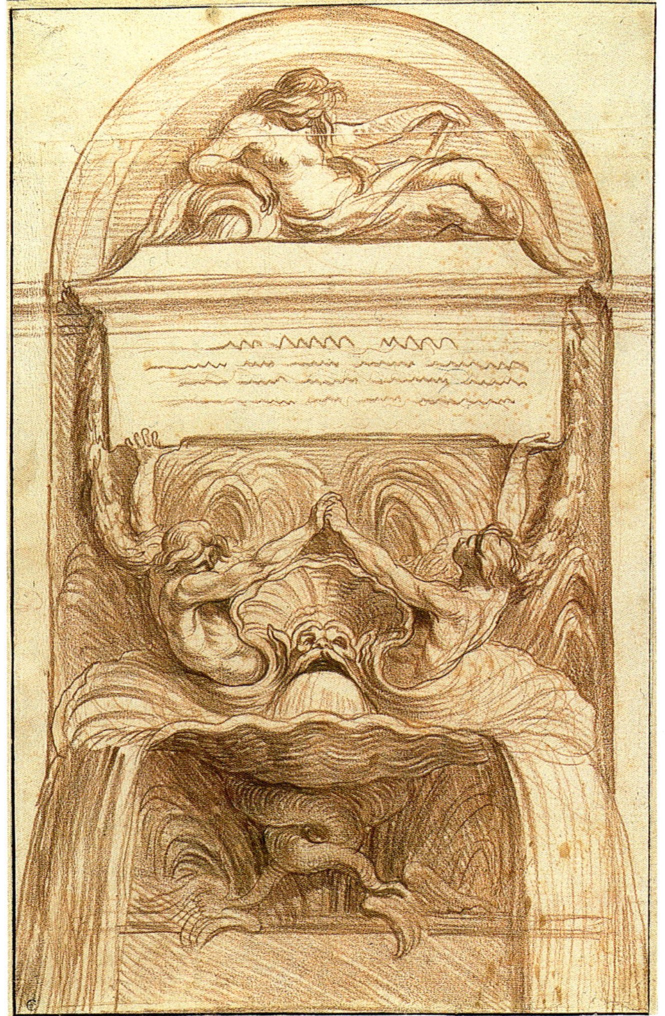

Among Bouchardon's numerous drawings for monuments and architectural structures, a particular place is held by his fountain designs, in which he gave full rein to his creative fantasy. Such compositions allowed him great freedom in the grouping of figures of seahorses, tritons and nymphs, all full of pronounced movement and surrounded by the play of streaming water. A red chalk drawing for the same fountain, including part of a building, is in the Louvre (inv. no. 24275). It is not known if the fountain shown here actually existed, but it has been suggested that the drawing should be linked with initial ideas for one designed for the rue de Grenelle in Paris, construction of which was begun in 1639 (Duclaux 1973).

In the Musée Mayence is a counterproof of this drawing (no. G.S. O 276). Weber (1968) linked it to the time when Bouchardon was working on a design for the tomb of Clement XI, and thus dated it to between 1728 and 1732. It seems more likely, however, that the mature skill and freedom of this drawing indicates a later date, c. 1740. I.N.

41, 42

Jacques de Lajoue

Paris 1687 – 1761 Paris

Two Decorative Compositions: 'Autumn' and 'Winter'

Autumn

Pen and ink, ink wash, watercolour, over a preparatory pencil sketch.
272 × 114 mm (without border);
384 × 223 mm (with border)

PROVENANCE: collection of Alfred Beurdeley, Paris (collector's mark L. 421); 1889 Baron Stieglitz School of Technical Drawing, St Petersburg; 1923 transferred to the Hermitage

Inv. no. 28116

OLD MANUSCRIPT CATALOGUES: 'Collection Beurdeley. Dessins d'architecture et d'ornements. École Française', p. 125, no. 441. 'Lajoue: Deux dessins: l'Automne et l'Hiver dans de riches encadrements rocaille. Les sujets sont rehaussés de tous à l'aquarelle. Les bordures sont tenités de jaune.'

EXHIBITIONS: 1995–6 St Petersburg, no. 31, ill.

LITERATURE: Shevchenko 1995a, p. 22, ill.

With its pair, *Autumn* forms part of a now divided group of *The Four Seasons*: since 1887 *Summer* has been in the Kunstbibliothek, Berlin (Berckenhagen 1970, pp. 210–11, no. 665; Roland Michel 1984a, D. 143, fig. 234), while *Spring*, which passed through the St Petersburg collection of Prince Vladimir Argutinsky-Dolgorukov (collector's mark L.2602d), was exhibited at the Galerie Cailleux, Paris, in 1989 (1989 Paris, no. 6).

All four drawings from this series are of the same format and share a common technique and compositional arrangement: the figures in the central group are arranged on a pedestal or pedestal-like object, and the whole is framed with a broad ornamental border, each element of which is unique. Moreover, Lajoue produced two versions of the border for each sheet, both of which incorporate decorative and symbolic elements relevant to the time of year. In all four cases the independently conceived frames were clearly executed on a large sheet of paper onto which the central subject compositions were then glued. The drawings in this cycle might be dated *c.* 1735 by analogy with an equally richly framed engraved series in Dijon (Roland Michel 1984a, D. 141, 142 figs 244, 245).

Autumn and *Winter* differ slightly from the two previously known to scholars. Both Hermitage compositions include a plaque suitable for an inscription.In addition, the rectangular frame in *Autumn* includes a panelled projection at the top, making it more like a doorway or window. Second, *Autumn* also has a large massy hill with a grotto covering most of the upper part of the sheet, an area that in the other drawings is left free or is occupied simply by roughly indicated branches. There is a less worked-up, but otherwise very close, signed preparatory sketch for the composition of the infant Bacchus and his ensemble in the Galerie Cailleux, Paris (inv. no. 950505).

Winter

Pen and ink, ink wash, watercolour, over a pencil preparatory sketch.
274 × 113 mm (without border);
388 × 225 mm (with border)

PROVENANCE: collection of Alfred Beurdeley, Paris (collector's mark L. 421); 1889 Baron Stieglitz School of Technical Drawing, St Petersburg; 1923 transferred to the Hermitage

Inv. no. 28115

OLD MANUSCRIPT CATALOGUES: 'Collection Beurdeley. Dessins d'architecture et d'ornements. École Française'; see cat. 41

EXHIBITIONS: 1995–6 St Petersburg, no. 32

LITERATURE: Shevchenko 1995a, pp. 22–3

Winter uses traditional devices, such as the bent figure of the naked old man warming himself by the coals of a huge brazier beneath him, which, like the vat in *Autumn*, serves as a pedestal. Both versions of the ornamental border for *Winter* include, among the *rocaille* twists, garlands and icicles, jets of water from a freezing fountain and (at top right) a walking-stick and crutch, for old age and the winter season are traditionally associated.

Lajoue made images of the Seasons on numerous occasions, for example the group of four drawings in the Nationalmuseum, Stockholm (Bjurström 1976, nos. 989–92), and various individual painted works, such as *Winter* in the Metropolitan Museum of Art, New York, probably relate to cycles on the same theme.

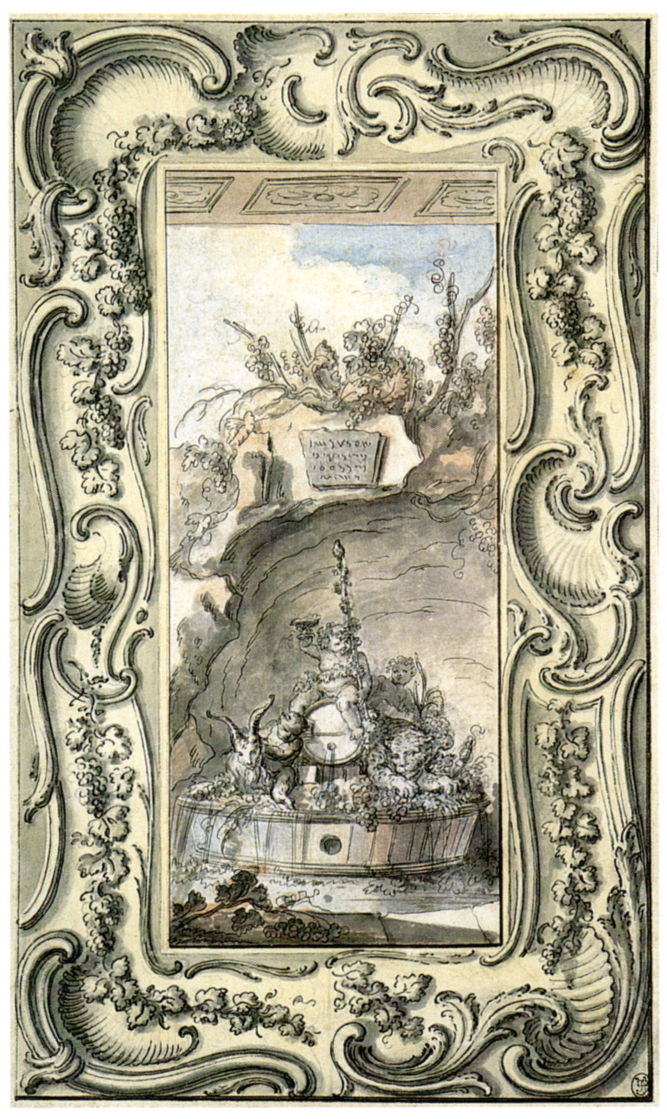

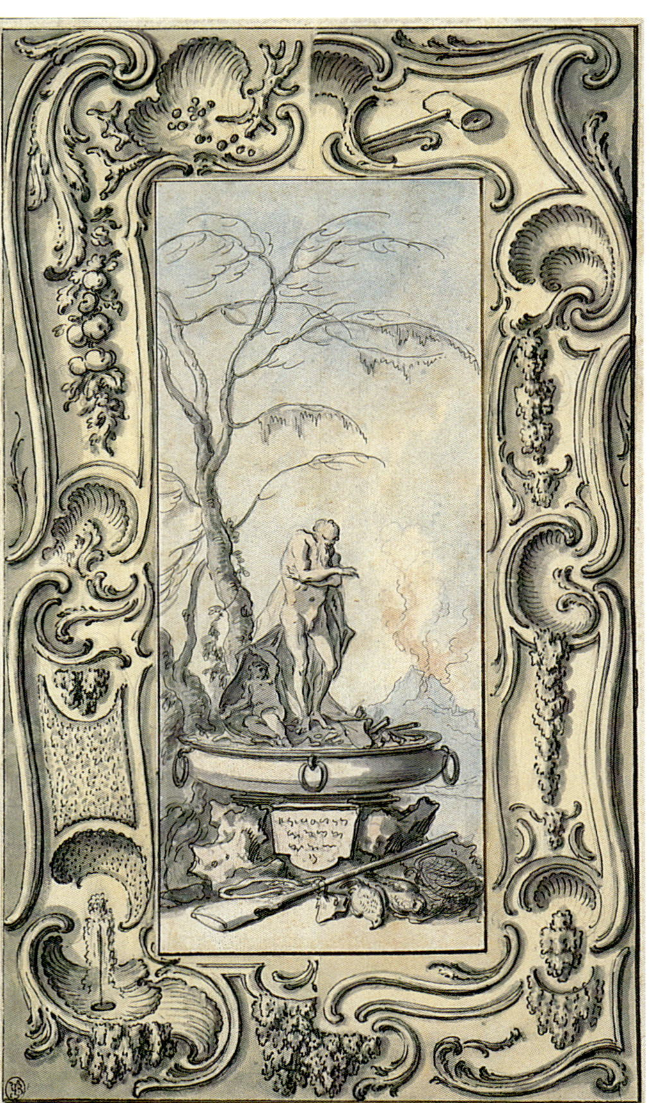

43

François Boucher

Paris 1703 – 1770 Paris

Landscape with a Pond

Oil on canvas. 51 × 65 cm
Signed and dated bottom right:
f. Boucher 1746

PROVENANCE: collection of Louis-Antoine Crozat, Baron de Thiers; 1772 acquired for the Hermitage; 1860–82 kept at Gatchina Palace, near St Petersburg

EXHIBITIONS: 1955 Moscow, p. 23; 1956 Leningrad, p. 10; 1970 Göteborg, no. 21; 1970 Leningrad, no. 2; 1972b Dresden, no. 2; 1977 Tokyo–Kyoto, no. 33; 1982 Tokyo–Kumamoto, no. 40; 1988 London, no. 6; 1995 Shizuoka–Tochigi–Okayama–Kumamoto, no. 18

LITERATURE: Cat. 1774, no. 1149; Cats 1863–1916, no. 1797; Réau 1929, no. 15; Cat. 1958, p. 261; Nemilova 1961, p. 306; Hermitage 1965, no. 72; Stuffmann 1968, p. 126; Nemilova 1975, p. 436; Ananoff 1976, vol. 1, p. 409, no. 300; Cat. 1976, p. 186; Nemilova 1982, no. 14; Nemilova 1985, no. 9; Laing, Rosenberg et al. 1986–7, p. 212

By the mid-18th century, French landscape painting was in decline, for no artist was the equal of Claude or Poussin. A small number of painters followed the example of their older contemporary Oudry, making sketches from nature in the environs of Paris, for instance in the romantically overgrown park of the Prince de Guise's château of Arcueil. Boucher, however, was probably the only member of this younger generation to pay serious attention to landscape.

It was after his stay in Italy (1727–31), where he lived in Rome and Venice, that Boucher made his landscapes something out of the ordinary. For instance, among the works he presented in 1737 to the Académie in order to be made professor, he included a number of landscape fantasies – a most unusual step. These paintings probably formed part of a series of landscapes produced that same year for the private apartments of the royal palace at Fontainebleau. At first Boucher preferred idealized views of the Veneto and Roman ruins, but apparently under Oudry's influence, in the late 1730s and early 1740s he turned to the French countryside – Charenton, Beauvais and Blois. His views of these places, mostly of Beauvais, were shown at the Paris Salons of 1742, 1743 and 1745. 'Pure' landscapes like this one – without Antique ruins, rural huts, watermills or his little bridges – are extremely rare in Boucher's work. *Landscape with a Pond* combines features of the early idealized Italianate views with those of later, 'French' views.

The sculptural group (male and female figures, overturned vessel pouring water) probably symbolizes the confluence of two rivers, as in *The Confluence of the Seine and Marne* carved for the cascade in the park at Saint-Cloud by Lambert Sigisbert Adam. The standing boy in a hat is repeated in the painting *Landscape with a Raft* of 1761 (private collection, Bielefeld, Germany).

Louis-Antoine Crozat de Thiers, a renowned collector, was a passionate admirer of Boucher's work and one of his first patrons. The catalogue of a posthumous sale of prints belonging to Gabriel Huquier, held 4 November 1772 in Paris lists at least 24 different compositions engraved by Crozat de Thiers after Boucher's paintings. According to the author of Boucher's life that appeared in *Galérie Françoise* (ed. J.-B.Collet de Messine, Paris, 1771, no. 5, Boucher, p. 1), Boucher 'painted several pictures for the cabinet of M. de Thiers', but nothing further is known regarding the Baron's commissions. It is puzzling, then, that the sale catalogue mentions only a 'Landscape' (undoubtedly this *Landscape with a Pond*) and *Frère Luce* (Pushkin Museum of Fine Arts, Moscow) and two drawings. Crozat de Thiers' other paintings by Boucher had presumably been sold earlier. E.D.

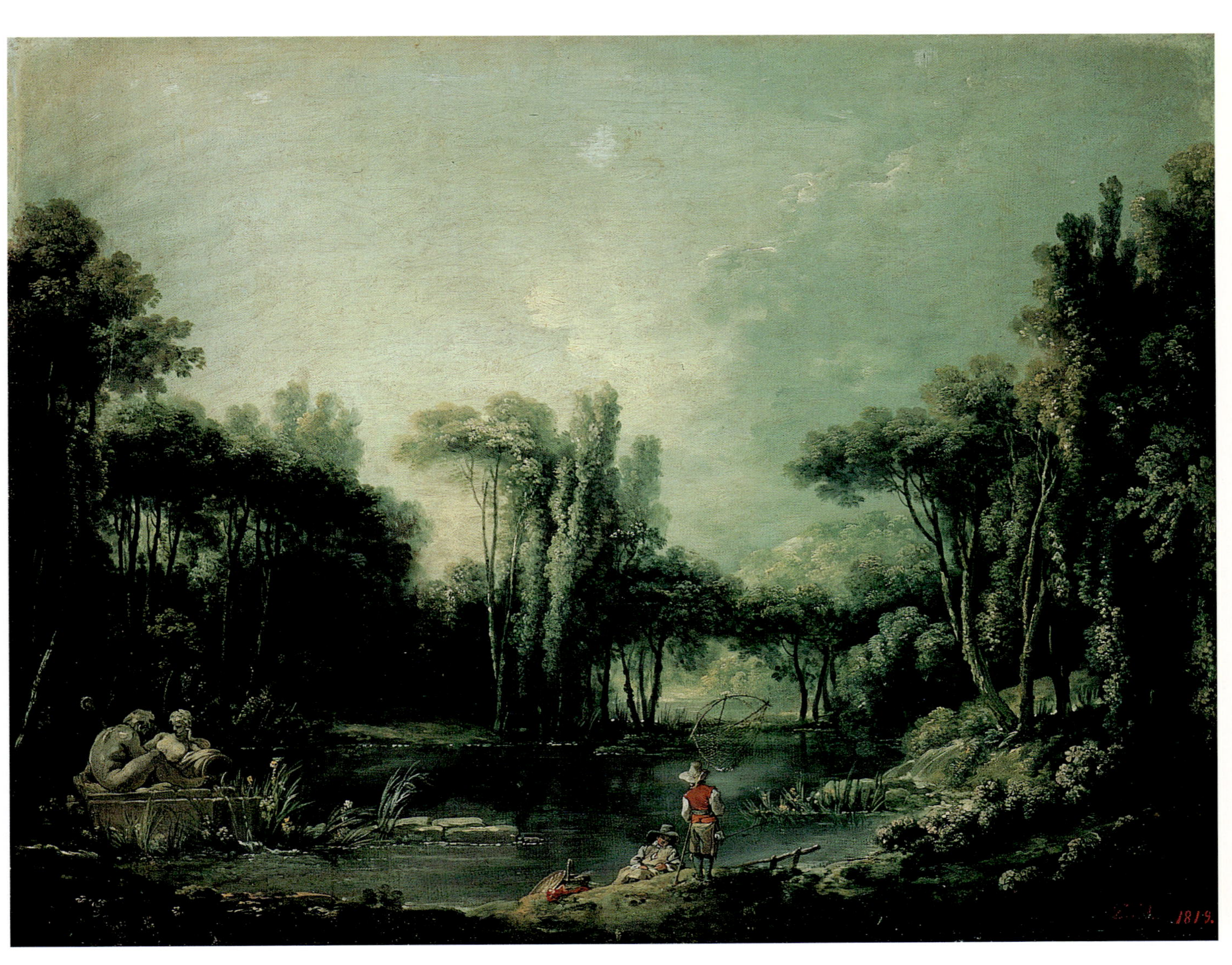
1819.

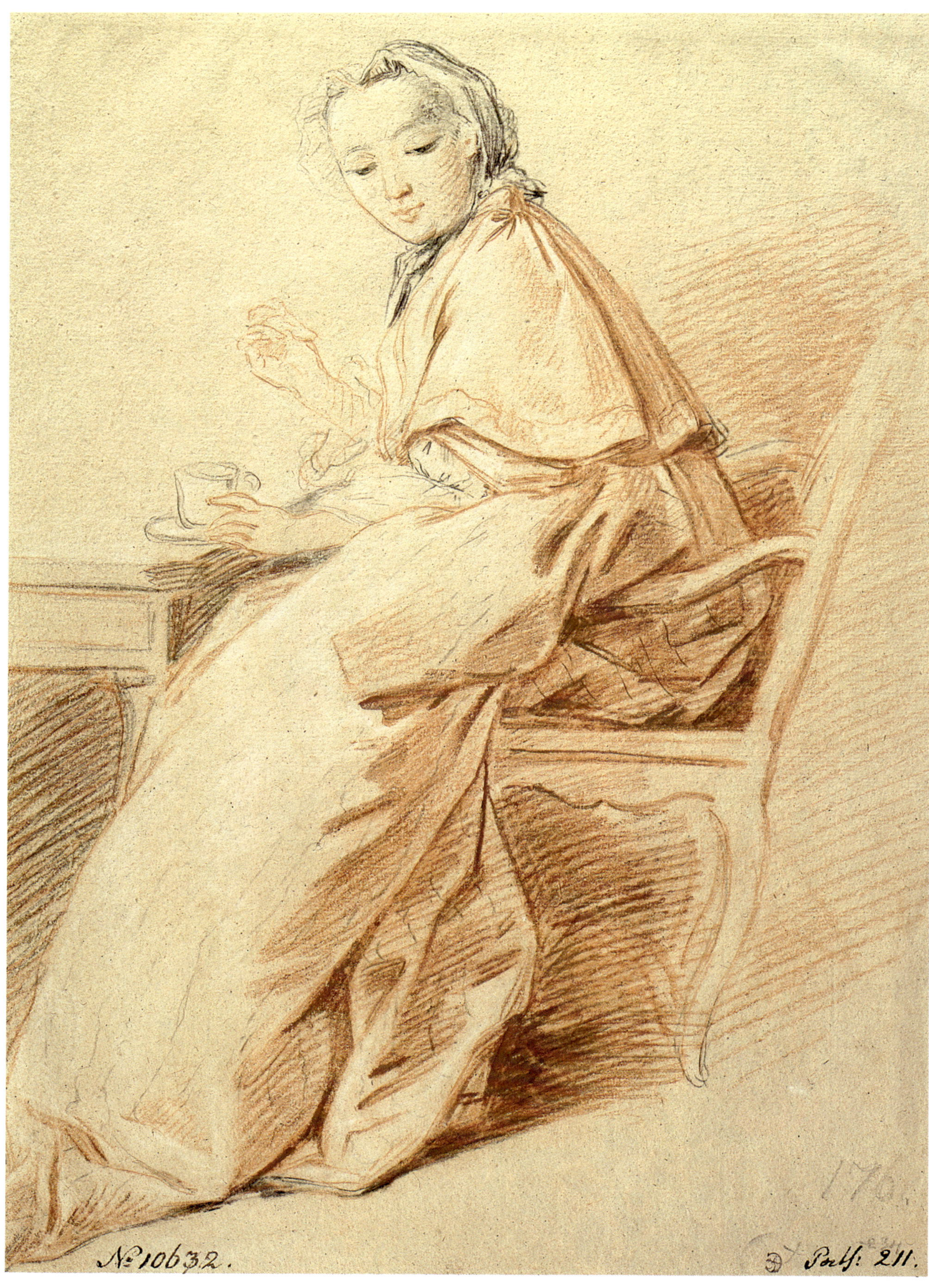
№ 10632.
Palf: 211.

44

François Boucher

A Young Woman Seated at a Table

Red, black and white chalk on pale brown paper. 346 × 253 mm. Lined

PROVENANCE: collection of V. P. Divov, St Petersburg; 1833 acquired for the Hermitage

Inv. no. OR 10632

EXHIBITIONS: 1926 Leningrad, no. 169; 1970 Leningrad, no. 17, ill.; 1972 Prague, no. 15, ill.; 1986 Bogota, ill.; 1986 Buenos Aires, no. 53, ill.; 1986 Montevideo, no. 53, ill.; 1987–8 Belgrade–Ljubliana–Zagreb, no. 65, ill.; 1996 Karlsruhe, no. 40, ill.

LITERATURE: Ananoff 1976, vol. I, pp. 284–6, no. 165, fig. 165/4; Novoselskaya 1973, pp. 64, 65

Boucher's skills as a draughtsman became increasingly virtuoso over the years, and his drawings more decorative and refined, acquiring the features now seen as typifying his style. *A Young Woman Seated at a Table* shows a figure who features in *Morning Coffee* (1739), which shows the artist's family at breakfast (fig. 36). The elegance and grace of the young woman accord with the fine, delicate use of colour (Boucher very consciously selected pale brown paper).

Boucher has paid most attention to the sitter's face (black chalk is used to pick out the eyes and headwear) and her morning dress, stressing the heavy folds with red chalk accents. The hands are only lightly marked, but their movement is full of grace. Intimate scenes of this sort are not often found in his work. I.N.

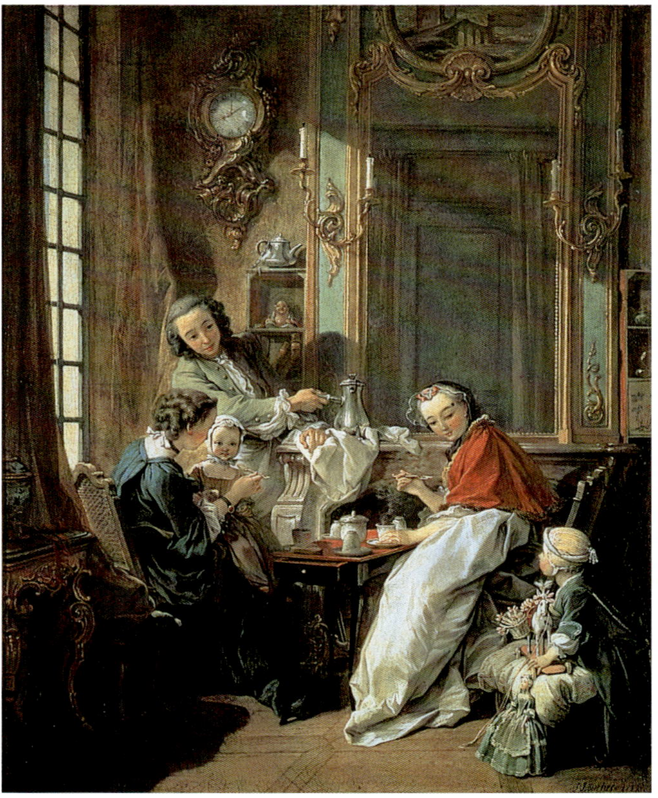

fig. 36
François Boucher
Morning Coffee, 1739
oil on canvas, 81.5 × 55.5 cm.
Musée du Louvre, Paris / Bridgeman Art Library

45

François Boucher

Clio, the Muse of History

Red chalk. 340 × 245 mm. Lined

PROVENANCE: private collection, Leningrad; 1938 acquired by the Hermitage through the Purchasing Commission

Inv. no. OR 42924

EXHIBITIONS: 1955 Moscow, p. 72; 1956 Leningrad, p. 84; 1968 Leningrad–Moscow, no. 7; 1970 Leningrad, no. 19; 1970 Budapest, no. 11, ill., 1975 Berlin, no. 91, ill.; 1983 Leningrad, no. 9; 1996 Karlsruhe, no. 41, ill.

LITERATURE: Novoselskaya 1961, pp. 40–42, ill.; Ananoff 1976, vol. II, p. 226, fig. 1545; Novoselskaya 1973, pp. 65, 66, ill.; Novoselskaya 1983, pp. 4, 19.

In the 1740s Boucher produced four overdoor paintings bearing allegorical images of Astronomy, Poetry, Rhetoric and History for the Royal Library at Versailles (Salon 1743). This sheet is a preparatory drawing for Clio, the Muse of History, writing a biography of Louis XV, whose portrait is held aloft by *putti*.

The sketches for such compositions, fixing the artist's initial ideas, are notable for the freedom with which the figures are grouped, the play of light and shade and the generalized nature of the silhouettes. *History* is one of the best such sheets. In this fluent drawing Boucher has established the figure's position and at the same time determined the distribution of light and shade with daring hatching. All the figures are shown in movement – the *putti* gambol, while Clio leans back in order to examine the portrait.

The paintings in the Royal Library were pear-shaped in form, and the design thus underwent small changes, although in the main its general character was preserved. None the less, the vividness of the drawing was somewhat lost in the resulting work, which was subjected to a greater degree of idealization. I.N.

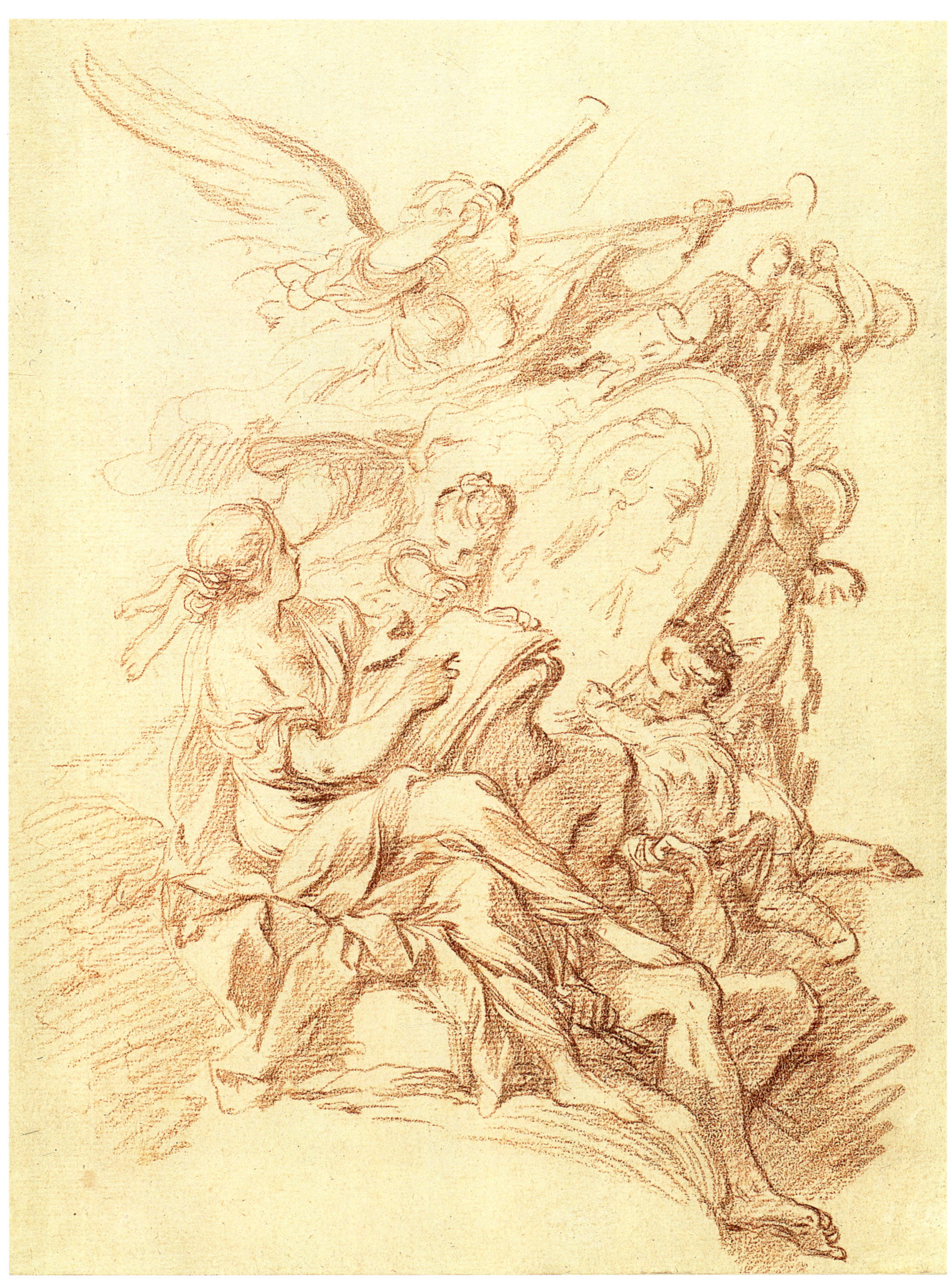

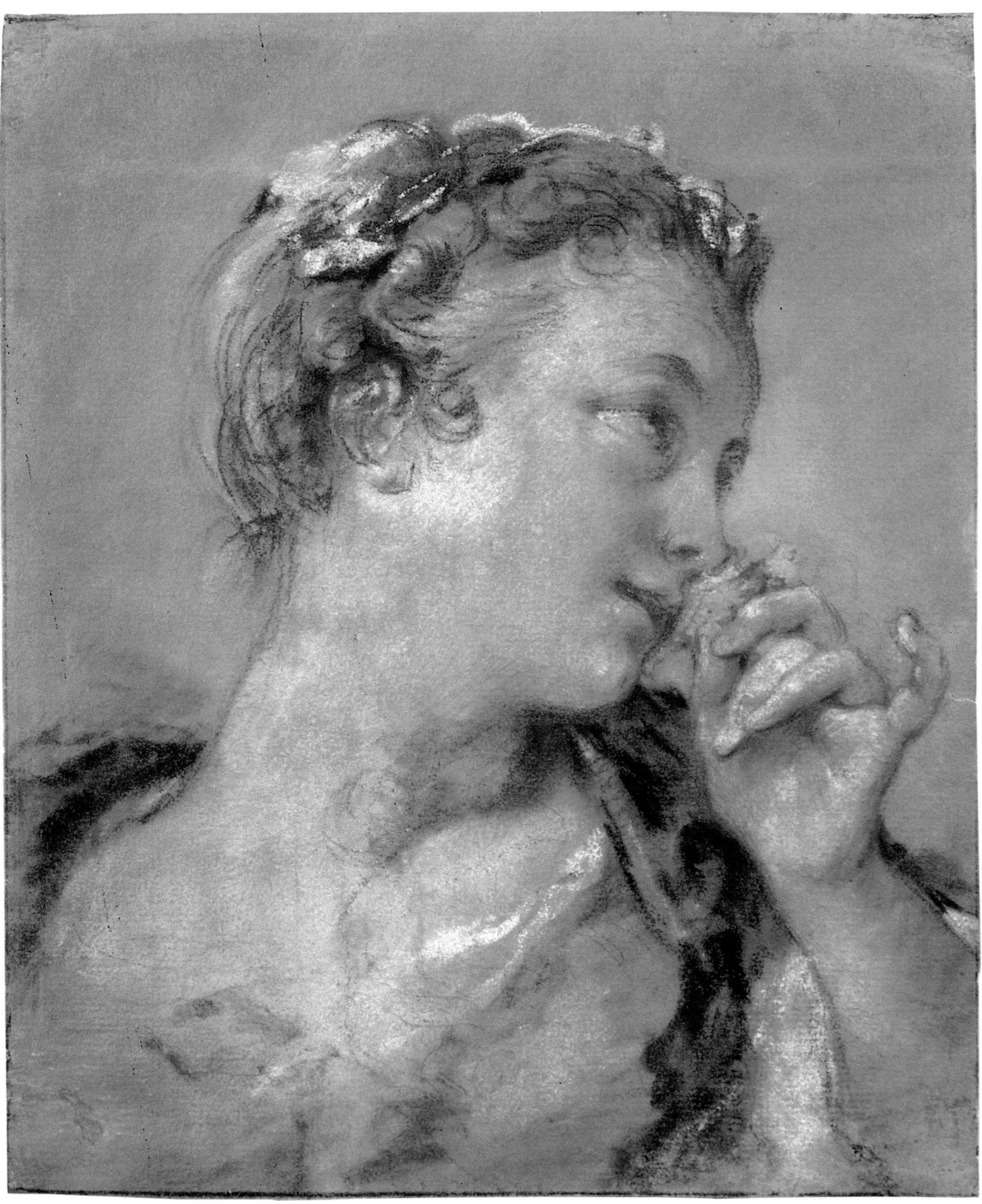

46

François Boucher

Girl with a Rose

Black and red chalk and pastel on toned brown paper. 225 × 181 mm

On the reverse: sketches of figures in the lower part of the sheet

Red and white chalk

PROVENANCE: collection of Pierre Crozat, Paris; collection of Louis-Antoine Crozat, Baron de Thiers; 1772 acquired for the Hermitage

Inv. no. OR 11416

EXHIBITIONS: 1867 St Petersburg, no. 485; 1926 Leningrad, no. 172; 1955 Moscow, p. 72; 1956 Leningrad, p. 84; 1970 Leningrad, no. 21

LITERATURE: Cat. 1774, no. LX; Kamenskaya 1960b, no. 20, ill.; Stuffman 1968, p. 126, no. 110, fig.; Novoselskaya 1973, p. 65; Ananoff 1976, vol. II, pp. 49–51, no. 350/6; Laing, Rosenberg et al. 1986–7, pp. 238–40, no. 54, note 5, ill.

A girl with a rose appears on the left side of Boucher's painting *The Rape of Europa* (exhibited at the Salon of 1747; fig. 37), but it is hard to say with any certainty whether this drawing is a preparatory work for the painting or if it was simply created on the basis of the motif. We know that variations of the drawing passed at different auctions (Laing, Rosenberg *et al.* 1986–7, p. 240, note 5) and that one of the versions was engraved by Gabriel Huquier under the title *Scent*.

Drawings such as *A Girl with a Rose* were often intended for domestic settings. Indeed, it was Boucher who was responsible for the fashion for hanging drawings in interiors. This charming image uses a combination of harmonious pastel tones – beige, pale blue, pink and brown – while sharper accents in black and white in the hair and clothing emphasize the gentleness of the face. I.N.

fig. 37

François Boucher

The Rape of Europa, 1747

oil on canvas, 160.5 × 193.5 cm. Musée du Louvre, Paris / Bridgeman Art Library

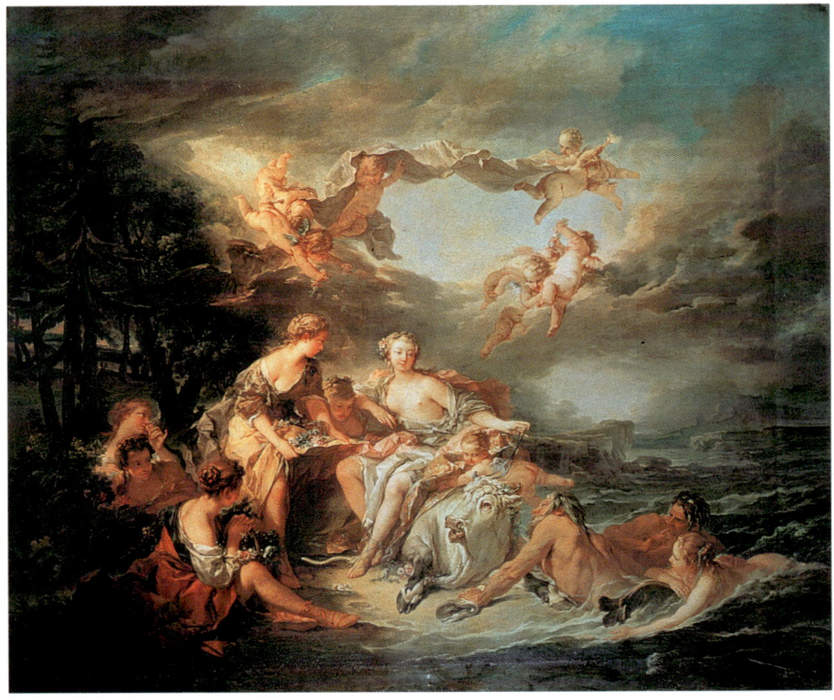

47

Jean-Baptiste-Marie Pierre

Paris 1714 – 1789 Paris

Sketch for a Ceiling in the Château of Saint-Cloud

Pen and ink, black wash, over a black chalk preparatory sketch, touched with watercolour in places. 416 × 537 mm

Signed in pen and brown ink in the bottom-right corner: *Pierre*

PROVENANCE: Library of the Baron Stieglitz School of Technical Drawing, St Petersburg; 1924 transferred to the Hermitage

Inv. no. OR 25066

LITERATURE: Novoselskaya 1996, pp. 80–85, ill.

Jean-Baptiste Pierre was a painter of decorative works as well as genre scenes, landscapes histories and religious works. Between the late 1740s and the 1760s he undertook a number of important decorative works in Paris and its environs: in 1749 he painted the cupola of the Chapel of the Madonna in the Church of St Roche, in 1753 the ceiling of the Palais Royale, and various overdoors for the Château de Fontainebleau.

In 1768–9 Pierre designed and painted a ceiling on the subject of Rinaldo and Armida for the Grand Salon of the Château of Saint-Cloud near Paris, then the property of Louis-Philippe, Duc d'Orléans. Mariette, noting the brilliance of his brushwork and the high quality of the artist's drawings, admiringly recorded that Pierre 'finished a large ceiling that the Duc d'Orléans commissioned from him for his Saint-Cloud apartments and this work received the acclaim that it deserved' (Mariette 1851–60, vol. IV, p. 155). Unfortunately it has not survived, having been destroyed when Saint-Cloud was the property of Marie-Antoinette. None the less, the Hermitage has this large signed drawing by the artist, apparently the preparatory sketch for the coffered ceiling.

In the central panel is Armida in a chariot; the spandrels contain four scenes within medallions, and at the angles are allegorical figures personifying the arts and sciences above shields bearing coats of arms. Pierre turned to subjects from Torquato Tasso's *Jerusalem Delivered* (1580) on a number of occasions. Among the most important works are *Erminia Disguised in the Armour of Clorinda Appearing to the Shepherds*, engraved in 1751 by Etienne Fessard (Rosenberg 1985, pp. 269–73), *The Danish Knight and Ubaldo at the Spring of Laughter* (Musée Bossuet, Meaux), an oil sketch for *Rinaldo and Armida* (sold at the Galerie Pardo, Paris, October 1980), and a drawing of the same title (sold at Charles et André Bailli, Paris, *Dessins et Esquisses de Maîtres anciens et modernes*, 17 May – 21 July 1989). These works were not preparatory works for the Saint-Cloud ceiling, since all of them, with the exception of the oil sketch, are finished works, and several of them were completed long before Pierre began at Saint-Cloud. Even so, the subjects of the Danish Knight and Ubaldo and Rinaldo and Armida appear in two of the ceiling medallions, albeit with some differences. No prototypes are known for the other two compositions, but both derive from the story of Rinaldo and Armida. One shows a reclining knight and a young woman standing above him. Tasso's verses, in Edward Fairfax's translation of 1600 (Book XIV. lxv–lxvi), describe the scene.*

The last composition in an oval clearly depicts the farewell of Armida and Rinaldo: 'But when her wooing fit was brought to end, / She congee took, kiss'd him, and went her way' (XVI. xxvi). This scene, watched in secret by the two knights who have arrived to rescue Rinaldo, is set in the gardens of the palace to which Armida had lured him; note the slender cypress trees in the distance and the architectural details. The theme of farewell thus seems to round off this excerpt from Tasso's narrative. I.N.

*
Then from her ambush forth Armida start,
Swearing revenge, and threat'ning
torments smart;
But when she lookéd on his face awhile,
And saw how sweet he breath'd,
how still he lay,
How his fair eyes though closéd seem to smile,
At first she stay'd, astound with great dismay;
Then sat her down (so love can art beguile),
And as she sat and look'd, fled fast away
Her wrath ...

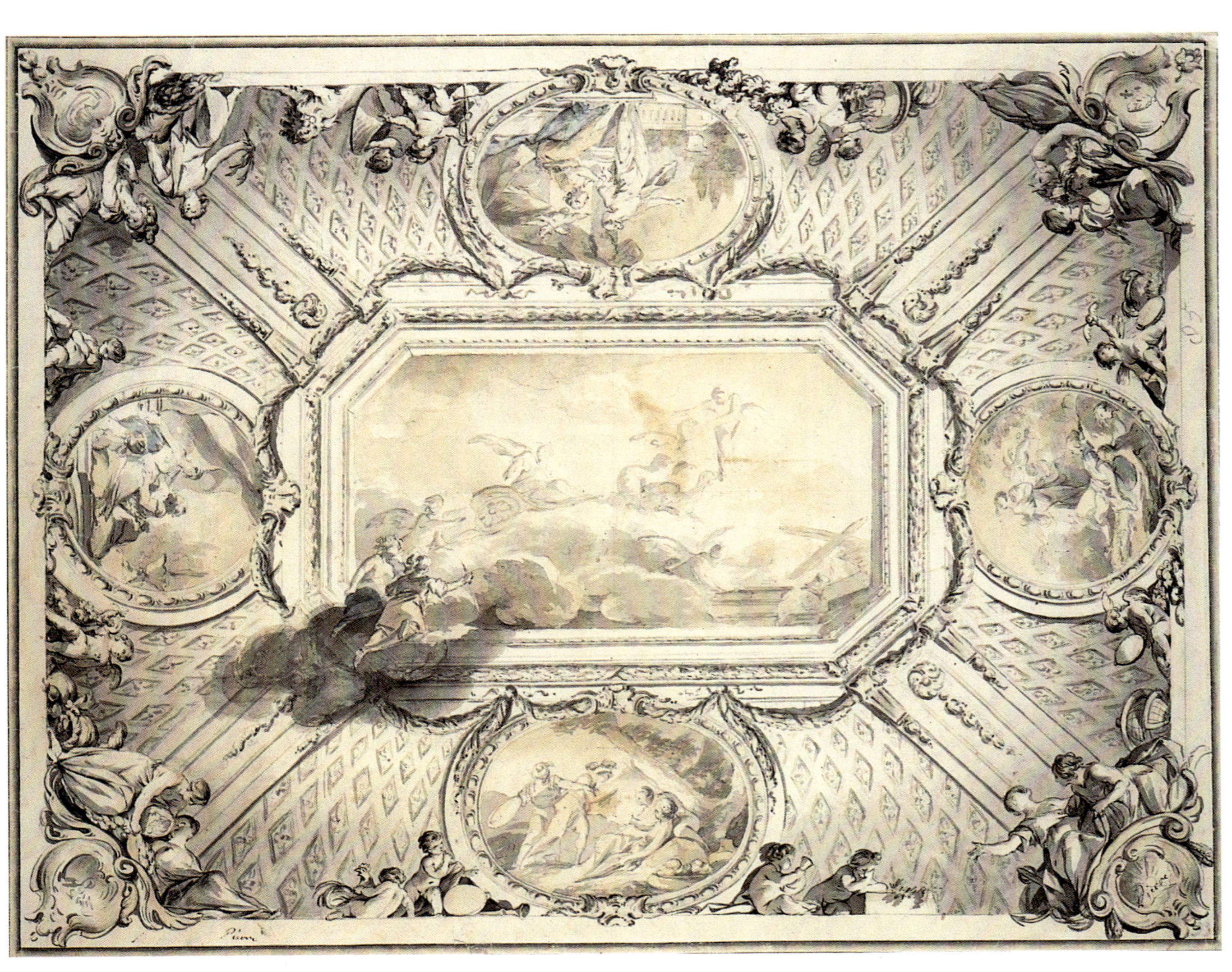

48

Gabriel de Saint-Aubin

Paris 1724 – 1780 Paris

Society Promenade

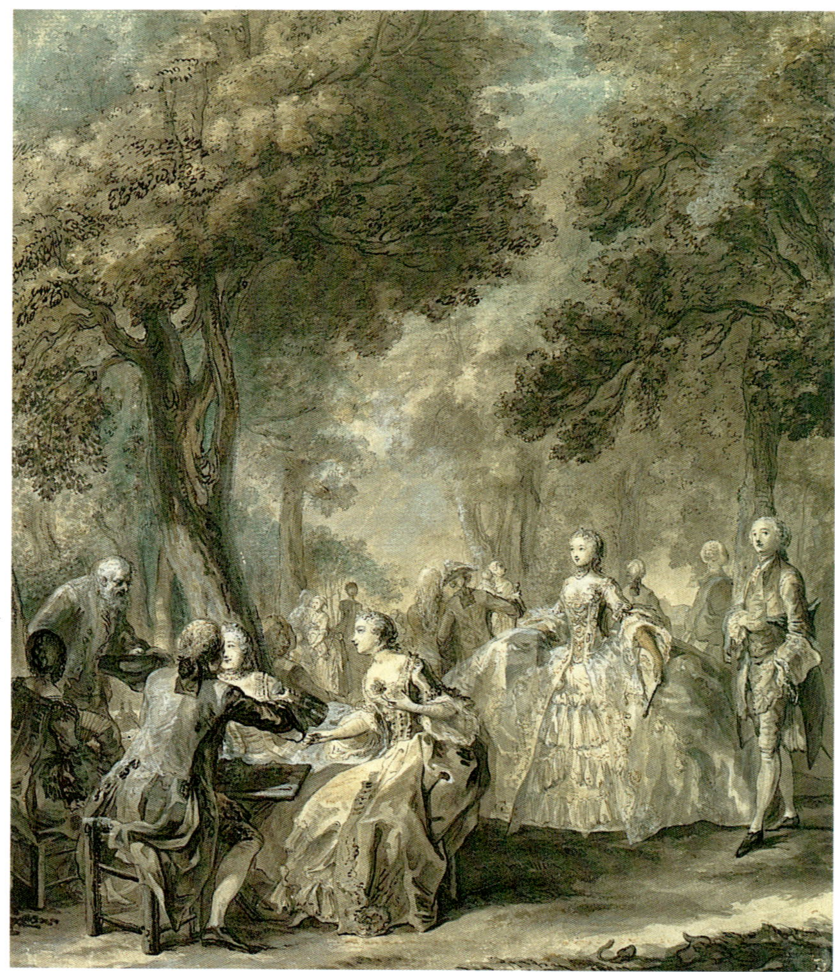

Pen and black and brown ink, black wash, watercolour and gouache. 314 × 258 mm. Lined

By the lower edge to right a date (cut off) and signature in pen and ink: *176... G.S.* Old inscription in pen and brown ink on the back of the lining: *execute à Paris aux environs*

PROVENANCE: Winter Palace, St Petersburg; 1932 transferred to the Hermitage

Inv. no. 27892

EXHIBITIONS: 1937 Leningrad, no. 96; 1955 Moscow, p. 84; 1956 Leningrad, p. 97; 1968 Leningrad–Moscow, no. 61; 1972 Vienna–Graz, no. 62, ill.; 1975 Aarhus, no. 88; 1975 Copenhagen, no. 88; 1975 Berlin, no. 93, ill.; 1982 Florence, no. 98, ill.; 1983 Leningrad, no. 57, ill.; 1996 Karlsruhe, no. 52, ill.

LITERATURE: Dobroklonsky 1954, pp. 26–8, ill.; Kamenskaya 1964, no. 130, ill.; Novoselskaya 1983, pp. 4, 55, ill.; Hermitage 1994, no. 353, ill.

This drawing was first identified and published as the work of Saint-Aubin by Mikhail Dobroklonsky (1954, pp. 26–8). The composition was engraved by A. J. Duclos with slight changes in the lower part of the sheet – the addition of two dogs and a stool to the right. This, one of Duclos' rarest etchings, confirms Saint-Aubin's authorship of the drawing by the inscription *G. de St Aubin pinxit*. It remains unclear, however, whether there was a painting that included the two dogs or whether the etching was taken from the drawing, since the signature ' St Aubin' also appeared on prints based on watercolours. Dacier supported the latter theory, but thought that the drawing had been lost (Dacier 1929–31, vol. I, p. 80, pl. XX; II, no. 527).

There are several versions of the composition *Society Promenade*, which Dacier dates to 1760–61. Closest to the Hermitage drawing are a painting in the Hyacinthe Rigaud Museum in Perpignan, *Society on the Boulevard*, which brings together a slightly altered version of the Hermitage composition, a drawing from a private collection in Paris (Dacier 1929–31, vol. II, nos. 529, 528; I, pl. V), and another drawing, *View of the Boulevard*, from the collection of the Fondation Custodia in Paris, repeating the left group from our drawing almost without alteration (Dacier 1929–31, vol. II, no. 525; I, pl. VI). I.N.

49

Gabriel de Saint-Aubin

'Armida' in the Old Hall of the Opéra

Pen and ink, ink wash, gouache, on greyish-brown paper. 315 × 537 mm. Cut out along the vertical edges of the scenery. Lined

Inscription in pen and ink in a rectangular frame beneath the drawing on the old mount: *Armide G. de S. Aubin*

PROVENANCE: collection of Counts Sheremetev, St Petersburg; Sheremetev Museum (Museum of Everyday Life), Leningrad; Russian Museum, Leningrad; 1932 transferred to the Hermitage

Inv. no. 40041

EXHIBITIONS: 1956 Leningrad, p. 97; 1983 Leningrad, no. 58, ill.; 1996 Karlsruhe, no. 53, ill.

LITERATURE: Dacier 1929–31, no. 746; Novoselskaya 1983, Catalogue, pp. 4, 56–7, ill.

An almost analogous drawing, but of slightly reduced dimensions (310 × 500 mm), showing the ceiling painting and a box cut off by the edge to right, is in the Museum of Fine Arts, Boston (Prints and Drawings 1975, no. 43, ill.). Dacier, who had seen only a photograph of the Hermitage drawing, called it a copy, while allowing that it might possibly be an original. But the virtuoso execution of this drawing, the brilliant colouring and Saint-Aubin's characteristic manner all indicate that it is in his hand.

On the mount of the Boston drawing, in a cartouche with an inscription, is the date '1747'. But Dacier proved that both drawings depict the revival of Lully's opera *Armida*, which took place with much pomp in 1761 in the old hall of the Opéra at the Palais Royale (Dacier 1929–31, vol. II, nos. 745, 746). Since he was renowned for his visual records of society life in Paris, Saint-Aubin could never have let such a magnificent event pass him by. I.N.

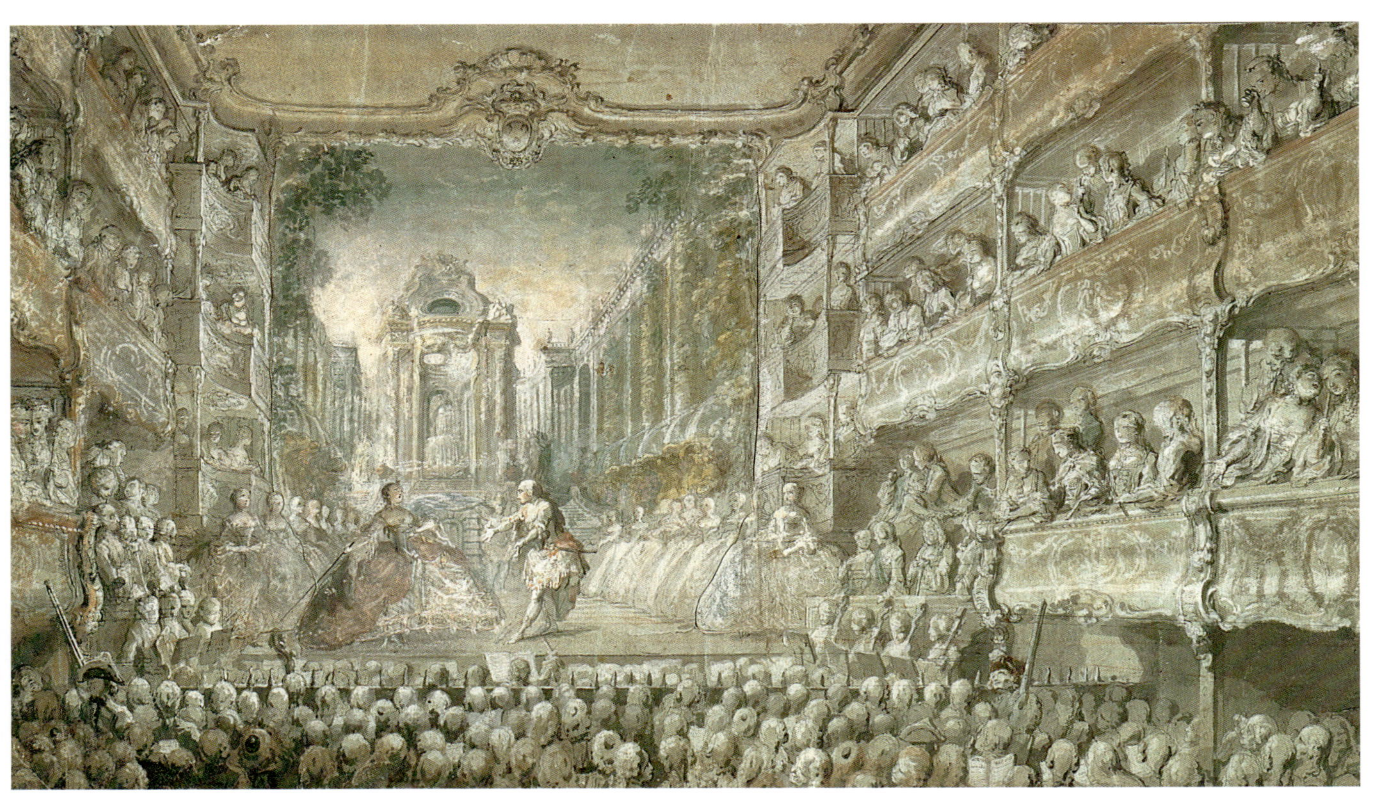

50

Jean-Baptiste Greuze

Tournus 1725 – 1805 Paris

Filial Piety (The Paralytic)

Oil on canvas. 115 × 146 cm
Monogram, barely readable, to right on the tablecloth: *J.G.* (?)

PROVENANCE: 1766 acquired from Greuze by Catherine II, through the mediation of Denis Diderot

EXHIBITIONS: 1763 Paris Salon, no. 140; 1955 Moscow, p. 28; 1956 Leningrad, p. 18; 1986–7 Paris, no. 318; 1987 Leningrad–Moscow, no. 382; 1987–8 Belgrade–Ljubliana–Zagreb, no. 9; 1990 New York–Chicago, no. 10

LITERATURE: Diderot 1763; Diderot 1765; Diderot 1968, p. 800; Aubert 1763; Grimm 15 January 1767; DuPont de Nemours 1771, vol. V, p. 52; cat. 1774, no. 22; Corberon 1776, vol. I, p. 156; Fortia de Piles 1796, vol. III, p. 190; Schnitzler 1828, pp. 45, 72–3; Mariette 1851–60, vol. II, p. 330; Cats 1863–1912, no. 1520; Waagen 1864, p. 306, no. 1520; Goncourt 1880, vol. I, pp. 324, 340, 351; Tourneux 1899, pp. 57–8; Mauclair 1906, pp. 69, 80–6, nos. 186, 1344–7, 1349, 1677, 1701, 1713, 1716, 1728; Réau 1920, pp. 274, 275, 281, 185; Réau 1929, no. 115; Gerts 1947; Brookner 1956, p. 161; Seznec, Adhémar 1957–67, vol. I, pp. 152, 153, 183–4, pl. 86; cat. 1958, p. 281; Garnaud 1963, pp. 47–8; Brookner 1972, pp. 62–3, 86, 103, 106–7, 118; Nemilova 1975, p. 434; cat. 1976, p. 197; Novoselskaya 1977, pp. 6–8; Schnapper 1977, pp. 86–7, 89; Bukdahl 1980, pp. 206, 207, 208, 283, 304, 310, 387, 388, 458, 485, 487; Fried 1980, pp. 54, 55–7, 65, 107, 108, 197–8; Schnapper 1980–81, pp. 599, 600; Bryson 1981, pp. 128–9, 131, 137, 190; Nemilova 1982, no. 123; Bukdahl 1982, pp. 175, 208, 215, 242, 261–2, 274, 287, 334, 335, 349, 353; Arquile-Bruley 1983, pp. 127, 128, 129, 132, 134–5, 137; Diderot 1984, pp. 232–7; Crow 1985, pp. 151–3, pl. 60; Nemilova 1985, no. 59

First exhibited at the Salon of 1763, *Filial Piety* received Diderot's enthusiastic praise. The long essay on the painting in the Livret for the exhibition is one of his best-known critical works, and in it Diderot warmly greeted the appearance of a new genre of painting:

> Firstly, I like the genre. This is moral painting. Has not the brush sufficiently and too long been consecrated to debauchery and vice? Should we not be satisfied to see it compete at last with dramatic poetry in touching us, instructing us, correcting us and inviting us to virtue? Courage, my friend Greuze! Make your painting moral, and do it always. When you shall be on the point of quitting life, there shall be none of your compositions which you cannot recall without pleasure.

Intriguingly, Munhall (Diderot 1984, p. 235) suggests that the relationship developed the other way round – that it was not Greuze who founded a new genre, but Diderot who founded his own concept of a new genre on *Filial Piety*. Certainly the increasing moralizing in Greuze's work between *L'Accordee de village* (Louvre, Paris) of just two years earlier and the truly high-toned *La Malediction paternelle* of a decade later (1777–8, Louvre), shows a startlingly swift development. In addition, Diderot paid close attention to the psychological portraits in *Filial Piety*, finding that 'each here gets that degree of interest which is suitable to his age and character', but limited his comments on the painting's execution to colour, as usual putting in a good word for the artist who embodied the ideal for him in this sphere: 'His colouring is good and strong, albeit it is not yet that of Chardin' (Diderot 1763).

A similarly passionate response was felt in the wider circle of connoisseurs, critics and art lovers; the Abbé Aubert even wrote a moralizing tale under the painting's influence (Aubert 1763). Nearly every commentator felt it necessary to dwell on an analysis of the composition overall and of the individual characters. And behind this work of fundamental importance both for Greuze and for the Enlightenment lay a long and complex evolution, reflected in the numerous studies he made for every part of it. A pen drawing touched with gouache, signed and dated 1760 (passed at the Revil sale, 1845, no. 30) probably represents the first dim glimmer of an idea, and it is clear that Greuze took several years to work up his subject. Substantial alterations were made between the occasion of one of the early versions – an almost caricature-like drawing in the Musée des Beaux-Arts, Le Havre – and the eventual canvas.

Central to the painting is the bourgeois family, its values and virtues. The critic of *Affiche de Paris*, in his review of the Salon of 1763, also indicated another source: a little known literary work, a Latin poem, *Parentum manibus*, by the 16th-century Italian poet Marco Girolamo Vida, Archbishop of Alba (1489–1566), lamenting the death of his parents, who for years had lived far from him. Munhall (Diderot 1984, p. 235) analyses the suggested link – after all it was made by a contemporary of Greuze – and concludes that the literary and painted works were related mainly in terms of the broader concepts. Some of the expressions ('O douleur! O piété filiale!..') and the emotions expressed, none the less indicate that Greuze may have been familiar with the text: 'your age should never cause me boredom, and the inconveniences inseparable from

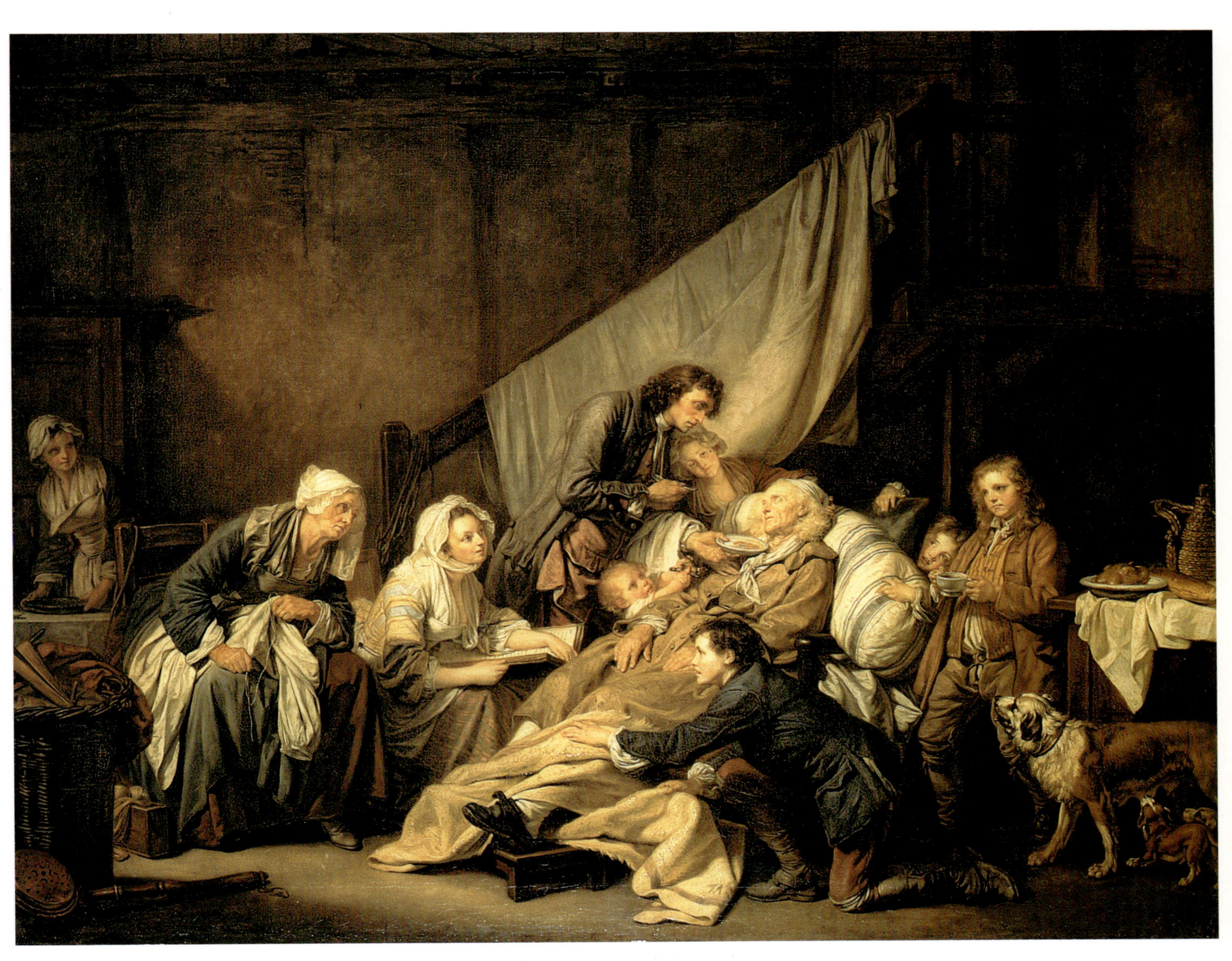

this age could never taint my affection, nor inspire disgust in me… nothing would have been more sweet to me in my whole house than to submit to your orders, to carry them out, to renounce grandeur in order to serve you alone' (*Les Vers à soie, poème de Jerome Vida de Cremone*, translated into French by J.-B. Levée, Paris, 1809, pp. 190, 194.) It remains purely hypothetical, however, since it is not clear how Greuze would made himself familiar with the Latin original, which was not available in French until 1809.

The sale of *Filial Piety* took no less time than its invention. In the Salon catalogue Greuze made an unusual note against the entry for his painting – 'Belongs to the author' – almost certainly a hint that he was willing to sell. According to Melchior Grimm, however, the price was unbelievably high, 2000 écus, and the painting remained unsold for a long time. One close contemporary suggested that the work was affordable only by wealthy collectors, but that such people preferred more pleasing subjects. In 1765 Diderot (1765) exclaimed in surprise: 'His Paralytic… is it not still in his studio?' To which Grimm replied, not without regret: 'Thanks to the Empress of Russia, the painting is no longer for sale. It is lost for France, but the artist has his recompense.' And he added, 'having not found a buyer for the painting, which cost him 200 louis in studies, he has allowed it to be sold to the Imperial Academy of Arts in St Petersburg in order to carry the painter's reputation to the furthest limits of Europe'. Diderot and Grimm also record that Greuze was invited to show *Filial Piety* to the court at Versailles, though not with its purchase in mind.

From the information provided by Grimm it follows that the painting was sold to Catherine in 1765, and it was traditionally thought within the Hermitage that it arrived in 1766, when it was entered in the inventory of the Imperial collection. But we know that Flipard, who began engraving the composition in 1764, didn't make his final alterations until 1767. *Filial Piety* probably arrived in Russia immediately afterwards. In passing, we should note that another engraver, Ingouf, in 1763–6 made a series of 'Heads of Different Characters' based on Greuze's figures. Undoubtedly the painting was also used as a study work for pupils at the Academy of Arts. In 1790 Fortia de Piles (1796) saw a marvellous Russian copy of it there. **E.D.**

51–58

Jean-Baptiste Greuze

Studies for Filial Piety (The Paralytic)

PROVENANCE: collection of Ivan Betskoy, St Petersburg; 1769 given by Betskoy to the Academy of Arts, St Petersburg (collector's mark L. 2699a); 1924 transferred to the Hermitage

Greuze's work on a painting was always preceded by a large number of preparatory drawings and sketches. According to Diderot in his review of the Salon of 1763 (at which *Filial Piety* was exhibited), Greuze 'draws like an angel … he makes studies endlessly; he spares neither effort nor expense in order to have the models which suit him… He is an endless observer in the streets, in churches, at markets and spectacles' (Diderot Salons 1957–67, vol. I, p. 233).

In addition to the nine drawings in the Hermitage, of which eight are included here, there is a long and impressive list of preparatory studies for *Filial Piety*. Of particular note is a sketch in ink for the overall composition (Musée des Beaux-Arts, Le Havre), several versions of the paralytic's head, and a study for the paralytic in red chalk (Hannema–de Stuers Foundation, Heino). As a body, these sheets are among Greuze's best drawings. Small alterations between the placing of the figures in a study and in the final painting can sometimes be seen, but in general each study is 'inserted' into its place.

Greuze's studies are almost always of large figures, heads or hands drawn on large sheets of paper. Strong, bold lines mould the forms and lend a sense of dynamism. He did not draw everything down to the tiniest detail, for these studies are generalized, yet they always capture quite expressively the most important features. Despite their very practical role in the preparation of his paintings, Greuze's drawings grew beyond their initially supplementary role as sketches and studies, and each stands as an independent work in its own right. Even so, when compared to the carefully finished portrait for the paralytic drawn in three chalks (cat. 51), the various figure studies in red chalk are of a more rapid, sketchy nature.

51

Head of an Old Man (Study for the Paralytic)

Red and black chalk with shading, touched with white chalk.
493 × 400 mm. Lined

Inv. no. 14727

EXHIBITIONS: 1956 Leningrad, p. 85; 1977a Leningrad, no. 57, ill.; 1986–7 Paris, no. 319, ill.; 1987 Leningrad–Moscow, no. 383, ill.; 1996 Karlsruhe, no. 66, ill.; 2000 Copenhagen, no. 2, ill.

LITERATURE: Monod 1922, no. 135, pl. LVI; Kamenskaya 1934a, pp. 79–93, ill.; Gerts 1948, p. 6, ill.; Novoselskaya 1977, pp. 14, 31, ill.; Novoselskaya 1985, p. 78; Novoselskaya 1987, pp. 5–7, fig.

There are a number of versions of the sick man's head; among them are two similar outstanding ones, this work in the Hermitage and one in the Nationalmuseum, Copenhagen. It is possible that the Hermitage drawing was the first of the two, and that the signed sheet in Copenhagen is a slightly improved repetition produced specifically for sale. Both heads are attractive in their expression and the nobility of the features, the old man's head being moulded softly with the aid of half-tones. Despite the limited colour – a consistent range of grey and brownish tones – both drawings are extremely painterly.

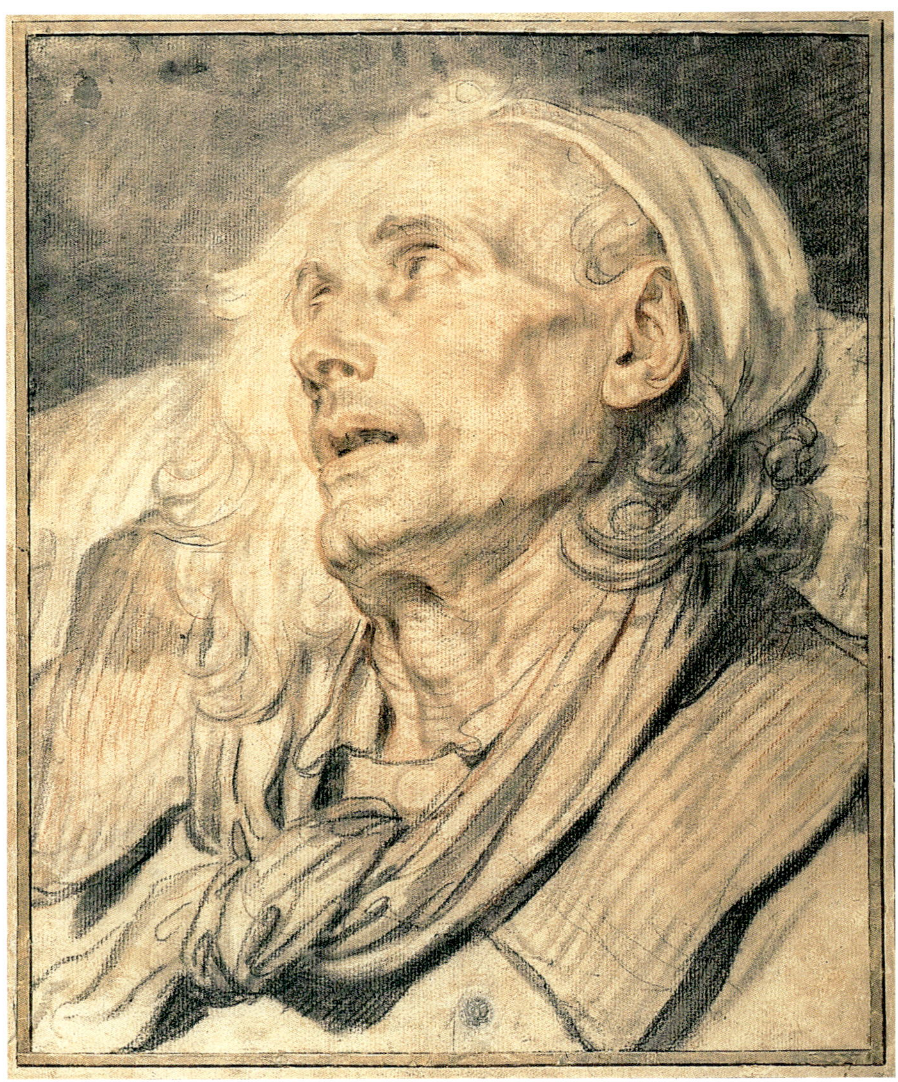

52

Study for the Paralytic's Wife

Red chalk. 388 × 294. Lined
Bottom left an old number in pen and ink: *9–48*
Old inscription in pen and brown ink on the back of the mount: *Etude du Paralitique*

Inv. no. 14802

EXHIBITIONS: 1956 Leningrad, p. 85; 1977a Leningrad, no. 58, ill.; 1986–7 Paris, no. 320, ill.; 1987 Leningrad–Moscow, no. 384, ill.; 1996 Karlsruhe, no. 67, ill.; 2000 Copenhagen, no. 3, ill.

LITERATURE: Monod 1922, no. 67; Kamenskaya 1934a, p. 86, ill.; Gerts 1948, p. 6; Novoselskaya 1977, pp. 14, 31, ill.; Novoselskaya 1985, p. 78; Novoselskaya 1987, pp. 4–7, fig.

Apart from the position of the hands, which were slightly altered for the painting, the seated wife's pose remained unchanged. Minor adjustments were made to her clothing.

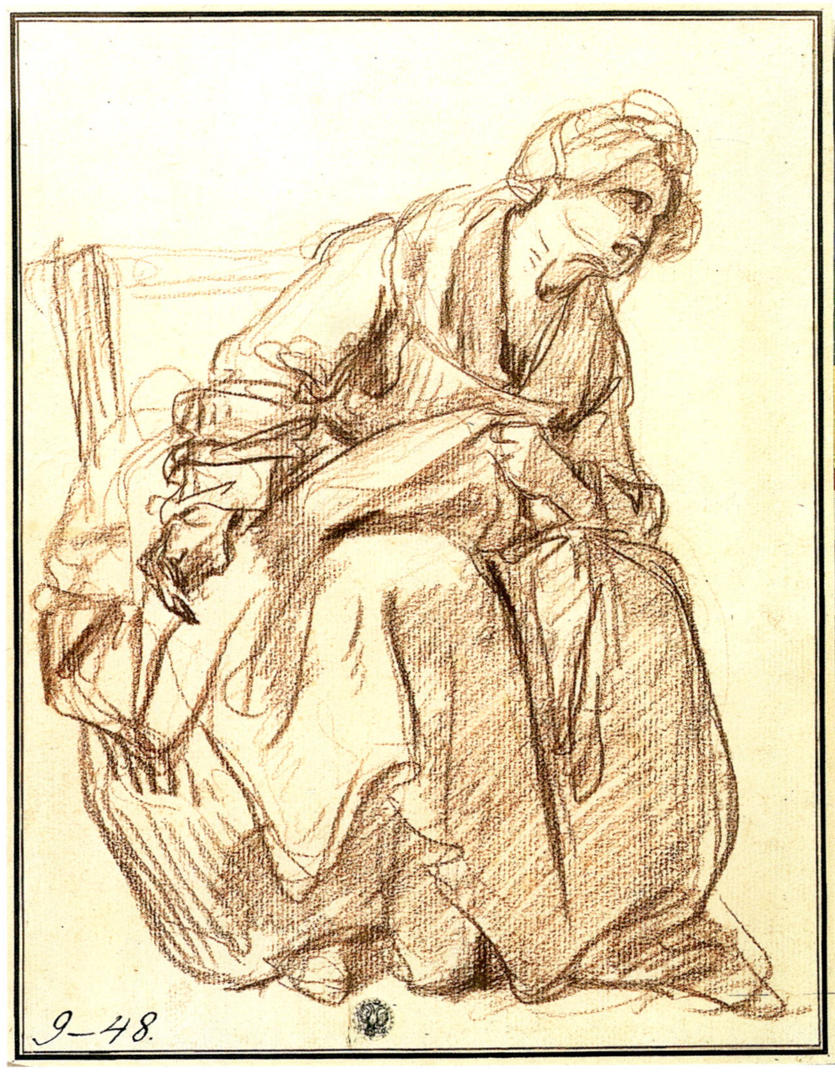

53

Study for the Son-in-Law

Red chalk. 492 × 316 mm. LinedBottom left an old number in pen and ink: *9–67* On the back of the mount an old inscription in pen and brown ink, cut off at the edge of the sheet: *Etude du tableau, La pieté, filiale, ou le Parali…*

Inv. no. 14794

EXHIBITIONS: 1977a Leningrad, no. 59, ill.; 2000 Copenhagen, no. 4, ill.

LITERATURE: Monod 1922, no. 54; Novoselskaya 1977, pp. 14, 31, ill.; Novoselskaya 1987, pp. 5–7

This preparatory study for the son-in-law feeding the sick man clearly represents the initial idea, for in the painting itself he is less bent over, the placing of the hands and details in the clothing have been altered, and the legs are hidden behind foreground figures. There is a study of the son-in-law's head in the Museum of the Academy of Arts, St Petersburg (inv. no. 2016).

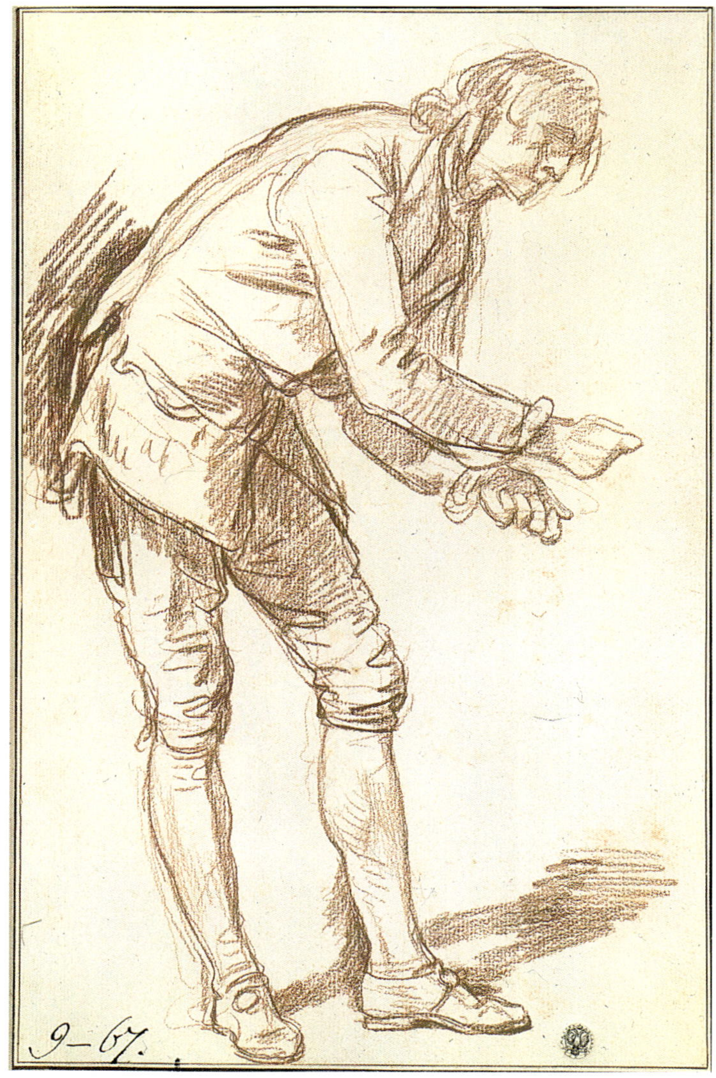

54

Study for the Son-in-Law (Second Version)

Red chalk. 481 × 320 mm. Lined
Bottom left an old number in pen and ink: *9–59*
Old inscription in pen and brown ink on the back of the mount: *Etude du Paralitique*

Inv. no. 14792

EXHIBITIONS: 1977a Leningrad, no. 60, ill.; 1986–7 Paris, no. 321, ill.; 1987 Leningrad–Moscow, no. 385, ill.; 1996 Karlsruhe, no. 68, ill.; 2000 Copenhagen, no. 5, ill.

LITERATURE: Monod 1922, no. 53, pl. XX; Novoselskaya 1977, pp. 31, ill.; Novoselskaya 1985, p. 78; Novoselskaya 1987, pp. 4–7, fig.

This was clearly made after the previous drawing, for this study is closer to the final painting, where the son-in-law stands with a plate in his hand, feeding the sick man. None the less, there are still some differences between the drawing and the painting in the pose, the placing of the hands and the costume.

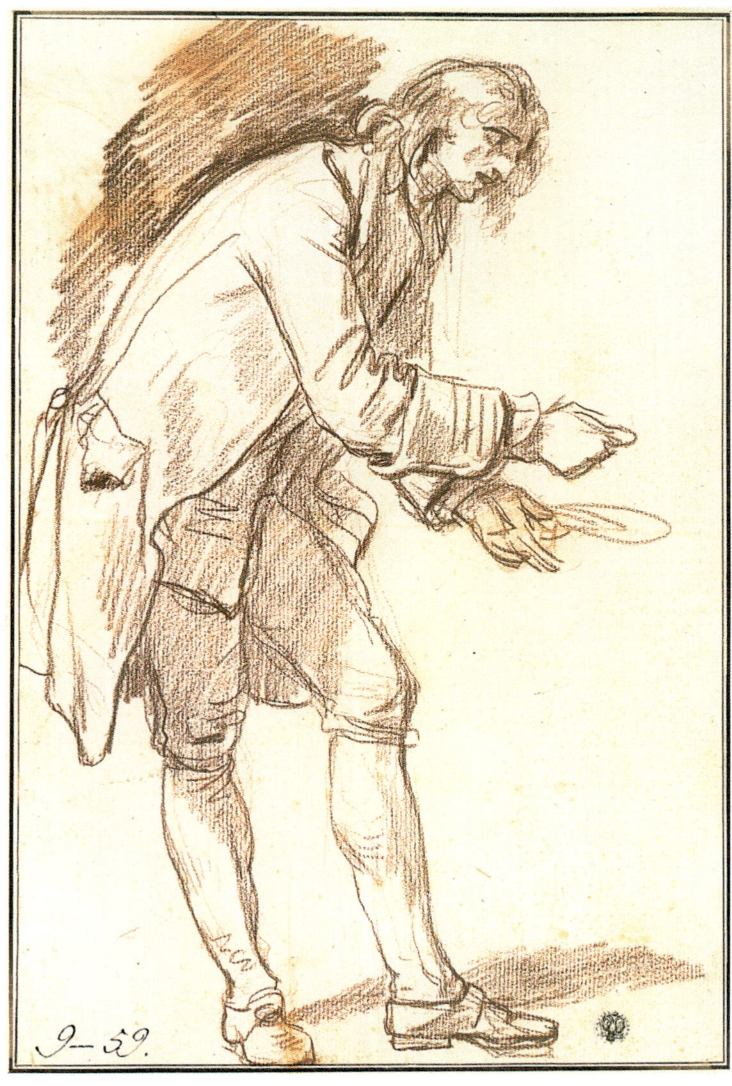

55

Study for the Boy Bearing a Cup

Red chalk. 388 × 294 mm. Lined
Bottom left an old number in pen and ink: *9–65*
Old inscription in pen and brown ink on the back of the mount: *Etude du Paralitique*

Inv. no. 14785

EXHIBITIONS: 1977a Leningrad, no. 61, ill.; 2000 Copenhagen, no. 6, ill.

LITERATURE: Monod 1922, no. 43; Novoselskaya 1977, pp. 14, 31, 32, ill.; Novoselskaya 1987, pp. 5–7, fig.

This is probably the first study for the boy who brings the patient a drink: in cat. 56, and in the painting itself, the boy is walking rather than standing. In this first drawing, however, the placing of the head and the boy's age are more in accordance with the painting.

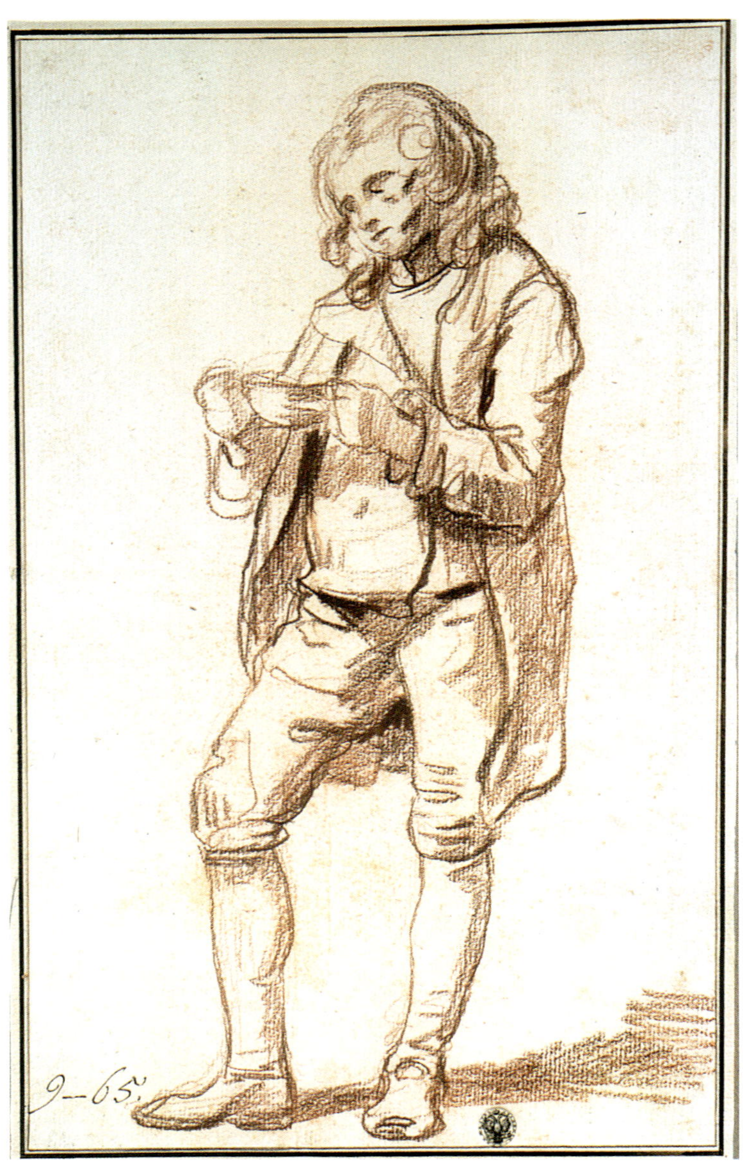

56

Study for the Boy Bearing a Cup (Second Version)

Red chalk. 433 × 299 mm. Lined
Bottom left an old number in pen and ink: *9–37*
Old inscription in pen and brown ink on the back of the mount: *Etude du Paralitique*

Inv. no. 14784

EXHIBITIONS: 1977a Leningrad, no. 62, ill.; 1986–7 Paris, no. 322, ill.; 1987 Leningrad–Moscow, no. 386, ill.; 1996 Karlsruhe, no. 69, ill.; 2000 Copenhagen, no. 7, ill.

LITERATURE: Monod 1922, no. 42; Kamenskaya 1934a, p. 86, ill.; Novoselskaya 1977, pp. 14, 32, ill.; Novoselskaya 1987, pp. 5–7

This second study is clearly closer to the painting, although the boy in this drawing could almost be standing, and his concentration is wholly on not spilling the cup's contents.

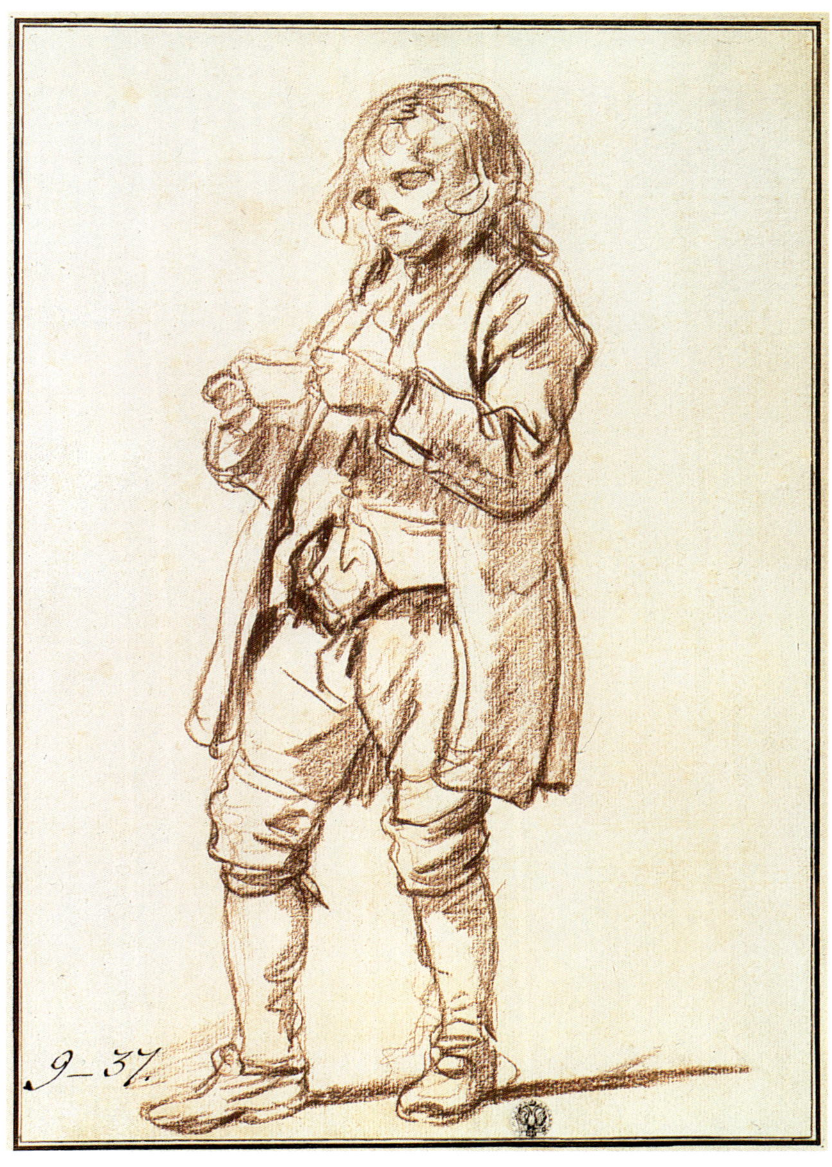

57

Study for the Boy Covering the Paralytic's Legs

Red chalk. 328 × 459 mm. Lined
Bottom left an old number in pen and ink: *9–62*
Old inscription in pen and brown ink on the back of the mount: *Etude du Paralitique*

Inv. no. 14798

EXHIBITIONS: 1977a Leningrad, no. 63, ill.; 1986–7 Paris, no. 323, ill.; 1987 Leningrad–Moscow, no. 387, ill.; 1996 Karlsruhe, no. 70, ill.; 2000 Copenhagen, no. 8, ill.

LITERATURE: Monod 1922, no. 59; Kamenskaya 1934a, p. 86, ill.; Novoselskaya 1977, pp. 14, 32, ill.; Novoselskaya 1987, pp. 5–7.

The boy's pose in this drawing is close to that of the painting, although the turn of the head differs slightly and the costume has been altered.

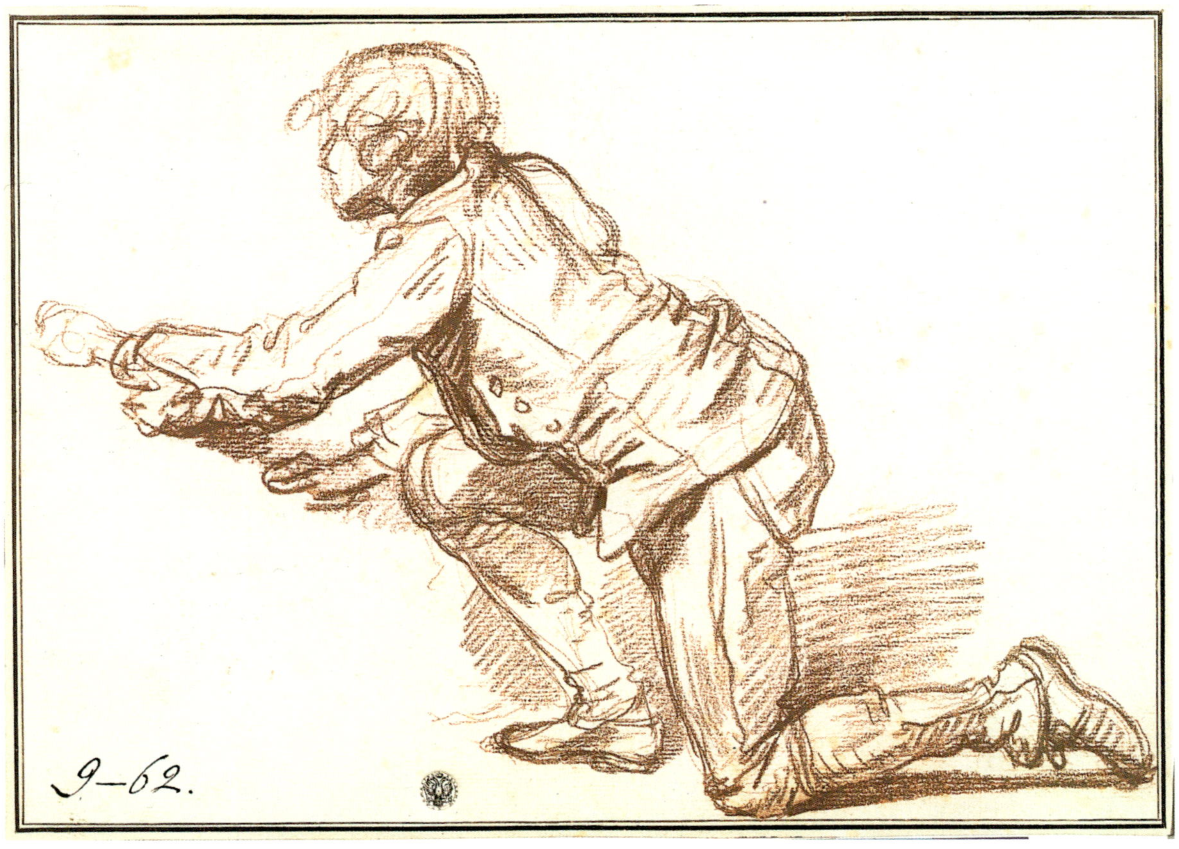

58

Study for the Dog

Red chalk. 328 × 453 mm. Lined
Bottom left an old number in pen and ink: *9–81*
On the back of the mount an old inscription in pen and brown ink: *Etude du Paralitique*

Inv. no. 14770

EXHIBITIONS: 1903 St Petersburg, p. 18; 1972 Prague, no. 45; 1974 Manchester, no. 38, ill.; 1975 Aarhus, no. 31; 1975 Copenhagen, no. 31; 1977a Leningrad, no. 64, ill.; 1978–9 Melbourne–Sydney–Adelaide, no. 22, ill.; 1986–7 Paris, no. 324, ill.; 1987 Leningrad–Moscow, no. 388, ill.; 1996 Karlsruhe, no. 71, ill.; 2000 Copenhagen, no. 10, ill.

LITERATURE: World of Art 1903, no. 12; Monod 1922, no. 18; Kamenskaya 1934a, p. 86, ill.; Novoselskaya 1977, pp. 14, 32, ill.; Novoselskaya 1987, pp. 5–7, fig.

This study of the bitch sympathetically gazing up at her master is closely followed in the painting, although with the addition there of suckling pups, reinforcing the painting's theme of care and benevolence between generations.
I.N.

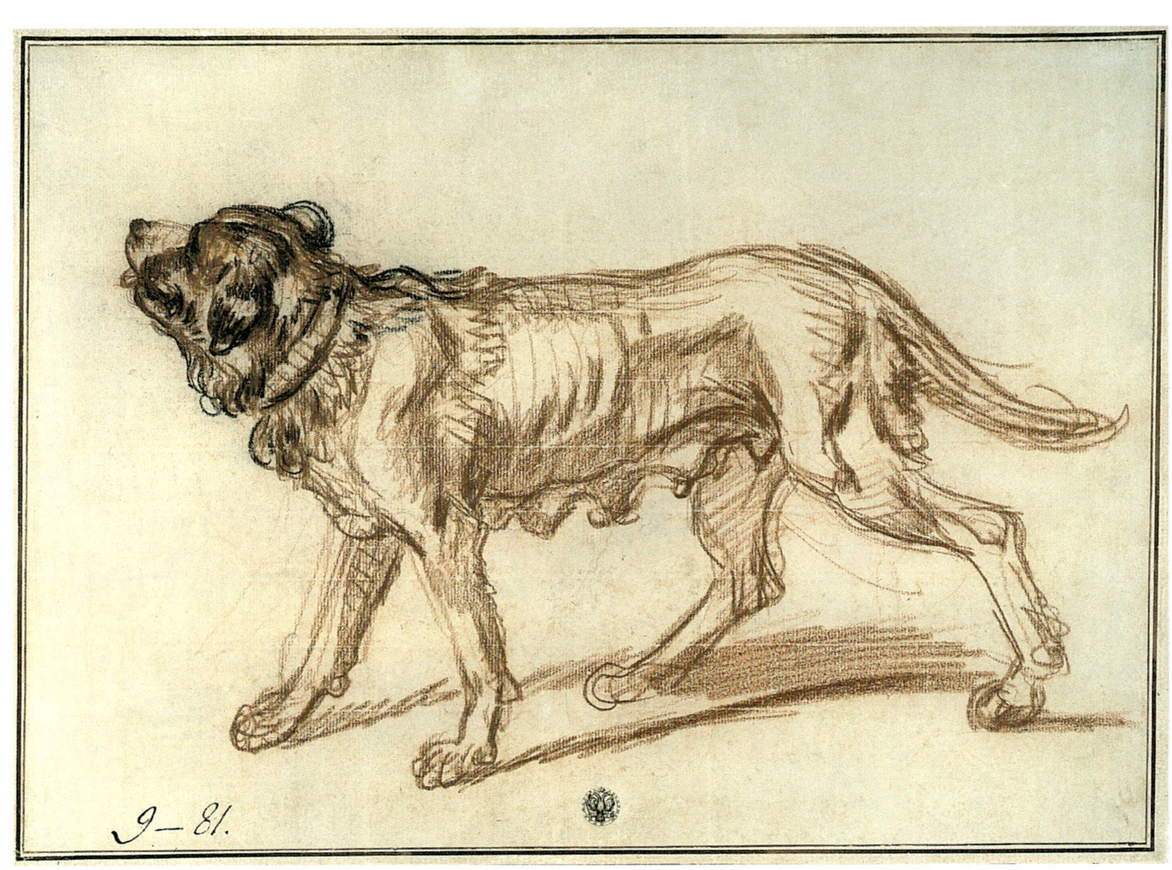

59

Jean-Baptiste Greuze

The Schoolteacher

Pen and ink, ink wash and brown wash. 330 × 444 mm. Lined

Signed in pen and brown ink bottom left and on the back of the child being punished in the centre: *J.B.Greuze*

PROVENANCE: collection of Count Carl Cobenzl, Brussels (collector's mark L. 2858b); 1768 acquired for the Hermitage: Collector's mark L. 2061

Inv. no. OR 3746

OLD MANUSCRIPT CATALOGUES: Cobenzl – 'Catal[ogue] de Cabin[et], Catalogue de Desseins, Troisième Grandeur' , p. 44v., Carton no. 5, no. 25, 'Greuze, La Maîtresse d'Ecole'

EXHIBITIONS: 1926 Leningrad, no. 205; 1955 Moscow, p. 73; 1956 Leningrad, p. 86; 1963 Stockholm, no. 44; 1969 Leningrad–Moscow, no. 17; 1977a Leningrad, no. 85, ill.; 1983 Leningrad, no. 25, ill.; 1996 Karlsruhe, no. 75, ill.; 1998–9 New York, no. 98, ill.

LITERATURE: Makarenko 1916, pp. 222, 224; Joffé 1932, p. 80; Kamenskaya 1934b, pp. 221, 222, ill.; Kamenskaya 1947, ill.; Novoselskaya 1975, p. 474, ill.; Novoselskaya 1977, pp. 37, 38, ill.; Novoselskaya 1983, pp. 31–3, ill.

T. D. Kamenskaya (1934b, pp. 221, 222) suggested that this drawing is a satirical depiction of the literary salon of Mme Geoffrin, who had mocked Greuze's painting *Dearly Beloved Mother* (Collection de Laborde, Madrid), calling it a 'fricassé of children' (a sketch for the painting was exhibited at the Salon in 1765 and the painting itself was announced for the Salon in 1769 but not actually exhibited that year). Greuze told Baron Grimm that he had made a portrait of Mme Geoffrin 'as a schoolteacher, her stick in her hand, and she shall frighten all the children both present and yet to be born' (recorded in Diderot 1876, vi/9, p. 443). Kamenskaya must be correct, and Mme Geoffrin's words must have been directed at the sketch exhibited in 1765. It is roughly to that time that this drawing should be dated, for it arrived at the Hermitage as early as 1768, before the painting *Dearly Beloved Mother* had been completed.

In the manuscript catalogue of the collection of Carl Cobenzl, this drawing is entitled 'La Maîtresse d'école' (i.e., 'The Schoolteacher'), but some later scholars (Dobroklonsky 1926; Kamenskaya 1947) preferred to call it 'The Country School'. Kamenskaya, however, suggested that Cobenzl's title had been the artist's own, and something of a play on words – 'La Maîtresse d'école' and 'La Maîtresse du Salon'. It is best, then, to keep to the original title.

Another drawing by Greuze also known as *The Schoolteacher* was formerly in the George III Gallery at Dresden. It showed a male teacher standing with a rod in one hand and an alphabet in the other; a little girl knelt before him while the remaining children continued with their lessons (Martin, Masson [1905], no. 326). Like many other themes, clearly this one, whether used for satirical ends or not, was taken up and varied in Greuze's work over a number of years. I.N.

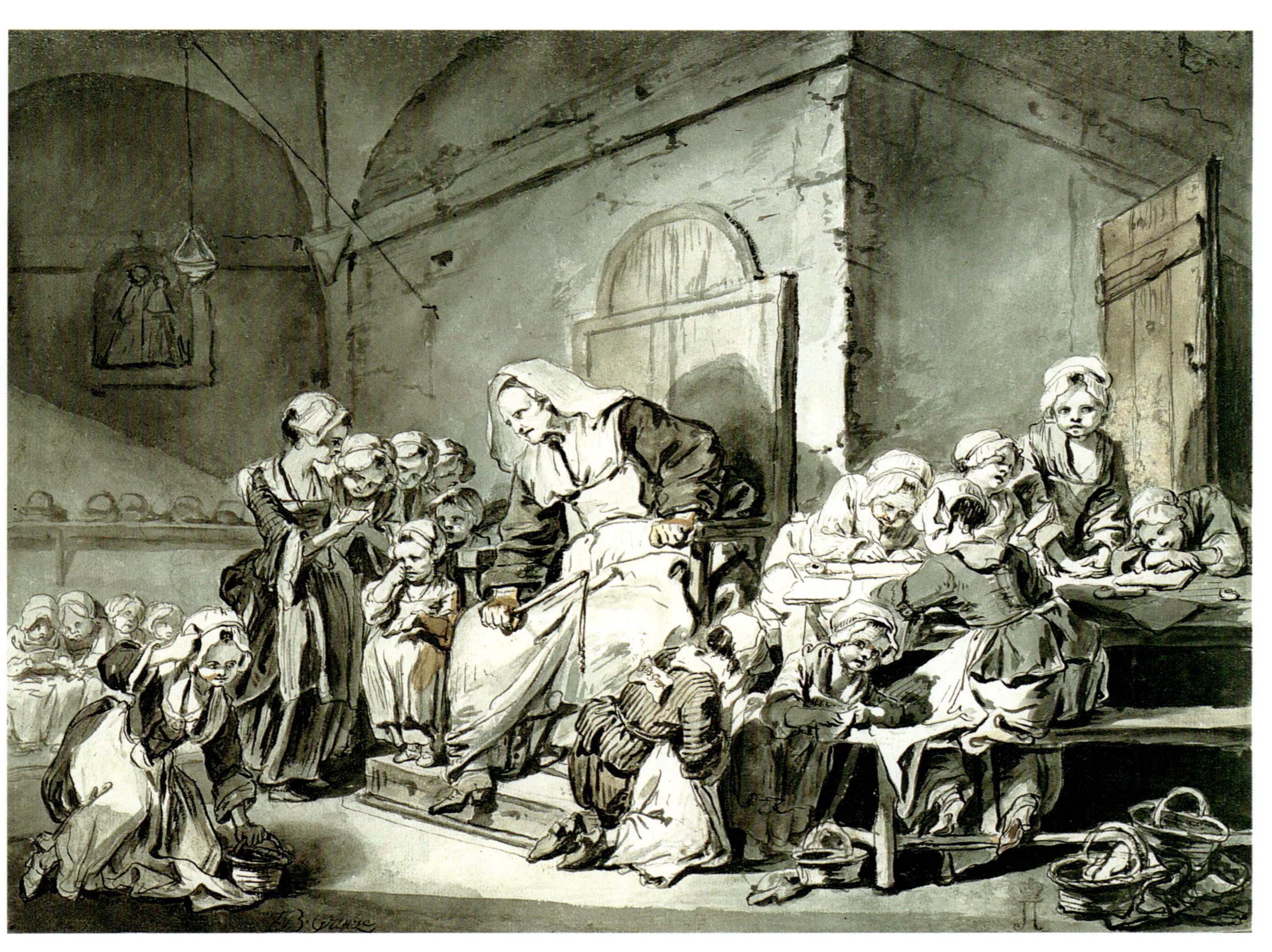

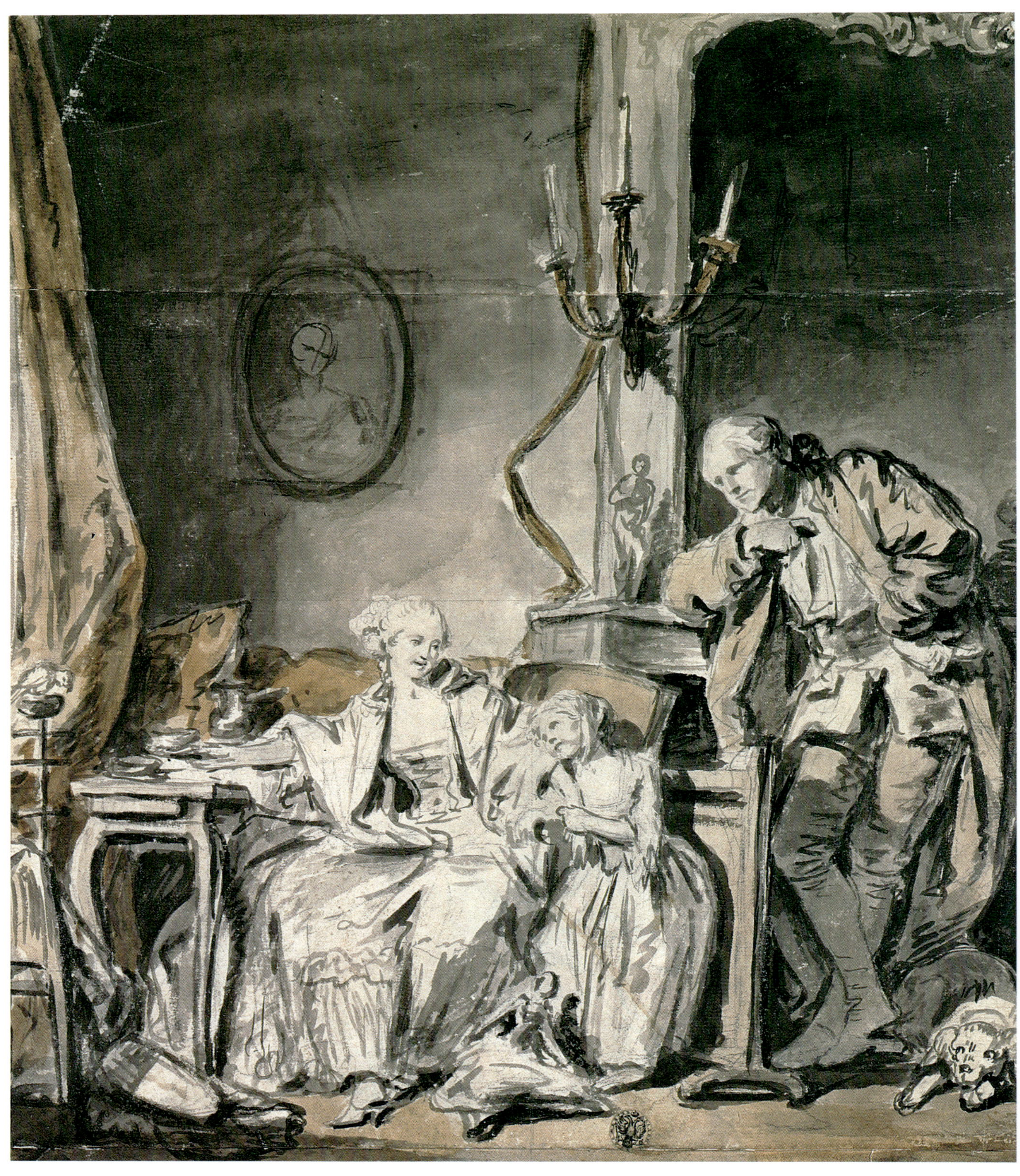

60

Jean-Baptiste Greuze

A Family Scene

Ink wash and brown wash over black chalk preparatory sketch.
457 × 400 mm.
Sheet glued together from three pieces arranged horizontally. Lined

PROVENANCE: collection of Ivan Betskoy, St Petersburg; 1769 given by Betskoy to the Academy of Arts, St Petersburg (collector's mark L. 2699a); 1924 transferred to the Hermitage

Inv. no. OR 14772

EXHIBITIONS: 1903 St Petersburg, no. 431; 1926 Leningrad, no. 206; 1977a Leningrad, no. 86, ill.; 1994 Ibaraki–Mie–Tokyo, no. 69, pl.; 1996 Karlsruhe, no. 76, ill.

LITERATURE: World of Art 1903, no. 12, p. 230, ill.; Martin, Masson [1905], no. 377 (under the title Tea, with the then incorrect indication of location as the Hermitage); Monod 1922, no. 25, pl. III; Novoselskaya 1977, pp. 38, 39, ill.; Novoselskaya 1985, p. 78

This drawing may well be a self-portrait of Greuze and his family. The likeness between the man shown here and known self-portraits of Greuze (Musée Greuze, Tournus; Louvre, Paris) is a close one, even though the artist was considerably shorter. The similarities between the woman and portraits of Greuze's wife in various drawings (*Young Woman in an Armchair*, Hermitage, inv. no. 14767; study of the fiancée in the painting *A Marriage Contract*, Musée Denon, Chalon-sur-Saône) should also be noted. Although female figures in Greuze's works often have something of his wife's features, the similarity here seems absolutely incontrovertible.

Between 1759 and 1764 Greuze's wife gave birth to three daughters, although the first died when very young. This drawing should clearly be dated to the mid-1760s, when Greuze was about 40 years old and the middle daughter, Anne-Geneviève, who was to go on to study under him, was about four. Since the drawing was produced for private purposes and was not a commissioned work, it remained in Greuze's family for some time. No painting from it is known.

In the Albertina, Vienna, is a version of this drawing entitled *Tea* (pen and wash in black and brown ink; inv. no. 12764). The Albertina drawing probably represents the artist's first ideas, which were then developed in the Hermitage sheet: the latter composition includes the man, while several features in the interior have been changed or added, such as the portrait hanging on the wall. The Hermitage sheet is somewhat more drawn out vertically (clearly the artist was determining the ideal proportions, adding pieces onto the original sheet to top and bottom) and the overall effect is more finished.

A Family Scene is executed in a free painterly manner and is suffused with a sense of warmth and affection. Its disingenuous and poetic nature adds to its enormous appeal. I.N.

61

Hubert Robert

Paris 1733 – 1808 Paris

Villa Madama

Pen and ink, ink wash and watercolour. 305 × 419 mm. Lined

PROVENANCE: collection of a. N. Vorobyov, St Petersburg; 1924 transferred to the Hermitage

Inv. no. OR 14307

EXHIBITIONS: 1926 Leningrad, no. 233; 1937 Leningrad, no. 93; 1955 Moscow, p. 83; 1956 Leningrad, p. 96; 1959 Leningrad, p. 29; 1963 Stockholm, no. 47; 1970 Budapest, no. 95, ill.; 1975 Berlin, no. 94, ill.; 1982 Florence, no. 97, ill.; 1983 Leningrad, no. 55, ill.; 1984b Leningrad, no. 55, ill.

LITERATURE: Kamenskaya 1939, pp. 8, 9, ill.; Novoselskaya 1975, p. 474; Novoselskaya 1981, p. 106, ill.

The Hermitage's holding of drawings by Hubert Robert, a pupil of Giovanni Panini (*c.* 1691–1766), comes mainly from his years in Italy, 1754–65. It was there that Robert made the numerous marvellous studies that later served as the basis for so many of his paintings.

One of Robert's favourite subjects in Rome and its environs was the Villa Madama, which had been built from 1517 to designs by Raphael, Giulio Romano and Antonio da Sangallo the Younger for Cardinal Giulio Medici (from 1521 Pope Clement VII). It was later owned by Margaret of Parma, daughter of the Holy Roman Emperor Charles V (hence the Villa's name: the title of Madame being given to the monarch's eldest daughter). The Villa Madama was never completed, and by the 18th century was in a semi-ruinous state.

In 1759–60 Robert made several red chalk drawings of the Madama from different points of view, showing various parts of the building. Of the surviving drawings, the counterproof in the Hermitage, *The Loggias of the Villa Madama* (Hermitage, inv. no. OR 25475), and a red chalk drawing in the Musée de Valence, *Washerwomen at the Villa Madama* (inv. no. D. 37), should be mentioned. This pen, wash and watercolour drawing in the Hermitage is dated to *c.* 1760 on the basis of a similar drawing in the Albertina, Vienna, which bears that date. Robert produced two painted versions based on his drawings (fig. 38), both entitled *The Villa Madama near Rome*, which today are in the Hermitage. I.N.

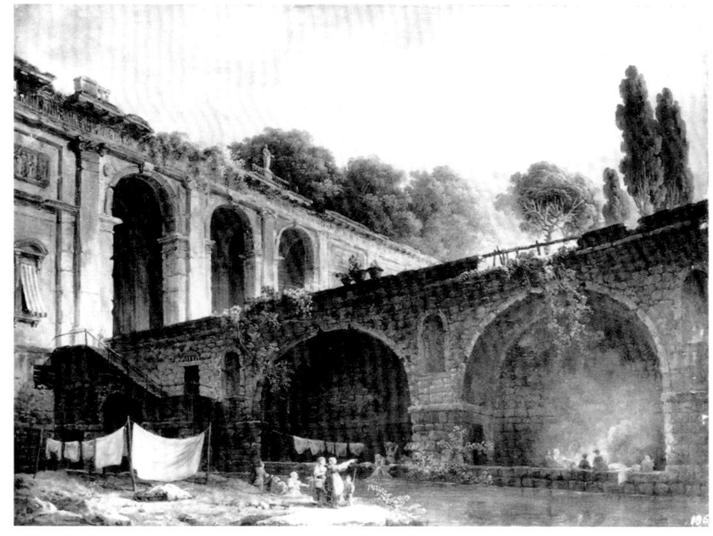

fig. 38
Hubert Robert
Villa Madama near Rome

oil on canvas
(inv. no. GE 5649)

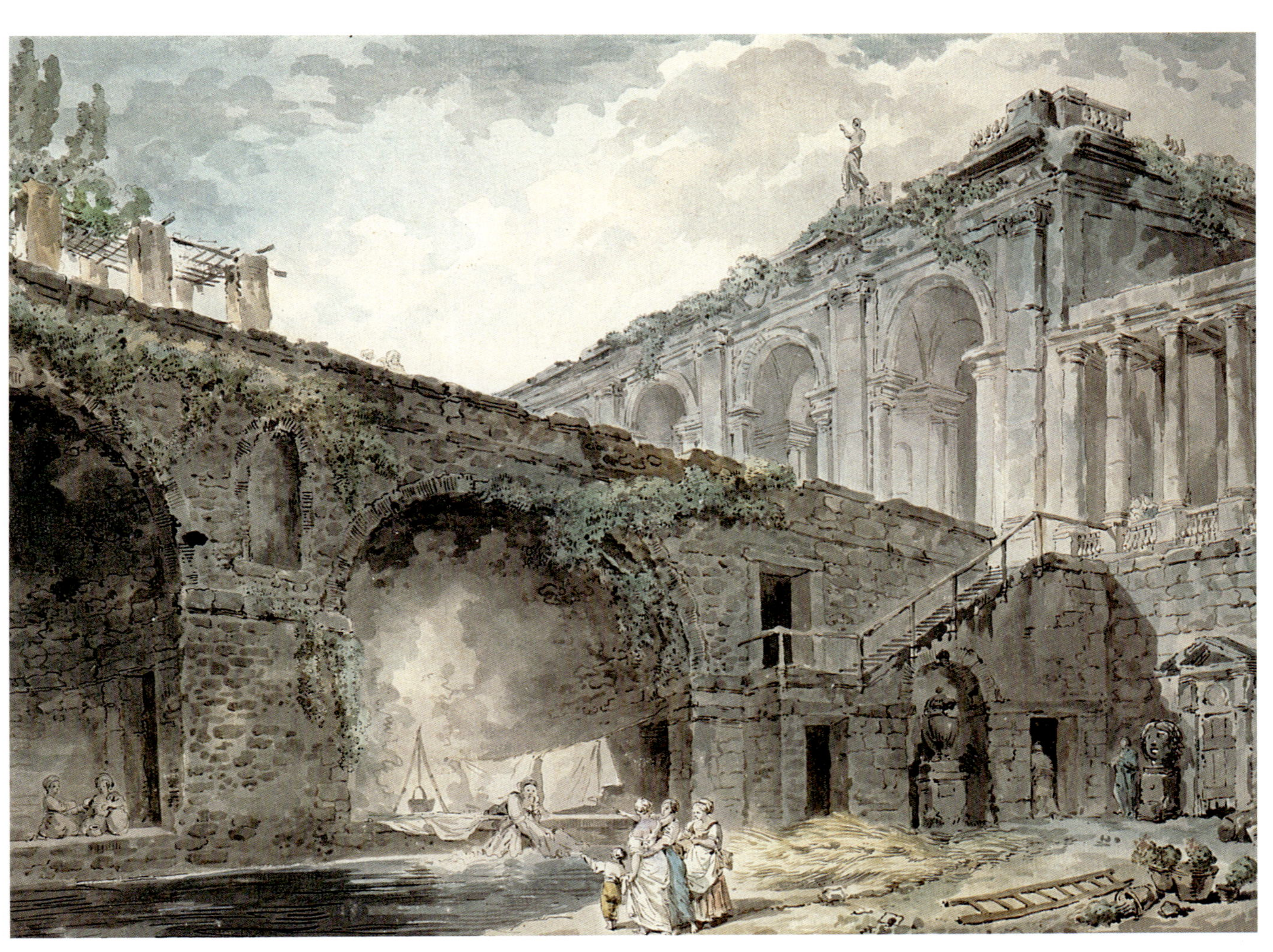

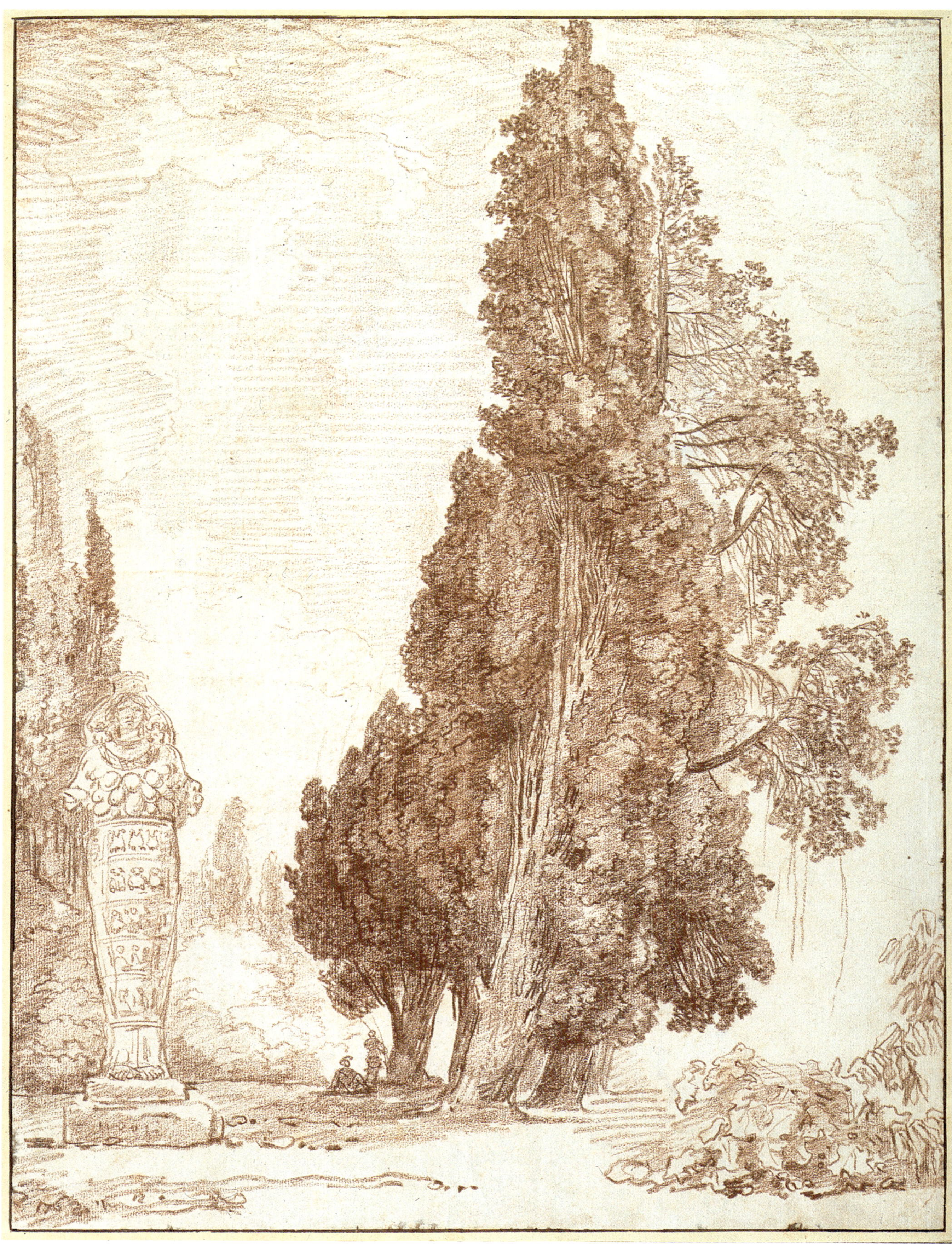

62

Hubert Robert

Landscape with Cypress Trees and a Statue of Diana of Ephesus

Red chalk. 448 × 335 mm. Lined
Dated in red chalk in the bottom left corner: *1762*

PROVENANCE: Russian Museum, St Petersburg; 1929 transferred to the Hermitage

Inv. no. OR 25474

EXHIBITIONS: 1955 Moscow, p. 83; 1956 Leningrad, p. 96; 1972 Vienna–Graz, no. 57, ill.; 1984b Leningrad, no. 85, ill.; 1990–91 Rome, no. 110, ill.; 1996 Karlsruhe, no. 56, ill.

Previously published: Gabillot 1895, pp. 216, 217

LITERATURE: Kamenskaya 1939, p. 9, ill.; Novoselskaya 1981, p. 103, ill.; Cayeux 1987, pp. 38, 40, fig.

In the early 1760s, when he was living in Italy, Robert often adopted the motif of some forgotten statue peeking out from amid the overgrowth in some quiet corner of a park, as in the drawing *Corner of a Park* (fig. 39). Although this *Landscape with Cypress Trees* at first seems to fit into this context, it is clearly conceived in a different spirit, inspired by the park of the Villa d'Este at Tivoli (although we do not know if Robert actually visited the Villa d'Este in 1762).

In the centre of the sheet is a group of cypress trees shooting upwards and forming a gigantic pyramid; the tall, slender tree in the centre, with tiny figures nearby, touches the edge of the sheet. Standing near to these monumental forms, the statue of Diana of Ephesus, goddess of fertility, is dwarfed, and there is a further sense of contrast between the sculpture's stillness and the dynamism of the cypress trees, between the dark silhouette of the latter and the pale, only lightly indicated carving.

As in many of his works, particularly those of his earlier period, Robert departed somewhat from reality in his depiction: we can presume that the cypresses were drawn from nature, but although a fountain statue of Diana of Ephesus has for centuries stood in the gardens at the Villa d'Este, it differs from the one shown here. The fountain statue actually occupies an arched niche, while Robert's has no architectural context.

Robert often dated his drawings without signing them, as here, where the numbers are woven into the pattern of the grass in the foreground. I.N.

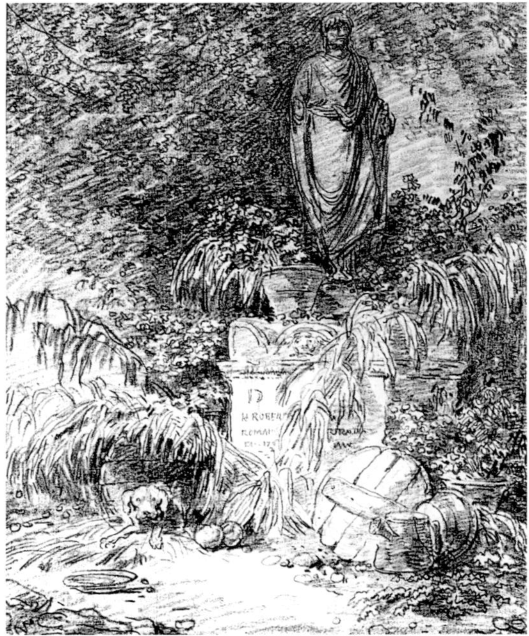

fig. 39
Hubert Robert,
Corner of a Park

(inv. no. OR 25335)

63

Hubert Robert

A Young Lady Drawing Amid Antique Ruins

Pen and ink, ink wash and watercolour. 263 × 376 mm

Signed and dated in pen and ink in large capitals in the lower part, on the stone: *H.ROBERT DELINEAVIT ANNO 1796*

PROVENANCE: collection of G. I. Byalik, Leningrad; 1977 acquired by the Hermitage through the Purchasing Commission

Inv. no. OR 46524

EXHIBITIONS: 1977b Leningrad, no. 56, ill.; 1986 Bogota, ill.; 1986 Buenos Aires, no. 63, ill.; 1986 Montevideo, no. 63, ill.; 1994 Ibaraki–Mie–Tokyo, no. 72, ill.; 1996 Karlsruhe, no. 69, ill.

LITERATURE: Novoselskaya 1981, p. 106, ill.

Robert's late period is represented in the Hermitage collection by this watercolour which, according to the Classical scholar Y. V. Mavleyev (personal communication), recalls the Greek architecture of southern Italy.

An artist – male or female – at work amid architectural monuments and ruins is a common subject in Robert's work. Thus in the Louvre's Département des Arts Graphiques is a watercolour composition dated 1786, *Two Young Women Drawing Amid Antique Ruins* (inv. no. RF 31695), and the Hermitage itself has a similar painting, *Artists* (inv. no. 6407). Many more such examples could be cited. This relatively late work stands apart from Robert's earlier undertakings in its greater compactness, the use of a single plane and the relatively large figures. We are drawn by the vividness of the depiction: the girl deeply involved in her painting and the young man in his hat and cape stretched out on a fractured frieze.

In comparison with earlier watercolours, such as the *Villa Madama* (cat. 61), Robert's colouring has undergone no radical changes: we see the same brown, grey and greenish tones with scatterings of white, pale blue and pink, but the colour has become purer and more transparent.

As in the Louvre drawing, the signature in large capitals and the date appear on one of the rocks. Dated drawings from Robert's later period are relatively rare: Cayeux notes that the date 1796 is found on only one drawing apart from this one in the Hermitage (Cayeux 1970, p. 103, note 24), and after 1796 no dates are found at all. All the greater, then, is the value of this high-quality work. I.N.

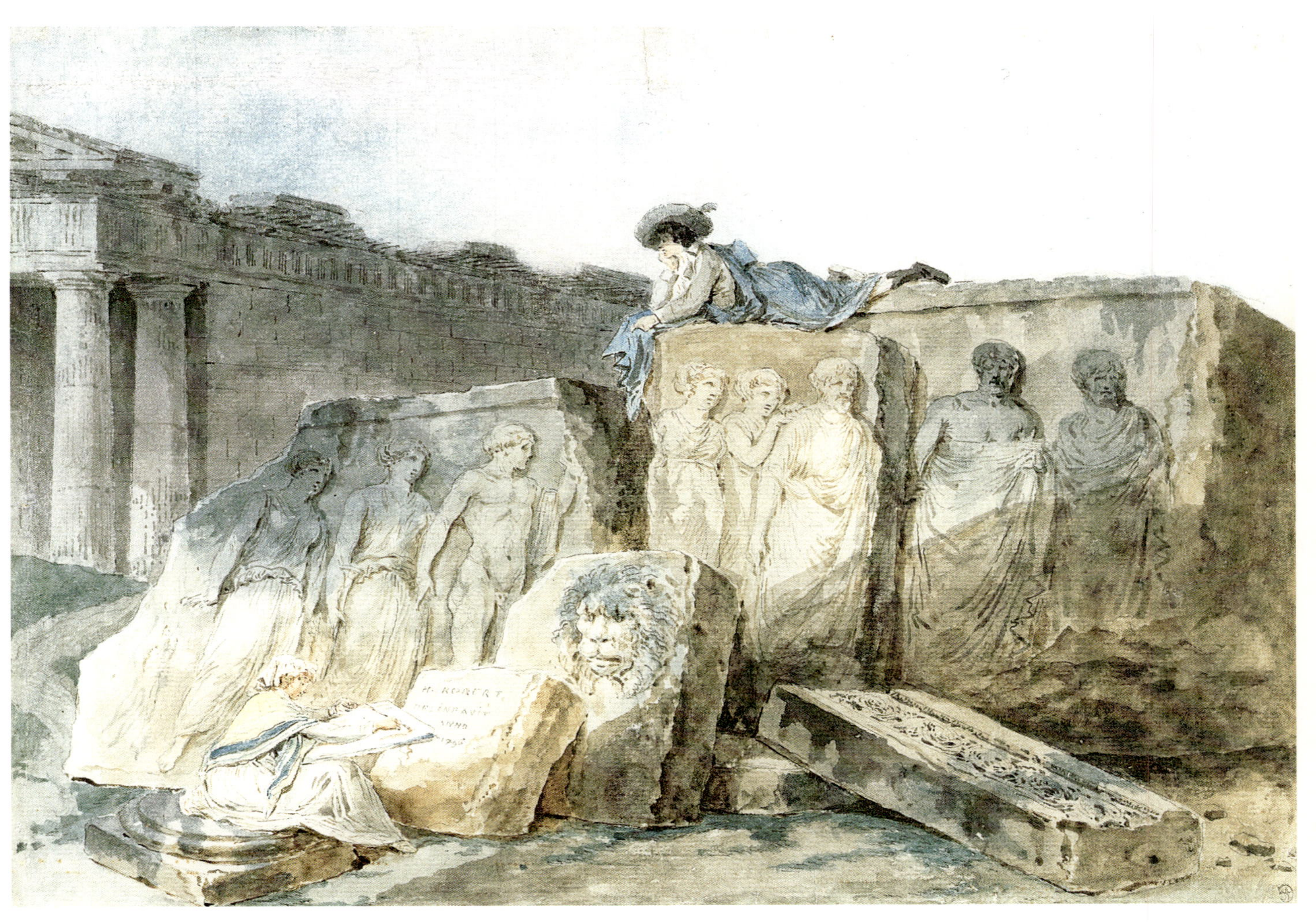
H. ROBERT

64

Charles de Wailly

Paris 1729 – 1798 Paris

Design for a Pavilion of the Arts and Sciences in an English-style Park (Élévation perspective du côté de l'entrée du temple de Minerve)

Pen and ink, wash. 562 × 923 mm; attached to a sheet in an album: 620 × 950 mm

PROVENANCE: 1773 gift to Catherine II from the author; before 1811 transferred from the Winter Palace to the Hermitage

Inv. no. 6869

OLD MANUSCRIPT CATALOGUES: listed in three manuscript inventory catalogues: 1811, 1821 and that 'corrected in 1839'. In the 'Inventory of Drawings by Various Original Masters Found in the Imperial Hermitage' of 1821, the album is listed as 'Book no. 152' with the pencil note 'To be done' (i.e., introduce corrections). In the title of the design, 'Pavilion of the Sciences and the Arts Beneath the Emblem of Minerva', is an addition in pencil: 'presented to Emp.[ress] Cath.[erine] II by archit.[ect] de Wailly'

EXHIBITIONS: 1971b Leningrad, no. 14, ill.; 1979 Paris–Leningrad, no. 296, ill.; 1986–7 Paris, no. 419; 1987 Leningrad–Moscow, nos. 260–2; 1998–9 Stockholm, p. 328, no. 294, ill. p. 322; 1999–2000 St Petersburg, no. 59, ill. p. 29

LITERATURE: Lavallée 1798, p. 19; SbRIO 1876, vol. XVII, p. 212; Hautecœur 1912, p. 41; Voronikhina 1971, pp. 32–3, ill.; Fuhring 1989, vol. II, p. 500, no. 786, ill.; Diderot Salons 1957–67, vol. IV, p. 204; Shevchenko 1997, p. 83, note 7; 1997 Venice, no. 91, ill.; GBA 1998, p. 12, no. 47, ill.; Starcky 1999, pp. 9–20, fig. 11; Dittscheid 1999, pp. 21–8

The prolific architect and talented draughtsman Charles de Wailly was well known both for the Théâtre de l'Odéon, Paris (built 1779–82), and for the regular exhibition of his works at the annual Salon. Among the many pupils from various countries who studied in his Paris studio were the Russian architects Vasily Bazhenov, Ivan Starov and Fyodor Volkov. How his drawings reached the Hermitage relates to Catherine the Great's desire to build a 'maison antique' in the park of her beloved summer residence at Tsarskoye Selo.

Catherine commissioned a design for a neo-Antique pavilion in 1773 from the architect Charles-Louis Clérisseau, but rejected the result for its impossibly huge scale (Hautecœur 1912, pp. 39–43; Shevchenko 1995c, pp. 66, 85; for information on the story behind the commission see Shevchenko 1997, p. 74). De Wailly had learned of Catherine's desire for a 'maison antique' early in 1772, before Clérisseau received his commission, from Prince Alexander Stroganov, the Russian ambassador in France. De Wailly's offering to Catherine is in many ways a repetition of his own design of ten years earlier for the Château de Montmusard de Dijon (partly destroyed during the French Revolution; Starcky 1999, pp. 9–20; Dittscheid 1999, pp. 21–8). Two of the new perspective views were exhibited at the Salon of 1773, and it was probably after this that one of them was put with other sheets in an album, bound in red morocco and sent to Catherine by the author. Such a timely gift (in November 1773), and one so richly bound, pleased the Empress (SbRIO 1876) mightily. Dittscheid suggested that Diderot, then at the Russian court, may have encouraged her to accept De Wailly's designs (Dittscheid 1999, p. 26). As a reward, Catherine sent the architect her portrait framed in diamonds, and later offered him the post of President of the Academy of Arts, with a salary of 8,000 roubles (Lavallée 1798, p. 19), but neither De Wailly's design nor that of Clérisseau were realized.

The album consists of 11 sheets (inv. nos. 6860–70), each accompanied by an explanatory text. On the title-page is 'Pavillon des Sciences et des Arts sous l'Emblème de Minerve susceptible d'être Exécuté dans un jardin à l'Anglaise, composé et dessiné par de Wailly architecte du ROI de France, contrôleur de ses bâtiments, et de ses Académies Roiales d'architecture, peinture et sculpture etc.', with the dedication 'la très Auguste CATHERINA ALEXIWNA II, Impératrice et Autocratrice de toutes les Russies de la part de son très humble et très obèissant serviteur Charles de Wailly'.

De Wailly was among those artist–architects (or rather 'architectes – non peintres', as they were called by Diderot in his review of the Salon of 1771), who were not only brilliant architectural draughtsmen but succeeded in 'enlivening' their designs with small genre scenes. This is the case for the album's two last sheets, perspective views of the façades. Imagining what it would be like if his park pavilion had indeed been built, in the one shown here De Wailly includes a visit by the Imperial suite, with people running forth to catch a glimpse of so magnificent a spectacle.

Clearly De Wailly himself was pleased with this drawing, and he repeated it, probably immediately afterwards (acquired in 1997 by the Musée des Beaux-Arts, Dijon: GBA 1998, p. 12, no. 47; Starcky 1999, pp. 9–20, note 19). The main differences

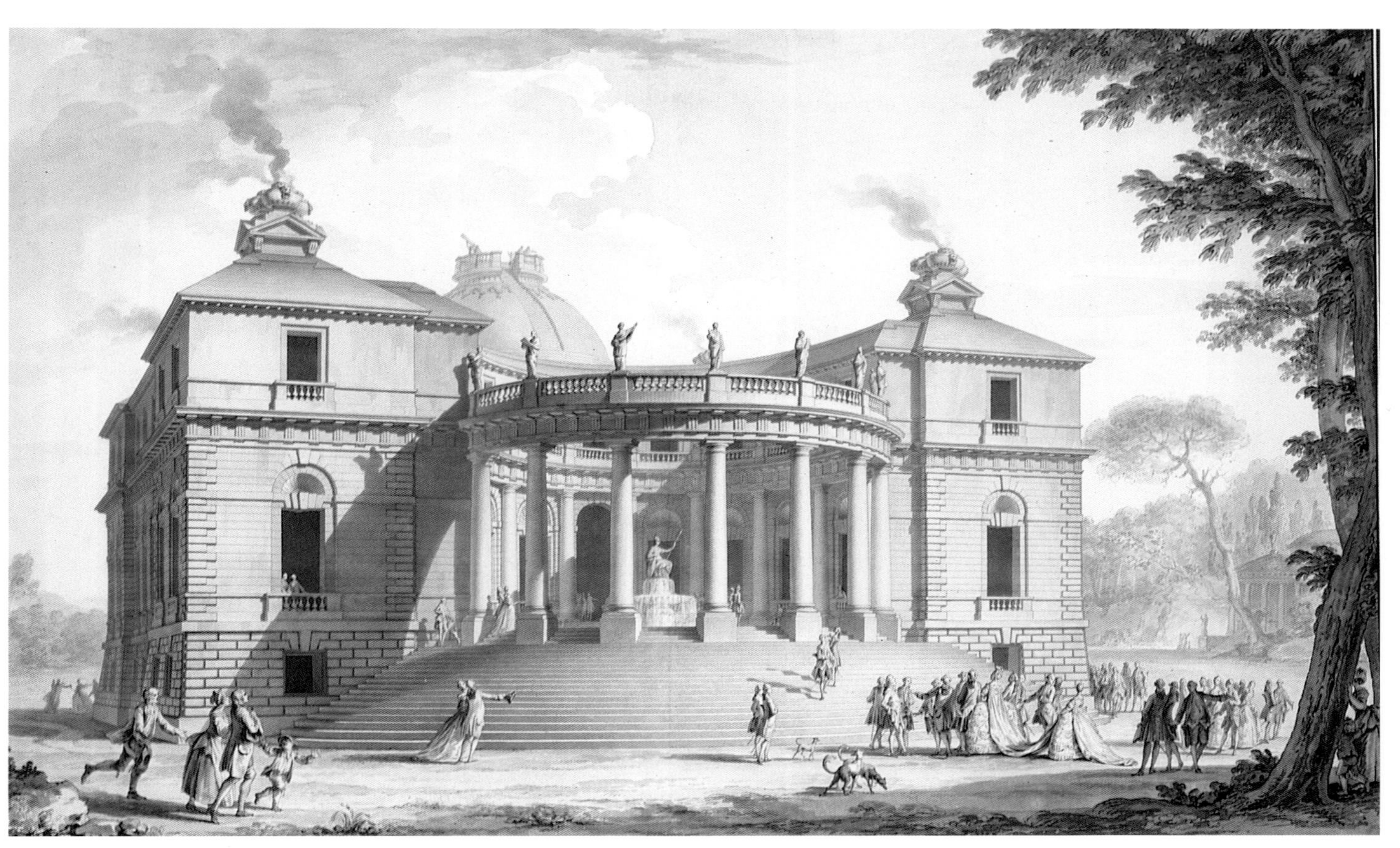

between the Dijon sheet and the one in the Hermitage are that the former is of slightly smaller dimensions and the space around the pavilion has been somewhat reduced. This is particularly visible to the top and right (Starcky considers that the sheet has been trimmed; Starcky 1999, p. 17, note 30). There are also differences in the number of figures, the inclusion of a dog near the couple to the right and the variant execution of the background trees.

The outstanding draughtsmanship, and possibly the theatrical presentation too, delighted not only Catherine. Piervaleriano Angelini has noted the great influence of the Hermitage album on her favoured architect, Giacomo Quarenghi, whose own copy of this sheet, done in St Petersburg in the early 1780s, is now in the Academia Carrara di Bergamo (Venice 1997, no. 91). Listing the four copies so far discovered, Angelini has suggested that the admiring Quarenghi probably copied all the sheets in the Hermitage album, and that the copies made from the other sheets may survive. V.S.

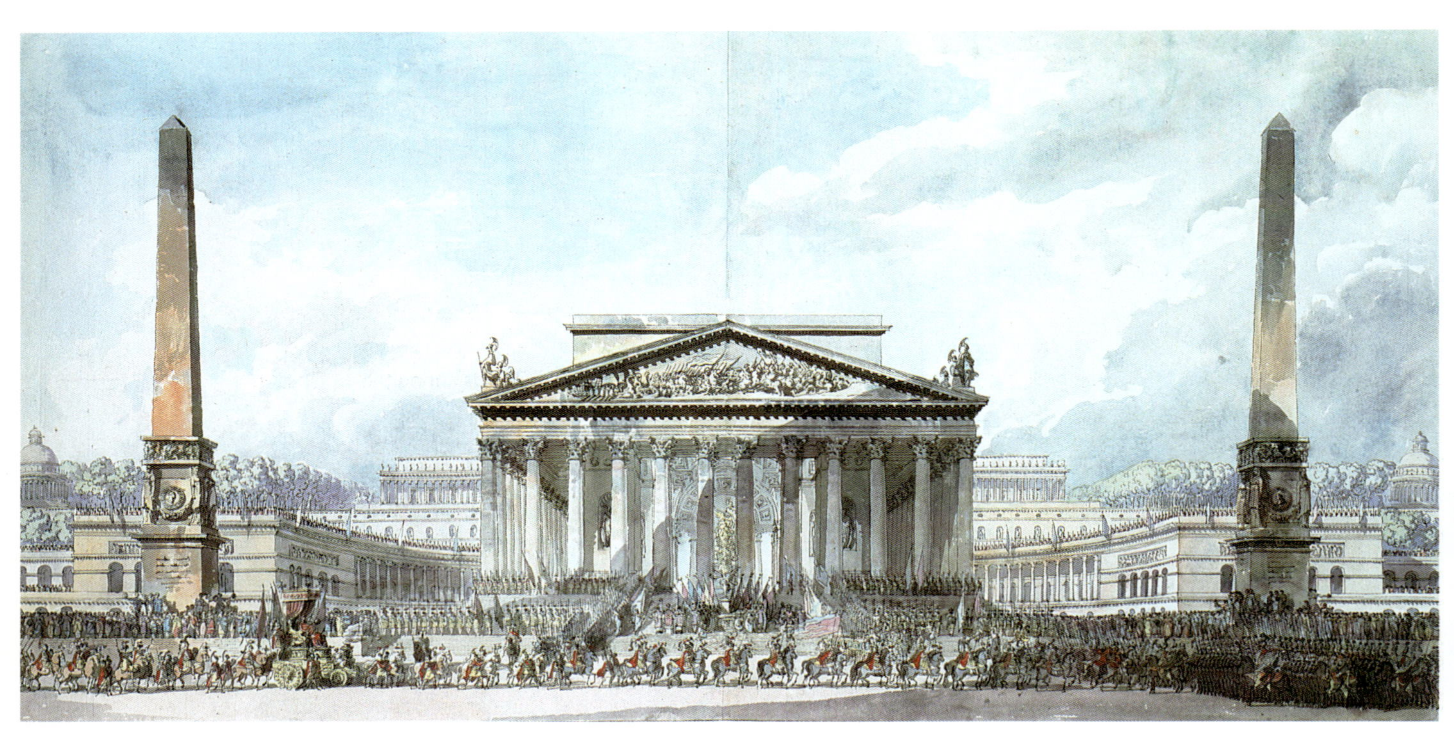

65

Louis-Jean Desprez

Paris 1743 – 1804 Auxerre

Inauguration of a 'Temple of Immortality'

Pen and ink, watercolour, over a black chalk outline. 643 × 1,006 mm

Inscription in pen and ink at the top: *Projet d'un temple de l'Immortalité*; at the bottom: *Inauguration du Temple de l'Immortalité*
Signed in pen and ink bottom left: Desprès inv:

PROVENANCE: c. 1790 gift to Catherine II from the author; before 1811 transferred from the Winter Palace to the Hermitage

Inv. no. 6675

OLD MANUSCRIPT CATALOGUES: listed in two manuscript inventories: 1811 and that 'corrected in 1839'. In the 'Inventory of Drawings by Various Original Masters Found in the Imperial Hermitage in St Petersburg' of 1821, the album is listed as 'Book no. 144' with the pencil note 'Checked'. In the inventory 'corrected in 1839' the drawing is entitled 'Façade of a Temple of Immortality and its Ceremonial Inauguration (in perspective)'

EXHIBITIONS: 1971b Leningrad, no. 24, ill.; 1998–9 Stockholm, p. 469, no. 475, ill. pp. 444–5, 471; 1999–2000 St Petersburg, no. 60, ill.

LITERATURE: Wollin 1939, pp. 208–16, ill. 201; Erensvärd 1962, pp. 14–18; Western European Drawing 1981, no. 94, ill.; 1992 Stockholm, ill. p. 119; 1994 Paris, p. 227, ill. p. 98

The album containing the design for this Temple of Immortality and two triumphal arches for it was made and presented to Catherine II – as was suggested by Nils Wollin – 'at the time of Gustav III, or more precisely nearer the time of the peace of Värälä' (a reference to conclusion of a peace treaty between Sweden and Russia signed at Värälä on 14 August 1790).

The first sheets in the album include a depiction of the Russian coat of arms and an extensive dedication that opens with the words 'À la Mageste [sic] l'Imperatrice de toutes les Russies', after which Desprez provides a general view of the projected ensemble. This artfully constructed architectural composition is not accompanied by a general plan, which would have provided a fuller idea of the architect's concept. Rather he presents the Temple of Immortality and its surrounding buildings during the inauguration ceremony: a procession with a chariot of heavy classical forms and proportions moves across a broad square before the monumental portico flanked by two obelisks. Desprez carefully organized the varied movements of a vast quantity of figures: the rhythmic repetition of the red cloaks of riders and weapon-bearers creates a sense of steady, ceremonial movement, while the immobility of the perfectly ranked soldiers is broken in places by the wild gesticulations of the jubilant crowd dressed in varicoloured collarless kaftans and sarafans. For all the expressive precision and virtuoso drawing of the figures, Desprez did not err in too strong a concentration on tiny details. Thus the resonant colours of the costumes, banners, shields and gilded carriage do not disrupt the unity of the composition. Surely his experience as a theatrical designer was coming into play here? Nils Wollin was inclined to see this composition as a magnificent stage backdrop, and he identified the participants as figures from a carousel or masquerade seen by Desprez in the suite of Gustav III, or perhaps borrowed from the numerous prints of the age of Louis XIV and the Renaissance (Wollin 1939, p. 211).

To offset the architectural symmetry, Desprez complicated the lighting by throwing a slanting shadow from the cloud to the right over the portico, obelisk and the crowd at its foot. The sense of festive bustle, the impressive richness of the background architectural ensemble and the monumentality of this Temple intended to immortalize the name of Catherine the Great have been skilfully unified.

This sheet is an impressive overture to the album's following drawings, which include views of the Temple's vast interior and a monumental sculpture of Catherine II on a gold chariot surrounded by soldiers and allegorical figures. Their large dimensions make the Temple all the more convincing, and enabled Desprez to brilliantly display his virtuoso technique, perhaps in the hope that he could charm the Empress into commissioning him to put his design into effect. She, however, 'deigned to express her high approbation of this audacious project in making a rich present to its author. But she manifested no intention of having it put into effect' (Wollin 1939, p. 216). V.S.

66

Jean-Guillaume Moitte

Paris 1746 – 1810 Paris

Design for a Bas-relief: The Judgement of Paris

Pen and ink, ink wash. 359 × 498 mm

PROVENANCE: collection of Charles-Eugene Bérard, Paris (collector's mark L. 75); 1891 Baron Stieglitz School of Technical Drawing, St Petersburg; 1924 transferred to the Hermitage

Inv. no. 28574

EXHIBITIONS: 1789 Salon de Paris, no. 269; 1900 St Petersburg, nos. 310–13; 1913 St Petersburg, no. 250; 1971b Leningrad, no. 62, ill.

LITERATURE: Bérard 1891, no. 276; Lacambre, Sérullaz et al. 1974–5, no. 102; Vilain 1976, p. 76; Campbell 1982, pp. 192–3, ill. 45; Bean 1986, no. 195; Gramaccini 1993, vol. II, pp. 89–90, no. 213, ill. 303; Hermitage 1994, no. 347, p. 424, ill.

Jean-Guillaume Moitte, a Neoclassical sculptor trained by Jean-Baptiste Pigalle (1714–85) and Jean-Baptiste Lemoyne (1704–78), was also a draughtsman and a designer of bas-reliefs. In addition he undertook designs for gold- and silversmiths. Around 1,000 of his ornamental drawings served as models for the most important works of Robert-Joseph Auguste, jeweller to the French monarch.

Gramaccini suggests that this drawing was for applied bronze ornament for furniture (Gramaccini 1993). Campbell dates it to between 1785 and 1789, since it was exhibited at the Salon in Paris in 1789 under number 269 (Campbell 1982) at the same time as another, now lost, drawing for similar applied bronze ornament with a relief also showing *The Judgement of Paris* (Gramaccini 1993, no. 148).

A similarly committed use of Antique architectural and sculptural elements in keeping with Neoclassical ideals is found in an analogous work in New York, an author's repetition of which is also in the Hermitage (fig. 40). In the Musée Vivenel at Compiègne is another similar drawing of three caryatids that, in the opinion of J. Vilain, were inspired by Raphael's caryatids in the Farnesina in Rome (Lacambre, Sérullaz *et al.* 1974–5). A comparison of the somewhat heavy female figures in all three drawings in terms of their type, pose, movements and proportions and the nature of their drapery, leaves us with no doubt that they are all Moitte's designs. V.S.

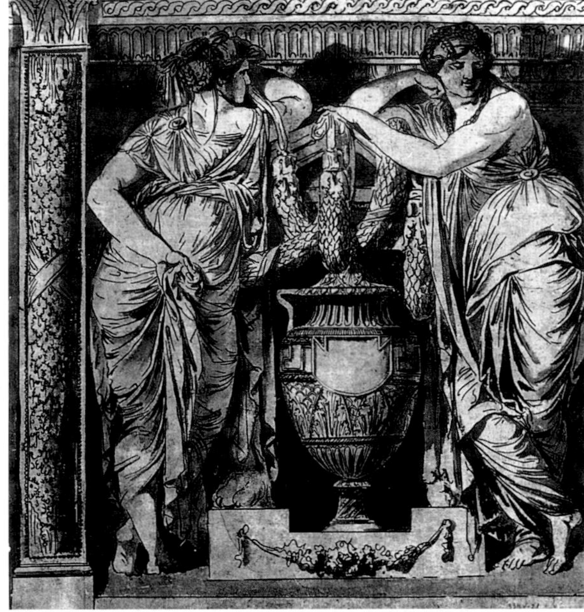

fig. 40
Jean-Guillaume Moitte
Variations on Caryatids from 'The Judgement of Paris' in the Metropolitan Museum of Art, New York
pen and ink, brown wash
338 x 302 mm
(inv. no. OR 30273)

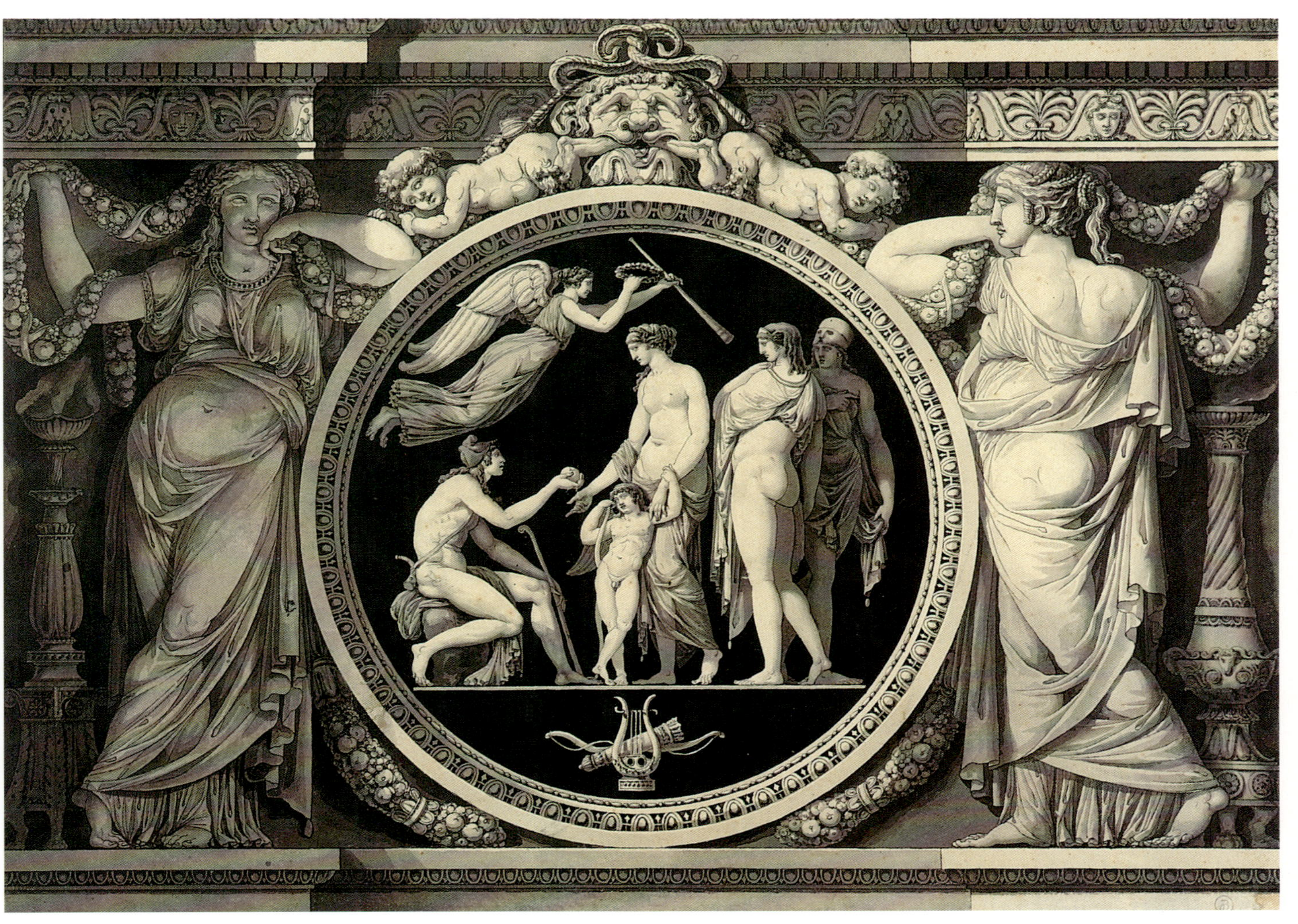

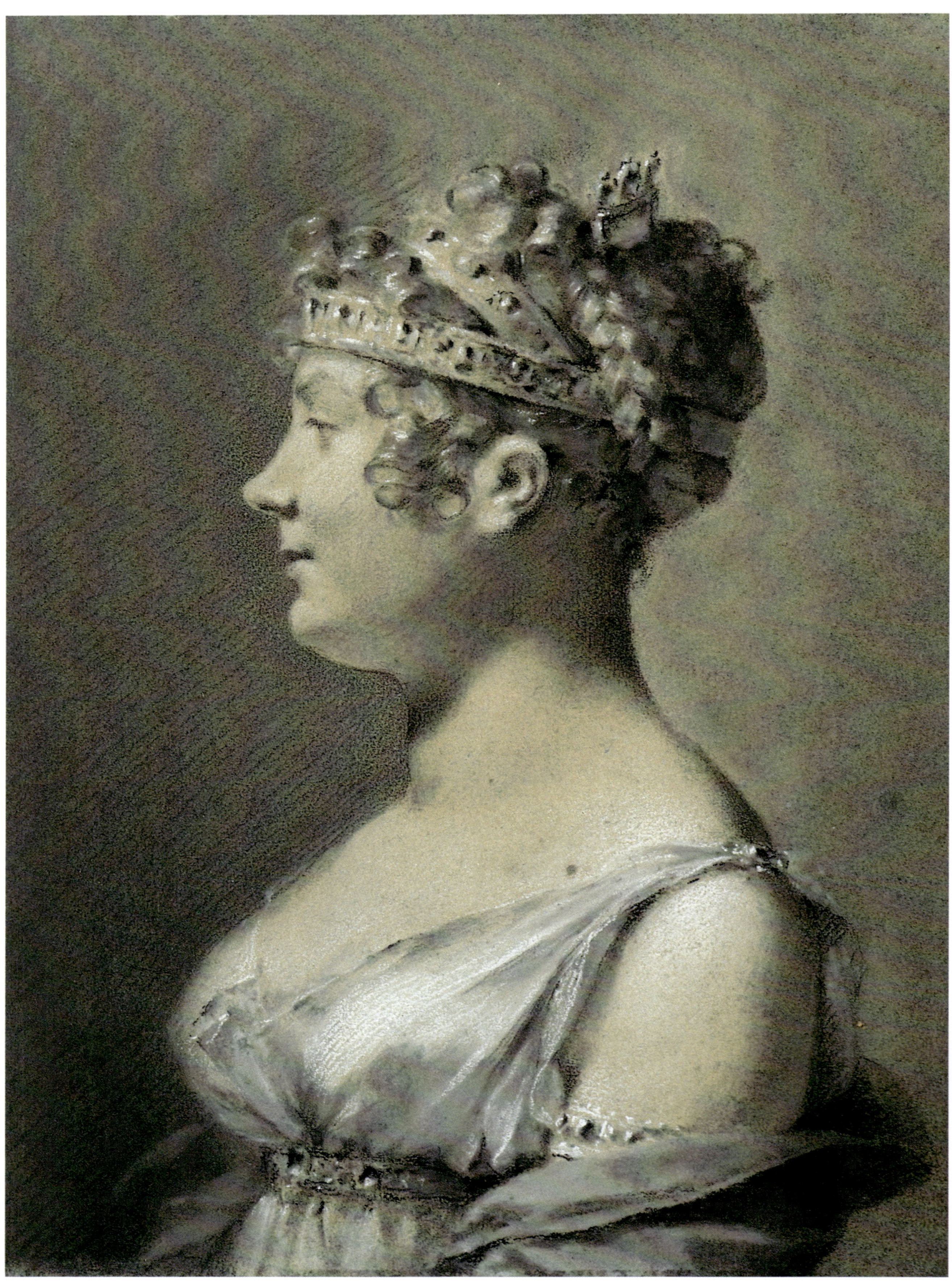

67

Pierre-Paul Prud'hon

Cluny 1758 – 1823 Paris

Princess Catherine Talleyrand

Black and white chalk on grey paper.
230 × 178 mm. Lined

PROVENANCE: private collection, Leningrad; 1939 acquired by the Hermitage through the Purchasing Commission

Inv. no. OR 43445

LITERATURE: Graphic Art 1961, no. 133, ill; Western European Drawing 1981, no. 96, ill.

The traditional attribution of this drawing and identification of the sitter are based on the portrait's style and technique and the subject's appearance. Her slightly vulgar beauty, the large blowsy forms, luxuriant hair and tipturned nose, the facial expression that suggests confidence in her own uniqueness – all were described by contemporaries of Catherine Talleyrand (?1762–1818), who attracted numerous admirers during her lifetime.

Born in India, at Tranquebar near Pondicherry, she was the daughter of Pierre Worley, an employee in the port administration. In 1777 she married George-Francis Grand, but after a scandalous legal case between her husband and her lover, Mme Grand moved to France, emigrating in 1792 to England but later returning to France, her peregrinations giving rise to suspicions that she was a spy. She was saved from arrest by her acquaintance with Charles-Maurice de Talleyrand-Périgord (from 1797 Minister of Foreign Affairs). She became his mistress in early 1798, marrying him in 1802 in a civil ceremony and later, thanks to various diplomatic machinations on Talleyrand's part, in a church ceremony. In 1806 he was created Prince of Benevento. Their marriage ended in divorce in 1815.

This drawing appears to have been made in 1806 or 1807, around the time Prud'hon was painting his portrait of Talleyrand (commissioned by Napoleon as one of a number of portraits of leading statesmen). A perceptive and lyrical artist, Prud'hon worked on this drawing in a soft and intimate style very unlike the pompous nature of the state portrait. Employing delicate gradations of black and white chalks, combining them with the grey of the paper, he created an image full of vital energy, of a woman no longer young but filled with bright sensual beauty, softly modelling forms with light strokes to set off the warm whiteness of her skin. A.K.-G.

68

Jean-Auguste-Dominique Ingres

Montauban 1780 – 1867 Paris

Portrait of a Young Girl

Graphite on laid paper. 285 × 207 mm

Signed and dated in the bottom right corner: *Ingres Del Roma 1815* (the top of the last figures cut off by the edge of the sheet)

PROVENANCE: 1920 transferred to the Hermitage from the Expert Committee

Inv. no. OR 27330

EXHIBITIONS: 1938 Leningrad, issue IV, no. 321, ill.; 1955 Moscow, p. 86; 1956 Leningrad, p. 99; 1967–8 Paris, no. 84, ill.; 1970 Budapest, no. 56; 1972 Prague, no. 53; 1975 Aarhus, no. 34; 1975 Berlin, no. 95, ill.; 1975 Copenhagen, no. 34, ill.; 1987 Delhi, no. 110

LITERATURE: Kamenskaya 1959, pp. 4–5; Kai Sass 1959–60, p. 14, ill.; Kai Sass 1960, p. 21, ill.; Naef 1960, pp. 35–6, ill.; Graphic Art 1961, no. 132, ill.; Naef 1977, vol. IV, no. 145; Western European Drawing 1981, no. 97, ill.; Hermitage 1994, vol. II, no. 354, ill.

Ingres' drawings, unlike his academic classical compositions, are always simple and sincere, embodying that 'probity of art' of which he himself wrote. Ingres was convinced that 'drawing is the sole principle capable of giving works of art their veritable form'. This example is linked with Ingres' work on a large group portrait in pencil of the family of Napoleon's brother Lucien (fig. 41). This young girl is very like the girl in the resultant group portrait, with her hand on the back of the chair of Lucien's second wife, Alexandrine, formerly the wife of a stockbroker named Jouberthon. None the less, it has proved to be difficult to establish her identity for certain.

Some scholars have identified the girl in the group portrait as Jeanne, daughter of Lucien and Alexandrine, who married the Marchese Honorati; others (Kai Sass 1960, pp. 19–20), suspect she is Anna Jouberthon, Alexandrine's daughter from her first marriage, who was born in 1799 or 1800, and who married first Prince Hercolani and then, after his death, the Polish Prince Maurizio Jablonowsky. Naef calls the girl Christine, and sees her as Lucien's daughter from his first marriage (to Christine Boyer), who later became Countess Arvid Posse, and then Mrs Dudley Coutts Stuart (Naef 1960, no. 146). Berezina (1977, p. 96) identifies her as Letitia Bonaparte (1804–71), daughter of Lucien and Alexandrine, who later became Lady Wyse, and who visited Napoleon in exile on the Island of Elba together with her aunt Pauline Borghese. Berezina explains the clear incompatibility in the ages of the figures in both the group portrait and the Hermitage drawing by suggesting a reading of the date on the drawing as 1819, rather than 1815. There can be no doubt, however, either that the girl was related to Lucien Bonaparte, or that the Hermitage drawing preceded work on the group portrait and that it was therefore produced in that same year, 1815. A.K.-G.

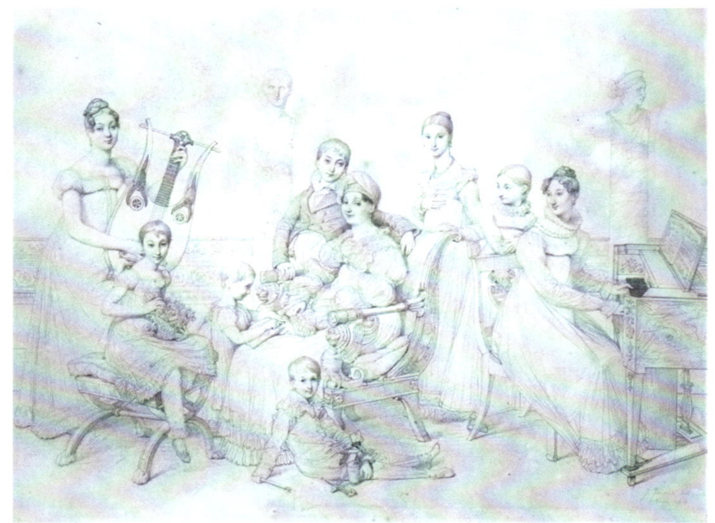

fig. 41
Jean-Auguste-Dominique Ingres
The Family of Lucien Bonaparte, 1815

graphite on white wove paper, 410 × 532 mm.
Courtesy of the Fogg Art Museum, Harvard University Art Museums, Cambridge, Mass., Bequest of Grenville L. Winthrop.
Photo: Katya Kallsen

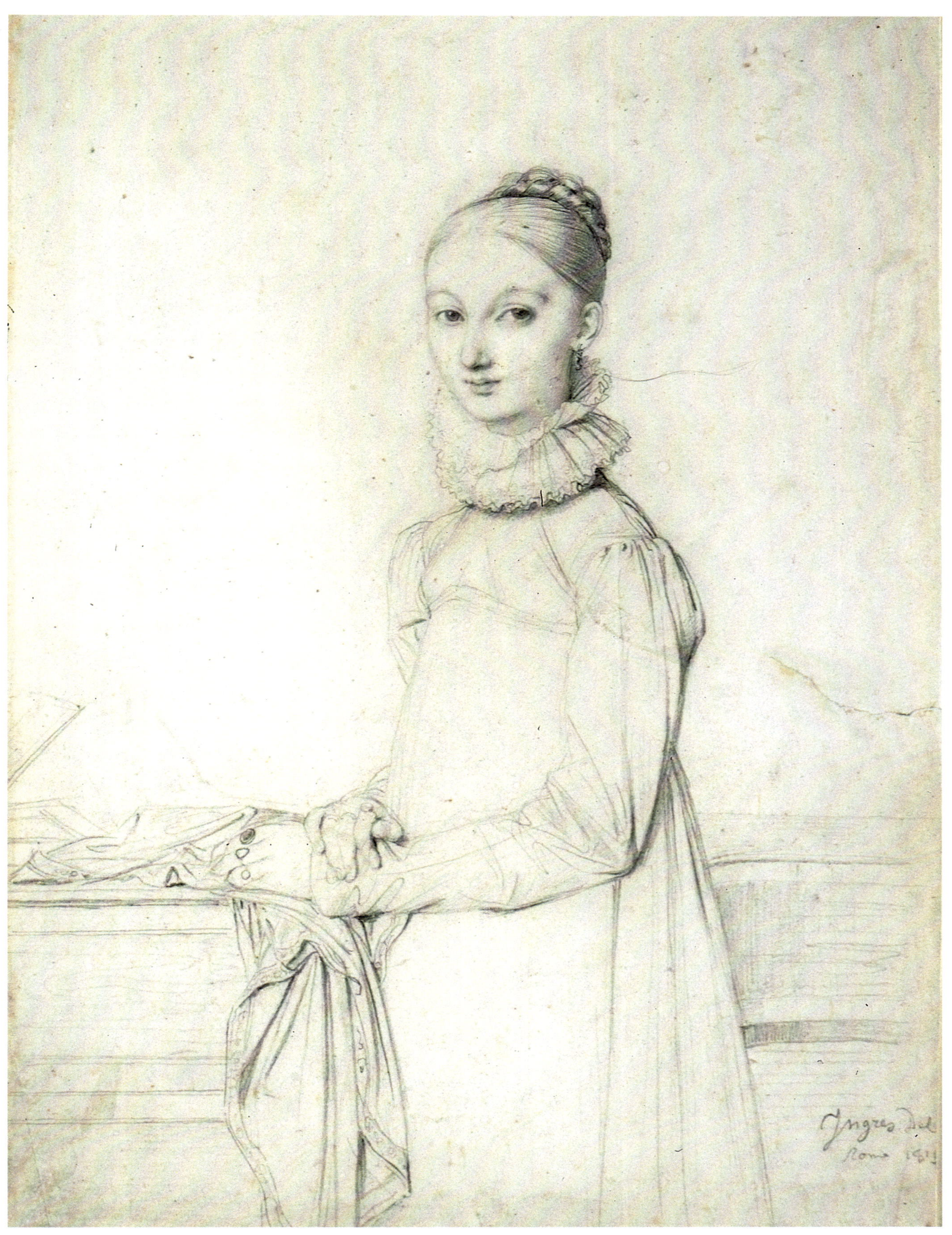
Ingres Del

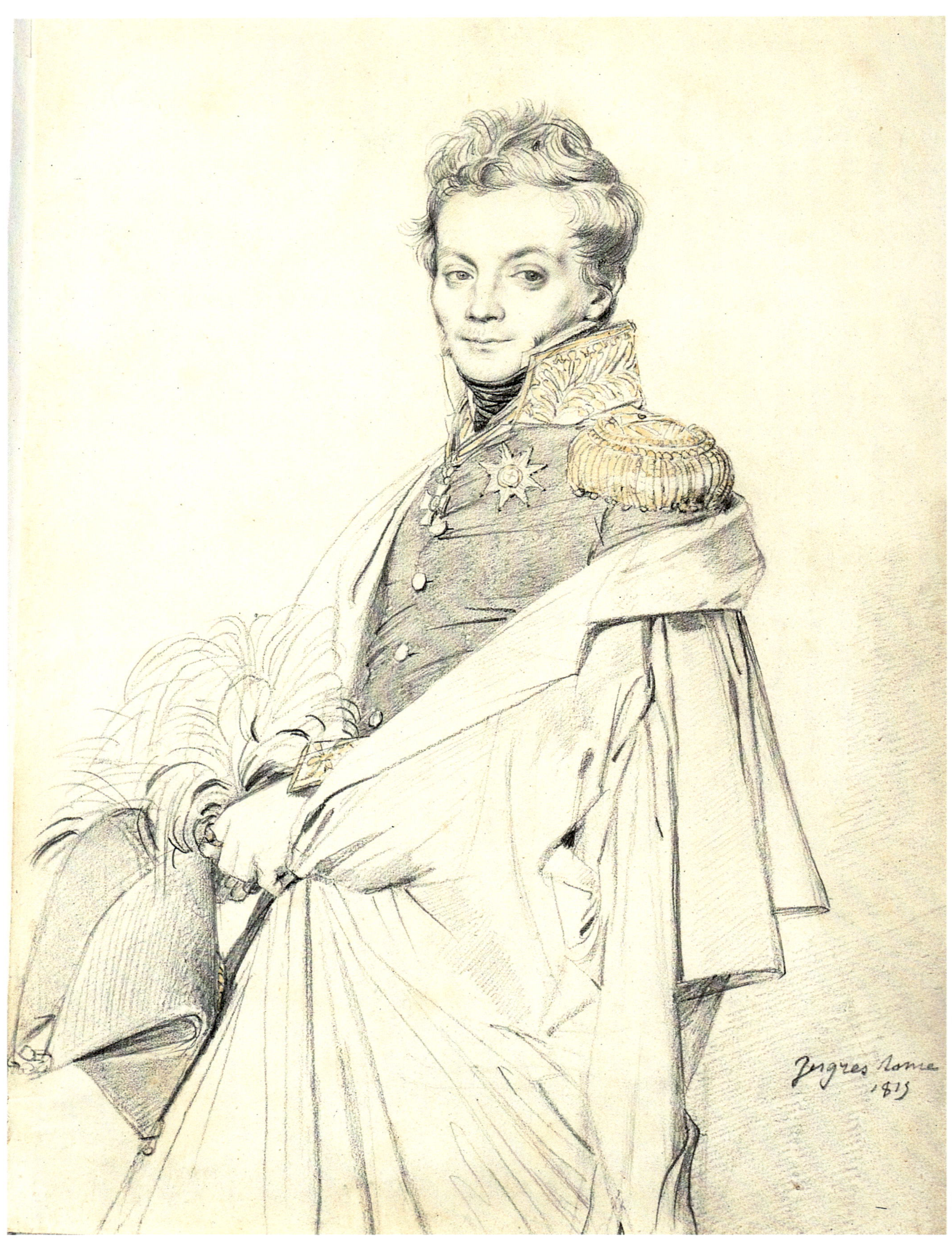
Ingres Rome
1815

69

Jean-Auguste-Dominique Ingres

Portrait of a Russian General

Graphite, with yellow watercolour in places, on laid paper. 296 × 220 mm

Signed and dated in the bottom right corner: *Ingres Roma 1815*

PROVENANCE: private collection, Moscow; 1977 acquired for the Hermitage through the Purchasing Commission

Inv. no. OR 46655

LITERATURE: Naef 1977, vol. V, no. 455; GBA 1978, p. 89, fig. 422; Foucart 1980, p. 11

The style of this drawing leaves no doubt that it is by Ingres. Foucart's lack of certainty regarding its authenticity is unfounded, and moreover he himself admitted that he had seen neither the drawing itself nor a good-quality photograph (Foucart 1980).

The General wears the Order of St George, 3rd Class, and the Star of the Order of St Andrew. It has not proved possible so far to establish his identity, but the nature of his uniform and the Orders he wears are evidence that he is Russian. The drawing is dated *1815*, the year of the Congress of Vienna, when Napoleon's departure from the historical scene left the Allies with the task of dividing up their newly conquered (or regained) territories. There would not have been anything surprising in the presence in Rome of a military representative of the Russian Emperor, Alexander I.

This time in Rome was something of a turning-point for Ingres: his French friends and patrons had returned to France and the artist found himself in severe financial straits, forcing him to suspend work on large oil canvases in order to undertake readily profitable pencil portraits. His fame as a skilled draughtsman drew clients of various nationalities to his studio.

This is a typical example of the virtuoso manner of Ingres' pencil portraits – the delicate working up of the face is very fine and careful, while the uniform, and more so the folds of the greatcoat pulled around the shoulders, are managed by means of a few simple lines. A.K.-G.

70

Jean-François Millet

Gruchy (nr. Cherbourg) 1814 – 1875 Barbizon

Death and the Woodcutter

Charcoal on pale-brown paper.
226 × 360 mm

The artist's initials bottom left: *J.F.M.*

PROVENANCE: 10–11 May 1875, posthumous sale of the artist's studio (collector's mark L. 1460) via Gallery Durand-Ruel, Paris; collection of Laurent-Richard Jacobsen, Paris; collection of J. S. Forbes, London; sale 10 December 1913, Frankfurt, no. 126; 1913 collection of Prince V. N. Argutinsky-Dolgorukov, St Petersburg; 1920 transferred to the Hermitage via the State Museums Fund

Inv. no. OR 25104

EXHIBITIONS: 1955 Moscow, p. 80; 1956 Leningrad, p. 92; 1968 Leningrad–Moscow, no. 46, ill.; 1970 Budapest, no. 78, ill.; 1972 Prague, no. 80, ill.; 1974 Manchester, no. 48, ill.; 1975 Aarhus, no. 59; 1975 Copenhagen, no. 59; 1975 Berlin, no. 98, ill.; 1978–9 Melbourne–Sydney–Adelaide, no. 30, ill.; 1985 Leningrad, no. 49, ill.; 1987 Sapporo–Fukuoka–Hiroshima, no. 52, ill.; 1999–2000 New York, no. 104, ill.

LITERATURE: Gudin 1913, no. 126, ill.; Graphic Art 1961, no. 134, ill.; Berezina 1963, pp. 30–33, ill.; Western European Drawing 1981, no. 98, ill.

This one of the preparatory studies undertaken for a painting in oils (fig. 42), its subject inspired by Jean de La Fontaine. In 1855 Millet and a group of artists then working at Barbizon gathered in the house of the writer Théodore Rousseau to discuss their ideas for a new illustrated publication of La Fontaine's *Fables* and to divide responsibility for the illustrations. Although the book never materialized, Millet was so inspired by the particular fable he had chosen that he produced a series of sketches, later used as a basis for the painting. For many years scholars of his work were largely unaware of the Hermitage drawing, but it none the less occupies a key place in preparatory work on the painting. A comparison with other extant drawings allows us to trace the emergence of the painting's compositional structure and to see how it was then endowed with emotional content.

The motif of Death carrying off a woodcutter first appears in two black chalk drawings on grey paper. In the first, and probably the earlier (Département des Arts Graphiques, Louvre, Paris, inv. no. R.F. 5707), the figure of Death, placed by the far-right edge, drags the woodcutter to the right, while the composition of the second (Louvre, inv. no. R.F. 5706) is closer to that in the Hermitage: Death stands in the left half of the sheet, and the movement of both figures is towards the left. The Hermitage drawing clearly came after the two Louvre drawings, for here the structure of the final composition is picked out and elements of the landscape background are indicated. The succeeding and final stage came with a large (309 × 413 mm) black chalk sketch (formerly Gallery Fisher, Lucerne), which is repeated with only minor changes in the painting.

The mark *J.F.M.* (L. 1460), placed on the Hermitage drawing by the artist's widow, is evidence that it formed part of the posthumous sale of works in Millet's studio, where it was acquired – along with the painting – by Laurent-Richard Jacobsen. Its further fate can be traced thanks to its publication in a catalogue of the joint sale in Frankfurt of the collections of Baron Th. J. Gudin and James S. Forbes on 10 December 1913. Here it was purchased by a certain 'noble Russian' – Prince Vladimir Nikolayevich Argutinsky-Dolgorukov. The owner of a celebrated art collection, he remained both a member of the Council of the Russian Museum and a member of staff at the Hermitage even after the Russian Revolution of 1917. He emigrated to France in the 1920s, and Millet's drawing arrived at the Hermitage with the remains of his collection via the State Museums Fund.

This is the sole drawing by Millet in the Hermitage, and despite its unfinished nature, in both subject and style it provides a true reflection of the artist's approach. The theme of hard peasant labour has poetic overtones in most of Millet's works, yet here acquires additional meaning. Hence the unusually gloomy, ascetic graphic style, the apparent carelessness of the thick, confused lines from which emerge the figures of the peasant broken by exhaustion but still holding onto life, and of Death, who appears at his involuntary cry. A.K.-G.

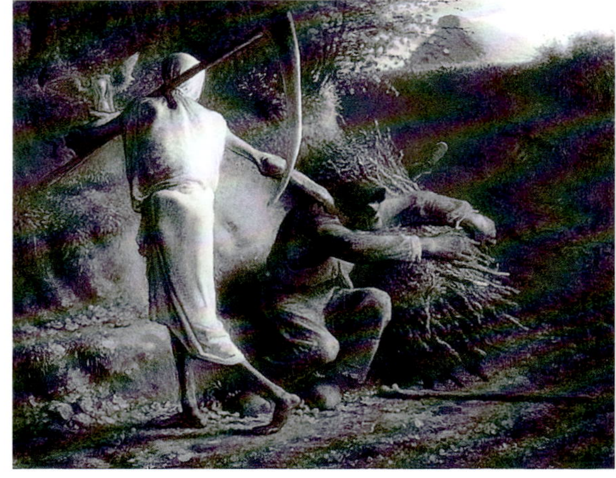

fig. 42
Jean-François Millet
Death and the Woodcutter, 1858–9

oil on canvas, 77.5 × 98.5 cm
Ny Carlsberg Glyptotek, Copenhagen

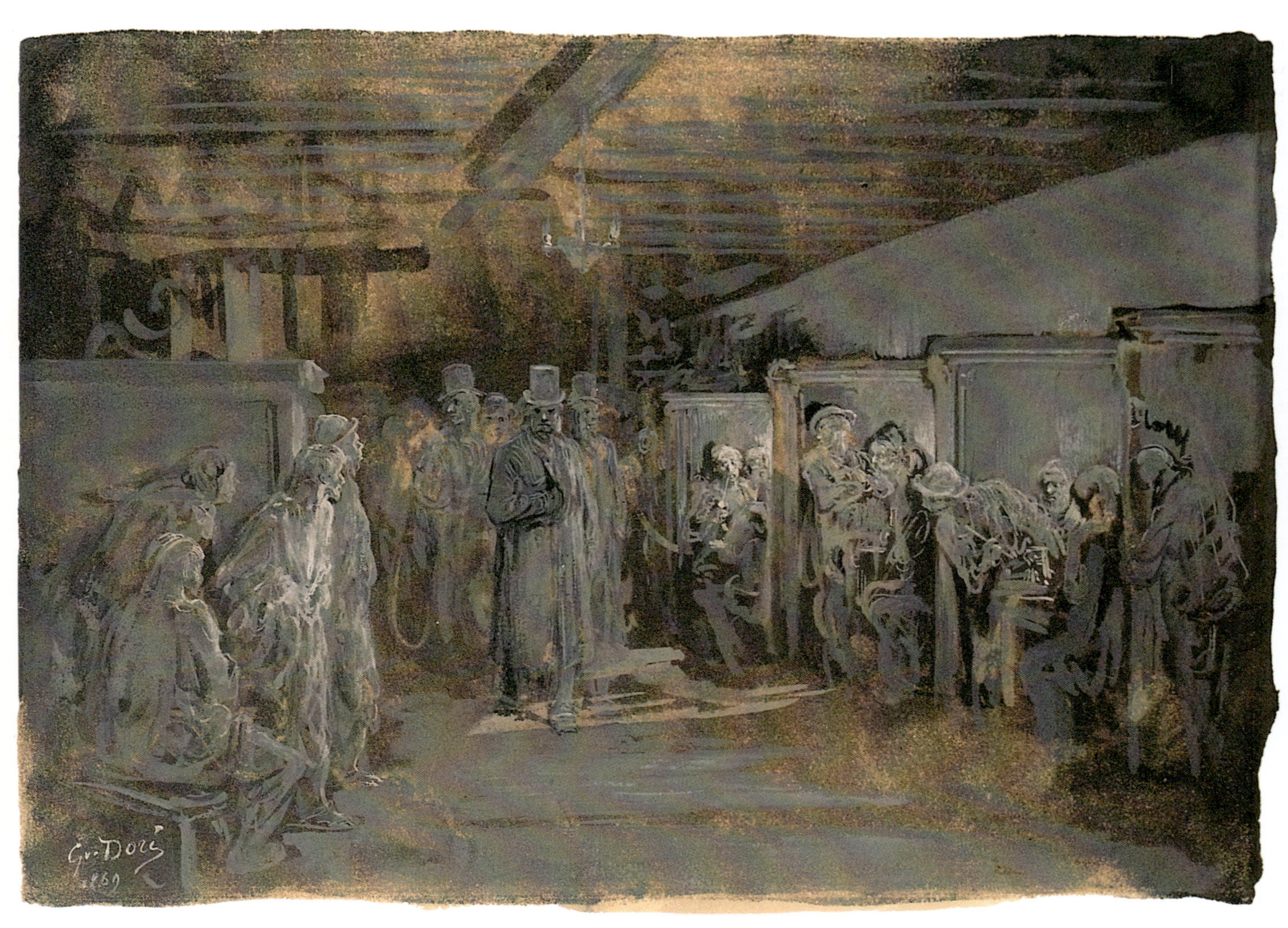
Gv. Doré

71

Gustave Doré

Strasburg 1832 – 1883 Paris

The Interior of an Inn at Whitechapel, London

Ink wash, gouache, heightened with white on paper covered with brown varnish. 255 × 359 mm. Lined

Signed and dated in white in the bottom left corner: *Gu Doré 1869*

PROVENANCE: 1935 acquired by the Hermitage through the Purchasing Commission

Inv. no. 42308

EXHIBITIONS: 1956 Leningrad, p. 88; 1968 Leningrad–Moscow, no. 17; 1970 Budapest, no. 31; 1972 Prague, no. 31; 1974 Manchester, no. 33, ill.; 1975 Aarhus, no. 22; 1975 Copenhagen no. 22; 1975 Berlin, no. 99, ill.; 1978–9 Melbourne–Sydney–Adelaide, no. 19, ill.; 1985 Leningrad, no. 23, ill.

LITERATURE: Doré and Jerrold 1872, p. 141; Drawings, Watercolours 1965, no. 89 ('Visit to the Night-shelter'); Farner 1963, vol. II, no. 226; Haskell 1968, no. 12; Western European Drawing 1981, no. 100, ill.

This drawing was made as a result of Doré's first visit to London in 1869. With the French journalist Blanchard Jerrold he had conceived the idea of a book on the British capital, its inhabitants and manners. Several trips were made to London during work on it, when the artist, accompanied by policemen from Scotland Yard, walked around the city, visiting the East End and one of its most colourful and impoverished districts, Whitechapel. He made sketches as he went, using them as the basis for compositions back in his studio.

Doré skilfully reproduces the gloomy tavern atmosphere, the ghostly figures of its regulars looking curiously at a group of unexpected visitors with the artist (?) in their midst. The drawing was reproduced (reversed) as a wood-engraving by Héliodore-Joseph Pisan, which forms the title illustration to Chapter XVIII of Jerrold and Doré's book *London* (1872), being entitled there *Café, Whitechapel* (p. 141). A partial version of the composition was engraved by Pisan for the same book (p. 114).

In the course of wood-engraving the drawing for the book, its painterly qualities were lost, the colour nuances were dimmed and the space flattened. A.K.-G.

72

Edouard Manet

Paris 1832 – 1883 Paris

Mme Jules Guillemet

Black chalk. 313 × 220 mm

Signed in black chalk bottom right: EM
Remains of a rubbed inscription in blue pencil on the reverse along the lower edge: *appartient à madame...*(?)

PROVENANCE: 1938 acquired by the Hermitage through the Purchasing Commission

Inv. no. OR 43094

EXHIBITIONS: 1955 Moscow, p. 59; 1956 Leningrad, p. 90; 1968 Leningrad–Moscow, no. 41, ill.; 1970 Budapest, no. 70, ill.; 1972 Otterlo, no. 65, ill.; 1972 Prague, no. 71, ill.; 1985 Leningrad, no. 29, ill.; 1999–2000 Rome, no. 4, ill.

LITERATURE: Vereysky 1938, pp. 153–4, ill.; Richardson 1958, no. 74, ill.; Graphic Art 1961, no. 137, ill.; Hermitage 1964, no. 156, ill.; Leiris 1969, no. 599; Western European Drawing 1981, no. 102, ill.; Impressionists and Post-Impressionists 1985, no. 6, ill.; Hermitage 1994, no. 357, ill.

This drawing served as a study for a pastel drawing, *Mme Jules Guillemet Wearing a Hat* of 1880 (St Louis Art Museum, St Louis, Missouri), although the latter is larger (550 × 330 mm) and shows the sitter at half-length.

Mme Guillemet and her husband, owners of a celebrated Paris fashion house, were close friends of the artist, for whom both they and her younger sister Marguérite posed on a number of occasions. The Guillemets are depicted in a painting of 1879, *In the Hothouse* (Nationalgalerie, Staatliche Museen Preussischer Kulturbesitz, Berlin), while the sisters appear in numerous pencil sketches, watercolours and pastels produced between the late 1870s and 1882. They exchanged light-hearted notes with Manet and visited him at Bellevue (where illness forced him to spend the summer months), never forgetting to wear the fashionable hats that so appealed to him. It is possible that one early portrait drawing of Mme Guillemet, produced before that in the Hermitage, is to be found in a small sketch of three female heads in various modish hats (Musée des Beaux-Arts, Dijon). One head, in the upper right corner, reveals – despite the somewhat summary nature of the image – an undoubted likeness to Mme Guillemet as presented in the Hermitage drawing. It has the same delicate profile, the same bonnet-like hat. Possibly this hasty sketch, made simply as an *aide-mémoire*, provided the stimulus for the Hermitage portrait and the succeeding pastel.

Judging by the manner of its execution, the portrait of Mme Guillemet was taken from life in one sitting, at a time when she was already so very familiar to Manet that the pencil seems to have glided lightly across the paper of its own accord. The technique is extremely simple and at the same time utterly confident: Mme Guillement has an indefinable, elusive expression that results from the turn of the head, the elegant profile marked with a fine soft line, combined with broad, energetic, hard-pressed lines that delineate her hat and tight-fitting dress.

In his portraits of Mme Guillemet, renowned for her beauty and – despite her American origins – for her absolutely Parisian charm, Manet not only captured her individual features, he created a generalized image of a young Parisian woman. Thus it is that a pastel portrait, *Mme Jules Guillemet, Bareheaded* (Ordrupgaardsamlingen, Charlottenlung, Copenhagen), is also known as *La Parisienne*. With this title it figured in 1884 at a posthumous exhibition of Manet's work at the Ecole des Beaux-Arts in Paris. *La Parisienne* is also the title given to another pastel portrait of the same sitter (1822; collection of Henry T. Madd, Los Angeles). A.K.-G.

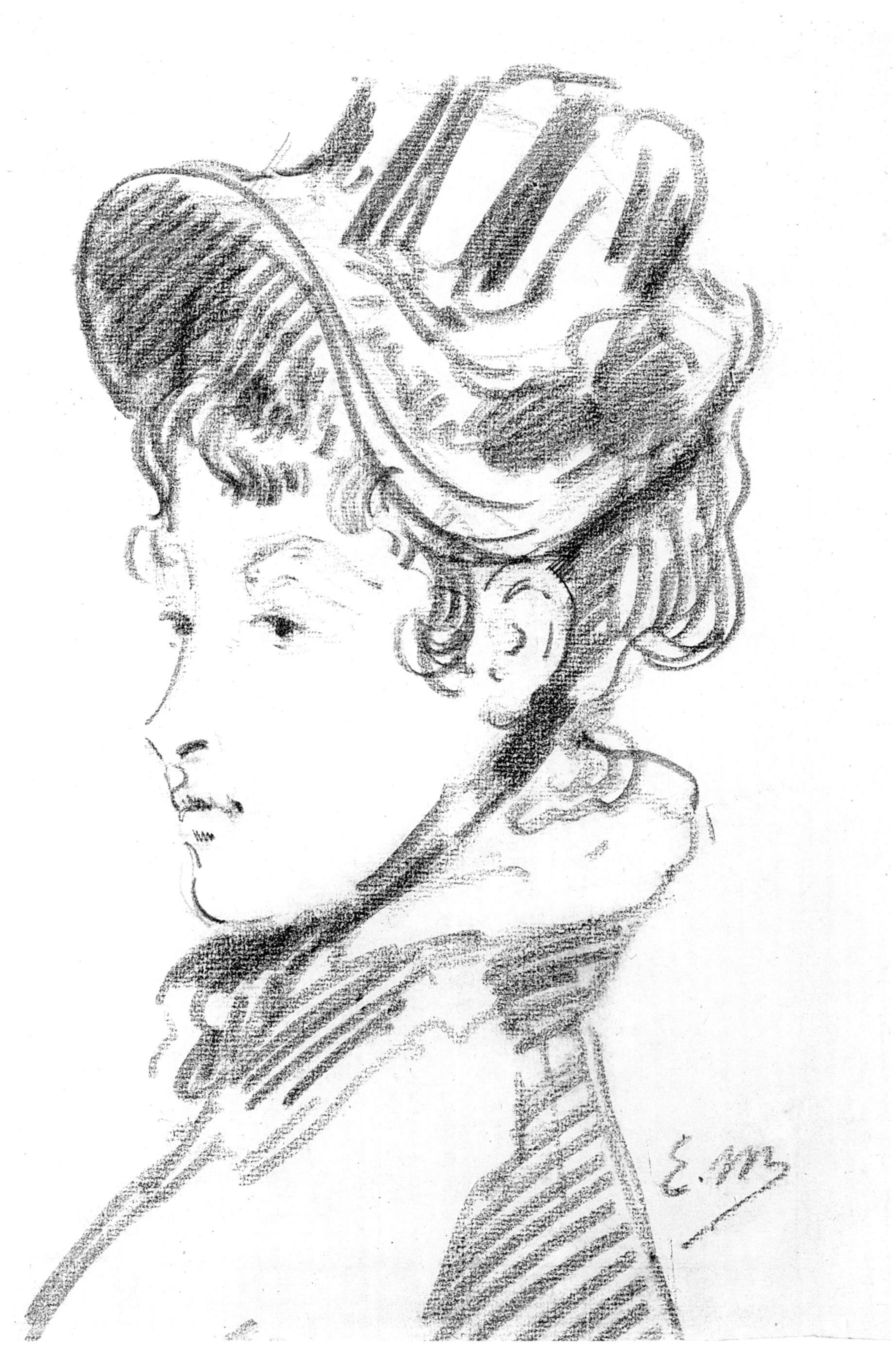

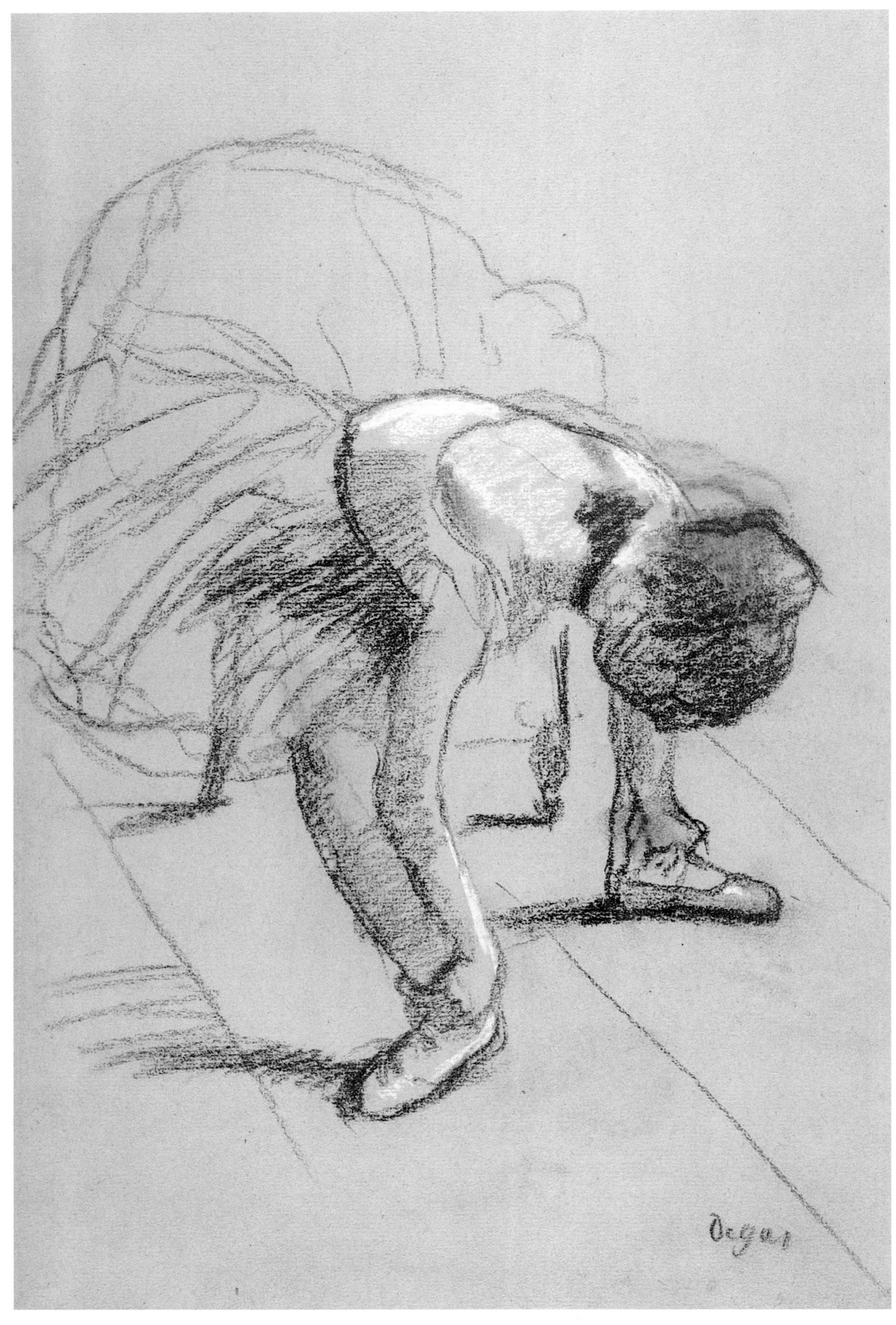
Degas

73

Edgar Degas

Paris 1834 – 1917 Paris

A Seated Dancer Tying her Shoes

Charcoal and chalk. 473 × 305 mm

Signed in charcoal bottom right: *Degas*
A pencil note in the middle of the lower edge: *16·40?*

PROVENANCE: 29 November 1898 acquired by Durand-Ruel (through the Paris dealer Camentron); 1898–1903 Gallery Durand-Ruel, Paris; 26 October 1903 bought by I. S. Ostroukhov (for 1,200 francs); 1918 Museum of Icons and Painting, Moscow; 1923 State Museum of New Western Art, Moscow; 1935 transferred to the Hermitage

Inv. no. 42160

EXHIBITIONS: 1901 Hamburg, no. 90; 1925 Moscow, no. 8, ill.; 1956 Leningrad, p. 87; 1968 Leningrad–Moscow, no. 14, ill.; 1972b Leningrad, no. 17; 1975 Aarhus, no. 17; 1975 Copenhagen no. 17; 1985 Leningrad, no. 10, ill.; 1987 Sapporo–Fukuoka–Hiroshima, no. 54, ill.; 1998–9 New York, no. 106, ill.; 1999–2000 Rome, no. 7, ill.

LITERATURE: New Western Art 1928, no. 813; Graphic Art 1961, no. 136, ill.; Grashchenkov 1961, no. 67, ill.; Western European Drawing 1981, no. 103, ill.; Kantor-Gukovskaya 1982, p. 7, ill.; Impressionists and Post-Impressionists 1985, no. 60

From the 1870s, ballet was a leitmotiv running throughout Degas' work, though he was never merely a chronicler of everyday stage life or a dry illustrator of the lexicon of dance. In his depictions he was the first artist to feel above all the beauty of line – sharp and soft, broken and smooth – in dance movements and poses, and to convey through them a keen mixture of prose and poetry. Ballet, as a synthetic art that arises and comes to life only in movement, was an endless source of inspiration to him. Following his artistic credo that nothing should seem to be superfluous or by chance, Degas selected and worked up – whether on paper or canvas – only the most essential, characteristic turns and gestures of the dance, whether from the magical world of spectacle and performance or from the prosaic hard work of rehearsal.

The ballerina seated in relaxed pose, tying her dance shoes, is a scene as ordinary backstage as is a complex step on the stage itself. Degas repeatedly made use of this motif in the early 1870s, varying it over many years in drawings, pastels and paintings. In its graphic 'handwriting', the Hermitage sheet is close to a hasty life drawing of 1874 in charcoal and chalk, showing a ballerina standing with her back to the viewer (formerly Nacenta collection, Paris; reproduced in Lemoisne 1946–9, vol. I, between pp. 74–5). In subject and manner of execution, however – the figure's arrangement in space, her posture, the drawn lines, the application of shadow, the diagonal crossed lines of the parquet – this drawing reveals greatest likeness to one of a ballerina adjusting the ribbons of her left shoe, dated 1881–3 (fig. 43). None the less, the Hermitage drawing is more like a life study, recalling a sketch of the young dancer Meline Darde (formerly Collection of Baroness Alain de Ginzburg, Paris), and was probably made in 1875–6.

It is possible that this drawing was the source for many variations of the motif, and indeed Degas repeated it – with the body turned the other way – in a monotype (Statens Museum for Kunst, Copenhagen, inv. no. 9157). Pastels with a similar motif are dated to 1878–9 (Lemoisne 1946–9, vol. II, nos. 530, 531). One of two dancers seated on a bench in a pastel of 1879 (Lemoisne 1946–9, vol. II, no. 559) is shown in almost the same pose, as are the figures in a series of pastels with a single dancer (Lemoisne 1946–9, vol. II, nos. 600, 658, 699), dated to *c.* 1881–3. Among the notable variations is a pastel of a dancer bending low to the left and almost touching with her head the ankle of her right leg (National Gallery of Victoria, Melbourne, inv. no. 537/4). Degas returned to the same motif in a late composition, *Two Dancers Seated on a Bench* (*c.* 1900–05; Lemoisne 1946–9, vol. III, no. 1256). It has been suggested that there is a link between the Hermitage drawing and the painting *Dancers in the Foyer (The Bass)* (Lemoisne 1946–9, vol. III, no. 905; Metropolitan Museum of Art, New York). A.K.-G.

fig. 43
Edgar Degas
Dancer Fixing her Slipper, *c.* 1881–3
pencil on paper
Musée Bonat, Bayonne / Giraudon / Bridgeman Art Library

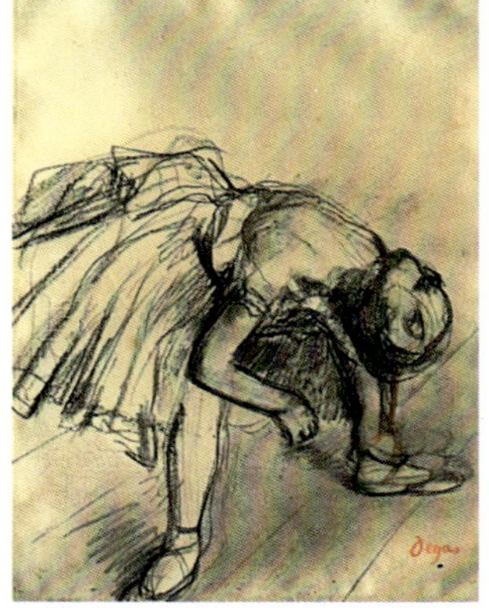

74

Henri Matisse

Le Cateau-Cambrésis 1869 – 1954 Nice

Lydia Delectorskaya

Oil on canvas. 64.3 × 49.7 cm
Signed and dated bottom right:
H. Matisse 47

PROVENANCE: from 1947 collection of Lydia Delectorskaya, Paris; 1967 Hermitage, gift of Lydia Delectorskaya

Inv. no. GE 10023

EXHIBITIONS: 1969 Moscow–Leningrad; 1977b Leningrad; 1988–9 Madrid–Barcelona, no. 25; 1991 Nagoya–Hiroshima–Kasama, no. 69; 1993 Moscow–St Petersburg, no. 73

LITERATURE: Matisse 1954, p. 147; Selz 1960, p. 88; Aragon 1971, vol. II, p. 339; Cat. 1976, p. 279; Matisse 1978, no. 55; Kostenevich 1999, pp. 385, 387, no. 258

Executed in Vence in 1947, this is a rare example of a painted portrait from Matisse's last years. Dividing the model's face into two zones, yellow and blue, he returned to those questions concerning colour that had preoccupied him at the time he produced *The Green Line* (1905, Statens Museum for Kunst, Copenhagen), although here his resolution is simpler and more rational.

In style this portrait was undoubtedly influenced by his work with *découpage*, in which he cut out pieces of ordinary coloured paper and glued them onto a ground. This emphasis on working with scissors during his last period was largely responsible for the linearity and the strikingly arbitrary (in terms of realism) use of colour, the division into different coloured planes.

In the same year as this portrait was painted, Matisse's book *Jazz* was published, containing a range of compositions for which the originals were all produced using the *découpage* technique. In the accompanying text, that reads something like a manifesto or declaration of principles, Matisse wrote: 'To draw with scissors. To cut out directly in colour reminds me of the direct carving of sculptors. This book has been conceived in this spirit.'

Yet despite the simplification and angular outlines, this painting has something in common with Matisse's pen drawings of Lydia Delectorskaya, notably a sheet of 1949 formerly in the collection of John Rewald, New York. According to Delectorskaya herself, Matisse began two portraits at the same time: the second, begun somewhat earlier than that in the Hermitage, remained unfinished and belongs to the artist's family. A.K.

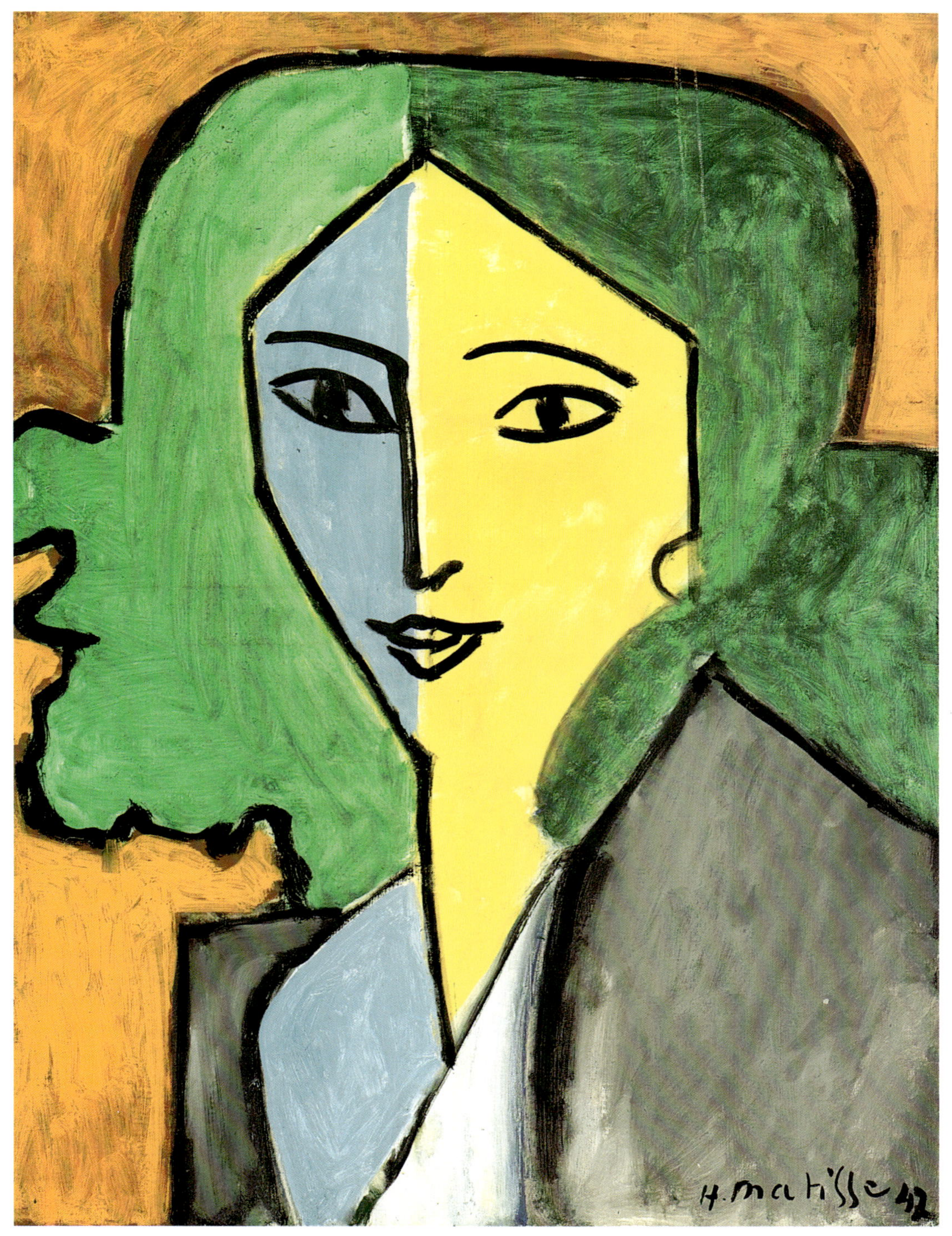
H. Matisse 47

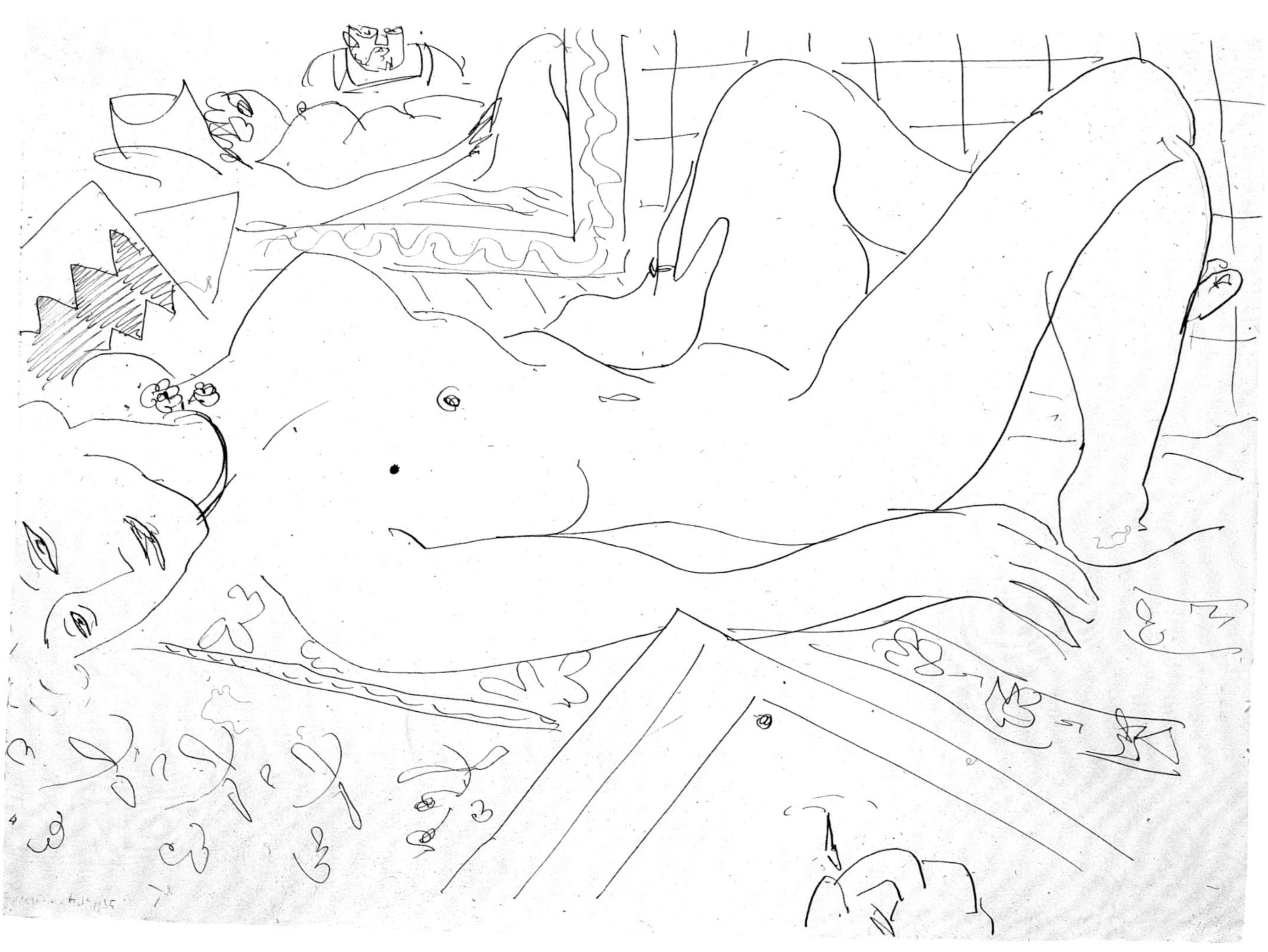

75

Henri Matisse

Reclining Nude in the Studio (The Painter and his Model)

Pen and ink. 378 × 505 mm

Signed and dated in pen in the bottom left corner: *Henri Matisse 1935*

PROVENANCE: collection of Lydia Delectorskaya, Nice; 1968 Hermitage, gift of Lydia Delectorskaya

Inv. no. 46047

EXHIBITIONS: 1936 London; 1975 Aarhus, no. 52; 1975 Copenhagen, no. 52; 1977 Leningrad, no. 129; 1984c Leningrad, no. 9; 1985 Leningrad, no. 34, ill.; 1988 Tokyo, no. 70, ill.; 1991 Nagoya–Hiroshima–Kasama, no. 90, ill.; 1993 Moscow–St Petersburg, no. 125, ill.; 1993–4 Stuttgart, no. 25, ill.; 1997 Retretti, no. 14, ill.; 1999–2000 Rome, no. 74, ill.

LITERATURE: Kantor-Gukovskaya 1975, pp.145–6; Delectorskaya 1986, p.77; Monod-Fontaine 1989, p. 223, ill.; Xavier 1991, p. 93, ill.

This is one of the most elegant in a series of pen drawings made in the second half of 1935, during work on the paintings *Large Reclining Nude* (Baltimore Museum of Art) and *Pink Nude – Prawn* (begun April 1935, abandoned and then destroyed by the artist). A version of the pose was also developed in the painting *La Verdure* (begun September 1935, completed only in 1940; Musée Matisse, Nice). As regards the Hermitage drawing, Girard Xavier cites it in connection with a later painting, *Nude Stretched on her Back* (Xavier 1991).

The various experiments Matisse undertook during work on the paintings found independent development and resolution in his series of graphic works (the first part of which was reproduced in the journal *Cahier d'Art*, 1936, nos. 3–6). Not only Matisse's method but also to a great extent the subject itself came to be understood differently; the appearance changed, even the very nature of the composition. One of the most important elements is the reflection in the mirror of both model and artist, which means that each component appears twice within the work. Near the lower edge of the sheet to the right, the composition includes only the artist's fingers, a pen and paper on a board; to top left, along the diagonal and within the frame of the mirror, we see his head above the faint outline of the model. Lydia Delectorskaya recalled in conversation with this author that the board did not form part of the original idea and emerged only by chance. Seated close up to the model, almost touching her with his board and paper, Matisse involuntarily took in the whole scene – model, board, his own fingers – and captured it there and then. The artist himself thus forms part of the overall compositional structure, while yet remaining outside it, among the viewers, who in their turn become witnesses to the act of creativity.

Matisse could not but appreciate the effect (he repeated it in other drawings in the series), which resulted not only from complex repetitions or a kind of witty dialogue between artist and model: this compositional device created specific spatial context, determined the distance between individual components and their rhythmic structure, while the interior seems to expand both in depth and height. Depicted close up, from different points of view simultaneously (from above and from the side), the model's body dominates all the scene's other components, occupying almost the whole of the space. The flexible pen line, following the sinuous outlines of the model, completes its movement in the creation of physical volume set within an arabesque, giving it mass and weight without destroying the decorative concept. Contact with the fine dark line turns the white of the paper into a source of light, which in its turn dictates the character of the line, its length, its brokenness, its intensity or fading quality. A.K.-G.

76

Henri Matisse

Lydia with her Hands Crossed Resting her Head on the Back of a Chair

Pencil. 248 × 325 mm

Signed in pencil in the bottom right corner: *HM*
Inscription in Matisse's hand on the reverse: *à L.D. HM*

PROVENANCE: presented to Lydia Delectorskaya by the artist; collection of Lydia Delectorskaya, Nice; 1968 Hermitage, gift of Lydia Delectorskaya.

Inv. no. OR 46061

EXHIBITIONS: 1970 Budapest, no. 73; 1972 Prague, no. 74; 1977 Leningrad, no. 130; 1984c Leningrad, no. 2; 1985 Leningrad, no. 33, ill.; 1986 Lille, no. 24, ill.; 1987 Sapporo–Hiroshima–Fukuoka, no. 60, ill.; 1989 Madrid–Barcelona, no. 29, ill.; 1991 Nagoya–Hiroshima–Kasama, no. 85, ill.; 1993 Moscow–St Petersburg, no. 106, ill.; 1993–4 Stuttgart, no. 30, ill.; 1997 Retretti, no. 12, ill.; 1999–2000 Rome, no. 33, ill.

LITERATURE: Kantor-Gukovskaya 1975, p. 141, ill.; Delectorskaya 1986, p. 16, ill.; Monod-Fontaine 1989, p. 86, fig. a; Xavier 1991, p. 93, ill.

In her memoirs Lydia Delectorskaya recalls that this drawing was made in Nice in 1934, a specific record of a chance moment. Entering his wife's room for a rest, Matisse saw Delectorskaya – then employed as his wife's companion and his own assistant – in a natural and relaxed pose that caught his attention.*

From February 1935 Delectorskaya posed for the artist regularly, and this contact with a new model stimulated a whole series of works united by a common motif. In 1935 Matisse produced two paintings one after the other: in late February–March *Blue Eyes* (Baltimore Museum of Art, Baltimore), and in April–May *The Dream* (fig. 44).

After completion of these canvases (or perhaps concurrently with work on them), Matisse turned again to graphic versions of the same subject. Two drawings in pencil are dated to 1935, one of them known from its publication by Roger Fry (*Henri Matisse*, Paris, 1935, pl. 58), the other given in Delectorskaya's book (1986, p. 44). In both cases, the figure of the model differs from both the Hermitage study and the paintings in that it is turned to the left. Similar placing of hand and heads to that in the original sketch is seen in a number of charcoal drawings, one of which, *Nude and Yellow Chair*, was begun in April 1935 and completed after various reworkings in 1936 (Delectorskaya 1986, pp. 49–51, ill.). Another pencil drawing developing the same motif, this time signed and dated 1936 (Baltimore Museum of Art), is in fact a variation on the painting *Blue Eyes*. Here the figure turns to the left, and the head fits almost entirely into the composition through the addition of a strip of paper along the top edge.

After he produced the Hermitage sketch and the two paintings, therefore, we see how Matisse returned to graphic versions of the composition, turning the figure and altering the pose and the placing of the hands to bring out in each work different aspects of one and the same motif. A.K.-G.

**Whilst I listened distractedly to the conversation, he suddenly said: 'Don't move!' And opening his book he drew me, fixing a pose which was quite usual to me: my head resting on my crossed arms leaning on the back of a chair … this is the very first drawing, which later became the origin for the canvas Blue Eyes, his first painting taken after me* (Delectorskaya 1986, p. 16).

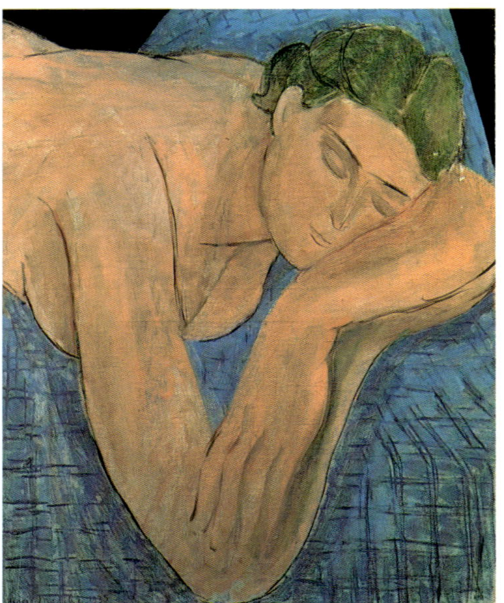

fig. 44
Henri Matisse
Le Rêve, 1935

oil on canvas, 81 × 65 cm.
Musée National d'Art Moderne, Paris / Bridgeman Art Library

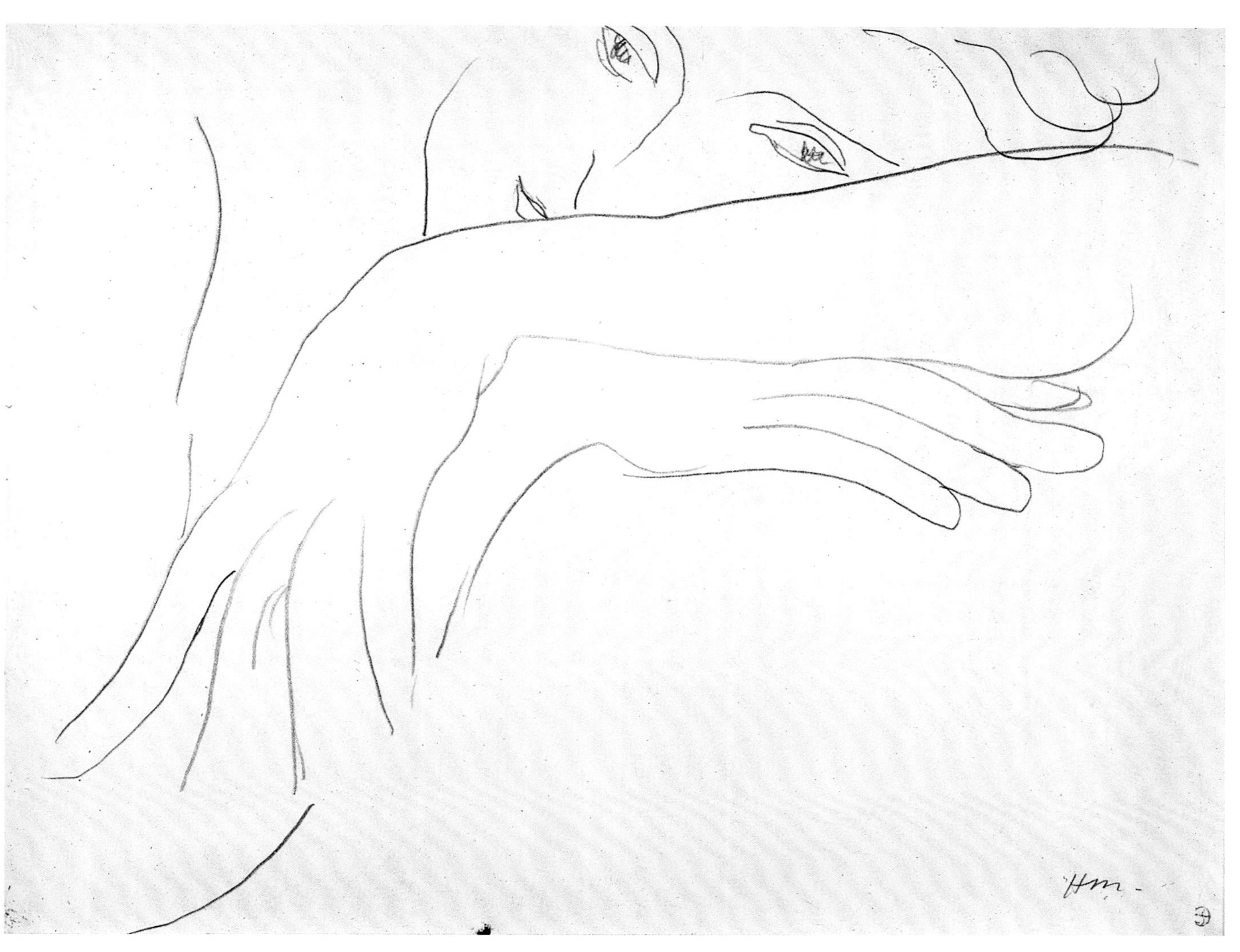

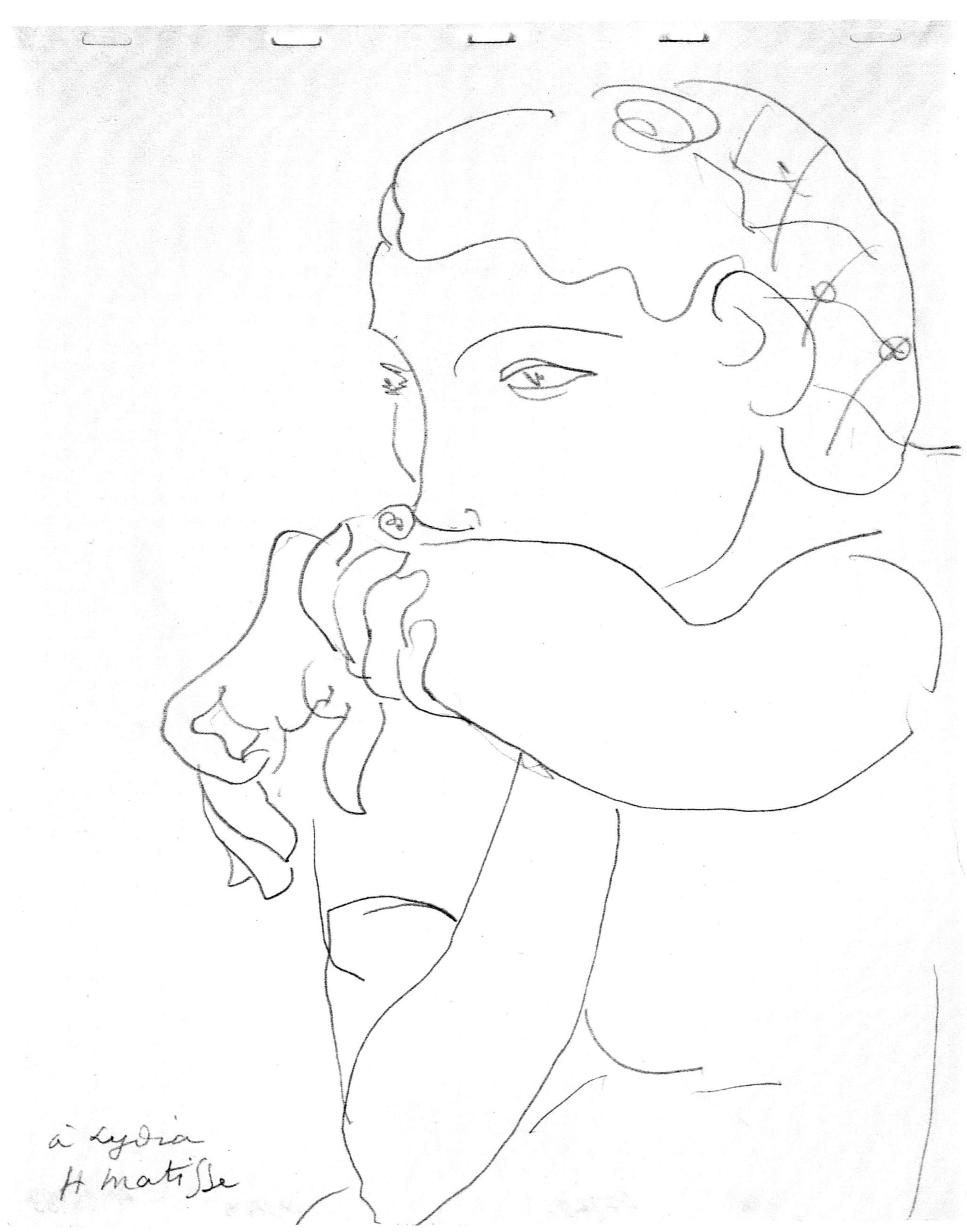
à Lydia
H Matisse

77

Henri Matisse

Lydia in a Hairnet

Pencil. 260 × 202 mm

Inscription in Matisse's hand in the bottom left corner: *à Lydia / H. Matisse*

PROVENANCE: presented to Lydia Delectorskaya by the artist; collection of Lydia Delectorskaya, Venice; 1984 Hermitage, gift of Lydia Delectorskaya

Inv. no. 47762

EXHIBITIONS: 1984c Leningrad, no. 14; 1985 Leningrad, no. 37, ill.; 1993 Moscow–St Petersburg, no. 132, ill.; 1993–4 Stuttgart, no. 32, ill.

Within the structure of this drawing is a clear vertical around which an arabesque unfolds gracefully. Lydia's pose, the incline of her head and placement of her hands are all closely grouped around an invisible axis; everything is subordinated to a single rhythmic structure. Woven into a complex ornamental pattern rather like an orchid blossom, the fingers droop down and seem to bring the tight spiralling movement to its close. Matisse's works do not contain the almost physical personification of an individual's hands common to some artists, instead he turned them into a sort of profound symbol or sign as dictated by the compositional resolution itself.

This drawing reminds one clearly of Matisse's comments to Louis Aragon on the long, flexible hands of Burmese statues, like those he himself depicted, in which, as he put it, the arm ends in a hand like a blossom on a stem. Matisse described it as the Burmese 'symbol' for a hand (Aragon 1971, vol. I, p. 153). A.K.-G.

78

Henri Matisse

Lydia Delectorskaya

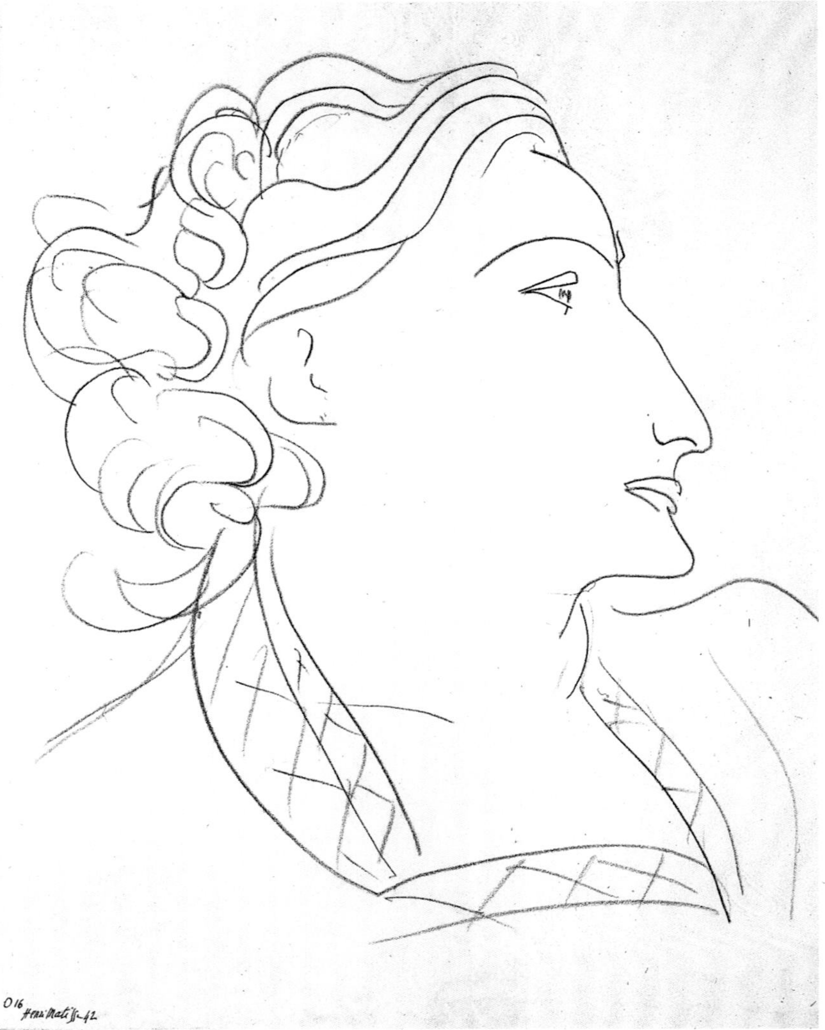

Pencil on laid ARCHES paper

530 × 407 mm

Signed and dated in pencil in the bottom left corner: *Henri Matisse 42*; a little to the left the figures: *016*

PROVENANCE: acquired by Lydia Delectorskaya from the artist; collection of Lydia Delectorskaya, Nice; 1968 Hermitage, gift of Lydia Delectorskaya

Inv. no. 46052

EXHIBITIONS: 1958 Paris, no. 49; 1972 Vienna–Graz, no. 42; 1974 Manchester, no. 74, ill.; 1975 Aarhus, no. 53, ill.; 1975 Copenhagen no. 53, ill.; 1977 Leningrad, no. 132; 1978–9 Melbourne–Sydney–Adelaide, no. 27, ill.; 1984c Leningrad, no. 17; 1985 Leningrad, no. 40, ill.; 1986 Lille, no. 28, ill.; 1987 Sapporo–Fukuoka–Hiroshima, no. 60, ill.; 1988 Tokyo, no. 71, ill.; 1991 Nagoya–Hiroshima–Kasama, no. 100, ill.; 1993 Moscow–St Petersburg, no. 142, ill.; 1997 Retretti, no. 18, ill.; 1999–2000 Rome, no. 78, ill.

LITERATURE: Thèmes et variations 1943, series O, 16th variation; Malingue 1949, p. 90, ill.; Kantor-Gukovskaya 1975, pp. 139–40, ill.; Western European Drawing 1981, no. 113, ill.; Hermitage 1994, no. 356, ill.

This is one of the drawings published in Matisse's *Thèmes et variations*, 158 sheets reproducing various series of drawings, selected for the album by Matisse himself. Each of the 17 series has an identifying letter and an opening drawing, *Thèmes*, usually in charcoal, after which come pencil or pen variations. The Hermitage sheet is the sixteenth in the series 'O': in his numerous variations, Matisse often departed from the original image, and in fact both the theme itself and the type of model in this series have almost nothing in common with many other drawings of the same sitter. As he explained:

> When I produce my 'Variation' drawings, the path made by my pencil across the piece of paper is partly something like the gesture of a man groping his way in the dark. What I wish to say is that there is nothing foreseen in my route: I am led, I do not lead. I move from one point of the model which is my object to another, seeing only that one point, independent of those other points to which my pen then moves on. Perhaps it is that I am moved solely by an inner exaltation … (Matisse, Fourcade 1972, p. 164).

Just such a sense of inner exaltation led to this profile portrait, one of numerous variations on the theme, on which the artist plays with virtuoso skill in different registers, using different harmonies, each revealing something new. The turn of the head, tossed slightly upwards, the movement of the shoulder, the sharp opening of the dress's collar, all allowed him through rhythmic repetition to convey the freedom and keen sense of joy Lydia radiated. A.K.-G.

79

Henri Matisse

Woman with Naked Breasts

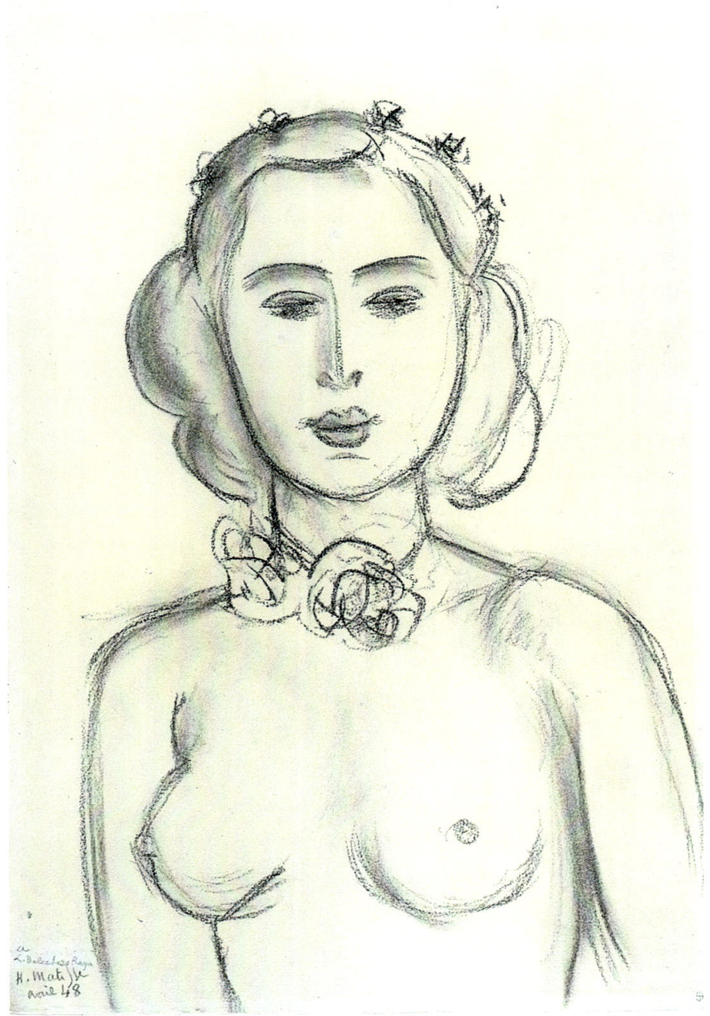

Charcoal. 604 × 405 mm

Pencil inscription in Matisse's hand in the bottom left corner: *à L.Delectorskaya / H. Matisse avril 48*

PROVENANCE: presented to Lydia Delectorskaya by the artist; collection of Lydia Delectorskaya, Vence; 1968 Hermitage, gift of Lydia Delectorskaya

Inv. no. OR 46046

EXHIBITIONS: 1958 Paris, no. 53; 1977 Leningrad, no. 133, ill.; 1984c Leningrad, no. 19; 1985 Leningrad, no. 41, ill.; 1986 Lille, no. 29, ill.; 1988–9 Tokyo-Kyoto-Nagoya, no. 73, ill.; 1993 Moscow-St Petersburg, no. 170, ill.; 1997 Retretti, no. 21, ill.; 1999–2000 Rome, no. 74, ill.

LITERATURE: Malingue 1949, p. 90, ill.; Kantor-Gukovskaya 1975, p. 144, ill.

Matisse made numerous portraits in charcoal, in which precisely drawn and often thick lines run across one another in places and tend towards an oval formation. These are combined with a soft, volumetric modelling of the face and body that is delicate and made up of gentle nuances, yet none the less consistently applied throughout. He had good reason to describe his drawings as 'painting with limited means', for he discovered in them a graphic language truly equivalent to painting. As in all his work, he found the break-up of colour and form unacceptable and he used 'sensitive' emotional and plastic lines to pick out forms and masses from the white of the paper, emphasizing the corporeal nature of his model.

The presentation inscription confirms that this drawing was made in or before April 1948. It later served as the basis for a print published *c.* 1950–51 in a run of 500 by the Maison de la Pensée Française, where a large exhibition of works by Matisse – paintings, drawings, *découpages* and sculptures – was held July to September 1950.

A.K.-G.

80

Pablo Picasso

Malaga 1881 – 1973 Mougins

Brick Factory at Tortosa

Oil on canvas. 50.7 × 60.2 cm

PROVENANCE: from 1909 Haviland collection, Paris; Kahnweiler Gallery; collection of Sergey Shchukin, Moscow; 1918 First Museum of New Western Painting, Moscow (from 1923 State Museum of New Western Art, Moscow); 1924 transferred to the Hermitage

Inv. no. GE 9047

EXHIBITIONS: 1954 Paris; 1960 London, no. 280; 1966–7 Paris, no. 63; 1970–71 New York, p. 170; 1972 Otterlo, no. 44; 1982 Leningrad–Moscow, no. 34; 1983 Tokyo–Kyoto, no. 52; 1987 Lugano, no. 40

LITERATURE: Tugendhold 1914, p. 35; Raynal 1921, no. 37; Stein 1933, p. 109; Zervos 1932–78, vol. II, no. 158; Kahnweiler 1954, no. 5; French 20th-Century Masters 1970, no. 81; Daix, Rosselet 1979, no. 279; Cat. 1976, p. 284; Podoksik 1989, pp. 101, 104, 107; Kostenevich 1999, pp. 355, 356, no. 306

Until comparatively recently this painting was known as *Factory at Horta de Ebro*. Between June and September 1909 Picasso was at Horta de Ebro (now Horta de San Juan), and the works he brought back from this trip were previously thought to all show this small town. Daix (Daix, Rosselet 1979) broke up this monolithic group, identifying several works painted during a stay in Barcelona and this painting too, although it was probably painted at Horta de Ebro, should also be set apart.

Palau i Fabre (1985) drew attention to the depiction of palms in the Hermitage work, although these do not grow in Horta de Ebro. Scholars have in general followed his lead in stating that Picasso invented this element, but this is not satisfactory: Picasso based his work on reality even in his deformations and distortions. The 'crystallizing' tendency that reached its culmination in landscapes made during the summer of 1909 grew out of the nature of the Tarragona landscape and architecture. In photographs he took and then sent to Leo and Gertrude Stein in Paris, we can clearly see the 'Cubist' structure of these localities, the small stuccoed houses scattered like wooden blocks or cubes. A comparison with these photographs reveals that Picasso depicted Horta not with literal precision, not even simplifying or geometricizing its details, but following the example of El Greco, whom he greatly admired and who moved or simply removed buildings in his views of Toledo. Picasso, too, subordinated his work not to topographical precision but to the demands of rhythm and composition, while reproducing the nature of the locality quite faithfully. This is underlined by the fact that he took and sent the photographs.

Picasso indeed had no reason to invent the palms, for they grow in Tortosa, the administrative centre of the region that includes Horta de Ebro. The town stands on the same River Ebro, and Picasso stayed there at the beginning of June on his way to Horta, from where he sent on 5 July a postcard with a view of Tortosa (perhaps he even went there a second time).

Tortosa was identified as the town shown in the Hermitage canvas by Maria Luisa Borras of Barcelona (personal communication). The town is even today famed for its brick factories built in the traditional manner: a small main block like a barn, porches for storing bricks and a chimney, usually rectangular. One such factory is shown here.

The landscapes of Horta de Ebro, although executed in the same manner, differ in the rocky nature of the locality: *Houses on a Hill, Horta de Ebro* (Museum of Modern Art, New York), and *Reservoir, Horta* (collection of David Rockefeller, New York, inv. no. Z.II.157). Both landscapes belonged at one time to Gertrude Stein, although in her memoirs she did not link them with any particularly place: 'That summer they [Picasso and Felix Fernandez] went again to Spain and he came back with some spanish [sic] landscapes and one may say that these landscapes, two of them still at the rue de Fleurus and the other one in Moscow in the collection that Stchoukine founded and that is now national property, were the beginning of Cubism' (Stein 1933, pp. 89–90). Together with *Houses on a Hill* and *Reservoir*, the *Brick Factory at Tortosa* forms a group of stylistically related architectural landscapes subordinated to the principle of reverse perspective.

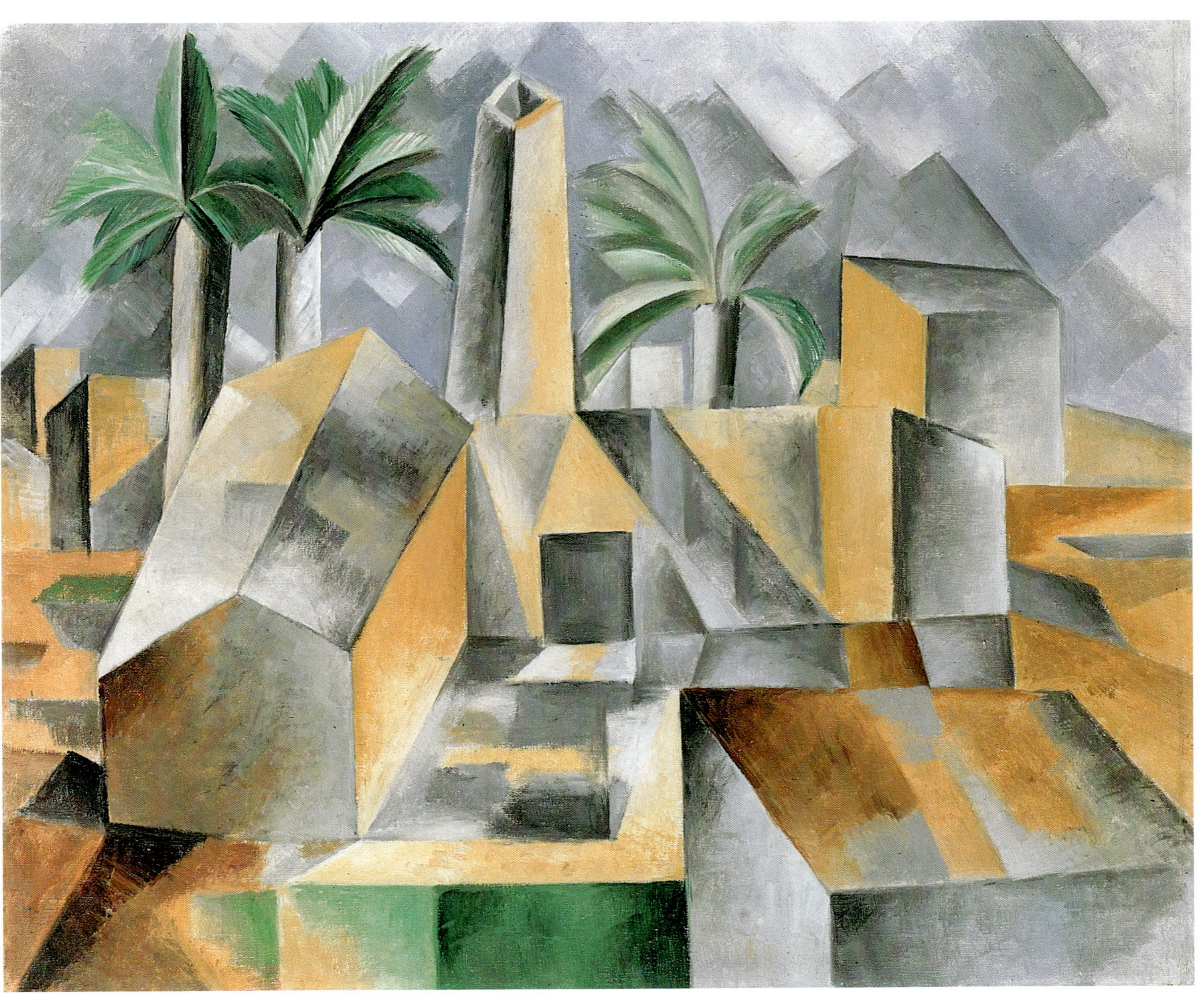

All of these landscapes are marked by precise crystalline articulation, to which even the sky is subjected in *Brick Factory*, expressing the grammar of Cubism with rare clarity. Such a painting overthrows all our preconceptions about landscape painting: one cannot 'enter into' it gradually, moving from the foreground, i.e., from the lower part of the canvas, to the middle, and then to the distant horizon, as was the way in paintings by the Old Masters, and even by many of Picasso's contemporaries. The sense of distance, without which such works cannot exist, has no point here. Now the landscape is perceived simultaneously, all at once, each individual detail being but part of the overall geometrical construction. Objects are not made precise in their details but are hammered out, the surfaces fashioned and faceted. The buildings are seen not from a single point of view but from a different points; they revolve and move apart, giving way before the will of the crystalline structure. In comparing this painting with photographs of the small brick factories that survive in Tortosa today, one understands the phantasmagorical nature of the painting, in which Picasso asserts the beauty and majesty of the simplest things by likening these stuccoed little houses to a precious crystal. A.K.

81

Pablo Picasso

Boy with a Dog

Gouache and pastel on brown card.
572 × 412 mm
Signed and dated top left: *Picasso 05*
On the reverse: *Study of Two Figures and a Male Head in Profile*

PROVENANCE: collection of Sergey Shchukin, Moscow; 1918 First Museum of New Western Painting, Moscow (from 1923 State Museum of New Western Art, Moscow); 1934 transferred to the Hermitage

Inv. no. OR 42158

EXHIBITIONS: 1956 Leningrad, p. 94; 1968 Leningrad, no. 53, ill.; 1982 Leningrad–Moscow, no. 45, ill.; 1985 Leningrad, no. 51; 1992 Barcelona–Bern, no. 43, ill.; 1995–6 Düsseldorf–Stuttgart, no. 30, ill.; 1999–2000 Rome, no. 85a, ill.

LITERATURE: Shchukin Catalogue 1913, no. 181; Tugendhold 1914, pp. 31, 65; Pertsov 1921, p. 95; Tugendhold 1923, pp. 113, 146; New Western Art 1928, no. 415; Réau 1929, no. 1005; Zervos 1932–78, vol. I, no. 306, ill.; Sterling 1957, pp. 196, 200, pl. 154; Daix, Boudaille 1966, XII: no. 16, ill.; French 20th-century Masters 1970, no. 66, ill.; Peinture française 1975, no. 200, ill.; Western European Drawing 1981, no. 116, ill.; Impressionists and Post-Impressionists 1985, no. 294, ill.; Podoksik 1989, no. 11, ill.; Hermitage 1994, no. 366, ill.

Although it is linked with a series of monumental compositions showing a group of travelling circus actors (*Saltimbanques*), begun at the end of 1904 (Zervos 1932–78, vol. I, no. 285), this study can also be seen as a fully independent work. Another work in the series (Zervos 1932–78, vol. I, no. 300; MoMA, New York), very close to this one but larger and more finished, shows two acrobats; one repeats this figure, with the same dog. The presence of a second (older) figure merely led the artist to twist the boy's body to the right, in order to unite the two.

The New York study was produced no later than mid-February 1905, since from 25 February to 6 March of that year it was exhibited at the Galerie Sérrurier in Paris and was reproduced in an essay by Guillaume Apollinaire, published in the journal *La Plume* (15 May 1905). *Boy with a Dog* relates to an earlier stage of work, and in all probability directly preceded the New York gouache.

As he worked on the painting, Picasso repeatedly altered his original concept, changing the figures accordingly. The final version, *Family of Saltimbanques* (Zervos 1932–78, vol. I, no. 285; NGA, Washington, DC), does not include the figures from either of these studies, yet that the original idea had the two acrobats and the dog is confirmed by x-ray analysis, where they can be seen through the upper layer of paint. Presumably it was during work on the composition that Picasso began to depart from subjects tied to the world of the poor and dispossessed, a world to which the figures in these studies undoubtedly belong.

The emotional resonance of the Hermitage drawing and the pale pink that flickers through the almost transparent greyish-blue tonality, allow us to see here the first signs of a transition from Picasso's Blue to Rose Period.

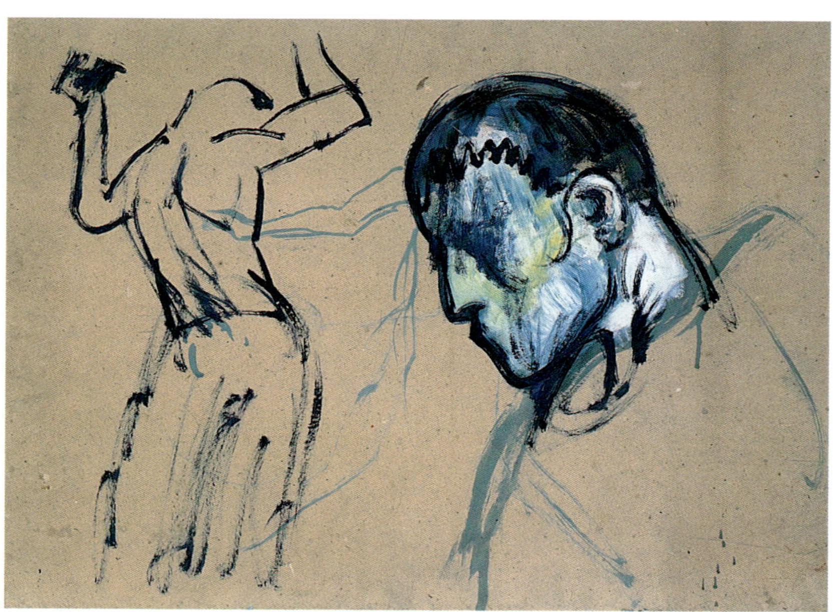

fig. 45
Study of Two Figures and a Male Head in Profile (reverse of cat. 81)

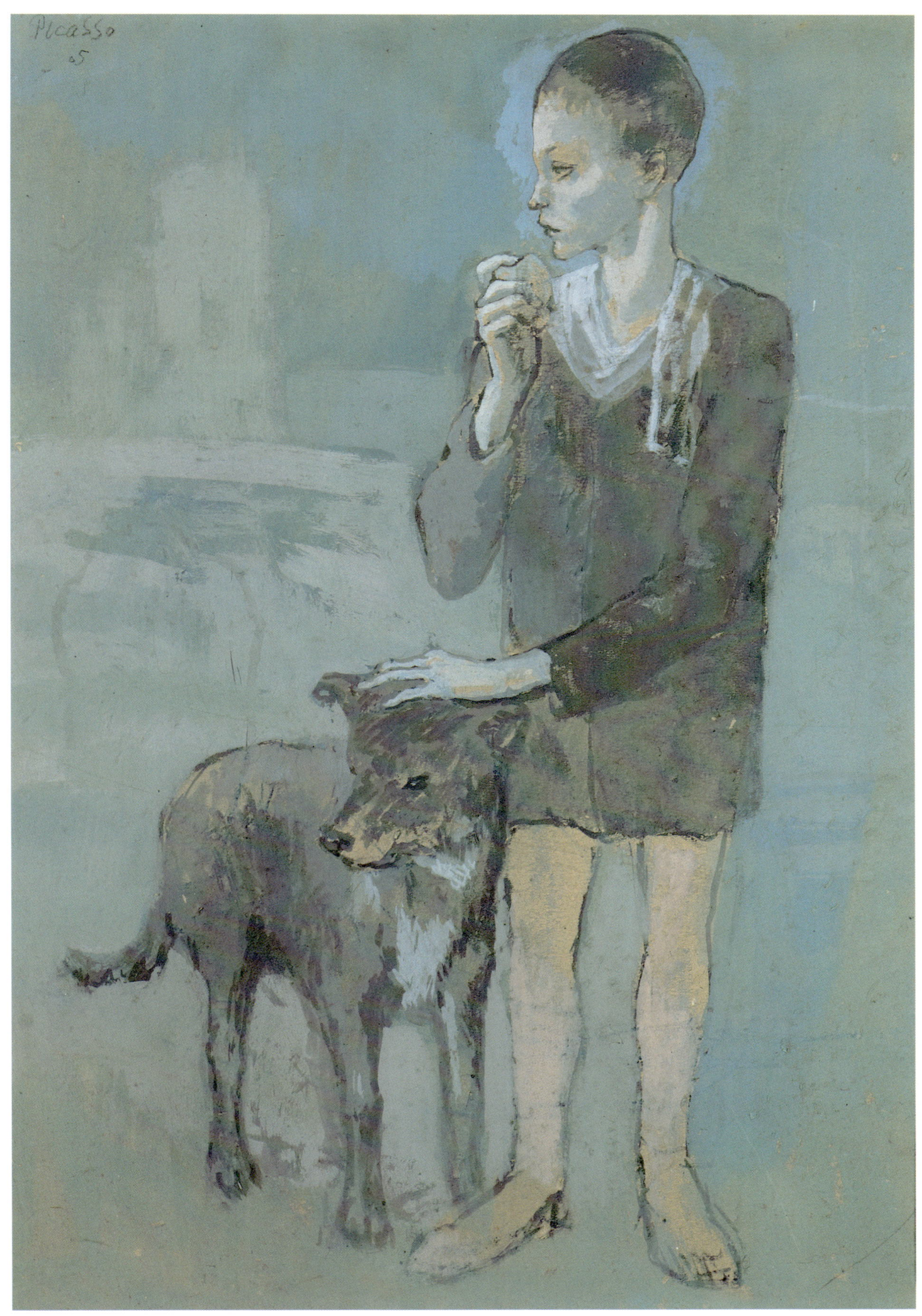
Picasso
05

On the reverse is *Two Figures, and a Male Head in Profile* (fig. 45), a sketch in tempera and oil that dates to the very end of 1904 or beginning of 1905, since *Boy with a Dog* is dated no later than mid-February 1905. Apparently the artist simultaneously conceived two compositions with travelling acrobats that were then worked up in a number of versions. One of these, showing a boy and dog, was not executed, while the other, linked with this sketch, reflects the earliest stage in work on the subject that resulted in the painting *Girl on a Ball* (1905, Pushkin Museum of Fine Arts, Moscow; Zervos 1932–78, vol. I, no. 290). Pokoksik's suggestion (1989) that the sketch be dated to the autumn of 1901 seems unconvincing. Both the athlete's powerful head and the youth's shaky pose, taken with the dark blue colours, indicate a link with the Moscow painting. Here the artist is taking only his first steps in a study from life and in positioning the figures: first he places the figure with hands flung out in the centre, then moves it to the left, covering it with the drawing of a male head. Later, moving away from the life drawings, Picasso replaced the gawky boy balancing on the ball with a girl, turning her face to the viewer, and made the horizontal format vertical, while yet remaining faithful to his original idea. The contrast between the unstable, slippery pose of the youthful acrobat's slender and flexible body, which keeps its balance only with difficulty, and the massive, heavy, immobile figure of the athlete, is clearly felt in this sketch. The composition gradually crystallized, and is reflected in a number of watercolours, gouaches and drypoint engravings produced that same year, 1905 (Zervos 1932–78, vol. I, no. 292; vol. XXII, no. 159; Daix, Boudaille 1966, XII: no. 20). A.K.-G.

82

Pablo Picasso

A Naked Youth

Gouache on brown card.
675 × 520 mm

Signed bottom right: *Picasso*
On the reverse: *Interior Scene: Reclining Female Nude with Seated Youth*

PROVENANCE: 1914 collection of Sergey Shchukin, Moscow; 1918 First Museum of New Western Painting, Moscow (from 1923 State Museum of New Western Art, Moscow); 1934 transferred to the Hermitage

Inv. no. OR 40777

EXHIBITIONS: 1925 Moscow, no. 64, ill.; 1982 Leningrad–Moscow, no. 46, ill.; 1985 Leningrad, no. 52; 1992 Barcelona–Bern, no. 126, ill.; 1995–6 Düsseldorf–Stuttgart, no. 47, ill.; 1999–2000 Rome, no. 86a, ill.

LITERATURE: Tugendhold 1923, p. 146; New Western Art 1928, no. 418; Réau 1929, no. 1008; Zervos 1932–78, vol. I, no. 268, ill.; Sterling 1957, pl. 155; Daix, Boudaille 1966, XIV: no. 8, ill.; Peinture française 1975, no. 221, ill.; Impressionists and Post-Impressionists 1985, no. 289, ill.; Podoksik 1989, no. 16, ill.

This study is characteristic of the end of Picasso's Rose Period, marked by the appearance of new, classically balanced forms and rhythms. This is the time when the world of travelling actors, of confused, transparent, sad figures, disappears from the artist's works. Picasso now began to draw and paint strong, stout, naked bodies, recalling Antique heroes in their proportions, albeit somewhat clumsy, with large hands and spreading, flat feet. Figures of athletes had appeared earlier in his compositions, but there they were intended to emphasize the fragility of the other figures, whose nakedness was a consequence of poverty. Here, on the contrary, we see a healthy youth.

The Hermitage study is one of the first of such works, which started a series of Paris (spring 1906) and Gosól (summer 1906) sketches and unfinished compositions with youths leading or washing horses (Zervos 1932–78, vol. I, nos. 264, 266; vol. XXII, nos. 266, 267, 269, 270 etc.).

On the reverse is *Interior Scene: Reclining Female Nude with Seated Youth* in gouache and charcoal (fig. 46). Although only summarily indicated, the objects in this interior are readily discernible: to the left is the corner of an overturned box used as a table, a single chair, a sofa, a kitten pressing into a woman's body, and a large bowl in which old journals were usually stored. Everything recalls Picasso's own room at Bateau-Lavoir, a refuge in Montmartre for impoverished artists, where from the summer of 1904 he lived with his mistress Fernande Olivier. Many years later, after she had parted from Picasso, she described in *Picasso et ses amis* (1933) how they met. Then a model for Othon Friesz and Raoul Dufy, she was returning one day to Bateau-Lavoir during a thunderstorm and bumped into Picasso in the corridor. Somewhat startled, he picked up a kitten from the floor and, holding out his hand, invited her in. So began nine years of life together.

It is not simply sentimental recollections that are associated with the name of Fernande, however, but the whole of the Rose Period – one of the most lyrical and poetic phases in Picasso's career. The soft, intimate manner of execution of this drawing, the modelling of form – fragile yet tactile and corporeal – the fullness of the contour, and the incorporation of the card's own brown tone into the pale blue colour scheme (warming it, depriving it of the severity inherent in the Blue Period), allow us to see this sketch as one of the first manifestations of the Rose Period.

It is possible that the figure of a youth washing his feet was added a little later as part of some new, unrealized composition in the spirit of the scenes from the life of travelling actors typical of Picasso's work in 1905. Although the figure recalls naked youths in other works of 1904 – in style, composition and emotion – it has no natural link with the scene. A.K.-G.

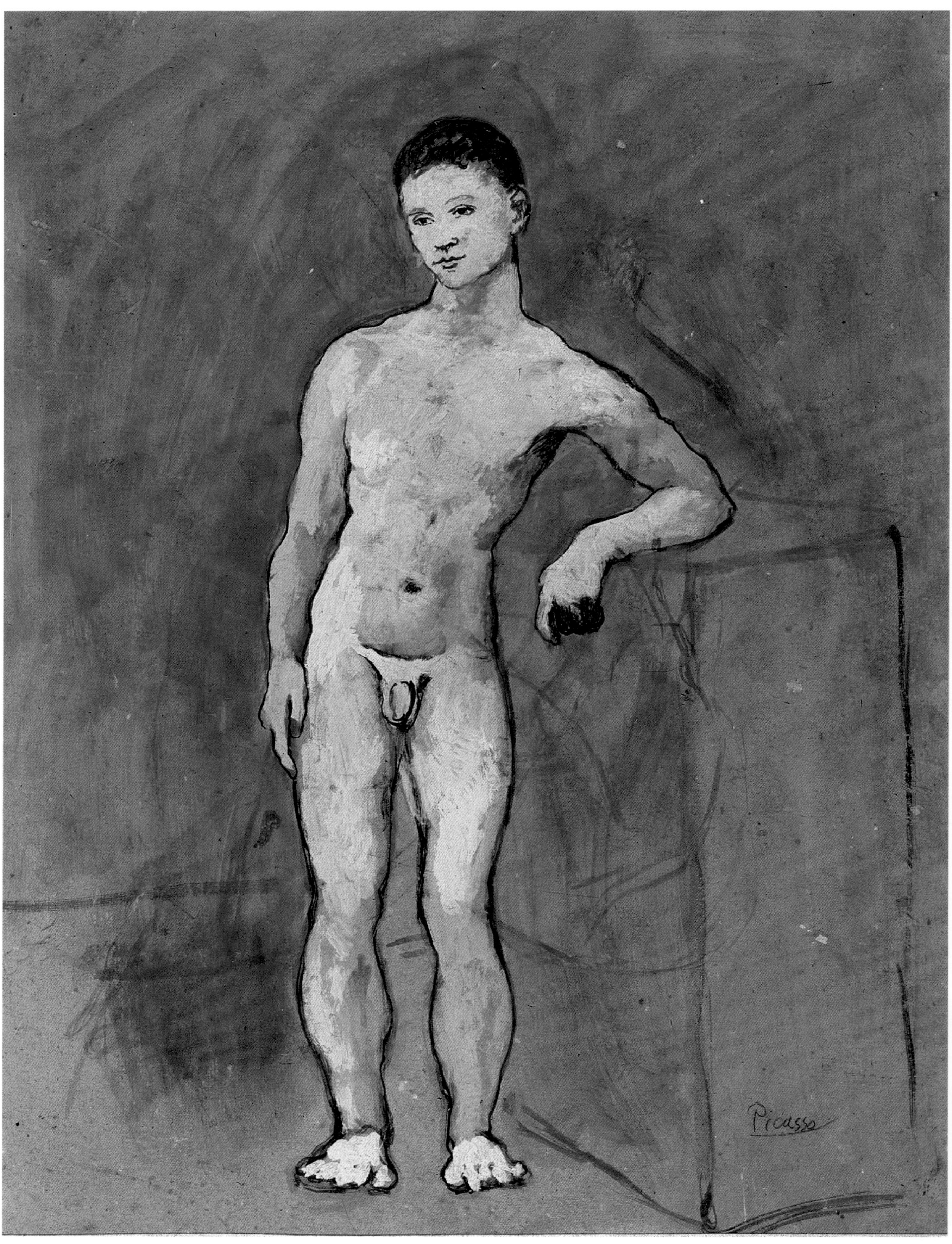
Picasso

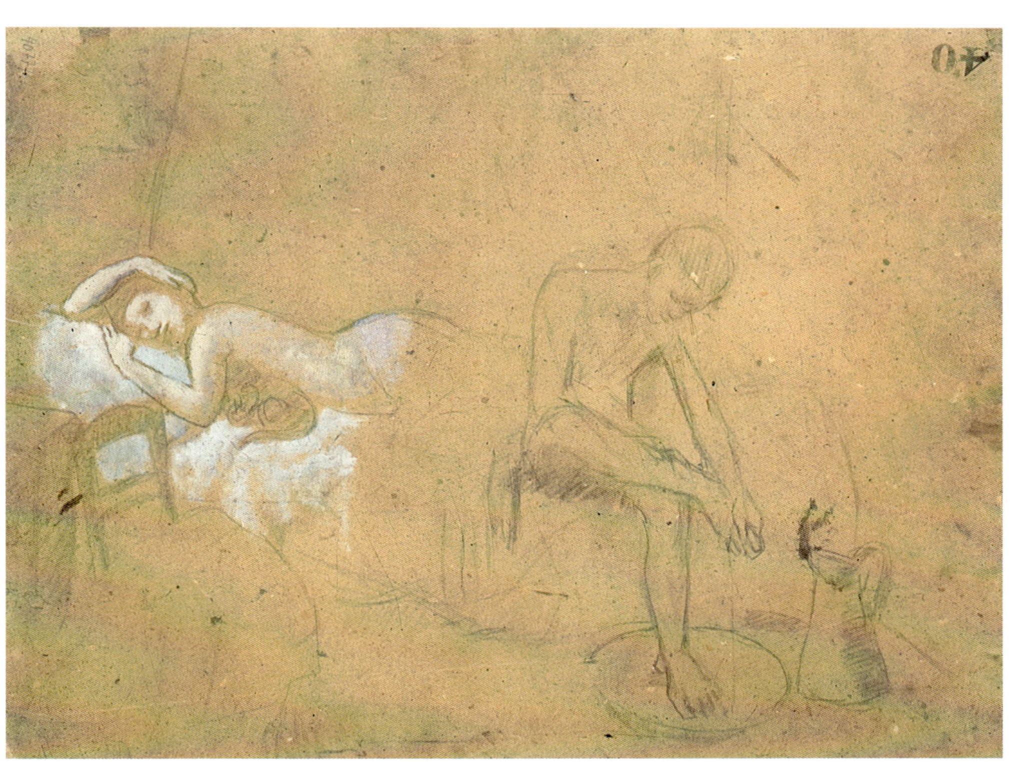

fig. 46
Interior Scene: Reclining Female Nude with Seated Youth (reverse of cat. 82)

83

Pablo Picasso

Leonid Massine and Lydia Lopukhova Rehearsing the Cancan in 'La Boutique Fantasque'

Pen and dark brown ink on brown paper. 288 × 408 mm

Inscription in dark brown ink in the artist's hand bottom right: *À Leonide Miassine Artiste qui j'aime son ami Picasso Londres 1919*
A vignette with Picasso's Barcelona address in reverse (mirror writing) to left: *3 calle de Merced Barcelona Julier 1919*

PROVENANCE: 1919 collection of Leonid Massine, Paris and New York; collection of Mikhail Baryshnikov, New York; 1991 presented by Baryshnikov to the Hermitage via the St Petersburg International Tele-Marathon

Inv. no. OR 48155

EXHIBITIONS: 1973 New York, no. 34, ill.; 1992 St Petersburg, no. 12, ill.; 1999–2000 Rome, no. 97, ill.

LITERATURE: Zervos 1932–78, vol. XXIX, no. 426; Cooper 1967, no. 154, ill.

In May 1919 Picasso arrived in London, where he was to design stage sets and costumes for a ballet, *La Tricorne* (based on the novel by the 19th-century Spanish writer Pedro de Alarcón), to be performed by Serge Diaghilev's Ballets Russes, then engaged for a season in the British capital. But when Picasso appeared, neither the music by Manuel de Falla nor Massine's choreography were ready. Work on *La Tricorne* was deferred and replaced with preparation of a one-act ballet, *La Boutique Fantasque*, with music by Gioachino Rossini arranged and orchestrated by Ottorino Respighi, and sets by André Derain. Massine was once again choreographer and main dancer, and he was totally occupied with rehearsals for *La Boutique Fantastique*, which had its premiere on 5 June 1919.

Throughout the whole of May, and later, when new performers were brought in, Picasso was a constant presence at rehearsals. According to Massine's memoirs, he liked to observe how the ballet was moulded and put together. Preferring rehearsals to the final finished stage performance, he made numerous sketches in pencil and pen: outline drawings of individual poses or groups that included famous dancers – Lydia Lopukhova, Vera Nemchinova, Tamara Karsavina; at times caricature-like portraits of the ballerinas and of Massine, Derain and Diaghilev, and of a temporary member of the troupe, Felix Fernandez.

Massine and Diaghilev had seen this young Spanish dancer in Madrid a year before their arrival in London, performing passionate flamenco dances in a small café. Full of admiration, they invited Fernandez to join the troupe in the hope that he could infuse something of his authentic Spanish style into their ballet performances. Fernandez proved unable to perform on the professional stage, but he was revealed to be an outstanding teacher, demonstrating the specific features of Spanish folk dance to Massine and the *corps de ballet*. Massine's pose in Picasso's drawing, his Spanish costume and flamenco dance shoes indicate that Felix's lessons had been incorporated into the balletic lexicon of *La Boutique Fantasque*.

More than just the elegant figure of a flamenco dancer, the Hermitage drawing reflects other aspects characteristic of Massine's work: the cancan itself, for instance, perceived by him as a sort of parody, a mocking *pas de deux*. It also shows the artist's no less characteristically subversive perceptions of the dance and dancers: the ballerina's grotesque 'flight', her fat calves, the rather comic pose of the dancer with the ballerina across his knee. Amid these rapid, spontaneous sketches that skilfully capture movements and poses, one's attention is drawn by the carefully worked up studies of hands. Strong and powerful, modelled with hatching, they recall Picasso's *The Italian Woman* (collection of Marina Picasso), painted that same year, 1919, and heralding the Neoclassical compositions of succeeding years. A.K.-G.

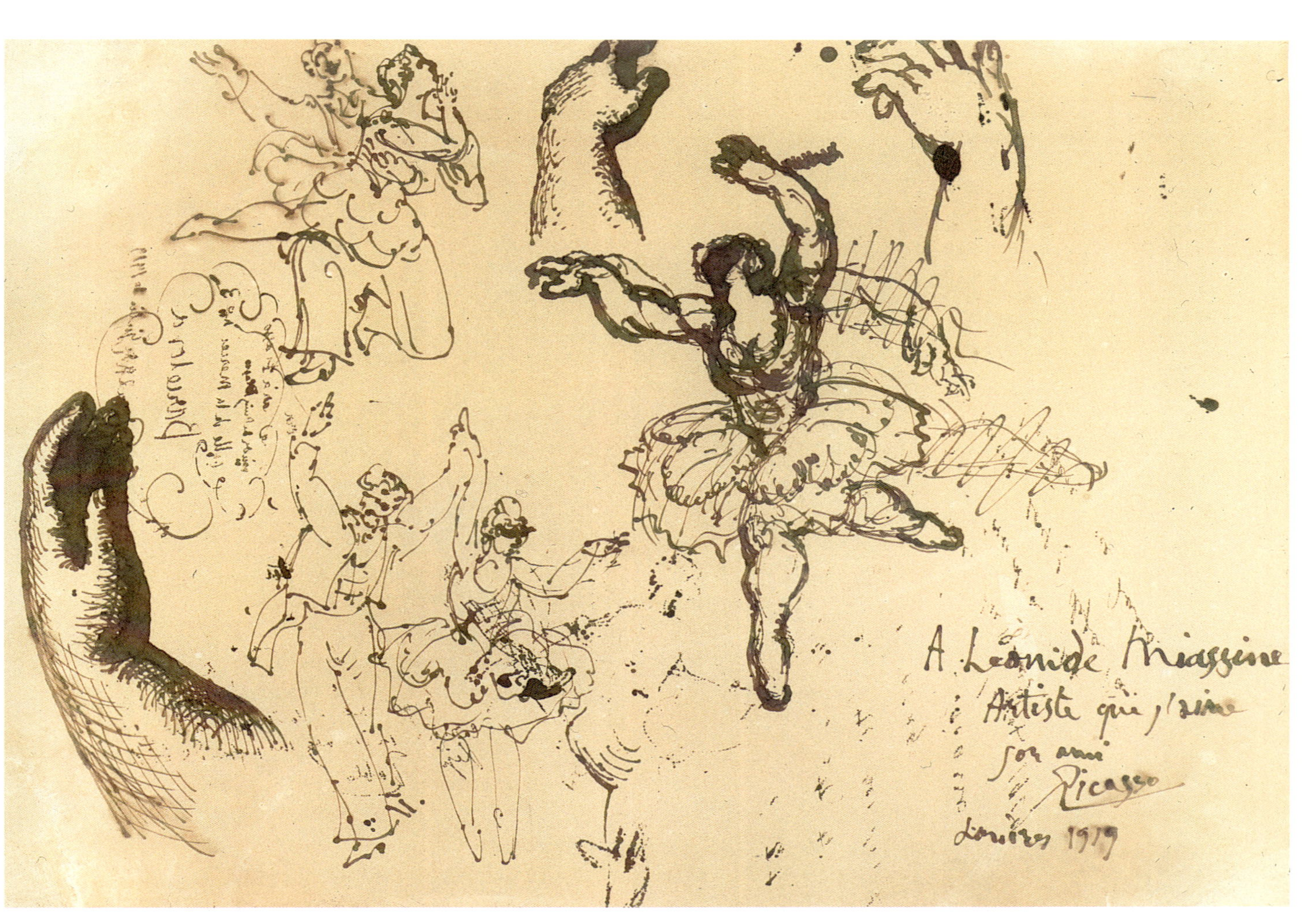
A Léonide Miassine
Artiste que j'aime
son ami
Picasso
Londres 1919

Exhibitions

1725 Paris, Exposition de la Jeunesse

1725 Paris, Salon
Collection des livrets des anciennes expositions depuis 1673 jusqu'en 1800. Salon, Paris, 42 vols, 1869

1860 St Petersburg
Muzey Imperatorskogo ermitazha. Opisaniye razlichnykh sobraniy, sostavlyayushchikh muzey [Museum of the Imperial Hermitage. Description of the Various Collections that Make up the Museum], St Petersburg, 1860

1867 St Petersburg
B. de Koehne: *Ermitage impérial. Collection des dessins. Galerie n. XII*, St Petersburg, 1867

1900 St Petersburg
Katalog risunkov masterov frantsuzskoy, ital'yanskoy, brabantskoy, gollandskoy i nemetskoy shkoly [Catalogue of Drawings by Masters of the French, Italian, Brabant, Dutch and German Schools], Museum of the Baron Stieglitz Central School of Technical Drawing, St Petersburg, 1900

1901 Hamburg
Paul Cassirer Art-Salon, Hamburg, 18 October – 18 December 1901 (title unknown)

1903 St Petersburg
Ukazatel vystavki 'Blanc et noir' imperatorskoy Akademii Khudozhestv [Index to the Exhibition 'Blanc et Noir' at the Imperial Academy of Arts], St Petersburg, October 1903

1912 St Petersburg
Katalog vystavki risunkov frantsuzskikh khudozhnikov epokhi Lyudovika XIV i Regentstva [Catalogue of an Exhibition of Drawings by French Artists of the Age of Louix XIV and the Regency], Museum of the Baron Stieglitz Central School of Technical Drawing, St Petersburg, 1912

1913 St Petersburg
Katalog vystavki risunkov frantsuzskikh khudozhnikov epokhi klassitsizma [Exhibition of Drawings by French Artists of the Age of Neoclassicism], Museum of the Baron Stieglitz Central School of Technical Drawing, St Petersburg, 1913

1925 Moscow
Gosudarstvenny Muzey Novogo Zapadnogo Iskusstva. Vystavka risunkov frantsuzskikh khudozhnikov kontsa XIX i nachala XX veka [State Museum of New Western Art. Exhibition of Drawings by French Artists of the Late 19th and Early 20th Centuries], compiled by S. Lobanov, Moscow, 1925

1926 Leningrad
M. Dobroklonsky: *Dessins des maîtres anciens*, Leningrad, 1927

1936 London
Leicester Gallery, London, January 1936

1937 Leningrad
Akvarel' XV–XIX vekov [Watercolours of the 15th to 19th Centuries], catalogue and introductory essay by T. D. Kamenskaya, State Hermitage Museum, Leningrad, 1937

1937 Paris
Chefs d'œuvre de l'art français, Palais National des Arts, Paris, 1937

1938 Leningrad
Vystavka portretov [Exhibition of Portraits], Hermitage Museum, Leningrad; issue III, *Portret epokhi vozrozhdeniya i barokko* [Portraiture of the Renaissance and Baroque Eras]; issue IV (untitled), 1938

1947 Leningrad
Arkhitekturnyye risunki i chertezhi ital'yanskoy i frantsuzskoy shkol XVI–nachala XIX veka [Architectural Drawings and Plans from the Italian and French Schools of the 16th to Early 19th Centuries], State Hermitage Museum, Leningrad, 1947; unpublished catalogue and introductory essay by G. G. Grimm, manuscript in the Academy of Arts, St Petersburg, Fund 20, *opis* 1, *delo* 172

1950 Paris
Claude Audran. Dessins du Nationalmuseum de Stockholm. Collections Tessin et Cronstedt, Bibliothèque Nationale, Paris, 1950

1954 Paris
Picasso. Œuvres des musées de Leningrad et de Moscou. 1900–1914, Maison de la Pensée Française, Paris, 1954

1955 Moscow
Vystavka frantsuzskogo iskusstva XV–XX vv. [Exhibition of French Art, 15th–20th Centuries], State Pushkin Museum of Fine Arts, Moscow, 1955

1956 Leningrad
Vystavka frantsuzskogo iskusstva XII–XX vv. [Exhibition of French Art, 12th–20th Centuries], Hermitage Museum, Leningrad; Moscow, 1956

1958 Paris
Chefs-d'œuvre de Henri Matisse. Au profit de 1'entraide des travailleurs intellectuels, Galerie Bernheim Jeune-Dauberville, Paris, 1958

1959 Leningrad
Zapadnoyevropeyskiy peyzazh XVI–XX vv. Zhivopis', grafika, prikladnoye iskusstvo. Katalog [Western European Landscape, 16th–20th Centuries. Painting, Graphic Art, Applied Art. Catalogue], Hermitage Museum, Leningrad, 1959

1960 London
Pablo Picasso, Tate Gallery, London, 1960

1960 Paris
Exposition Nicolas Poussin, Louvre, Paris, 1960

1963 Stockholm
Mastarteckninger från Ermitaget, Leningrad, Nationalmuseum, Stockholm, 1963

1965 Bordeaux
Chefs-dîœuvre de la Peinture française dans les Musées de Leningrad et de Moscou, Bordeaux, 1965

1965–6 Paris
Chefs-d'œuvre de la Peinture française dans les Musées de Leningrad et de Moscou, Paris, 1965–6

1966–7 Paris
Hommage à Pablo Picasso. Peintures, Grand Palais, Paris, 1966–7

1967–8 Paris
Ingres. Exposition, Petit Palais, Paris, 1967

1968 Leningrad: see 1968 Leningrad–Moscow (work exhibited only in Leningrad)

1968 Leningrad–Moscow
Ot Dyurera do Pikasso. 50 let sobiraniya i izucheniya zapadnoyevropeyskogo risunka v Ermitazhe [From Dürer to Picasso. 50 Years of Collecting and Studying Western European Art in the Hermitage], Hermitage Museum, Pushkin Museum for Fine Arts, Leningrad–Moscow, 1968

1968–9 Belgrade
Narodni muzej u Beogradu. Drzhavni Ermitazh u Leningradu. Dela Zapadnoevropskikh slikara 16.–18. veka iz zbirki Drzhavnog Ermitazha [National Museum in Belgrade. State Hermitage in Leningrad. Works of Western European Art of the 16th to 18th Centuries from the Collection of the State Hermitage]; 1968–9; Ljubljana, 1969 (no catalogue)

1969 Leningrad
Vystavka frantsuzskogo karandashnogo portreta XV–XVI vekov [Exhibition of French Crayon Portraits of the 15th to 16th Centuries]; Hermitage Museum; Leningrad, 1969

1969 Leningrad–Moscow
Izbrannyye risunki iz sobraniya Gosudarstvennogo Ermitazha. Sobraniye K. Kobentslya. Katalog vystavki [Selected Drawings from the Collection of the State Hermitage. Collection of C. Cobenzl. Exhibition Catalogue]; Hermitage Museum, Leningrad; Pushkin Museum of Fine Arts, Moscow; Leningrad, 1969

1969 Moscow–Leningrad
Anri Matiss. Zhivopis'. Skul'ptura. Grafika. Pis'ma. Vystavka, posvyashchyonnaya 100-letiyu so dnya rozhdeniya khudozhnika [Henri Matisse. Painting. Sculpture. Graphic Art. Letters. Exhibition on the 100th Anniversary of the Artist's Birth]; Pushkin Museum of Fine Arts, Moscow; Hermitage, Leningrad; Leningrad, 1969

1970 Budapest
Kiállitás a Leningrai Ermitazs legzebb rajzaiból, Szepmuveszeti Museum, Budapest, 1970

1970 Göteborg
Hundra målmingar och teckninger från Eremitaget, Leningrad, 1968; *Eremitaget i Leningrad. 100 malningar och teckningar fran ranassans till 1700-tal*, Konstmuseum, Göteborg, 1970

1970 Leningrad
Fransua Bushe (1703–1770). Zhivopis'. Grafika. Prikladnoye iskusstvo [François Boucher (1703–1770). Painting. Graphic Works. Applied Art], Hermitage Museum, Leningrad, 1970

1970–71 New York
Four Americans in Paris, The Museum of Modern Art, New York, 1970–71

1971a Leningrad
Izbrannyye risunki iz sobraniye Gosudarstvennogo Ermitazha. Kollektsiya G. Bryulya [Select Drawings from the Collection of the State Hermitage. The G. Brühl Collection], Hermitage Museum, Leningrad, 1971

1971b Leningrad
Proyekty i risunki frantsuzskikh arkhitektorov i ornamentalistov XVIII–nachala XIX veka. Gosudarstvennyy Ermitazh [Designs and Drawings by French Architects and Ornamentalists of the 18th to Early 19th Centuries. State Hermitage], catalogue and introductory essay by A. N. Voronikhina, State Hermitage Museum, Leningrad, 1971

1972a Dresden
Zeichnungen alter Meister aus der Ermitage zu Leningrad. Die Sammlung Brühl, Staatliche Kunstsammlungen, Dresden; Kupferstichkabinett, Dresden, 1972

1972b Dresden
Meisterwerke aus der Ermitage, Leningrad und aus dem Puschkin–Museum, Moscau, Dresden, 1972

1972a Leningrad
I. Nemilova, N. Biryukova: *Vatto i yego vremya. Zhivopis', grafika, skul'ptura, prikladnoye iskusstvo* [Watteau and his Age. Painting, Graphic Art, Sculpture, Applied Art], Hermitage Museum, Leningrad, 1972

1972b Leningrad
Pasteli zapadnoyevreopeyskikh masterov XVII–XX vekov [Pastels by Western European Masters of the 17th to 20th Centuries], compiled by A. Kantor-Gukovskaya, Hermitage Museum, Leningrad

1972 Otterlo
From Van Gogh to Picasso: Nineteenth- and Twentieth-century Paintings and Drawings from the Pushkin Museum in Moscow and the Hermitage in Leningrad, Rijksmuseum Kröller-Müller, Otterlo, 1972 (in Dutch and English)

1972 Paris 1972–3
Sylvie Béguin: *L' École de Fontainebleau*, Grand Palais, Paris, 1972–3; Paris, 1972

1972 Prague
Kresby evropsk?ch mistr? ze sbirek Státni Ermitáze v Leningrad?, Narodni Galerie v Praze, Prague, 1972

1972 Vienna–Graz
Meisterzeichnungen aus der Ermitage in Leningrad, dem Puschkin Museum und der Tretjakow Galerie in Moskau, Graphische Sammlung Albertina, Vienna; Neue Gallery, Graz; Vienna, 1972

1973a Leningrad
Karavadzho i Karavadzhisty. Katalog vystavki kartin iz muzeyev SSSR [Caravaggio and Caravaggisti. Catalogue for an Exhibition of Paintings from Museums in the USSR], Hermitage, Leningrad, 1973

1973b Leningrad
Vystavka pamyatnikov, restavrirovannykh v Gosudarstvennom Ermitazhe [Exhibition of Objects Restored in the State Hermitage], Hermitage, Leningrad, 1973

1973 New York
Stravinsky–Diaghilev, Cordier Ekstrom Gallery, New York, May – June 1973

1974 Manchester
Drawings by West European and Russian Masters, Whitworth Art Gallery, Manchester, 1974

1975 Aarhus
Tegninger frå Leningrad, Aarhus Kunstmuseum, 1975

1975 Copenhagen
Tegninger frå Leningrad, Thorvaldsens Museum, Copenhagen, 1975

1975 Berlin
Zeichnungen aus der Ermitage zu Leningrad. Werke des XV. bis XIX. Jahrhunderts, Kupferstichkabinett der Staatlichen Museen zu Berlin; Berlin, 1975

1975 Washington, DC
Jacques Callot. Prints and Related Drawings, National Gallery of Art, Washington, DC, 1975

1975–6 Washington, DC–Detroit–Los Angeles–Houston
Master Paintings from the Hermitage and the State Russian Museum, Leningrad; National Gallery of Art, Washington, DC; M. Knoedler and Co., Inc., New York; The Detroit Institute of Arts, Detroit; LA County Museum of Art, Los Angeles; The Museum of Fine Arts, Houston; 1975–6; New York, 1975

1976 Mexico
Pinturas Maestras de Los Museos Estatales del Ermitage y Ruso, Leningrado, Mexico, 1976

1976 Montreal
Chefs-d'œuvres de l'Ermitage et du Musée Russe de Leningrad, Montreal, 1976

1976 Winnipeg
Master Paintings from the Hermitage and the State Russian Museum, Leningrad, Winnipeg, 1976

1977a Leningrad
I. Novoselskaya: *Zhan-Batist Gryoz. Risunki iz sobraniya Ermitazha* [Jean-Baptiste Greuze. Drawings from the Hermitage Collection], Hermitage Museum, Leningrad, 1977

1977b Leningrad
Gosudarstvennyy Ermitazh. Novyye postupleniya 1966–1977 [State Hermitage. New Acquisitions 1966–77], Leningrad, 1977

1977 Tokyo–Kyoto
Master Paintings from the Hermitage Museum, Leningrad, The National Museum of Western Art, Tokyo; Kyoto Municipal Museum of Art; Tokyo, 1977

1978 Düsseldorf
Nicolas Poussin (1594–1665), Stadtische Kunsthalle, Düsseldorf, 1978

1978–9 Melbourne–Sydney–Adelaide
Hermitage and Tretiakov Gallery. Master Drawings and Watercolours, National Gallery of Victoria, Melbourne; Art Gallery of New South Wales, Sydney; Art Gallery of South Australia, Adelaide; Adelaide, 1978

1979 Paris–Leningrad
Charles De Wailly, peintre, architecte dans l'Europe des Leningrad lumières, Caisse Nationale des Monuments Historiques et des Sites, ed. Monique Mosser and Daniel Rabreau, Grand Palais, Paris, 1979

1981 Vienna
Gemälde aus der Eremitage und dem Puschkin–Museum. Ausstellung von Meisterwerken des 17. Jahrhunderts aus den Staatlichen Museen von Leningrad und Moskau; Kunsthistorisches Museum, Vienna; Vienna, 1981

1982 Florence
Disegni dell'Europa occidentale dall'Ermitage di Leningrado, Catalogue by I. Grigorieva, J. Kuznetzov, I. Novoselskaja, Introduction by J. Kusnetzov, Cabinet of Drawings and Prints of the Uffizi, LVII, Florence, 1982

1982 Leningrad–Moscow
Pablo Pikasso 1881–1973. K stoletiyu so dnya rozhdeniya [Pablo Picasso 1881–1973. On the 100th Anniversary of his Birth]; Hermitage Museum, Leningrad; Pushkin Museum of Fine Arts, Moscow; Leningrad, 1982

1982 Paris
H. Opperman: *Jean-Baptiste Oudry. 1686–1755*, Galeries National du Grand Palace, Paris, 1982

1982 Tokyo–Kumamoto
François Boucher (1703–1770); Tokyo Metropolitan Art Museum; Kumamoto Prefectural Museum of Art; Tokyo, 1982

1983 Leningrad
I. Novoselskaya: *Frantsuzskiy risunok XVIII veka v sobranii Ermitazha* [18th-century French Drawings in the Hermitage Collection], Leningrad, 1983

1983 Tokyo–Kyoto
Picasso, The National Museum of Modern Art, Tokyo; Kyoto Municipal Museum, 1983

1984a Leningrad
Antuan Vatto. K 300-letiyu so dnya rozhdeniya. Prospekt vystavki [Antoine Watteau. On the 300th Anniversary of his Birth. Exhibition Outline], Hermitage Museum, Leningrad, 1984

1984b Leningrad
Gyuber Robert i arkhitekturnyy peyzazh vtoroy poloviny XVIII veka. Zhivopis'. Grafika [Hubert Robert and Architectural Landscapes of the Second Half of the 18th Century. Paintings. Graphic Art], Hermitage Museum, Leningrad, 1984

1984c Leningrad
A. S. Kantor-Gukovskaya: *Anri Matiss. Risunki i estampy v sobranii Gosudarstvennogo Ermitazha* [Henri Matisse. Drawings and Prints in the State Hermitage Collection], Hermitage Museum, Leningrad, 1984

1984–5 Washington, DC–Paris–Berlin
Watteau. 1684–1721, National Gallery of Art Washington, DC; Grand Palais, Paris; Château de Paris–Berlin; Charlottenburg, Berlin; Paris, 1984–5

1985 Sapporo
Works by Western European Masters from the Collection of the Hermitage; The Hokkaido Museum of Modern Art, Sapporo; Sapporo, 1985 (in Japanese with some Russian)

1985 Leningrad
A. S. Kantor-Gukovskaya: *Risunok, akvarel', pastel' frantsuzskikh khudozhnikov vtoroy poloviny XIX–XX v. v sobranii Ermitazha* [Drawings, Watercolours and Pastels by French Artists of the Second Half of the 19th Century to the 20th Century in the Hermitage Collection], Hermitage Museum, Leningrad, 1985

1986 Bogota
Dibujos de Maestros europeos de los siglos XV al XVIII. Colección del Museo Estatal Ermitage de Leningrado, Museo de Arte Modemodo de Bogota, 1986

1986 Buenos Aires
Dibujos de los maestros de Europa occidental de los siglos XV al XVIII. Colección del Ermitage de Leningrado, Museo National de Arte Decorative, Buenos Aires, 1986

1986 Lille
Matisse, peintures et dessins du Musée Pouchkine et du Musée de 1'Ermitage. Musée des Beaux-Arts, Lille, 1986

1986 Montevideo
Dibujos de los maestros de Europa occidental de los siglos XV al XVIII. Colección del Ermitage de Leningrado, Museo National de Artes Visuales, Montevideo, 1986

1986–7 Paris
La France et la Russie au Siècle des Lumières. Relations culturelles et artistiques de la France et de la Russie au XVIIIe siècle, Grand Palais, Paris, 1986–7

1987 Delhi
Masterpieces of Western European Art from the Hermitage, Leningrad, The National Museum, New Delhi; Leningrad, 1987

1987 Leningrad–Moscow
Rossiya–Frantsiya. Vek Prosveshcheniya. Russko–frantsuzskiye kul'turnyye svyazi v 18 stoletii [Russia–France. The Age of Enlightenment. Russo–French Cultural Links in the 18th Century], Hermitage Museum, Leningrad, 1987

1987 Lugano
Capolavori impressionisti e postimpressionisti dai musei sovietici, Collezione Thyssen-Bornemisza, Villa Favorita, Lugano, 1987

1987 Sapporo–Hiroshima–Fukuoka
Masterpieces of Western Art of the 19th and 20th Centuries from the Collection of the State Hermitage, Leningrad, The Hokkaido Museum of Modem Art, Sapporo; The Fukuoka Prefectural Museum of Art; The Hiroshima Museum of Art, 1987

1987–8 Belgrade–Ljubliana–Zagreb
Svetski majstori iz riznica Ermitaza od XV–XVIII veka. Hermitage Masterpieces. Paintings and Srawings, XV – XVIII Century; Narodni muzej, Belgrade; Narodna Galerija, Ljubliana; Muzejski Prostor, Zagreb; 1987–8; Belgrade, 1987

1988 Leningrad
N. K. Masulionite, I. N. Novoselskaya: *Risunki i gravyury Kloda Mellana v sobranii Ermitazha* [Drawings and Prints by Claude Mellan in the Hermitage Collection], Hermitage Museum, Leningrad, 1988

1988 London
French Paintings from the USSR. Watteau to Matisse; The National Gallery, London; London, 1988

1988 Meaux
De Niccolo dell'Abate à Nicolas Poussin: aux sources du Classicisme, 1550–1650, Meaux, 1988

1988–9 Tokyo–Kyoto–Nagoya
Barbizon School, Impressionist, Early Modern Painting from the Hermitage Museum, Seiji Togo Memorial Jasuda Kasai Museum of Art, Tokyo; Kyoto Municipal Museum of Art; Nagoya City Art Museum; 1988–9; Tokyo, 1988

1988–9 Madrid–Barcelona
Henri Matisse. Pinturas y dibujos de los museos Pushkin de Moscu y el Ermitage de Leningrado; Centre de Arte Reina Sofia, Madrid; Museo Picasso, Barcelona; 1988–9; Madrid, 1988

1989 Moscow
Frantsuzskiy risunok XVII–XX vekov iz natsional'nogo muzeya v Varshave i Gravyurnogo kabineta Biblioteki Varshavskogo universiteta [French Drawings of the 17th to 20th Centuries from the National Museum in Warsaw and the Print Cabinet of Warsaw University]; Pushkin Museum of Fine Arts, Moscow; Moscow, 1989

1989 Paris
Les Étapes de la création. Esquisses et dessins de Boucher à Isabey, Galerie Cailleux, Paris, 1989

1990 Edinburgh
Cézanne and Poussin: the Classical Vision of Landscape, National Gallery of Scotland, Edinburgh, 1990

1990 New York–Chicago
From Poussin to Matisse. The Russian Taste for French Painting. A Loan Exhibition from the USSR, The Metropolitan Museum of Art, New York; The Art Institute of Chicago; New York, 1990

1990–91 Rome
J. H. Fragonard et H. Robert a Roma, Academia di Francia a Roma, Villa Medici, 1990–91; Rome, 1990

1991 Nagoya–Hiroshima–Kasama
Matisse Retrospective; Nagoya City Art Museum; Hiroshima Museum of Art; Kasama Nichido Museum of Art; Tokyo, 1991

1991 Paris
Le Rouge et le noir. Cent dessins français de 1700 à 1850, Galerie Cailleux, Paris, 1991

1992 Birmingham
Dangerous Liaison. Poussin's 'Tancred and Erminia' in Context, Birmingham Museum and Art Gallery, Birmingham, 1992–3; Birmingham (UK), 1992

1992 Barcelona–Bern
Picasso 1905–1906. From the Rose Period to the Ochres of Gosól, Barcelona, Museum Picasso; Berne, Kunstmuseum; Barcelona, 1992

1992 St Petersburg
Pamyatniki kul'tury i iskusstva, priobretyonnyye Ermitazhem v 1991 godu [Cultural and Artistic Monuments Acquired by the Hermitage in 1991], Hermitage, St Petersburg, 1992

1992a Nancy
P. Choné, D. Temois: *Jacques Callot. 1592–1635*, Musée Historique Lorrain, Nancy; Nancy, 1992

1992b Nancy
L'Art en Lorraine au temps de Jacques Callot, Musée des Beaux-Arts, Nancy; Nancy, 1992

1992 Stockholm
Louis-Jean Desprez. Tecknare, Teaterkonstnär, Arkitekt. Katalog, Nationalmuseum, Stockholm, 1992

1993 Moscow–St Petersburg
Anri Matiss. 1869–1954. Zhivopis'. Risunkok. Dekupazhi [Henri Matisse. 1869–1954. Paintings. Drawings. Découpages], Pushkin Museum of Fine Arts, Moscow; Hermitage Museum, St Petetersburg; Moscow, 1993

1993–4 Stuttgart
Henri Matisse. Zeichnungen und Gouaches decoupées, Graphische Sammlung, Staatsgalerie, Stuttgart, 1993–4

1994 Ibaraki–Mie–Tokyo
French Baroque and Rococo Art from The State Hermitage Museum, The Museum of Modem Art, Ibaraki; Mie Prefectural Art Museum; Toby Museum of Art, Tokyo; 1994 (in Japanese)

1994 Paris
La Chimère de Monsieur Desprez, Louvre, Paris, 1994

1994–5 Paris
Nicolas Poussin. 1594–1665, by Pierre Rosenberg, Grand Palais, Paris, 1994–5; Paris, 1994

1995 London
Nicolas Poussin, Royal Academy of Arts, London, 1995

1995 St Petersburg
N. Petrusevich: *Nikola Pussen. 1594–1665. Risunki iz sobraniya Ermitazha. Katalog vystavki k 400-letiyu so dnya rozhdeniya khudozhnika* [Nicolas Poussin. 1594–1665. Drawings from the Hermitage Collection. Catalogue of an Exhibition on the 400th Anniversary of the Artist's Birth], Hermitage Museum, St Petersburg, 1995

1995 Shizuoka – Tochigi – Okayama – Kumamoto
Stikhiya vody [The Watery Elements], exhibition of paintings and prints from the collection of the State Hermitage, Shizuoka Prefectural Museum of Art; Tochigi Prefectural Museum of Fine Arts; The Okayama Prefectural Museum of Art; Kumamoto Prefectural Museum of Art, 1985 (catalogue in Japanese with some Russian)

1995–6 St Petersburg
V. G. Shevchenko: *Sto risunkov frantsuzskikh ornamentalistov (pervaya polovina XVII–nachalo XVIII veka). Gosudarstvennyy Ermitazh* [One Hundred Drawings by French Ornamentalists (First Half of the 17th to Early 18th Century). State Hermitage], State Hermitage Museum, St Petersburg, 1995

1995–6 Düsseldorf–Stuttgart
Picasso Welt der Kinder, Herausgegeben und mit einer Einfuhrung von Werner Spies, mit Beitragen von Doris Krystofund Sigrid Metken, sowie Erinnerungen von Maya Picasso; Kunstsammlung Nordhein–Westfallen, Düsseldorf; Staatsgalerie, Stuttgart; Munich–New York, 1995

1996 Karlsruhe
Vom Glück des Lebens. Französische Kunst des 18. Jahrhunderts aus der Staatlichen Eremitage St. Petersburg, Städtische Galerie in PrinaMaxPalais, Karlsruhe, 1996

1996–7 Washington, DC–Fort Worth
Georges de La Tour and his World; National Gallery of Art, Washington, DC; Kimbell Art Museum, Fort Worth; 1996–7

1997 Bonn
Zwei Gesichter der Eremitage. Von Caravaggio bis Poussin, 2 vols, Bonn, 1997

1997 Retretti
Matisse. La belle Epoque et 1'avantegarde, Taidekeskus Retretti, Punkaharju, 1997

1997 Venice
Disegni di Giacomo Quarenghi. Vedute e capricci, Gallerie dell'Accademia di Venezia, Venice, 1997

1998–9 New York
Master Drawings from the Hermitage and Pushkin Museum; The Pierpont Morgan Library, New York, 1998–9; New York, 1998

1998–9 Stockholm
Catherine the Great & Gustav III, Nationalmuseum, Stockholm, 1998–9

1999 St Petersburg
I. Novoselskaya: *Frantsuzskiy risunok XVII veka v sobranii Ermitazha / Le Dessin français du XVIIe siècle dans les collections du Musée de l'Ermitage*, Hermitage Museum, St Petersburg; St Petersburg, 1999

1999–2000 Rome
I Cento Capolavori dell'Ermitage. Impressionisti e Avangardie alle Scuderie Papali al Quirinale, Scuderie Papali al Quirinale, Rome; Milan, 1999

1999–2000 St Petersburg
Ot voyny k miru. Rossiya – Shvetsiya. XVIII vek [From War to Peace. Russia – Sweden. 18th Century], Part 5: *Kollektsii Yekateriny II i Gustava III* [The Collections of Catherine II and Gustav III]; State Hermitage Museum, St Petersburg, 1999–2000; St Petersburg, 1999

2000 Copenhagen
Greuze. Hjertets dannelse, Statens Museum for Kunst, Copenhagen, 2000

2001 Rennes
J. Thuillier: *Jacques de Bellange*; Musée des Beaux-Arts, Rennes; Rennes, 2001

Literature

ALEXEYEVA, VODO 1977
V. Alekseyeva, N. Vodo: *Frantsuzskiy risunok XVI–XVIII vekov iz sobraniya Gosudarstvennogo muzeya izobrazitel'nykh iskusstv im. A. S. Pushkina* [French Drawings of the 16th to the 18th Centuries from the Collection of the Pushkin Museum of Fine Arts, Moscow], 1977

ALPATOV 1960
M. Alpatov: 'Poussin – peintre d'histoire', *Nicolas Poussin (Actes du Colloque International, Paris, 19–21 Septembre 1958)*, 2 vols, Paris, 1960, vol. I, p. 189

ALPATOV 1963A
M. Alpatov: 'Pussen – istoricheskiy zhivopisets' [Poussin as History Painter], in *Etyudy po istorii zapadnoyevropeyskogo iskusstva* [Studies in the History of Western European Art], Moscow, 1963, pp. 288–92

ALPATOV 1963B
M. Alpatov: 'Klassicheskoye techeniye vo frantsuzskoy zhivopisi XVII veka'The Classical Trend in French 17th-century Painting], in *Etyudy po istorii zapadnoyevropeyskogo iskusstva* [Studies in the History of Western European Art], Moscow, 1963, pp. 282

ALPATOV 1967
M. Alpatov: 'Tancred and Herminia', in *Studies in Renaissance and Baroque Art Presented to Anthony Blunt on his 60th Birthday*, London, 1967

ALPATOV 1979
M. Alpatov: '"Tankred i Erminiya" Pussena v Ermitazhe' [Poussin's 'Tancred and Herminia' in the Hermitage], in *Etyudy po vseobshchey istorii iskusstv* [Studies in the General History of the Arts], Moscow, 1979

ANANOFF 1976
A. Ananoff: *François Boucher*, avec la collaboration de M. Daniel Wildenstein, 2 vols, Lausanne–Paris, 1976

ANIKIYEVA 1947
V. Anikiyeva: 'Ot zamysla k kartine (Nikola Pussen)' [From Concept to Painting (Nicolas Poussin)], *Trudy Vserossiyskoy Akademii Khudozhestv* [Papers of the All-Russian Academy of Fine Arts], issue I, Moscow–Leningrad, 1947, pp. 67–86

ARAGON 1971
Louis Aragon: *Henri Matisse, Roman*, Paris, 1971

ARQUILE-BRULEY 1983
F. Arquile-Bruley: 'Documents notaries inédits sur Greuze', *Bulletin de la Société de l'Histoire de l'Art Français, Année 1981*, 1983

AUBERT 1763
Abbé Aubert: *L'Amour filial. Conte moral dont l'idée est prise du tableau de M. Greuze exposé au Salon du Louvre*, Paris, 1763

B.V. 1901
?.?.: 'Nikola Pussen, Tankred i Erminiya' [Nicolas Poussin, Tancred and Herminia], *Khudozhstennyye sokrovishcha Rossii* [The Artistic Treasures of Russia], 1901

BADT 1969
K. Badt: *Die Kunst des Nicolas Poussin*, 2 vols, Cologne, 1969

BEAN 1986
J. Bean (with the assistance of L.Tur?ic): *15th to 18th-century French Drawings in the Metropolitan Museum of Art*, New York, 1986

BENESCH 1939–40
O. Benesch: 'Jean Cousin fils, Dessinateur', *Promethée*, 1939–40, nos. 9–10

BENOIS [1910]
A. Benua [Benois]: *Putevoditel po kartinnoy galeree imperatorskogo Ermitazha* [Guide to the Picture Gallery of the Imperial Hermitage], St Petersburg [1910]

BÉRARD 1891
Catalogue des dessins anciens [...] des maîtres ornemanistes des écoles française, italienne et allemande du XVe au XIXe siècle [...] de la collection de feu M. Ch.-Eug. Bérard, architecte, Hôtel Drouot, Paris, 1891

BERCKENHAGEN 1970
E. Berckenhagen: *Die Französischen Zeichnungen der Kunstbibliothek Berlin*, Berlin, 1970

BEREZINA 1963
V. Berezina: 'Risunok J.-F. Mille' [A Drawing by J.-F. Millet], *Soobshcheniya Gosudarstvennogo Ermitazha* [Bulletin of the State Hermitage], issue XXIV, 1964

BEREZINA 1977
V. Berezina: *Zhan-Ogyust-Dominik Engr* [Jean-Auguste-Dominique Ingres], Moscow, 1977

BIRKE 1986
Veronika Birke: *Graphische Sammlung Albertina, Vienna. Zeichenkunst aus sechs Jahrhunderten*, Vienna, 1986

BJURSTRÖM 1976
P. Bjurström: *French Drawings: Sixteenth and Seventeenth Centuries, Drawings in Swedish Public Collections*, II, Nationalmuseum, Stockholm, 1976

BLUNT 1960
A. Blunt: 'Poussin Studies XI: Some Addenda to the Poussin Exhibition', *The Burlington Magazine*, CII, 1960

BLUNT 1965
A. Blunt: 'Poussin and his Roman Patrons', *Walter Friedlaender zum 90. Geburstag*, Berlin, 1965

BLUNT 1966
A. Blunt: *The Paintings of Nicolas Poussin. A Critical Catalogue*, London, 1966

BLUNT 1967
A. Blunt: *Nicolas Poussin*, 2 vols, London and New York, 1967

BLUNT 1979
A. Blunt: *The Drawings of Poussin*, New Haven and London, 1979

BODKIN 1939
T. Bodkin: 'A Rediscovered Picture by Nicolas Poussin', *The Burlington Magazine*, June 1939

BOERNER 1931
Handzeichnungen alter Meister des XVI bis XVIII Jahrhunderts aus den Bestanden der Ermitags in Leningrad und anderer staatlicher Sammlungen der Soviet Union, C. G. Boerner in Leipzig, 29 April 1931, Leipzig 1931

BONNAFÉ 1882
E.Bonaffé: *Les Amateurs de l'ancienne France. Le surintendant Foucquet*, Paris and London, 1882

BRAME, REFF 1984
P. Brame, T. Reff: *Degas et son œuvre. A Supplement*, New York and London, 1984

BREJON DE LAVERGNÉ 1985
?. Brejon de Lavergnée: 'Portraits dessinés de Claude Mellan conservés du Musée de 1'Ermitage', *Gazette des Beaux-Arts*, January 1985

BREJON DE LAVERGNÉ 1987
B. Brejon de Lavergnée: *Musée du Louvre. Cabinet des dessins. Inventaire général des dessins. Ecole française. Dessins de Simon Vouet. 1590–1649*, Paris, 1987

BROOKNER 1956
A. Brookner: 'Jean-Baptiste Greuze', *The Burlington Magazine*, May 1956

BROOKNER 1972
A. Brookner: *Greuze*, London, 1972

BRUWAERT 1912
E. Bruwaert: *Vie de Jacques Callot, Graveur Lorrain, 1592–1635*, Paris, 1912

BRYSON 1981
N. Bryson: *Word and Image. French Painting of the Ancien Regime*, Cambridge, 1981

BUKDAHL 1980
E. M. Bukdahl: *Diderot Critique d'Art, I: Théorie et pratique dans les Salons de Diderot*, Copenhagen, 1980

BUKDAHL 1982
E. M. Bukdahl: *Diderot Critique d'Art, II: Les Saloniers et les estheticiens de son temps*, Copenhagen, 1982

CAMPBELL 1982
R. J. Campbell: 'Jean-Guillaume Moitte. The Sculpture and Graphic Art. 1785–1799', PhD thesis, Brown University, Rhode Island, 1982

CARRÉ 1888
Catalogue des dessins anciens de toutes les écoles relatifs à la décoration et l'ameublement formant la collection de feu M.J. Carré..., Paris, 1888

CAT. 1774
[E. Münich]: *Catalogue des tableaux qui se trouvent dans les galeries et dans les cabinets du Palais Impérial de St. Pétersbourg*, 1774

CATS 1863–1912

CAT. 1958
Gosudarstvennyy Ermitazh. Otdel Zapadnoyevropeyskogo iskusstva. Katalog Zhivopis' [The State Hermitage. Department of Western European Art. Catalogue of Painting], vol. I (Italy, Spain, France, Switzerland), vol. II (Netherlands, Flanders, Belgium, Holland, Germany, Austria, England, Sweden, Denmark, Norway, Finland, Hungary, Czechoslovakia), Leningrad–Moscow, 1958

CAT. 1976
Gosudarstvennyy Ermitazh. Zapadnoyevropeyskaya zhivopis. Katalog 1. Italiya, Ispaniya, Frantsiya, Shveytsariya [The State Hermitage. Western European Painting. Catalogue 1. Italy, Spain, France, Switzerland], Leningrad, 1976

CAT. CROZAT 1755
Catalogue des tableaux du Cabinet de M. Crozat, baron de Thiers, Paris, 1755

CAYEUX 1970
J. de Cayeux: 'Dessins d'Hubert Robert', *Revue de l'Art*, no. 7, 1970

CAYEUX 1987
J. de Cayeux: *Hubert Robert et les jardins*, Paris, 1987

CHAMPEAUX 1888/9–97/8
A. de Champeaux: *Portefeuille des Arts décoratifs*, 10 vols, Paris 1888/9–1897/8

CHOUIX 1973–4
J. Chouix: *Jacques Bellange*, MAS, III, 1973–4, pp. 235–6

CLIFFORD 1973
T. Clifford: 'Un disegno del Bellange al British Museum', *Art illustrata*, 1973, pp. 377–80

COMER 1980
C. D. Comer: *Studies in Lorrain Art, 1580–1625*, Princeton University, January 1980

COOPER 1967
D. Cooper: *Picasso. Theatre*, Paris, 1967

CORBERON 1776
Chevalier de Corberon: *Journal Intime*, Paris, 1776, vol. I, p. 156

DACIER 1928
E. Dacier: 'Gillot (1673–1722)', in *Les Peintres français du XVIIIe siècle*, sous la direction de M. Louis Dimier, 2 vols, Paris and Brussels, 1928–30, Vol. I (1928), pp. 157–216

DACIER 1929–31
E. Dacier: *Gabriel de Saint-Aubin, peintre, dessinateur et graveur. 1724–1780*, 2 vols, Paris and Brussels, 1929–31

DACIER, VUAFLART 1922
E. Dacier, A. Vuaflart: *Jean Jullienne et les graveurs de Watteau du XVIIIe siècle*, Paris, 1922

DAHLBÄCK, PARISET 1954
B. Dahlbäck, F.-G.Pariset: 'Dessins de costumes de théâtre de Jacques de Bellange et de l'Ecole Lorraine', *Revue d'histoire du Théâtre*, 1954

DAIX, BOUDAILLE 1966
P. Daix, G. Boudaille: *Picasso. 1900–1906. Catalogue raisonné de l'œuvre peint*, Neuchâtel, 1966

DAIX, ROSSELET 1979
P. Daix, J. Rosselet: *Le Cubisme de Picasso. 1907–1916*, Neuch,tel, 1979, no. 279

DANIEL 1979
S. M. Daniel: 'Pussen i teatr' [Poussin and the Theatre], in *Teatral'noye prostranstvo* [Theatrical Space], Moscow, 1979

DELECTORSKAYA 1986
L. Delectorskaya: *L'apparente facilité: Henri Matisse, peintures de 1935 à 1939*, Paris, 1986

DESCARGUES 1961
P. Descargues: *Le Musée de l'Ermitage*, Paris, 1961; English edn, London and New York, 1961

DESGUINES 1950
A. Desguines: *L'Œuvre de J.-B. Oudry sur le parc et jardins d'Arcueil*, Paris, 1950

DIDEROT 1763, 1765 etc.
Salon reviews; *see* Diderot Salons 1957–67

DIDEROT 1968
Denis Diderot: *Pensées détachées sur la peinture*, ed. 1968, p. 800

DIDEROT 1984
Diderot et l'art de Boucher à David. Les Salons 1759–1781, exh. cat., Hôtel de la Monnaie, Paris, 1984

DIDEROT SALONS 1957–67
Denis Diderot: *Salons*, Texte établi et présenté par Jean Seznec et J.Adhemar, 4 vols, Oxford, 1957–67

DIDEROT 1876, VOL. IX
D. Diderot: *Œuvres complètes*, Paris, 1876, vol. IX

DIMIER 1924–6
L. Dimier: *Histoire de la peinture de portrait en France au XVIe siècle*, 3 vols, Paris–Brussels, 1924–6

DITTSCHEID 1999
H. C. Dittscheid: 'Le château de Montmusard: une realisation à Dijon – une idée pour l'Europe', *Bulletin des Musées de Dijon*, no. 5, 1999, pp. 21–8

DOBROKLONSKY 1932
M. Dobroklonsky: 'Unbekannte Zeichnungen Jean Cousin's des Älteren in der Ermitage', *Zeitschrift für Kunstgeschichte*, I, Berlin–Leipzig, 1932, pp. 44–7

DOBROKLONSKY 1954
M. Dobroklonsky: '"Obshchestvo na progulke" Grabielya de Sent-Obena' [Gabriel de Saint-Aubin's 'Society Promenade'], *Soobshcheniya Gosudarstvennogo Ermitazha* [Bulletin of the State Hermitage], issue VI, 1954

DOBROKLONSKY 1961
M. Dobroklonsky: 'The Drawings of Claude Lorrain in the Hermitage', *The Burlington Magazine*, September 1961

DORÉ AND JERROLD 1872
Gustave Doré, Blanchard Jerrold: *London. A Pilgrimage*, London, 1872

DRAWINGS, WATERCOLOURS 1965
M. V. Dobroklonsky: *Gosudarstvennyy Ermitazh. Risunki i akvareli. Album* [The State Hermitage. Drawings and Watercolours. Album], Leningrad and Moscow, 1965

DUCLAUX 1973
L. Duclaux: *La Statue équestre de Louis XV. Dessins de Bouchardon, sculpteur du rois, dans les collections du Musée du Louvre*, exh. cat., Louvre, Paris, 1973

DUCLAUX 1975
L. Duclaux: *Inventaire général des dessins: École française. Musée du Louvre. Cabinet des Dessins*, vol. 12, *Nadar–Ozanne*, Paris, 1975

DUPONT DE NEMOURS 1771
P.-S. DuPont de Nemours: *Ephemerides du citoyen; ou bibliothèque raisonnée des sciences morales et politiques*, Paris, 1771, vol. V

DUSSIEUX 1856
L. Dussieux: *Les Artistes français à l'etranger*, Paris, 1856

EIDELBERG 1984
M. P. Eidelberg: 'Gabriel Huquier – Friend or Foe of Watteau?', *The Print Collector's Nevsletter*, Vol. XV, no. 5, Nov–Dec 1984

ERENSVÄRD 1962
U. Erensvärd: *Svenska arkitecturritningar i Ermitaget och andra samlingar i Leningrad*, *NM Skriftserie* 8, Stockholm, 1962

FARNER 1963
K. Farner: *Gustave Doré – der industrialisierte Romantiker*, 2 vols, Dresden, 1963

FISCHER 1990
E. Fischer: *Melchior Lorck i Tyrkiet*, Statens Museum for Kunst, Copenhagen, 1990

FORTIA DE PILES 1796
Comte A. Fortia de Piles: *Voyage de deux Français en Allemagne, Danemark, Suède, Russie et Pologne fait en 1790–1792*, 5 vols, Paris, 1796

FOUCART 1980
J. Foucart: 'L'Ingrisme dans le monde en 1978', *Bulletin de Musée d'Ingres*, no. 45, Montauban, 1980

FRENCH 20TH-CENTURY MASTERS 1970
A. Barskaya, A. Izerghina, B. Zernov: *The Hermitage. French 20th-century Masters*, Prague, 1970

FRIED 1980
M. Fried: *Absorption and Theatricality. Painting and the Beholder in the Age of Diderot*, Berkeley, Cal., 1980

FRIEDLÄNDER 1965
W. Friedländer: *Nicolas Poussin. A New Approach*, London, 1966

FRIEDLÄNDER, BLUNT 1939–74
The Drawings of Nicolas Poussin. Catalogue raisonné, ed. W. Friedländer and A. Blunt, 5 vols, London, 1939–74

FUHRING 1989
P. Fuhring: *Design into Art. Drawings for Architecture and Ornament. The Lodewijk Houthakker Collection*, 2 vols, London, 1989

FUHRING 1992
P. Fuhring: 'Designs for and after Boulle Furniture', *The Burlington Magazine*, CXXXIV, no. 1071, June 1992, pp. 350–62

GABILLOT 1895
J. Gabillot: *Hubert Robert et son temps*, Paris, 1895

GARNAUD 1963
F. Garnaud: 'La Douleur dans l'art', *Aesculape*, April 1963

GBA 1998
Gazette des Beaux-Arts, 140e année, March 1998

GEORGEL 1985
P. Georgel: *Le Musée des Beaux-Arts de Dijon*, Dijon, 1985

GERTS 1947
V. K. Gerts: *Nikola Pussen. Tankred i Erminiya* [Nicolas Poussin, 'Tancred and Herminia'], Leningrad, 1947

GERTS 1948
V. Gerts: *Gryoz. Paralitik* [Greuze, 'The Paralytic'], Leningrad, 1948

GLIKMAN 1959
A. Glikman: *Zhak Kallo* [Jacques Callot], Leningrad, 1959

GLIKMAN 1964
A. Glikman: *Nikola Pussen* [Nicolas Poussin], Leningrad, 1964

GONCOURT 1980
E. & J. Goncourt: *L'Art du dix-huitième siècle*, Paris, 1880, vol. I

GRAMACCINI 1993
G. Gramaccini: *Jean-Guillaume Moitte (1746–1810). Leben und Werk*, 2 vols, Berlin, 1993

GRAND 1965
P. M. Grand: 'The Russian Delegation to Paris', *Art News*, October 1965

GRAPHIC ART 1961
Gosudarstvennyy Ermitazh. Grafika [State Hermitage. Graphic Art], album compiled by M. B. Dobroklonsky, Leningrad, 1961

GRASHCHENKOV 1961
V. N. Grashchenkov: *Risunki zapadnoyevropeyskikh khudozhnikov XIX veka* [Drawings by 19th-century Western European Artists], Moscow, 1961

GRAUTOFF 1914
O. Grautoff: *Nicolas Poussin: sein Werk und sein Leben*, 2 vols, Munich, 1914

GRIMM 1767
M. Grimm: *Correspondance littéraire*, 16 vols, Paris, 1877–82, vol. VII

GRIMM 1958
G. G. Grimm: 'Neizvestnoye proizvedeniya Zh.L. Depre' [An Unknown Work by J.-L. Desprez], *Soobshcheniya Gosudarstvennogo Ermitazha* [Bulletin of the State Hermitage], issue XIV, 1958, pp. 42–5

GUDIN 1913
Katalog der Sammlung des Herrn Baron Th. J. Gudin mit Beständen aus der Sammlung J. S. Forbes – London und anderen Besitz. Gemälde und Zeichnungen Alter Meister und von Meistern der Barbizon-Schule…, December 1913, Frankfurt

GUICHARD 1881
E. Guichard: *Dessins de decoration des principaux maîtres*, Paris, 1881

GUIFFREY [1900]
J. Guiffrey: *Les Modèles et le Musée des Gobelins*, 2 vols, Paris [1900]

HASKELL 1968
F. Haskell: 'Doré's London', *Architectural Design*, no. 12, 1968

HAUTECŒUR 1912
L. Hautecœur: *L'Architecture classique à Saint-Pétersbourg à la fin du XVIIIe siècle*, Paris, 1912

HERMITAGE 1964
'Eduard Mane. Portret g-zhi Giyme' [Eduard Manet, 'Portrait of Madame Guillement'], *Ermitazh*, Leningrad, 1964

HERMITAGE 1965
The Hermitage, Leningrad. Baroque and Rococo Masters, Leningrad and Prague, 1965

HERMITAGE 1994
The State Hermitage. Masterpieces from the Museum's Collection, 2 vols, London, 1994

HOURTICQ 1937
L. Hourticq: *La Jeunesse de Poussin*, Paris, 1937

IMPRESSIONISTS AND POST-IMPRESSIONISTS 1985
Impressionists and Post-Impressionists in Soviet Museums, Leningrad, 1985

INV. AVED 1766
'Inventaire dressé après le décès de J.-A.-J. Aved, 16 juin 1766', in G. Wildenstein: *Le Peintre Aved, sa vie et son œuvre*, Paris, 1922

INVENTAIRE 1988
Inventaire du fonds français. Bibliothèque Nationale. Departement des Estampes. Graveurs du XVIIe siècle, vol. XVII, by M. Préaud, Paris, 1988

JEAN-RICHARD 1978
P. Jean-Richard: *L'Œuvre gravée de François Boucher dans la collection Edmond de Rothschild [Musée du Louvre, Cabinet des Dessins]*, in the series *Inventaire général des gravures. Ecole française*, Paris, 1978

JOFFÉ 1932
I. Joffé [Ioffe]: *Frantsuzskoye iskusstvo epokhi razlozheniya feodalizma* [French Art of the Age of the Collapse of Feudalism], Leningrad, 1932

JOLLET 1997
E. Jollet: *Jean et François Clouet*, Paris, 1997

JOUANNY 1911
Correspondance de Nicolas Poussin, publiée d'après les originaux par Ch. Jouanny, in the series *Nouvelles Archives de 1'art français*, V, Paris, 1911

JOUIN 1889
H. Jouin: *Charles Le Brun et les arts sous Louis XIV*, Paris, 1889

JULLIAN 1960
R. Jullian: 'Poussin et le caravagisme', *Nicolas Poussin (Actes du Colloque International, Paris, 19–21 Septembre 1958)*, 2 vols, Paris, 1960, vol. I

KAHNWEILER 1954
D.-H. Kahnweiler: *Les Années héroiques du cubisme*, Paris, 1954

KAI SASS 1959–60
Else Kai Sass: 'Omkring Ingres' tegning af Lucien Bonapartes familie – Der Laerde Selskab (Société des sciences et des lettres d'Aarhus)', *Aarhus Arbog*, I, 1959–60

KAI SASS 1960
E. Kai Sass: 'Ingres Drawings of the Family of Lucien Bonaparte', *The Burlington Magazine*, January I960

KAMENSKAYA 1929
?. Kamenskaya: 'Les dessins de Jacques Bellange au Musée de 1'Ermitage', *Gazette des Beaux-Arts*, II, 1929

KAMENSKAYA 1934A
T. Kamenskaya: 'Cherty realizma v risunkakh Zh.-B. Gryoza' [Features of Realism in the Drawings of J.-B. Greuze], *Iskusstvo* [Art], no. 5, 1934

KAMENSKAYA 1934B
?. Kamenskaya: 'Greuze et Madame Geoffrin', *Gazette des Beaux-Arts*, November 1934

KAMENSKAYA 1939
T. Kamenskaya: *Gyuber Rober* [Hubert Robert], Leningrad, 1939

KAMENSKAYA 1947
T. Kamenskaya: *Zhan-Batist Gryoz. Sel'skaya shkola (Mest' khudozhnika)* [Jean-Baptiste Greuze. The Rural School (An Artist's Revenge)], Leningrad, 1947

KAMENSKAYA 1949
T. Kamenskaya: 'Portret Karla IX' [Portrait of Charles IX], *Sokrovishcha Gosudarstvennogo Ermitazha* [Treasures of the State Hermitage], Leningrad, 1949

KAMENSKAYA 1957
T. Kamenskaya: 'Neizvestnyye risunki Kloda Vin'yona i Zhaka Bellanzha' [Unknown Drawings by Claude Vignon and Jacques Bellange], *Soobshcheniya Gosudarstvennogo Ermitazha* [Bulletin of the State Hermitage], issue XII, 1957

KAMENSKAYA 1959
T. Kamenskaya: 'Les Œuvres d'Ingres au Musée de 1'Ermitage', *Bulletin de Musée d'Ingres, Montauban*, December 1959

KAMENSKAYA 1960A
T. Kamenskaya: 'Les Dessins inédits de Jacques de Bellange au Musée de 1'Ermitage', *Gazette des Beaux-Arts*, February 1960

KAMENSKAYA 1960B
T. D. Kamenskaya: *Gosudarstvennyy Ermitazh. Pasteli khudozhnikov shkol XVI–XIX vekov* [The State Hermitage. Pastels by Artists of Schools of the 16th to 19th Centuries], Leningrad, 1960

KAMENSKAYA 1962
T. Kamenskaya: 'Frantsuzskiy karandashny portret' [A French Crayon Portrait], *Khudozhnik* [Artist], no. 12, 1962

KAMENSKAYA 1964
T. Kamenskaya, in I. S. Nemilova: *Vatto i yego proizvedeniya v Ermitazhe* [Watteau and his Works in the Hermitage], Leningrad, 1964

KAMENSKAYA 1971
T. Kamenskaya: *Risunki Pussena v sobranii Ermitazha. Katalog* [Drawings by Poussin in the Hermitage Collection. Catalogue], Leningrad, 1971

KAMENSKAYA 1973
T. Kamenskaya, in Zolotov 1973

KAMENSKAYA 1985
T. Kamenskaya, in Y. Zolotov: *Antoine Watteau. Catalogue raisonné des tableaux et des dessins dans les musées russes* (notice par T. Kamenskaya), Leningrad, 1985

KAMENSKAYA, NOVOSELSKAYA 1969
T. Kamenskaya, I. Novoselskaya: *Frantsuzskiy risunok XV–XVI vekov. Katalog* [French Drawings of the 15th and 16th Centuries. Catalogue], Hermitage Museum, Leningrad, 1969

KANTOR-GUKOVSKAYA 1975
A. Kantor-Gukovskaya: 'Risunki Matissa v Ermitazhe' [Drawings by Matisse in the Hermitage], in the anthology: *Iskusstvo Frantsii XV–XX vekov. Sbornik statey* [French Art of the 15th to 20th Centuries. Anthology of Essays], Leningrad, 1975, pp. 131–49

KANTOR-GUKOVSKAYA 1981
A. Kantor-Gukovskaya: 'O nabroske Pikasso v sobranii risunkov Ermitazha' [On a Sketch by Picasso in the Hermitage Collection of Drawings], *Soobshcheniya Gosudarstvennogo Ermitazha* [Bulletin of the State Hermitage], issue XLVI, 1981

KANTOR-GUKOVSKAYA 1982
A. Kantor-Gukovskaya: *Degas*, Leningrad and New York, 1982

KANTOR-GUKOVSKAYA 1985
[1985 Leningrad] A. S. Kantor-Gukovskaya: *Risunok, akvarel', pastel' frantsuzskikh khudozhnikov vtoroy poloviny XIX–XX v. v sobranii Ermitazha* [Drawings, Watercolours and Pastels by French Artists of the Second Half of the 19th to 20th Centuries in the Hermitage Collection], Hermitage Museum, Leningrad, 1985

KANTOR-GUKOVSKAYA 1999–2000
[Rome 1999–2000] *I Cento Capolavori dell'Ermitage. Impressionisti e Avangardie alle Scuderie Papali al Quirinale*, Scuderie Papali al Quirinale, Rome; Milan, 1999

KAUFMANN 1978
E. Kaufmann: *Trois Architectes des Lumières: Boullée, Ledoux, Lequeu*, introduction and notes by G. Erouart and G. Teissot, Paris, 1978 (translated from the English by F. Revers); original English publication: *Three Revolutionary Architects: Boullée, Ledoux, Lequeu*, Philadelphia, 1952

KEAZOR 1996
H. Keazor: 'A Reconsideration of Nicolas Poussin's Drawings for the Conversion of St Paul', *Gazette des Beaux-Arts*, December 1996

KNAB, OBERHUBER 1968–9
E. Knab, K. Oberhuber: *Jacques Callot und sein Kreis. Werke aus dem Besitz der Albertina und Leihgaben aus den Uffizien*, exh. cat., Vienna, 1968–9

KNAB, WIDAUER 1993
E. Knab, H. Widauer: *Die Zeichnungen der französischen Schule von Clouet bis Le Brun. Beschreibender Katalog der Handzeichnungen in der graphischoen Sammlung Albertina. Wien*, Vienna, 1993

KOJINA, GERTS 1977
?usée de l'Ermitage. Peinture d'Europe Occidentale des XVII–XVIII siècles, preface by E. Kojina, Leningrad, 1977 (note by V. Gerts [Herz])

KOSTENEVICH 1999
A. Kostenevich: *French Art at the Hermitage. Bouguereau to Matise. 1860–1950*, London, 1999

KROL 1938
A. Krol: 'Vystavka portreta' [Exhibition of Portraits], *Iskusstvo* [Art], no. 4, 1938

KUZNETSOV 1970
Yu. Kuznetsov: 'Ot Dyurera do Pikasso' [From Dürer to Picasso], *Soobshcheniya Gosudarstvennogo Ermitazha* [Bulletin of the State Hermitage], issue XXXI, 1970

LABENSKY 1805–9
Galérie de l'Ermitage. Gravée au trait d'après les plus beaux tableaux qui la composent avec la description historique. Ouvrage publié par F. X. De Labensky, St Petersbourg, 1805–9, parallel French and Russian edn in 2 vols

LACAMBRE, SÉRULLAZ ET AL. 1974–5
J. Lacambre, A. Sérullaz *et al.*: *Le Néo-Classicisme français. Dessins des Musée de Province*, exh. cat., Paris, 1974–5

LAING, ROSENBERG ET AL. 1986–7
A. Laing, P. Rosenberg *et al.*: *François Boucher 1703–1770*, The Metropolitan Museum of Art, New York; the Detroit Institute of Arts, Detroit; Galerie National de Grànd Palais, Paris; 1986–7; New York, 1986

LANDON 1814
C. P. Landon: *Vie et œuvre complète de Nicolas Poussin*, Paris, 1814

LAVALLÉE 1798
Notice historique sur Charles DeWailly, architecte, ...par Joseph Lavallée, Paris, AN VII (Paris, 1798)

LE BRETON 1809
Le Breton: 'La Galerie de l'Ermitage', *Mercure de France*, May 1809

LEE 1967
R. W. Lee: 'Mola and Tasso', in *Studies in Renaissance and Baroque art Presented to Anthony Blunt on his 60th Birthday*, London, 1967

LEIRIS 1969
A. Leiris: *The Drawings of Edouard Manet*, Berkeley, Cal., 1969

LEMOISNE 1946–9
P.-A. Lemoisne: *Degas et son œuvre*, 4 vols, Paris, 1946–9

LEVINSON-LESSING 1965
The Hermitage, Leningrad: Baroque and Rococo Masters, introduction and notes by V. F. Levinson-Lessing and the staff of the State Hermitage Leningrad, Prague and Leningrad, 1965

LICHT 1954
F. S. Licht: *Die Entwicklung der Landschaft in der Werken von Nicolas Poussin*, Basel and Stuttgart, 1954

LINNIK 1973A
I. V. Linnik: ''Oplakivaniye' Zhaka Bellanzha' [Jacques Bellange's 'Lamentation'], *Soobshcheniya Gosudarstvennogo Ermitazha* [Bulletin of the State Hermitage], issue XXXVI, 1973

LINNIK 1973B
I. V. Linnik: 'Un Tableau de Jacques Bellange nouvellement decouvert', *Revue de l'Art*, 20, 1973, pp. 65–70

LIVRET 1838
Livret de la Galerie Imp»riale de l'Hermitage de Saint-Pétersbourg. Contenant l'explication des Tableaux qui la composent, avec de courtes notices sur les autres objects d'art ou de curiosité qui y sont exposés, St Petersburg, 1838

LOCQUIN 1912
J. Locquin: *Catalogue raisonné de l'œuvre de Jean-Baptiste Oudry*, Paris, 1912

MAGNE 1914
E. Magne: *Nicolas Poussin, premier peintre du Roi. 1594–1665*, Brussels and Paris, 1914

MAHON 1960
D. Mahon: 'Poussin's Early Development: An Alternative Hypothesis', *The Burlington Magazine*, CII, 1960

MAHON 1962
D. Mahon: 'Poussiniana. Afterthoughts Arising from the Exhibition', *Gazette des Beaux-Arts*, July–August 1962, pp. 1–138; Volume séparé avec même pagination et introduction, Paris, New York and London, 1962

MAKARENKO 1916
M. Makarenko: *Khudozhestvennyye sokrovishcha Imperatorskogo Ermitazha* [Artistic Treasures of the Imperial Hermitage], St Petersburg, 1916

MALINGUE 1949
Matisse. Dessins, preface by M. Malingue, Paris, 1949

MALTSEVA 1958
N. Maltseva: 'Frantsuzskiy karandashnyy portret perioda rastsveta' [French Crayon Portraiture at its Height], *Iskusstvo* [Art], no. 6, 1958

MALTSEVA 1963
N. Maltseva: *Klue* [Clouet], Moscow, 1963

MALTSEVA 1978
N. Maltseva: *Frantsuzskiy karandashnyy portret XVI veka* [French Crayon Portraiture of the 16th Century], Moscow, 1978

MARIETTE 1741
Pierre-Jean Mariette: *Description sommaire des dessins des grands maîtres d'Italie, des pays-bas et de France de feu M. de Crozat, avec des réflexions sur la manière de dessins des principaux maîtres*, Paris, 1741

MARIETTE 1851–60
Abecedario de P.J. Mariette et autres notes inédites de cet amateur sur les arts et les artists, publié par Ph. de Chennevières et A. de Montaiglon, 6 vols, Paris, 1851–60; vols 2, 4, 6, 8, 10, 12 in the series *Archives de l'art français*

MAROT ŒUVRE 1712
Œuvre du Marot architecte de Guillaume III Roy de la Grande Bretagne contenant plusieurs pensées utiles aux Architectes, Peintres, Sculpteurs, Orfèvres, Jardiniers et autres: Le tout en faveur de ceux qui s'appliquerent aux Beaux-Arts, Amsterdam, 1712

MAROT 1958
P. Marot: 'Le Jardin de la Cour de Nancy dessiné et gravé par Jacques Callot', in *Le Pays Lorrain*, Nancy, 1958

MARSEL 1911
P. Marcel: 'Frantsuzskiye risunki. II. Shestnadtsatoye stoletiye' [French Drawings. II. 16th Century], *Staryye gody* [Days of Yore], November 1911

MARCEL 1912
P. Marcel: 'Frantsuzskiye risunki. III. Pervaya polovina XVII veka' [French Drawings. III. First Half of the 17th Century], *Staryye gody* [Days of Yore], October 1912

MARTIN, MASSON [1905]
M. J. Martin, M. Ch. Masson: *Catalogue raisonné de 1'œuvre peint et dessiné de Jean-Baptiste Greuze*, Paris [1905]

MATHEY 1959
J. Mathey: *Antoine Watteau, peinture réapparures..., identification par les dessins, chronologie*, Paris, 1959

MATISSE 1954
Henri Matisse. Portraits, Monte Carlo, 1954

MATISSE 1978
Henri Matisse: Peintures et scuptures dans les musées soviétiques, Leningrad, 1978, no. 55

MATISSE, FOURCADE 1972
'Notes de Matisse sur les dessins de la série "Thèmes et variations"', in *Henri Matisse. Écrits et propos sur l'art*, text, notes and index by D. Fourcade, Paris, 1972

MAUCLAIR 1906
C. Mauclair: *Jean-Baptiste Greuze, Avec un Catalogue raisonné de l'œuvre paint et dessiné de J.-B. Greuze par J. Martin et C. Masson*, Paris, 1906

MEAUME 1860
E. Meaume: *Recherches sur la vie et les ouvrages de J. Callot*, 2 vols, Paris, 1860

MÉROT 1990
A. Mérot: *Nicolas Poussin*, Paris, 1990

MONOD 1922
F. Monod, L. Hautecœur: *Les Dessins conservés à 1'Academie des Beaux-Arts de Saint-Pétersbourg*, Paris, 1922

MONOD-FONTAINE 1989
Œuvres de Henri Matisse, Centre Georges Pompidou, Collections du Musée National d'Art Moderne, Catalogue by J. Monod-Fontaine, A. Baldassari and G. Laugier, Paris, 1989

MONTAGU 1962
J. Montagu: 'The Tapestries of Maincy and the Origin of the Gobelins', *Apollo*, September 1962

MOREAU-NÉLATON [1908]
E. Moreau-Nélaton: *Le Portrait à la cour des Valois. Crayons français du XVIe siècle conservés au Musée Condé à Chantilly*, 5 vols, Paris [1908]

MOREAU-NÉLATON 1908A
E. Moreau-Nélaton: *Les Frères Du Monstier*, Paris, 1908

MOREAU-NÉLATON 1908B
E. Moreau-Nélaton: *Les Clouet. Peintres officiels des rois de France*, Paris, 1908

MOREAU-NÉLATON 1924
E. Moreau-Nélaton: *Les Clouet et leurs émules*, 3 vols, Paris, 1924

MOUREY 1910
G. Mourey: 'Un Mobilier de l'époque de la Régence', *Les Arts*, no. 97, January 1910, pp. 29–32

NAEF 1960
H. Naef: 'Vier Ingres Zeichnungen', *Pantheon*, XVIII, 1, Munich, 1960

NAEF 1977
H. Naef: *Die Bildniszeichnungen von J.-A.-D. Ingres*, 4 vols, Bern, 1977

NEMILOVA 1961
I. S. Nemilova: 'Novaya kartina Fransua Bushe' [A New Painting by François Boucher], *Trudy Gosudarstvennogo Ermitazha* [Papers of the State Hermitage], issue 6, 1961

NEMILOVA 1975
I. Nemilova: 'Contemporary French Art in Eighteenth-century Russia', *Apollo*, June 1975

NEMILOVA 1982
I. S. Nemilova: *Frantsuzskaya zhivopis' XVIII veka v sobranii Ermitazha. Nauchnyy katalog* [French 18th-century Paintings in the Hermitage Collection. A Scholarly Catalogue], Leningrad, 1982

NEMILOVA 1985
The Hermitage Catalogue of Western European Painting. French Painting: Eighteenth Century, Florence, 1986

NEUSTROYEV 1898
A. A. Neustroyev: *Kartinnaya galereya imperatorskogo Ermitazha*, [The Picture Gallery of the Imperial Hermitage], St Petersburg, 1898

NEW WESTERN ART 1928
Katalog Gosudarstvennogo Muzeya Novogo Zapadnogo Iskusstva [Catalogue of the State Museum of New Western Art], Moscow, 1928

NOTHAFT 1936
Ye. G. Nothaft [Notgaft]: *Frantsuzskiye karandashnyye portrety XVI–XVII vekov* [French Crayon Portraiture of the 16th to 17th Centuries], Leningrad, 1936

NOTHAFT 1941
Ye. Nothaft [Notgaft]: 'Zhan-Batist Udri i yego proizvedeniya v Ermitazhe' [Jean-Baptiste Oudry and his Works in the Hermitage], *Gosudarstvennyy Ermitazh. Trudy otdela zapadnoyevropeyskogo iskusstva* [State Hermitage. Papers of the Western European Department], vol. II, 1941

NOVOSELSKAYA 1961
I. Novoselskaya: 'Eskiz Bushe k desyudeportu "Istoriya"' [Boucher's Sketch for the Dessu-de-porte 'History'], Soobshcheniya Gosudarstvennogo Ermitazha [Bulletin of the State Hermitage], issue XX, 1961

NOVOSELSKAYA 1962
I. Novosselskaya: 'Les Dessins de Claude Mellan au Musée de 1'Ermitage', *Gazette des Beaux-Arts*, May 1962

NOVOSELSKAYA 1970
I. Novoselskaya: 'Risunki Sharlya Lebrena v Ermitazhe' [Drawings by Charles Lebrun in the Hermitage], *Zapadnoyevropeyskoye iskusstvo. Sbornik statey* [Western European Art. Anthology of Essays], Leningrad, 1970

NOVOSELSKAYA 1972
I. Novoselskaya in W. F. Levinson-Lessing, I. Novoselskaya: *Masterpieces of Painting in the Hermitage Museum*, Leningrad, 1972

NOVOSELSKAYA 1973
I. Novoselskaya: 'Risunki Fransua Bushe v sobranii Ermitazha' [Drawings by François Boucher in the Hermitage Collection], *Trudy Gosudarstvennogo Ermitazha* [Papers of the State Hermitage, issue 14, 1973

NOVOSELSKAYA 1975
I. Novosselskaya: 'French Drawings from Watteau to Greuze', *Apollo*, June 1975

NOVOSELSKAYA 1977
[1977 Leningrad] I. Novoselskaya: *Zhan-Batist Gryoz. Risunki iz sobraniya Ermitazha* [Jean-Baptiste Greuze. Drawings from the Hermitage Collection], exh. cat., Leningrad, 1977

NOVOSELSKAYA 1981
I. Novoselskaya: 'Risunko Gyubera Robera v Ermitazhe' [Drawings by Hubert Robert in the Hermitage], *Muzey* [Museum], no. 2, 1981

NOVOSELSKAYA 1983
[1983 Leningrad] I. Novoselskaya: *Frantsuzskiy risunok XVIII veka v sobranii Ermitazha* [18th-century French Drawings in the Hermitage Collection], Leningrad, 1983

NOVOSELSKAYA 1985
I. Novoselskaya: 'Rol risunka v tvorchestve Zhana-Batista Gryoza' [The Role of Drawing in the Work of Jean-Baptiste Greuze], *Zapadnoyevropeyskaya grafika XV–XX vekov. Sbornik statey* [Western European Graphic Art of the 15th to 20th Centuries. Anthology of Essays], Leningrad, 1985

NOVOSELSKAYA 1987
I. Novoselskaia: *Jean-Baptiste Greuze*, Leningrad, 1987

NOVOSELSKAYA 1996
I. Novosselskaya: 'A Drawing by Pierre for the Ceiling of the Grand Salon at Saint-Cloud', *Master Drawings*, XXXIV, no. 1, Spring 1996

NOVOSELSKAYA 1999
[1999 St Petersburg] I. Novoselskaya: *Frantsuzskiy risunok XVII veka v sobranii Ermitazha / Le dessin française du XVIIe siècle dans les collections du Musée de l'Ermitage*, St Petersburg, 1999

OPPERMAN 1970
H. N. Opperman: 'The Genesis of the "Chasses Royales"', *The Burlington Magazine*, April 1970

OPPERMAN 1977
H. N. Opperman: *Jean-Baptiste Oudry*, 2 vols, New York and London, 1977

OTTOMEYER, PRÖSCHEL 1987
H. Ottomeyer, P. Pröschel: *Vergoldete Bronzen: Die Bronzearbeiten des Spätbarock und Klassizismus*, 2 vols, Munich, 1987

PALAU Ì FABRE 1985
J. Palau Ì Fabre: *Picasso. The Early Years, 1881–1907*, Barcelona, 1985

PARISET 1948
F.-G. Pariset: *Georges de la Tour*, Paris, 1948

PARISET 1950
F. G. Pariset: 'Dessins de Jaques de Bellange', *La Critica d'arte*, 3e série, année VIII, no. 5, January 1950

PARISET 1962
F. G. Pariset: 'Jacques de Bellange', *L'Œil*, no. 93, 1962

PARISET 1963
F. G. Pariset: 'Bellange et Lagneau', in *Studies in Western Art. Actes du 20. Congrès international d'histoire de l'art (1961)*, 1963

PARKER 1931
K. T. Parker: *The Drawings of Antoine Watteau*, London, 1931

PARKER–MATHEY 1957
K. T. Parker, J. Mathey: *Antoine Watteau. Catalogue complet de son œuvre dessiné*, 2 vols, Paris, 1957

PATTISON 1884
Mrs. Mark Pattison [Emilia Francis Strong Dilke]: *Claude Lorrain, sa vie et ses œuvres d'après des documents inédits*, Paris, 1884

PEINTURE FRANÇAISE 1975
A. Izerghina, A. Barskaïa: *La Peinture française. Seconde moitié du XIXe debut du XXe siècle. Musée de 1'Ermitage*, Leningrad, 1975

PERTSOV 1921
P. Pertsov: *Shchukinskoye sobraniye frantsuzskoy zhivopisi* [The Shchukin Collection of French Painting], Museum of New Western Art, Moscow, 1921

PETRUSEVICH 1995
[1995 St Petersburg] N. Petrusevich: *Nikola Pussen. 1594–1665. Risunki iz sobraniya Ermitazha. Katalog vystavki k 400-letiyu so dnya rozhdeniya khudozhnika* [Nicolas Poussin. 1594–1665. Drawings from the Hermitage Collection. Catalogue of an Exhibition on the 400th Anniversary of the Artist's Birth, Hermitage Museum, St Petersburg, 1995

PEYRE 1965
H. Peyre: 'Painter's Painter to the Age', *Art News*, February 1965

PODOKSIK 1989
A. Podoksik: *Picasso: the Eternal Quest. The Artist's Works in Soviet Museums*, New York and Leningrad, 1989

POSNER 1977
D. Posner: 'Jacques Callot and the Dances Called Sfessania', *The Art Bulletin*, LIX, issue 2, 1977, pp. 203–16

PRINTS AND DRAWINGS 1975
Prints and Drawings by Gabriel de Saint-Aubin, Davison Art Center, Middletown, Conn.; Baltimore Museum of Art, 1975

PROKOFYEV 1962
V. N. Prokofyev: *Frantsuzskaya zhivopis' v muzeyakh SSSR* [French Painting in Museums of the USSR], Moscow, 1962

RAYNAL 1921
M. Raynal: *Pablo Picasso*, Munich, 1921

RÉAU 1912
L. Réau: ëLa Galerie de tableaux de l'Ermitage et la collection Semenov 1', *Gazette des Beaux-Arts*, 54e année, 2e semestre, 1912, pp. 379–96

RÉAU 1913
L. Réau: *St. Pétersbourg. (Les Villes d'Art célèbres)*, Paris, 1913

RÉAU 1920
L. Réau: 'Greuze et la Russie', *L'Art et les Artistes*, vol. I, July 1920

RÉAU 1929
L. Réau: *Catalogue de l'art français dans les musées russes*, Paris, 1929

REMY 1766
P. Remy: *Catalogue raisonné des tableaux de differents bons maîtres ... qui composent le cabinet de feu M. Aved, peintre du Roi et de son Académie*, Paris, 1766; republished in G. Wildenstein: *Le Peintre Aved, sa vie et son œuvre*, Paris, 1922

REMY 1767
P. Remy: *Catalogue raisonné des tableaux, dessins ... après le décès de M.de Jullienne*, 2 vols, Paris, 1767

RICHARDSON 1958
J. Richardson: *Edouard Manet. Paintings and Drawings*, London, 1958

ROLAND MICHEL 1984A
M. Roland Michel: *Lajoue et l'Art rocaille*, Paris, 1984

ROLAND MICHEL 1984B
M. Roland Michel: *Un Artiste du XVIIIe siècle*, Paris and London, 1984

ROLAND MICHEL 1987
M. Roland Michel: *Le Dessin français au XVIIIe siècle*, Fribourg, 1987

ROSENBERG 1985
P. Rosenberg: 'Un Pierre retrouvé', *Paragone*, 36, May 1985, pp. 269–73

ROSENBERG 1984–5
P. Rosenberg in 1984–5 Washington, DC–Paris–Berlin

ROSENBERG 1988
[1988 Meaux] *De Niccolo dell'Abate à Nicolas Poussin: aux sources du Classicisme, 1550–1650*, Musée Bossuet, Meaux, 1988

ROSENBERG, PRAT 1994
P. Rosenberg, L.-A. Prat: *Nicolas Poussin. 1594–1665. Catalogue raisonné des dessins*, 2 vols, Milan, 1994

ROSENBERG, PRAT 1996
P. Rosenberg, L.-A.Prat: *Antoine Watteau. 1684–1721. Catalogue raisonné des dessins*, 2 vols, Milan, 1996

RÖTHLISBERGER 1961
M. Röthlisberger: *Claude Lorrain: The Paintings*, 2 vols, London, 1961

RÖTHLISBERGER 1968
M. Röthlisberger: *Claude Lorrain. The Drawings*, 2 vols, Berkeley and Los Angeles, 1968

RÖTHLISBERGER 1977
M. Röthlisberger: 'Le Paysage comme idéal classique', in *Tout l'œuvre peint de Claude Lorrain*, Introduction and *catalogue raisonné* by M. Rothlisberger with Doretta Cecchi, Paris, 1977

ROUCHES 1921
G. Rouches: 'L'Interpretation du "Roland furieux" et de la "Jerusalem delivrée" dans les arts plastiques', *Etudes Italiennes*, III, 1921

SAMOYAULT 1979
J.-P. Samoyault: *André-Charles Boulle et sa famille. Nouvelles recherches, nouveaux documents*, Geneva, 1979

SANDRART 1675–9
J. von Sandrart: *Teutsche Academie*, Nürnberg, 1675–9; cited from Joachim von Sandrart: *Die teutsche Academie*, ed. A. R. Peltzer, Munich, 1925

SBRIO 1876
'Perepiska Imperatritsy Yekateriny II s baronom Grimmom (1744–1796), izdannaya s poyasneniyami i primechaniyami I. Grota' [The Correspondence of Empress Catherine II and Baron Grimm (1744–1796), published with explanations and notes by J. Groot], in *Sbornik Imperatorskogo russkogo istoricheskogo obshchestva* [Anthology of the Imperial Russian Historical Society], vol. XVII, 1876

SCHNAPPER 1977
A. Schnapper: 'Greuze, un Précurseur?', *Connaissance des Arts*, June 1977

SCHNAPPER 1980–81
A. Schnapper: 'Greuze, peintre d'histoire ou peintre de genre?', *Commentaire*, no. 12, Hiver, 1980–81

SCHNITZLER 1828
[J. H. Schnitzler:] *Notice sur les principaux tableaux du Musée Impérial de l'Ermitage à Saint-Pétersbourg*, St Petersburg and Berlin, 1828

SELZ 1960
J. Selz: *Matisse*, Paris, 1960

SERRE, LEEGENHOEK 1988
J.-C. Serre, J. Leegenhoek: *Exposition de Tableaux des XVIIe et XVIIIe siècles. Catalogue*, Société Labatut, Paris, 1988

SEZNEC, ADHEMAR 1957–67
Commentary by J. Seznec and J. Adhemar in Diderot *Salons*, 1957–67

SHCHUKIN CATALOGUE 1913
Katalog kartin sobraniya S. I. Shchukina [Catalogue of Paintings in the Collection of S. I. Shchukin], Moscow, 1913

SHEVCHENKO 1995A
[1995 St Petersburg] V. G. Shevchenko: *Sto risunkov frantsuzskikh ornamentalistov (pervaya polovina XVII-nachalo XVIII veka). Gosudarstvennyy Ermitazh* [One Hundred Drawings by French Ornamentalists (First Half of the 17th Century to the Early 18th). State Hermitage], State Hermitage Museum, St Petersburg, 1995

SHEVCHENKO 1995B
V. G. Shevchenko: 'Risunki Zhilya-Mari Oppenora v gravyurakh Gabrielya Yuk'ye' [Drawings by Gille-Marie Oppenord in the Prints of Gabriel Huquier], *Soobshcheniya Gosudarstvennogo Ermitazha* [Bulletin of the State Hermitage], issue LVI, 1995, pp. 16–24

SHEVCHENKO 1995C
V. Shevchenko, in *Charles-Louis Clérisseau. (1721ñ1820) Dessin du Musée de l'Ermitage. Saint-Pétersbourg*, exh. cat., Musée du Louvre, Paris, 1995

SHEVCHENKO 1997
[1997 St Petersburg] V. G. Shevchenko: *Sharl'-Lui Klerisso – arkhitektor Yekateriny Velikoy. Risunki iz sobraniya Gosudarstvennogo Ermitazha* [Charles-Louis Clérisseau – Architect to Catherine the Great. Drawings from the Collection of the State Hermitage], exh. cat., State Hermitage Museum, St Petersburg, 1997

SMITH 1829–42
A Catalogue Raisonné of the Works of the Most Eminent Dutch, Flemish and French Painters..., by John Smith, 8 parts and Supplement, London, 1829ñ42

STARCKY 1999
E. Starcky: 'De Montmusard à Catherine II: trois dessins pour le Musée des Beaux-Arts', *Bulletin des Musées de Dijon*, no. 5, 1999, pp. 9–20

STEIN 1933
Gertrude Stein: *The Autobiography of Alice B. Toklas*, New York, 1933, p. 109

STERLING 1957
C. Sterling: *Musée de 1'Ermitage. La peinture française de Poussin à nos jours*, Paris, 1957

STUFFMAN 1968
M. Stuffmann: 'Les Tableaux de la collection de Pierre Crozat. Historique et destinée d'un ensemble célèbre, établis en partant d'un inventaire après décès inédit (1740)', *Gazette des Beaux-Arts*, July–September 1968, pp. 11–143

TERNOIS 1961
D. Ternois: 'Jacques Callot', *L'Information d'Histoire de 1'Art*, 1961

TERNOIS 1962A
D. Ternois: *L'Art de Jacques Callot*, Paris, 1962

TERNOIS 1962B
D. Ternois: *Jacques Callot. Catalogue complet de son œuvre dessiné*, Paris, 1962

THÈMES ET VARIATIONS 1943
Henri Matisse. Dessins. Thèmes et variations, Paris, 1943

THUILLIER 1974
J. Thuillier: *Tout l'œuvre peint de Poussin*, Paris, 1974

THUILLIER 1990–91
J. Thuillier: *Simon Vouet*, exh. cat., Grand Palais, Paris, 1990–91; Paris, 1990

THUILLIER 1992
[1992b Nancy] *L'Art en Lorraine au temps de Jacques Callot*, Musée des Beaux-Arts, Nancy, 1992

THUILLIER 2001
[2001 Rennes] J. Thuillier: *Jacques de Bellange*, Musée des Beaux-Arts, Rennes, 2001

TOURNEUX 1899
M. Tourneux: *Diderot et Catherine II*, Paris, 1899

TUGENDHOLD 1914
J. Tugendhold [Ya. Tugendkhold]: 'Frantsuzskoye sobraniye S. I. Shchukina' [The French Collection of S. I. Shchukin], *Apollon* [Apollo], nos. 1/2, 1914

TUGENDHOLD 1923
J. Tugendhold [Ya. Tugendkhold]: *Pervyy Muzey Novoy Zapadnoy Zhivopisi, byvsheye sobraniye S. I. Shchukina* [The First Museum of New Western Painting, Formerly the Collection of S. I. Shchukin], Moscow, 1923

UGLOFF 1935
L. Ugloff: 'Drawings by Jaques Callot for the "Temptation of St Antony"', *The Burlington Magazine*, LXVII, 1935, pp. 220–24

VERDI 1992
R. Verdi: *Nicolas Poussin. Tancred and Erminia. The Birmingham and St Petersburg Paintings in Context*, exh. cat., Birmingham Museum and Art Gallery, Birmingham, 1992

VEREYSKY 1938
G. Vereysky: 'Risunok Eduarda Mane. Novoye priobreteniye Gosudarstvennogo Ermitazha' [A Drawing by Eduard Manet. New Acquisition by the State Hermitage], *Iskusstvo* [Art], no. 5, 1938

VERGNET-RUIZ 1930
J. Vergnet-Ruiz: 'Oudry', in *Les Peintres français du XVIIIe siècle*, sous la direction de M. Louis Dimier, 2 vols, Paris and Brussels, 1928–30, vol. II (1930)

VILAIN 1976
J. Vilain, J. Lacambre: 'Dessins neoclassique,' *Revue du Louvre*, XXVI, no. 2, 1976

VOL'SKAYA 1946
V. Vol'skaya: *Nikola Pussen* [Nicolas Poussin], Moscow, 1946

VORONIKHINA 1971
A. N. Voronikhina: 'Graficheskiye raboty arkhitektora Sharlya De Vayi v Ermitazhe' [Graphic Works by the Architect Charles de Wailly in the Hermitage], *Soobshcheniya Gosudarstvennogo Ermitazha* [Bulletin of the State Hermitage], issue XXXIII, 1971, pp. 33–8

WAAGEN 1864
G. F. Waagen: *Die Gemäldesammlung in der Kaiserlichen Ermitage zu St. Petersburg nebst Bemerkungen über andere dortige Kunstsammlungen*, Munich, 1864, 2nd edn, St Petersburg, 1870

WALCH 1971
N. Walch: *Die Radierungen des Jacques Bellange*, Munich, 1971

WATTE 1960
A. Watte: 'Paris Commentary', *Studio*, XI, 1960

WEBER 1968
G. Weber: 'Etudes et documents. Quelques dessins inédits d'Edme Bouchardon', *Bulletin de la Société de l'Histoire de l'Art Français*, 1968, pp. 191–200

WESTERN EUROPEAN DRAWING 1981
Western European Drawing. The Hermitage, Leningrad, 1981 (also German and French editions, e.g., *Ermitage. Westeuropäische Zeichnung*, Leningrad, 1981)

WILD 1966
D. Wild: 'Charles Mellin ou Nicolas Poussin', *Gazette des Beaux-Arts*, October 1966

WILD 1980
D. Wild: *Nicolas Poussin*, 2 vols, Zurich, 1980

WILDENSTEIN 1924
G. Wildenstein: *Le Salon de 1725. Compte rendu par Mercure de France de l'exposition faite au Salon Carré du Louvre..., Publié avec des notes et documents nouveaux...*, Paris, 1924

WOLLIN 1939
Nils G. Wollin: *Desprez en Suède. Sa vie et ses travaux en Suède, en Angleterre, en Russie etc. 1784–1804*, Stockholm, 1939

WORLD OF ART 1903
Mir iskusstva [The World of Art], no. 12, 1903

WORTHEN 1976
A. L. N. Worthen: 'Jacques Bellange: Some Questions', *Print Collector's Newsletter*, no. 5, 1976, p. 124

XAVIER 1991
G. Xavier: *Les Chefs-d'œuvre du Musée Matisse, Nice*, exh. cat., Musée des Beaux-Arts de Dijon; Paris, 1991

ZAHN 1923
L. Zahn: *Die Handzeichnungen des Jacques Callot unter besonderer Berucksichtigung der Petersburger Sammlung*, Munich, 1923

ZERVOS 1932–78
Christian Zervos: *Pablo Picasso*, 33 vols, Paris, 1932–78

ZOLOTOV 1973
Antuan Vatto [Antoine Watteau], by Yu. Zolotov, I. Nemilova, Yu. Kuznetsov, T. Kamenskaya, V. Alexeyeva, Leningrad, 1973

ZOLOTOV 1979
Y. K. Zolotov: 'O khudozhestvennoy sisteme Pussena' [On Poussin's Artistic System], *Iskusstvo* [Art], no. 1, 1979

ZOLOTOV 1985A
Y. K. Zolotov: 'Tankred i Erminiya i apologiya poezii v tvorchestve Pussena' [Tancred and Erminia and an Apologia for Poetry in the Work of Poussin], *Muzey* [Museum], issue 5, 1985

ZOLOTOV 1985B
Y. K. Zolotov: *Nikola Pussen* [Nicolas Poussin], Leningrad, 1985

ZOLOTOV 1988
Yu. K. Zolotov: *Pussen* [Poussin], Moscow, 1988

ZOLOTOV, SEREBRIANNAIA ET AL. 1990
Y. Zolotov, N. Serebriannaia, N. Petroussevitch, M. Maiskaia, I. Kouznetsova: *Nicolas Poussin dans les musées de l'Union Sovietique. Peintures. Dessins*, Leningrad, 1990

CAT. 1773–85
[E. Munich:] 'Catalogue raisonné des tableaux qui se trouvent dans les Galeries, Sallons et Cabinets du Palais Impérial de S.Pétersbourg, commencé en 1773 et continué jusqu'en 1785', MS, in 3 vols: vols 1–2, 1773–83, vol. 3, 1785; Hermitage Archives: Fund 1, *Opis'* VI-A, *delo* 85

CAT. 1797
'Katalog kartinam, khranyashchimsya v Imperatorskoy galeree Ermitazha, v Tavricheskom i Mramornom dvortsakh, sochinyonnyy [...] pri uchastii F. I. Labenskogo' [Catalogue of Paintings Kept in the Imperial Hermitage Gallery, the Tauride and Marble Palaces, compiled... with the participation of F. I. Labensky], 1797, MS, in 3 vols; Hermitage Archives: Fund 1, *Opis'* VI-A, *delo* 87

INVENTORY 1859
'Opis' kartinam i plafonam, sostoyashchim v zavedovanii II otdeleniya imperatorskogo Ermitazha' [Inventory of Paintings and Ceilings in the Care of the II Department of the Imperial Hermitage], MS, 1859–1929; Hermitage Archives, Fund 1, *Opis'* XI-?, *delo* 1

Index of Artists

Founders of the Hermitage Rooms

Principal Benefactors
Mikhail Khodorkovsky and Yukos Oil

Founder Patrons
Sir David Alliance CBE
The Dellal Foundation
Donald and Jeanne Kahn
Henry and Marie-Josée Kravis
Lord Rothschild GBE
Mrs Charles Wrightsman

Major Donors
The Clore Duffield Foundation
Sir Harry Djanogly CBE
The Linbury Trust

Benefactors
Mr and Mrs Sid Bass
Mrs Oscar de la Renta *in honour of Mrs Charles Wrightsman*
Sandler Capital Management Charitable Foundation

Donors
Mr Kenneth Lipper
Dr Eileen Guggenheim

Corporate Founder Sponsor
Morgan Stanley

Corporate Supporter
IBM

We also thank the following for their support of the Hermitage Rooms at Somerset House

American Friends of the Hermitage
BSkyB
Finers Stephens Innocent
Somerset House Arts Fund
Somerset House Art History Foundation
Somerset House Trust